INTERNATIONAL
LABOUR LAW REPORTS

This volume covers the period 1 October 2015 to 30 September 2016.

INTERNATIONAL LABOUR LAW REPORTS

VOLUME 36

Editor
JANE AEBERHARD-HODGES
Geneva, Switzerland

Editorial Board

Prof. ALVIN GOLDMAN
University of Kentucky

Prof. JEAN-MAURICE VERDIER
University of Paris, Nanterre

Prof. MANFRED WEISS
University of Frankfurt

Founding Editor
The late JUSTICE ZVI H. BAR-NIV

Former Editors
Felice Morgenstern
Alan Gladstone

BRILL
NIJHOFF

Printed on acid-free paper.

ISBN 978-9004-34770-0
E-ISSN 2211-6028

(c) Copyright 2017 by Koninklijke Brill NV, Leiden, The Netherlands.
Koninklijke Brill NV incorporates the imprints Brill, Brill Hes & De Graaf, Brill Nijhoff, Brill Rodopi, Brill Sense and Hotei Publishing.

All rights reserved. No part of this publication may be reproduced, stored in a retrieval system, or transmitted in any form or by any means, electronic, mechanical, photocopying, microfilming, recording or otherwise, without written permission from the Publisher.

Authorization to photocopy items for internal or external use is granted by Brill Academic Publishers provided that the appropriate fees are paid directly to The Copyright Clearance Center, 222 Rosewood Drive, Suite 910, Danvers MA 01923, USA.
Fees are subject to change.

CONTENTS

LIST OF REPORTERS	vii
LIST OF CASES – BY JURISDICTION	xi
LIST OF CASES – BY SUBJECT MATTER	xv

Part One
GENERAL PRINCIPLES OF LABOUR LAW
AND KEY CONCEPTS   1

Part Two
BASIC RIGHTS PERTAINING TO LABOUR   65

Part Three
MANPOWER   121

Part Four
INDIVIDUAL EMPLOYMENT RELATIONSHIP   159

Part Five
COLLECTIVE LABOUR RELATIONS   249

Part Six
ADMINISTRATION – JUDICIAL AND GENERAL   299

REPORTERS

International

COURT OF JUSTICE OF THE EUROPEAN COMMUNITIES	Prof. Mia Rönnmar Lund Univ. (Sweden)
HUMAN RIGHTS BODIES	Dr. Martin Oelz International Labour Office Geneva

National

AUSTRALIA	Prof. Shae McCrystal Univ. of Sydney
AUSTRIA	Prof. Nora Melzer Univ. of Graz
BELGIUM	Prof. Chris Engels Catholic Univ. of Leuven
CANADA	Prof. Brian Langille Univ. of Toronto
FINLAND	Prof. Niklas Bruun Univ. of Helsinki
FRANCE	Prof. Philippe Auvergnon Univ. of Bordeaux
GERMANY	Dr. Christoph Gyo Goethe Univ., Frankfurt

HUNGARY	Dr. Jószef Hajdú Univ. of Szeged
INDIA	Prof. Kamala Sankaran Univ. of Delhi
IRELAND	Prof. Anthony Kerr Univ. College, Dublin
ISRAEL	Judge Stephen Adler Former President, National Labour Court
ITALY	Prof. Mariella Magnani Univ. of Pavia
JAPAN	Prof. Ryoko Sakuraba Kobe University
NETHERLANDS	Prof. A.T.M. Jacobs Univ. of Tilburg Dr. Famke Laagland Nijmegen Univ.
NEW ZEALAND	Prof. Pam Nuttall Auckland Univ. of Technology
NORWAY	Prof. Stein Evju Univ. of Oslo
POLAND	Dr. Malgorzata Kurzynoga Univ. of Lodz Dr. Monika Smusz-Kulesza Univ. of Lodz
SOUTH AFRICA	Prof. Emeritus Halton Cheadle Univ. of Capt Town

SPAIN	Prof. F. Ferrando García Univ. of Murcia
	Prof. F. Gómez Abelleira Univ. of Murcia
	Prof. Belén Garcia Romero Univ. of Murcia
SWEDEN	Prof. Ronnie Eklund Univ. of Stockholm
UNITED KINGDOM	Prof. M. Freedland St. John's College, Oxford
	Dr. Nicola Countouris Univ. College London
	Dr. Astrid Sanders London School of Economics and Political Science
UNITED STATES OF AMERICA	Prof. A.L. Goldman Univ. of Kentucky
	Prof. Robert Covington Vanderbilt Univ.

CASES REPORTED BY JURISDICTION

INTERNATIONAL

Court of Justice of the European Union
(Grand Chamber)
    Dansk Industri (DI), acting on behalf
    of Ajos A/S v. Estate of Karsten Eigil
    Rasmussen, Case C441/14   C.J.E.C.1   9
European Court of Human Rights
    Çam v. Turkey (Application no. 51500/08)   H.R. 1   21

NATIONAL

Australia

Fair Work Commission
    Four Yearly Review of Modern Awards –
    Penalty Rates   Austral. 1   179

Austria

Supreme Court
    25 May 2016 9 ObA 117/15v   Aust. 1   83
Supreme Court
    29 November 2016, 9 ObA 53/16h   Aust. 2   123

Belgium

Labour Court Brussels, Summary Proceedings
    28 January 2016, GR n° 2015/CB/14   Bel. 1   131

Canada

Supreme Court of Canada
    Wilson v. Atomic Energy of Canada Limited
    2016 SCC 29, [2016] 1 S.C.R. 770   Can. 1   213

Finland

Supreme Court 2016:12
   3.3.2016 (S2013/757)   Fin. 1   271

France

Supreme Court, Labour Division
   Mr Jean-François X… v. Mr Serge Y… et alia
   1 June 2016   Fr. 1   97

Germany

Federal Labour Court
   Decision of 10 May 2016 – 9 AZR 347/15   Ger. 1   203

India

Supreme Court of India
   Cardamom Marketing Corporation and Anr
   v. State of Kerala and Ors   Ind. 1   301

Ireland

The Supreme Court
   Stephen Miley, Devil's Glen Equestrian Centre
   Ltd and Devil's Glen Partnership v. Employment
   Appeals Tribunal, Paul Bourke and the
   Attorney General   Ire. 1   309
The Employment Appeals Tribunal
   Gregory Crowe v. An Post   Ire. 2   227
The Workplace Relations Commission
   Senelisiwe Buthelezi v. Coy Dlamini, Thobeka
   Dlamini and the Republic of South Africa   Ire. 3   233

Israel

The National Labour Court
   Koach LaOvdim Democratic Workers'
   Organization v. Z.L.F. Industries Inc.
   NLC 51407-07-15   Isr. 1   67

Italy

Court of Cassation, Labour Division		
Decision no. 8068 of 21 April 2016	It. 1	173
Court of Cassation, Labour Division		
Decision no. 24157 of 26 November 2015		
Agrigento Industrial Development		
Consortium v. C.S.	It. 2	241
Constitutional Court		
Decision no. 5126 of March 2015	It. 3	263

Japan

Supreme Court (Second Petty Bench)		
19 February 2016	Jap. 1	141

The Netherlands

Supreme Court		
Decision of 18 September 2015		
The State of the Netherlands v. an employee	Neth. 1	3

Norway

Supreme Court		
Rt. 2015 p. 1332	Nor. 1	149

Poland

Supreme Court		
The resolution of seven judges of		
28 September 2016, III PZP 3/16	Pol. 1	31
Supreme Court		
Judgement of 17 November 2016, II PK 227/15	Pol. 2	193

South Africa

Labour Appeal Court of South Africa		
ADT Security (Pty) Ltd v. National Security &		
Unqualified Workers Union and Others [2012]		
ZALAC 52; [2014] 11 BLLR 1096; (2015) 36 ILJ		
152 (LAC)	S.A. 1	277

Spain

Supreme Court Social Chamber (acting as a General Chamber) Decision of 25 October 2016, Appeal No 881/2016	Sp. 1	43
Supreme Court Social Chamber Decision No 961/2016 of 16 November 2016	Sp. 2	285
Supreme Court Social Chamber Decision of 3 May 2016	Sp. 3	105

Sweden

Labour Court AD 2015 No. 74	Swe. 1	59

Great Britain

Court of Appeal Windle v. Secretary of State for Justice [2016] EWCA Civ 459	G.B. 1	161

United States of America

Court of Appeals for the District of Columbia Circuit Hyundai Am. Shipping Agency, Inc. v. NLRB	U.S.A. 1	75
Court of Appeals for the District of Columbia Circuit HTH Corp. v. NLRB	U.S.A. 2	317
Court of Appeals for the Fifth Circuit Associated Builders and Contractors of Texas v. NLRB	U.S.A. 3	251
Court of Appeals for the Eleventh Circuit Suazo v. NCL (Bahamas) Ltd.	U.S.A. 4	331
Federal Supreme Court Tyson Foods v. Bouaphakeo 136 S.Ct. 1036 (2016)	U.S.A. 5	345
Federal Supreme Court Heffernan v. City of Paterson, N.J 136 S.Ct.1412 (2016)	U.S.A. 6	355

CASES REPORTED BY SUBJECT MATTER

CUMULATIVE VOLUMES 30–33*

(For a cumulative list of cases reported in Volumes I to VII see Volume VII; for a cumulative list of cases reported in Volumes VIII to XIII see Volume XIII; for Volumes XIV to XVIII see Volume XVIII; for Volumes XIX to XXIV see Volume XXIV; and for Volumes XXV to XXIX see Volume XXIX)

PART ONE

GENERAL PRINCIPLES OF LABOUR LAW AND KEY CONCEPTS

Conflict of Laws

Discrimination claim of foreign national employed abroad – contractual choice of law	U.S.A. 6	XXXI	3
Dutch dismissal law – international context	Neth. 2	XXXII	3
Cross-border services – EU law	Nor. 1	XXXIII	3
Protection of remuneration for work of posted workers	Pol. 1	XXXIV	3
Global work and jurisdiction	Sp. 2	XXXIV	13
Transposition of EU Directive 2003/88/EC on the Organisation of Working Time – conditions for claiming monetary compensation for denied paid annual leave	Neth. 1	XXXVI	3

* Cases touching on multiple subjects may be found under two or more headings.

Equal treatment (see also Basic Rights pertaining to Labour)

Limited or open list of discrimination criteria – burden of proof	Pol. 1	XXXIII	31
Prohibition of age discrimination – Directive 2000/78 – maximum entry age for fire service	C.J.E.C. 1	XXX	3
Blue and white collar workers – equal treatment	Bel. 1	XXXI	15
Blue collar worker fixed-term contract – unfair dismissal provision – equal treatment	Bel. 1	XXXII	11
Principle of equal treatment – seniority bonus – reserved to professional category – justification	Fr. 1	XXXI	27
Labour contract – execution – power of management – restrictions of fundamental freedoms – restriction of religious freedom – secularism – unjustified dismissal	Fr. 1	XXXIII	27
Social policy – information and consultation – Directive 2002/14/EC – Charter of Fundamental Rights of the European Union – Article 27 – subjecting the setting up of bodies representing staff to certain thresholds of employees – calculation of the thresholds – national legislation contrary to European Union law – role of the national court	C.J.E.C. 1	XXXIV	23
Maternity leave – EU Directives 92/85/EEC and 96/34/EC – conditions governing the continued receipt of full pay during maternity leave – equal treatment of men and women – employment contract – national collective agreements	Fin. 1	XXXIV	33
Articles 8 and 14 of the European Convention for the Protection of Human Rights and Fundamental Freedoms – respect for private and family life – termination of employment – discrimination based on health (HIV status)	H.R. 1	XXXIV	41
Employment offence – discrimination on grounds of sexual orientation and family-related reasons – inherent requirement of job being applied for – employment contract – protection of privacy in working life	Fin. 2	XXXV	3

Social policy – Charter of Fundamental Rights
  of the European Union – Directive 2000/78/EC
  – principle prohibiting discrimination on
  grounds of age– national legislation
  incompatible with the Directive – possibility
  for a private person to bring proceedings to
  establish the liability of the State for breach of
  EU law – dispute between private persons
  – principles of legal certainty and the
  protection of legitimate expectations – role
  of the national court   C.J.E.C.1   XXXVI   9
Article 14 of the European Convention for the
  Protection of Human Rights and Fundamental
  Freedoms and Article 2 of its Protocol No. 1
  – interface of regional and U.N. norms – right
  to education and discrimination based
  on disability   H.R. 1   XXXVI   21
The claim for compensation for a discriminatory
  termination of an employment contract – age
  discrimination – time limits when
  lodging cases   Pol. 1   XXXVI   31
Surrogate motherhood and right to maternity/
  paternity benefits   Sp. 1   XXXVI   43
Temporary agency work – equal treatment
  principle – interpretation of collective
  agreement   Swe. 1   XXXVI   59

Employee and employer

Relationship between manufacturing company
  and its contractor's employees – retaliation
  against employee for his report to
  Labour Office   Jap. 2   XXX   13
Employer liability for acts of "supervisors"   U.S.A. 3   XXXIII 49
Definition of employee – child labour   U.S.A. 5   XXXI   35
Employment status – volunteer –
  whether employee   Ire. 2   XXXIII 59
Collective redundancies – Directive 98/59/EC –
  winding up – consultation – equivalence
  between employer and liquidator   C.J.E.C. 1 XXXI   49
Opera chorus member – worker under
  Labour Union Act   Jap. 2   XXXI   59

Home care of older people – employed and self-employed – integration in household	Aust. 1	XXXII	25
Victimisation – engaging in lawful industrial activity – causal connection between trade union activity and termination of employment	Austral. 2	XXXIV	53
Nature of employment relationship – nature of partnership – what constitutes discrimination in human rights law – mandatory retirement age	Can. 1	XXXIV	63
Employment status – whistle-blowers – workers – limited liability partnerships	G.B. 1	XXXIV	75
Contracting for services – labour-only contracting – temporary agency work – right to employment with user undertaking	Nor. 1	XXXIV	91
Employment intermediary – provider of bookkeeping/accounting services or employer – independent contractor or employee – service provider – temporary employment agencies – social welfare tax payments	Isr. 2	XXXV	9

PART TWO

BASIC RIGHTS PERTAINING TO LABOUR

Freedom of association

European Convention of Human Rights – freedom of association – discrimination	Fin. 1	XXXI	67
Victimisation – engaging in industrial activity – causal connection between trade union activity and suspension – onus of proof	Austral. 1	XXXII	33
Employment contract – exercise of the right to strike – business closure – non-forced situation – unlawful lockout – obstruction of the exercise of the right to strike – consequences of a lockout declared unlawful – compensation for damages	Fr. 1	XXXIV	103
Right to strike (see previous volumes) freedom of speech (see previous volumes) – unlawful employer payments to labor organizations or their officers	U.S.A. 1	XXXIV	111

Freedom of association – agency shop –
persons choosing not to belong to a trade
union representing personal assistants of
persons with disability U.S.A. 6 XXXIV 125

National Labor Relations Act – power of
president to appoint members of National
Labor Relations Board U.S.A. 7 XXXIV 141

Constitutional law – Charter of Rights –
freedom of association – right to strike –
public service employees – whether right to
strike is protected by guarantee of freedom of
association – whether prohibition on essential
services employees participating in strike
action amounts to substantial interference with
meaningful process of collective bargaining
and therefore violates freedom of association –
if so, whether such violation is justified as a
reasonable limitation on
freedom of association Can. 2 XXXV 17

Freedom to associate as trade unions –
ILO Convention No. 87 Pol. 1 XXXV 39

Demonstrating on employer's sidewalk – right
of access to courts U.S.A. 6 XXXV 51

Right to union organization – union recognized
bargaining agent – union de-recognition –
protected period of union recognition –
employer's anti-union activities – penalty for
employer anti-union activity Isr. 1 XXXVI 67

Employer handbook rules – interference with
right to engage in concerted activity U.S.A. 1 XXXVI 75

Right to privacy

Public employees right of privacy –
constitutionality of review of police
department review of officers' text messages U.S.A. 2 XXX 23

Employee records – confidential information –
evidence of gender discrimination U.S.A. 3 XXXI 73

Employer's power to monitor employees –
by private agency It. 1 XXXI 89

Right of employees of government contractor
to informational privacy U.S.A. 7 XXXI 95

Computer monitoring in the workplace	Sp. 2	XXXII	43
Labour arbitration – scope of "management rights" clause in collective agreement – health and safety requirements – unilateral imposition of alcohol testing	Can. 2	XXXIV	149
Employer's liability for failing to pay due care to an employee's health and safety – whether damages may be reduced because the employee had not provided the employer with full information concerning her mental health condition	Jap. 1	XXXIV	163
Workplace privacy and employee monitoring – dismissal based on the capture of the employee images on a video camera recorded without the knowledge of affected worker and with a different purpose from the one declared by the company	Sp. 1	XXXIV	171
Violation of the rights of human dignity and development of one's personality – stakeout by a private investigator – hidden video recordings and photographs	Ger. 1	XXXV	61
Remote employee surveillance – concealed monitoring for protection – Article 4 Workers' Statute – protection of company assets – dignity and privacy of the employee – dismissal	It. 2	XXXV	71
Employee data protection – employee's consent – abusive provision in individual employment contract	Sp. 2	XXXV	81

Freedom of occupation

Covenant restricting competition by former employee – trade secrets	U.S.A. 4	XXX	35
Withdrawal from non-competition clause	Czech. 1	XXXII	53

Discrimination

Religious discrimination – discrimination on grounds of sexual orientation – direct and indirect discrimination – dismissal	G.B. 1	XXX	43
Religious discrimination – employment status – arbitration agreements	G.B. 1	XXXII	69

Non-discrimination on grounds of sex – difference in retirement age for men and women	Pol. 2	XXX	59
Gender discrimination – equal pay – comparable worth	U.S.A. 6	XXX	65
Transgender discrimination	U.S.A. 6	XXXII	101
Exclusion of male military personnel from parental leave – European Convention	H.R. 1	XXXII	111
Age discrimination – age specified by party discriminated against considered governing	Hun. 2	XXXI	103
Maximum age for entry into fire service – genuine and determining occupational requirement	C.J.E.C. 1	XXX	3
Mandatory retirement age – pension scheme	Nor. 1	XXXI	109
Retaliation under Title VII by third party	U.S.A. 2	XXXI	119
Retaliation under Title VII – burden of proof	U.S.A. 5	XXXIII	75
Discrimination based on "view of life" ("weltanschauung")	Aust. 2	XXX	75
Limits on class actions in discrimination cases	U.S.A. 1	XXXI	123
Dress code – sex discrimination	Sp. 1	XXXI	133
Indirect sex discrimination – pensions – part-time workers	Sp. 1	XXXIII	85
Equal pay – comparators – same employment	G.B. 1	XXXIII	109
Defence of Marriage Act – discrimination	U.S.A. 4	XXXIII	121
Gender discrimination and variable pay	Sp. 2	XXXIII	129
Nature of employment relationship – nature of partnership – what constitutes discrimination in human rights law – mandatory retirement age	Can. 1	XXXIV	63
Dismissal protection of an HIV-positive employee beyond the scope of general dismissal protection	Ger. 2	XXXIV	179
Articles 8 and 14 of the European Convention for the Protection of Human Rights and Fundamental Freedoms – respect for private and family life – termination of employment – discrimination based on health (HIV status)	H.R. 1	XXXIV	41

Equal remuneration – not lawful if an employer pays different wages to employees employed in the same position, the nature of the work performed, its quality and quantity, working conditions, efforts and responsibilities being identical	Hun. 2	XXXIV	195
Whistle blower protection of hospital interns – intern status as an employee	U.S.A. 3	XXXIV	201
Duty to accommodate employees' religious dietary restrictions	U.S.A. 4	XXXIV	219
Articles 8 and 14 of the European Convention for the Protection of Human Rights and Fundamental Freedoms – discrimination based on sex – termination of employment in the civil service	H.R. 1	XXXV	93
Victimisation – exercising 'workplace right' – acting because of exercise of workplace right or effect of exercise of workplace right	Austral. 2	XXXV	103
Employment offence – discrimination on grounds of sexual orientation and family-related reasons – inherent requirement of job being applied for – employment contract – protection of privacy in working life	Fin. 2	XXXV	3
Maternity protection and workplace discrimination – dismissal after in-vitro fertilisation	Ger. 2	XXXV	115
Validity of disciplinary suspension and subsequent demotion of employees who engaged in sexual harassment	Jap. 2	XXXV	125
Equal pay – pay equity – comparator group	N.Z. 2	XXXV	133
Discrimination on grounds of age – no justification found under exception provisions – impact of European Union law	Swe. 1	XXXV	141
Religious discrimination in the workplace – headscarf and company policy on headgear – employer's obligation even when no request to accommodate has been made – shifting burden of proof under Title VII of the Civil Rights Act	U.S.A. 2	XXXV	151

Social policy – Charter of Fundamental Rights of the European Union – Directive 2000/78/EC – principle prohibiting discrimination on grounds of age– national legislation incompatible with the Directive – possibility for a private person to bring proceedings to establish the liability of the State for breach of EU law – dispute between private persons – principles of legal certainty and the protection of legitimate expectations – role of the national court	C.J.E.C. 1	XXXVI	9
Lawful dismissal due to refusal to remove a full-face veil or an Islamic headscarf at the workplace – discrimination on ground of religion?	Aust. 1	XXXVI	83
Occupational health and safety – employers' safety obligations – psychological harassment of employees – employer's liability – grounds for exemption	Fr. 1	XXXVI	97
Article 14 of the European Convention for the Protection of Human Rights and Fundamental Freedoms and Article 2 of its Protocol No. 1 – interface of regional and U.N. norms – right to education and discrimination based on disability	H.R. 1	XXXVI	21
The claim for compensation for a discriminatory termination of an employment contract – age discrimination – time limits when lodging cases	Pol. 1	XXXVI	31
Dismissal of sick employee – discrimination – disability – Directive 2000/78	Sp. 3	XXXVI	105

PART THREE

MANPOWER

Free mobility of labour (see previous volumes)

Summary termination for serious reasons – linguistic requirements –freedom of movement of workers	Bel. 1	XXXIV	239

Employment contracts containing trial periods – termination – language requirements – freedom of movement of workers   Bel. 1   XXXV 159

Manpower operations

Validity of transfer of part of undertaking – organisational structure of the transferee employer   It. 2   XXXII 125

"Hand-over" employment – character and purpose – entitlement to severance allowance on termination of employment   Sp. 2   XXX 87

Prison work – European Convention   H.R. 1   XXXI 151

Employer duty of loyalty – employment protection   H.R. 1   XXXIII 143

Penalties for wage dumping   Aust. 2   XXXIV 245

Transfer of part of an undertaking – economic, functional and organisational autonomy – existence of the requirement prior to the transfer   It. 1   XXXIV 251

"Deemed working hours" scheme designed for workers who work outside their regular workplace denied to tour conductors of a travel agency   Jap. 2   XXXIV 257

Social policy – Article 4(1) of Directive 2008/104/EC on temporary agency work – prohibitions or restrictions on the use of temporary agency work – justification – grounds of general interest – obligation to review   C.J.E.C. 1   XXXV 167

Successor company's liability for vested pensions of prior business' employees   U.S.A. 5   XXXV 175

Wage dumping through temporary work of an Austrian employee in Germany – applicability of the German minimum wage law   Aust. 2   XXXVI 123

Transfer of a business or part of a business – retention of employment relationship with entity taking over business – competence of court in summary proceedings   Bel. 1   XXXVI 131

Validity of employees' consent to changes to their retirement benefits as prescribed in work rules   Jap. 1   XXXVI 141

Business reorganization – redundancy –
dismissal – scope of circle of employees to
be considered for selection   Nor. 1   XXXVI 149

PART FOUR

INDIVIDUAL EMPLOYMENT RELATIONSHIP

Individual contract of employment

Housekeeper tasks – employment relationship –
employer instruction and control   Hun. 3   XXXI 167

On-call categorization of employment
relationship – superannuation   Austral. 2   XXXI 175

The employer's duty to rehire an employee after
retirement at 60 – legality of excluding him
from the "continued employment"
arrangement required by a statute to promote
the employment of elderly persons   Jap. 2   XXXIII 157

Employment status – shams –
mutuality of obligations   G.B. 1   XXXI 187

Forced or compulsory labour – domestic
servitude – European Convention   H.R. 1   XXXIII 167

Fixed-term contract of disabled worker – failure
to state technical, organisational, production
or replacement reasons in the employment
contract – lawfulness   It. 1   XXX 105

Fixed-term contract – temporary agency work   Fin. 1   XXXII 133

Fixed-term contract   It. 3   XXXIII 165

Employment contract between individual and
diplomatic mission – state immunity   H.R. 1   XXX 387

Change of terms and conditions in the contract –
employer's right to direct and supervise the
work – termination   Fin. 2   XXX 111

Succession of employment contract upon
company split   Jap. 1   XXX 115

Repudiation by employee – third party –
remedy available to employer   Austral. 1   XXXI 207

Sex workers – enforcement of illegal employment contract – constitutional protection – applicability of Labour Relations Act – remedies	S.A. 1	XXX	123
Framework Agreement on fixed-term work – EC Directive – successive fixed-term contracts	C.J.E.C. 1	XXXII	139
Contract of employment – whether contains implied term of trust and confidence	Austral. 1	XXXIV	267
Contract of Employment – non-competition clause – restraint of trade – enforceability of covenant	Ire. 1	XXXIV	277
Constitutionality of indefinite-term employment contract in support of entrepreneurs introduced by Spanish Act 3/2012	Sp. 3	XXXIV	285
Non-competition clause – contractual penalty/ liquidated damages – legal reduction of excessive penalties by the courts	Aust. 2	XXXV	195
Non-competition agreement – how to calculate compensation when a sum does not qualify as wages	Hun. 1	XXXV	201
Whether workers employed by a contractor in a statutory canteen on the premises of the principal employer are employed by such principal employer	Ind. 1	XXXV	207
Employment intermediary – provider of bookkeeping/accounting services or employer – independent contractor or employee – service provider – temporary employment agencies – social welfare tax payments	Isr. 2	XXXV	9
Employee data protection – employee's consent – abusive provision in individual employment contract	Sp. 2	XXXV	81
Employment contracts – breach of contract – psychiatric injury – duty of care	G.B. 1	XXXV	217
Employment status – mutuality of obligation – casual and intermittent workers	G.B. 1	XXXVI	161
Agency work – sham labour intermediation – posting	It. 1	XXXVI	173

Remuneration

Statutory minimum remuneration – Labour Court – joint committees	Ire. 1	XXXI 215
Entitlement to severance allowance on termination of "hand-over" employment contract	Sp. 2	XXX 87
Modern awards – minimum standards – safety net – penalty rates in retail and hospitality sectors	Austral. 1	XXXVI 179
The concept of drivers' flat rate for overnight subsistence allowance in international transport	Pol. 2	XXXVI 193

Hours of work

Dividing up of working time period – extent of employer discretion – protection against changes in scheduling of working hours	Swe. 1	XXX 137
Right to rest as a personal right – violation of employee's dignity	Pol. 1	XXX 147
"Deemed working hours" scheme designed for workers who work outside their regular workplace denied to tour conductors of a travel agency	Jap. 2	XXXIV 257
Hours of work – compensation for on-call workers – exclusion of sleep time from 24-hour shifts	U.S.A. 4	XXXV 257

Weekly rest and annual leave

Right to adoption leave and social security benefits in case of adoption by one partner of same sex couple of the other's biological child	Sp. 3	XXX 157
Calculation of attendance rate to get annual paid holidays	Jap. 1	XXXIII 173

Safety and health including maternity (previously under "individual contract of employment")

The Right to Sit at Work Law – failure to provide chairs for workers collective or individual dispute	Isr. 2	XXX 169
Possibility of serious injury	U.SA. 4	XXXI 227
Employees' refusal to perform work exposing them to physical harm	It. 2	XXXIII 179

Civil responsibility for work accidents of self-employed sub-contactors	Neth. 1	XXXII 151
Works outing – connection to employment – minimum numerical participation	Aust. 2	XXXII 159
Employee on sick leave – pressure to return – dismissal void	Sp. 3	XXXI 241
Family and Medical Leave Act – immunity of states	U.S.A. 1	XXXII 165
Disabilities – equal treatment – UN and EU standards – obligation to provide accommodation	C.J.E.C. 1	XXXIII 187
Psychological harassment – employer's responsibility – obligation of actual safety – sexual harassment	Fr. 1	XXX 175
Parental leave – difference of treatment – biological and adoptive father – transferable right of leave	Sp. 2	XXXI 253
Retired workers suffering from asbestos – considered as workers	Jap. 1	XXXII 175
Risk during breast feeding	Sp. 3	XXXII 181
Dismissal of medical marijuana user – statutory protection of use	U.S.A. 7	XXXII 197
Maternity leave – EU Directives 92/85/EEC and 96/34/EC – conditions governing the continued receipt of full pay during maternity leave – equal treatment of men and women – employment contract – national collective agreements	Fin. 1	XXXIV 33
Employment status – whistle-blowers – workers – limited liability partnerships	G.B. 1	XXXIV 75
Fixed-term contracts – annual bonuses and productivity bonus – payable only to employees on open-ended contracts – unequal treatment – lawfulness	It. 2	XXXIV 309
Employer's liability for failing to pay due care to an employee's health and safety – whether damages may be reduced because the employee had not provided the employer with full information concerning her mental health condition	Jap. 1	XXXIV 163

Maternity protection and workplace discrimination – dismissal after in-vitro fertilisation	Ger. 2	XXXV 115
Validity of demotion of an employee who requested a lightened workload during her pregnancy	Jap. 1	XXXV 269
Occupational health and safety – employers' safety obligations – psychological harassment of employees – employer's liability – grounds for exemption	Fr. 1	XXXVI 97
Occupational health and safety – tobacco smoke-free workplace	Ger. 1	XXXVI 203
Surrogate motherhood and right to maternity/paternity benefits	Sp. 1	XXXVI 43

Termination of employment

Dismissal of church employees – infringement of loyalty	Ger. 1	XXXI 269
Disciplinary termination of mentally troubled employee – prolonged absence from work	Jap. 2	XXXII 205
Dismissal for justified reasons – reduction of personnel	It. 4	XXXI 283
Employee's notice of absence in case of illness – penalties for default	Aust. 2	XXXI 291
Dismissal of university professor – tenure – fair procedures	Ire. 2	XXX 181
Abolition of job – tasks given to other employees – lawful cause of dismissal	Hun. 1	XXX 191
Abusive dismissal – concept – blue-collar workers	Bel. 1	XXX 197
Employer's duty of loyalty	Swe. 1	XXXIII 199
Non-renewal of fixed-term contract – successive contracts – justified reason	Fin. 1	XXX 203
Unlawful "extraordinary dismissal" – failure to take up work – reinstatement	Hun. 3	XXX 207
Collective redundancy – reprisal against exercise of right to strike	Sp. 3	XXXIII 203
Duty of loyalty – right to criticise	It. 1	XXXII 211
Wrongful dismissal – employee refusal to violate law	U.S.A. 4	XXXII 217

Right of government employee to publicly criticise employing agency with respect to matters of public interest	U.S.A. 5	XXXII 225
Unlawful dismissal by company in group of companies – reinstatement in parent company – capacity as actual employer	It. 2	XXXI 297
Victimisation – reinstatement – subsequent termination	Austral. 3	XXXII 227
Limitation on reinstatement as a remedy – review of arbitration award – corporate employer's right to dismiss its head lawyer	U.S.A. 5	XXX 213
Limits on freedom of employee to resign – minimum guaranteed contract length clause – admissibility	It. 2	XXX 227
Employee's voluntary resignation – retraction of resignation	Sp. 1	XXX 231
Termination by retirement – holding outside office – protective status	Fr. 1	XXXII 247
Winding-up of public service	Pol. 1	XXXI 303
Additional employment – notification – grounds for "ordinary" dismissal	Hun. 1	XXXI 315
Summary termination for serious reasons – linguistic requirements –freedom of movement of workers	Bel. 1	XXXIV 239
In a labour lawsuit it cannot be examined whether the economic situation of the employer really justified reorganization and layoff	Hun. 3	XXXIV 315
Termination of employment contract – sports – law and economics considerations	Swe. 1	XXXIV 323
Continuation of wage payment during suspension of work – types of circumstances when work is suspended – obligation to conclude an interim employment contract – deduction of unemployment benefits	Aust. 1	XXXV 279
Employment contract – termination of an employment contract for economic reasons – reduction of wages	Fin. 1	XXXV 287

Employee publicly revealing work-related experience on own Internet website – conduct qualifies as jeopardizing the legitimate economic interests of the employer – it can constitute a lawful reason for ordinary dismissal by the employer	Hun. 2	XXXV 293
Dismissal – breach of email policy – workplace privacy – whether employer acted reasonably in dismissing employee – appropriate remedy	Ire. 1	XXXV 301
Dismissal on disciplinary grounds – non-existence of the alleged material fact – unlawfulness – reinstatement – Article 18, section 4 of the Workers' Statute	It. 1	XXXV 317
Redundancy – statutory test for justified dismissal – Court may inquire into substantive justification for dismissal – objective assessment of substantive justification	N.Z. 1	XXXV 323
Judicial termination of the employment contract at the request of the employee, based on breach by the employer – Workers' Statute Article 50 – exceptions to the requirement of continuing to work until judgement is rendered	Sp. 3	XXXV 335
Unjust dismissal – statutory protection – non-unionized workers – scope of protection under statute as compared to common law	Can. 1	XXXVI 213
Dismissal – criminal conviction – offence committed outside workplace – whether sufficient nexus between offence and employment – whether dismissal fair and reasonable	Ire. 2	XXXVI 227
Diplomatic immunity – complaint of discriminatory dismissal – embassy staff – vicarious liability	Ire. 3	XXXVI 233
Dismissal – public sector employment – Art. 18 of Act no. 300/1970 – Amendment Act no. 92/2012 – applicability	It. 2	XXXVI 241

PART FIVE

COLLECTIVE LABOUR RELATIONS

Parties

Trade union dues – check-off – credit transfer – employer refusal – anti-union behaviour	It. 3	XXXII 257
Union fees and dues – members and non-members – using fees and dues for political purposes	U.S.A. 3	XXXII 263
Criteria for determining the bargaining unit – union rivalry	Isr. 1	XXX 247
Duty to bargain with contractor's employees	Jap 1	XXXI 323
Retiree benefits – scope of union representational authority	U.S.A. 1	XXXIII 225
Collective labour relations – union organization of workers employed through individual labour contracts – division of a bargaining unit – definition of a labour union	Isr. 1	XXXIV 333
Freedom of association – agency shop – persons choosing not to belong to a trade union representing personal assistants of persons with disability	U.S.A. 6	XXXIV 125
Collective labour relations – inter-union disputes – changing trade union – union rivalry – role of works council – definition of bargaining agent – collective bargaining – good faith and stability in labour relations – election to determine bargaining agent	Isr. 1	XXXV 347

Collective bargaining

Promulgation and normative effect of the collective agreement	Aust. 1	XXXIII 233
Competence to collectively bargain – alliance of trade unions	Ger. 2	XXXI 329
Good faith bargaining requirements – employee meetings – employer proposal put to ballot unilaterally	Austral. 1	XXX 259
Employer prerogatives – ban on smoking – interpretation of collective agreement	Fin. 2	XXXI 349

Duty to bargain – bargaining orders	Austral. 2	XXXII 273
Lawful subjects	U.S.A. 2	XXXIII 239
Prohibited employer activities during union organizing campaign – limitations on employer freedom of speech	Isr. 2	XXXIII 251
Trade union participation in bargaining – refusal to sign agreement	It. 1	XXXIII 261
Consultation rules – unlawfulness can be established in the framework of non-contentious proceedings –consultation, however, cannot be forced	Hun. 1	XXXIV 341
Unitary trade union representation body (RSU) – right to call workplace meetings – competence of a single RSU member	It. 3	XXXIV 347
Collective bargaining – termination of enterprise agreement – 'public interest' considerations in terminating enterprise agreement	Austral. 1	XXXV 353
Constitutional law – Charter of Rights – freedom of association –right to collective bargaining – challenge to constitutionality of legislation excluding RCMP members from public service labour relations regime and imposing non-unionized regime – legislatively imposed regime not independent from management and not providing for employee choice of association or input into selection of collective goals – whether impugned legislation substantially interferes with right to meaningful process of collective bargaining and thereby infringes constitutional guarantee of freedom of association – if so, whether infringement justifiable	Can. 1	XXXV 367
Collective bargaining – refusal to bargain – remedy for unfair labor practice – reimbursement of union's bargaining-related expenses	U.S.A. 3	XXXV 387
Right to union organization – union recognized bargaining agent – union de-recognition – protected period of union recognition – employer's anti-union activities – penalty for employer anti-union activity	Isr. 1	XXXVI 67

Timing of representation elections – timing of hearing to challenge voter eligibility – providing unions with information for contacting individual employees – privacy   U.S.A. 3   XXXVI 251

Collective agreements

Company and territorial agreements – *erga omnes* effect distribution of labour law powers between State and Regional authorities   It. 4   XXXII 287

Concurrency of collective agreements   Ger. 1   XXX 271

Disagreement as to scope of proposed collective agreement   Austral. 3   XXX 291

Collective agreement – accessory peace obligation – secondary collective action   Nor. 1   XXX 371

Collective agreements – "satzung"(statute) – relationship with agreements   Aust. 1   XXX 299

Successorship – enforcement of arbitration provision (in collective agreement)   U.S.A. 3   XXX 309

Breach of agreement – duty to produce entire text   It. 3   XXXI 355

Effects of collective agreement – retroactivity   Aust. 1   XXXI 363

Equal treatment regarding terms and conditions in collective agreement   Fin 1   XXXIII 271

Revocation of adjudication of capacity to conclude agreements   Aust. 2   XXXIII 279

Sectoral wage setting – extension of collective agreements   Ire. 1   XXXIII 291

Labour arbitration – scope of "management rights" clause in collective agreement – health and safety requirements – unilateral imposition of alcohol testing   Can. 2   XXXIV 149

Enforceability of employer imposed arbitration in claims for overtime pay – employer prohibition of employee claims brought in class action format – right to engage in or refrain from mutual aid and protection   U.S.A. 2   XXXIV 355

Collective bargaining agreements – differences between professional categories – observance of equal treatment – presumption – evidence to the contrary – justification outside any consideration of a professional nature   Fr. 1   XXXV 401

Measures to curb public spending – freeze of all pay increases for public sector employees for 2011-2014 – infringement of Arts. 3 and 36 of Constitution – freezing of collective bargaining for 2011-2013 and extension of freeze to 2014 and 2015 – infringement of Art. 39 of Constitution – supervening constitutional unlawfulness   It. 3   XXXV 409

Extension of the applicability of an expired collective bargaining agreement and maintenance of wage conditions that had applied under that agreement   Sp. 1   XXXV 419

Collective bargaining agreement – court interpretation of retirees' contribution-free health benefits scheme where there exists a general duration clause   U.S.A. 1   XXXV 429

Collective agreement – worker members of cooperatives – minimum wage – reference to collective agreements signed by the comparatively more representative organizations – Art. 39 of Italian Constitution requiring commensurate and sufficient – remuneration   It. 3   XXXVI 263

Industrial conflict

Protected industrial action – suspension because of apprehended injury to third parties – balancing of interests of unions and third parties   Austral. 2   XXX 323

Responsibility for damages caused by illegal strike   Pol. 2   XXXIII 309

Right of public servants (Beamte) to engage in industrial action   Ger. 1   XXXII 295

Right to strike in church-run establishments   Ger. 1   XXXIII 309

Picketing – location of picket – whether employer or carries on business at location of picketing   Ire. 1   XXX 337

Picketing – dismissal – exclusion	It. 3	XXX 357
Protected industrial action – protected action ballot – genuine efforts to reach agreement – matters pertaining to the employer/employee relationship	Austral. 4	XXX 363
Right of employer(s) to take industrial action – positive right of association on employer side	Swe. 2	XXXIII 345
Strike in essential services – minimum services in TV – Technological strike breaking	Sp. 1	XXXII 317
Strikes in essential services	Isr. 1	XXXIII 355
Strikes – employer response – withholding of pay – whether includes denial of access to employer-provided accommodation	Austral. 1	XXXIII 365
Secondary collective action – accessory peace obligation	Nor. 1	XXX 371
Trade union right to bring action on behalf of employee – with or without consent of employee	Pol. 2	XXXI 371
Collective dispute – mass resignation – right to strike by group of workers not recognised as bargaining agent – strike in essential services	Isr. 1	XXXI 381
Illegal threat – freeing employer from the legal consequences of declaration of intent – doctors "leaving" patients	Pol. 1	XXXII 335
Determination of bargaining agent – changing trade union – period of protection against challenge	Isr. 1	XXXII 345
Employment contract – exercise of the right to strike – business closure – non-forced situation – unlawful lockout – obstruction of the exercise of the right to strike – consequences of a lockout declared unlawful – compensation for damages	Fr. 1	XXXIV 103

Cases Reported by Subject Matter   xxxvii

Call for strike via the employer's intranet	Ger. 1	XXXIV	369
Constitutional law – Charter of Rights – freedom of association – right to strike – public service employees – whether right to strike is protected by guarantee of freedom of association – whether prohibition on essential services employees participating in strike action amounts to substantial interference with meaningful process of collective bargaining and therefore violates freedom of association – if so, whether such violation is justified as a reasonable limitation on freedom of association	Can. 2	XXXV	17
The right to take collective action – preconditions for the exercise of the right to strike	Neth. 1	XXXV	435
The right of workers and trade unions to boycott an enterprise in which there is a collective conflict	Neth. 2	XXXV	445
Lockout – employees not party to dispute – may not be locked out	S.A. 1	XXXV	451
Employment contract – employment benefits – bonuses – discrimination – industrial action	Fin. 1	XXXVI	271
Demonstration outside of working hours aimed at placing pressure on an employer in a collective bargaining dispute – union not exercising rights under the Labour Relations Act but under the constitutional right to demonstrate – constitutes a circumvention of the dispute procedures of the Labour Relations Act – accordingly unlawful	S.A. 1	XXXVI	277
Strike, contractor and main company – forbidden cases of strikers' replacement by hiring another contractor	Sp. 2	XXXVI	285

Workers' participation

Rules on election of works council – effect on formation of Central Works Council	Hun. 2	XXX	379
Collective redundancies – Directive 98/59/EC – judicial decision ordering dissolution – consultation required – employer and liquidator	C.J.E.C. 1	XXXI	49

Works Council – protected worker – merit based salary increases	Bel. 1	XXXIII	375
Dismissal of a member of the works council	Aust. 1	XXXIV	377
Social policy – information and consultation – Directive 2002/14/EC – Charter of Fundamental Rights of the European Union – Article 27 – subjecting the setting up of bodies representing staff to certain thresholds of employees – calculation of the thresholds – national legislation contrary to European Union law – role of the national court	C.J.E.C. 1	XXXIV	23
Consultation rules – unlawfulness can be established in the framework of non-contentious proceedings – consultation, however, cannot be forced	Hun. 1	XXXIV	341
Unitary trade union representation body (RSU) – right to call workplace meetings – competence of a single RSU member	It. 3	XXXIV	347
Unlawful employer payments to labor organizations or their officers	U.S.A. 1	XXXIV	111

PART SIX

ADMINISTRATION – JUDICIAL AND GENERAL

Right of access to court – disputes arising out of employment contracts between individuals and diplomatic missions – state immunity	H.R. 1	XXX	387
Enforceability of provision in employment contract which delegates to arbitrator authority to resolve any dispute relating to the contract's enforceability – Federal Arbitration Act	U.S.A. 1	XXX	405
Scope of judicial deferral to arbitrator – Federal Arbitration Act	U.S.A. 6	XXXIII	385
Limitation on class actions in Title VII discrimination cases	U.S.A. 1	XXXI	407

Migrant worker – lack of permit – statutory entitlements	Ire. 1	XXXII 359
Application of Americans with Disabilities Act to religious/educational institutions	U.S.A. 2	XXXII 369
Penalties for wage dumping	Aust. 2	XXXIV 245
Dismissal protection of an HIV-positive employee beyond the scope of general dismissal protection	Ger. 2	XXXIV 179
Global work and jurisdiction	Sp. 2	XXXIV 13
Enforceability of employer imposed arbitration in claims for overtime pay – employer prohibition of employee claims brought in class action format – right to engage in or refrain from mutual aid and protection	U.S.A. 2	XXXIV 355
Jurisdiction over the claims of persons who are not U.S.A. residents who allege that they were injured in another country by the wrongful acts of a foreign company with U.S.A. subsidiary – extraterritorial application of U.S.A. law	U.S.A. 5	XXXIV 385
National Labor Relations Act – power of president to appoint members of National Labor Relations Board	U.S.A. 7	XXXIV 141
Employment rights – migrant worker – lack of employment permit – whether worker able to claim statutory entitlements	Ire. 2	XXXV 459
Qualification of collective labour law disputes for court legal action – differentiating between cases that can be heard before civil or labour courts	Pol. 2	XXXV 469
Judicial termination of the employment contract at the request of the employee, based on breach by the employer – Workers' Statute Article 50 – exceptions to the requirement of continuing to work until judgement is rendered	Sp. 3	XXXV 335
Whether additional court fees can be collected from litigants in order to finance social security benefits for persons in the legal profession	Ind. 1	XXXVI 301

Employment tribunal – judicial review of decision – applicant securing order of certiorari – whether applicant entitled to costs – whether tribunal acted mala fide or improperly   Ire. 1   XXXVI 309

Employer handbook rules – interference with right to engage in concerted activity   U.S.A. 1   XXXVI 75

Remedies for unfair labor practices – public reading of notice of wrongdoing – wrongdoer's liability for costs of enforcing the law   U.S.A. 2   XXXVI 317

Suit for non resident employee's maritime claims barred by arbitration agreement   U.S.A. 4   XXXVI 331

Employer failed to keep certain worktime records – damages awarded to a certified class – can court rely on expert evidence estimating the time worked under Federal Rules of Procedure   U.S.A. 5   XXXVI 345

Demotion of a public employee in the mistaken belief that the employee has exercised a right protected by the United States Constitution – a wrongful act for the purpose of federal law   U.S.A. 6   XXXVI 355

PART ONE

GENERAL PRINCIPLES OF LABOUR LAW AND KEY CONCEPTS

THE NETHERLANDS

Supreme Court decision of 18 September 2015
The State of the Netherlands v. an employee

Transposition of EU Directive 2003/88/EC on the Organisation of Working Time – conditions for claiming monetary compensation for denied paid annual leave

HEADNOTES

Facts

This case involved the claim of a disabled employee who under the existing statutory rules had only been granted a partial right to paid annual leave. In a procedure against the State of the Netherlands, he claimed monetary compensation of €2651 for denied annual leave, asserting that the action was contrary to Article 7(1) of the European Union (EU) Directive 2003/88/EC on the Organisation of Working Time. The Court of First Instance of The Hague found in favour of this claim on the basis of the so-called *Francovich* doctrine. The State of The Netherlands appealed to the Court of Appeal of The Hague. This Court confirmed the judgement of the Court of First Instance, but on a different legal basis, namely the general law of civil liability of public authorities for illegal legislation. The State then petitioned the Dutch High (Supreme) Court to overturn the lower Court decision ("cassation").

Decision

The Dutch Supreme Court confirmed the judgement of the Court of Appeal of The Hague.

Law Applied

- Art. 7 (1) of EU Directive 2003/88/EC on the Organisation of Working Time
- Art. 7:654 (4) of the Dutch Civil Code (as it stood at that time)

JUDGEMENT

The High Court confirmed the judgement of the Court of Appeal of The Hague that, according to Dutch law, to issue and maintain on the statute book rules which are contrary to higher sources of legislation is a "tort", which implies a fault and opens the right to compensation. There is insufficient reason not to apply this rule in the case where the rule in question is an Act of Parliament which is contrary to an EU Directive. There was also no reason for the Court of Appeal to judge the claim of the employee on the basis of the criteria developed by the Court of Justice of the European Union in the cases of *Francovich* and *Brasserie du Pêcheur*.

ANNOTATION

In the Netherlands since the 1960s there exists a number of provisions in the Civil Code granting all employees a minimum of four weeks annual paid leave (Articles 7:634 to 7:645 of the Dutch Civil Code). However this entitlement has always been somewhat limited for employees who are not working because of a lengthy sickness or disability. At the date of the claim (2010) the relevant provision essentially said that the entitlement to annual paid leave of an employee who is unable to work because of sickness only is accrued during the last 6 months of the non-performance of work (Article 7:635 (4) of the Dutch Civil Code).

A comparable limitation was contained in the German legislation on annual paid leave. This provision was questioned in the case *Schultz-Hoff* (C-350/06). In its judgement dated 20 January 2009 the Court of Justice of the European Union ruled that this German provision was contrary to Article 7(1) of Directive 2003/88/EC on the Organisation of Working Time. Immediately after this judgement in literature and in parliament many persons in The Netherlands took the position that, as a consequence of the *Schultz-Hoff* judgement, the Dutch rules on the annual paid leave entitlement of ill and disabled workers had to be changed.

The Government took this problem to heart, but – as legislative procedures always take time – it was only in 2013 that Art. 7:635 (4) of the Dutch Civil Code was changed. Dutch lawyers immediately took the position that, now that the legislator had recognised that the Dutch law in this field, like the German legislation, was contrary to EU law, the employees concerned by this limitation of the paid leave entitlement, could claim compensation for the denied annual paid leave from the State on the basis of the so-called *Francovich* doctrine. According to this doctrine, developed for the first time by the Court of Justice of the European Union notably in the case of *Francovich* (ECJ 19 November 1991, C-6/90), a Member State is required to make good loss and damage caused to individuals by failure to transpose a Directive into national law, provided that three conditions are fulfilled: the first being that the result prescribed by the Directive should entail the grant of rights to individuals; the second being that it should be possible to identify the content of those rights on the basis of the provisions of the Directive; and thirdly the existence of a causal link between the breach of the State's obligation and the loss and damage suffered by the injured parties. In a later case, *Brasserie du Pêcheur* (ECJ 5 March 1996, C-46/93), the ECJ slightly refined these three conditions, stating that "where a breach of EU law by a Member State is attributable to the national legislature acting in a field in which it has a wide discretion to make legislative choices, individuals suffering loss or injury thereby are entitled to reparation where the rule of EU law breached is intended to confer rights upon them, the breach is sufficiently serious, and there is a direct causal link between the breach and the damage sustained by the individuals." Consequently law suits were initiated on this basis, from which the law suit concerned here was one of the fruits.

In the case under discussion the Court of First Instance indeed granted the claim of the employee on the basis of the doctrine developed by the Court of Justice of the European Union in the *Francovich/Brasserie du Pêcheur* cases. It considered, among other issues, that the Dutch authorities should not have waited until the *Schultz-Hoff* judgement was issued in order to realise that the Dutch implementation within domestic law was not in accordance with EU law. Already in 2001 there had been the judgement in the *Bectu* case (CJEU 26 June 2001, C-173/99), which should have alerted the Government to the fact that restrictions on the accrual of rights to paid leave are not allowed under the EU Directive on the Organisation of Working Time.

The State then brought an appeal to the Court of Appeal of the The Hague. This Court affirmed the granting of the employee's claim, but based its reasoning concerning State responsibility no longer on the fulfilment of the *Francovich/Brasserie du Pêcheur* conditions, but on the Dutch national system of state responsibility for illegal legislation.

Then the case moved to the Dutch High Court (Supreme Court) where all attention no longer focused on the question whether the *Francovich/Brasserie du Pêcheur* conditions were fulfilled in this case of improper implementation of the EU Working Time Directive. All attention was now targeted on this new basis for the accepting the claim. The State of The Netherlands did not contest that the Dutch judiciary in principle could base the State responsibility for the defective annual leave regulation on the Dutch national system of state responsibility because the CJEU itself in the *Brasserie du Pêcheur* case had recognised that a Member State may compensate victims of the violations of EU law with a more advantageous regime of compensation. The compensation according to the *Francovich/Brasserie du Pêcheur* doctrine should be seen as a minimum requirement for the Member States. The Dutch national system of state responsibility is seen as more advantageous for victims because it operates less onerous criteria for recognising State responsibility.

However the debated issue here was, whether there existed already such a general system of national State responsibility for illegal legislation in the Netherlands. Up to the time of this judgement – as the Advocate-General to the High Court pointed out – Dutch law on State compensation for damages as a result of illegal legislation was not so clear cut. Earlier precedents on the issue were only concerned with illegal legislation of lower State authorities *vis-à-vis* Acts of the Dutch Parliaments. The question was: Should it be extended to the case of illegal legislation of Acts of Parliaments *vis-à-vis* EU Directives?

In its final judgement the High Court overruled these hesitations and the query raised by its Advocate-General. The High Court judgement simply extended without any qualification the rudimentary Dutch general law on civil liability of the State for illegal legislation to cases of improper implementation of EU rules in Dutch national statutory law. No limitations or criteria according to the *Francovich/Brasserie du Pêcheur* doctrine are necessary.

The commentator of this Annotation doubts whether the High Court has ruled wisely to "upgrade" the rudimentary Dutch national law on State responsibility for illegal legislation in the relationship between lower authorities and the Acts of Parliament, to govern also the relationship between national legislation and EU Directives. As the Advocate-General of the Dutch High Court quite rightly argued: "EC rules sometimes are consciously framed in an unclear and ambiguous way, that its interpretation is assigned to the ECJ; that in that interpretation usually legal arguments but also integration-political arguments play a role and therefore it is difficult to avoid conflicts with EU law which only later emerge." In this context the Advocate-General recalled that the relevant EU norm terminates with the words "[…] in accordance with the conditions for entitlement to, and granting of, such leave laid down by national legislation and/or practice." Moreover he pointed at the fact that the ECJ judgment in the *Bectu* judgement dates back more than 12 years after the final date for implementation of the same norm in Directive 93/104/EC and that the Dutch norm, like similar norms in other Member States, had never incited the European Commission to start infraction procedures based on improper transposition of the Directive.

The clarifications given by the Court of Justice of the European Union in *Brasserie du Pêcheur* especially about the criterion that the breach must be sufficiently serious, contain wise limitations (considerations given at points 55-58, C-46/93), which were not at that time explicitly contained in Dutch national rules on illegal legislation. The decision states "As to the second condition, as regards both Community liability under Article 215 and Member State liability for breaches of Community law, the decisive test for finding that a breach of Community law is sufficiently serious is whether the Member State or the Community institution concerned manifestly and gravely disregarded the limits on its discretion. The factors which the competent court may take into consideration include the clarity and precision of the rule breached, the measure of discretion left by that rule to the national or Community authorities, whether the infringement and the damage caused was intentional or involuntary, whether any error of law was excusable or inexcusable, the fact that the position taken by a Community institution may have contributed towards the omission, and the adoption or retention of national measures or practices contrary to Community law. On any view, a breach of Community law will clearly be sufficiently serious if it has persisted despite a judgement finding the infringement in question to be established, or a preliminary ruling or settled case-law of the Court on the matter, from which it is clear that the conduct in question constituted an infringement. While, in the present cases, the Court cannot substitute its assessment for that of the national courts, which have sole jurisdiction to find the facts in the main proceedings and decide how to characterize the breaches of Community law at issue, it will be helpful to indicate a number of circumstances which the national courts might take into account." Finally in points 59-64 of its *Brasserie du Pêcheur* ruling (C-46/93) the ECJ has given some interesting indications.

It is submitted that the judgements of the Dutch Courts should have given much more attention to these factors than they have done. For the sake of a level playing field between the EU Member States it does not seem wise to surpass the minimum conditions laid down in the *Francovich/Brasserie du Pêcheur* cases. In the case commented on here, the damages awarded by the High Court were calculable at € 2650; similar claims will presumably not surpass a few million Euros for the Dutch taxpayer. However, the day may come that the Dutch taxpayer has to suffer much more substantial losses because of the very generous character of the Dutch law on compensation for other examples of conflicts between Dutch statutory law and EU legislation.

This decision gives rise to reflection and hopefully further academic research regarding to what extent in the various EU Member States civil liability claims against the State for deficient implementation of EU labour law are effectively made and honoured.

C.J.E.C 1.

EUROPEAN UNION

Court of Justice of the European Union (Grand Chamber)
Dansk Industri (DI), acting on behalf of Ajos A/S v.
Estate of Karsten Eigil Rasmussen, Case C441/14

Social policy – Charter of Fundamental Rights of the European Union – Directive 2000/78/EC – principle prohibiting discrimination on grounds of age – national legislation incompatible with the Directive – possibility for a private person to bring proceedings to establish the liability of the State for breach of EU law – dispute between private persons – principles of legal certainty and the protection of legitimate expectations – role of the national court

HEADNOTES

Facts

The judgement relates to the interpretation of Article 2(1) and (2)(a) and Article 6(1) of European Union (EU) Council Directive 2000/78/EC of 27 November 2000 establishing a general framework for equal treatment in employment and occupation (banning direct and indirect discrimination on the ground of age, as well laying down the scope for justification of differential treatment on age grounds) and the principle prohibiting discrimination on the ground of age and the principles of legal certainty and the protection of legitimate expectations.

The reference for a preliminary ruling was made in the course of the proceedings between Dansk Industri (DI), acting on behalf of Ajos A/S (Ajos) and the legal heirs of Mr Rasmussen concerning Ajos's refusal to pay Mr Rasmussen a severance allowance.

Mr Rasmussen was dismissed by his employer, Ajos, on 25 May 2009 at the age of 60. He left his job at the end of June 2009, and was subsequently employed by another undertaking. Mr Rasmussen had been employed by Ajos since 1 June 1984, and was, in principle, entitled to a severance allowance equal to three months' salary under Paragraph 2a(1) of the Danish Law on salaried employees (*funktionærloven*). However, since he had reached the age of 60 by the date of his departure and was entitled to an old-age pension payable by the employer under a scheme which he had joined before reaching the age of 50, Paragraph 2a(3) of that law, as interpreted in consistent national case-law, barred his entitlement to the severance allowance, even though he remained on the employment market after his departure from Ajos.

In March 2012, the trade union Dansk Formands Forening brought an action on Mr Rasmussen's behalf against Ajos claiming payment of a severance allowance equal to three months' salary, as provided for in Paragraph 2a(1) of the Law on salaried employees. The trade union relied on the judgement of the Court of Justice of 12 October 2010 in *Ingeniørforeningen i Danmark* (C499/08, EU:C:2010:600). On 14 January 2014, the Maritime and Commercial Court upheld the claim brought on behalf of Mr Rasmussen, now represented by his legal heirs, for payment of the severance allowance in question. That Court stated that it was clear from the judgement in *Ingeniørforeningen i Danmark* that Paragraph 2a(3) of the Law on salaried employees was contrary to EU Directive 2000/78 and it found that the previous national interpretation of Paragraph 2a was inconsistent with the general principle, enshrined in EU law, prohibiting discrimination on grounds of age.

Ajos appealed against that decision before the Danish Supreme Court, contending that any interpretation of Paragraph 2a(3) of the Law on salaried employees that was consistent with the provisions interpreted in the 2010 judgement of *Ingeniørforeningen i Danmark* would, in any event, be *contra legem*. It also maintained that the application of a rule as clear and unambiguous as that laid down in Paragraph 2a(3) of that Law could not be precluded on the basis of the general principle of EU law prohibiting discrimination on grounds of age without jeopardising the principles of the protection of legitimate expectations and legal certainty.

The Supreme Court decided to stay the proceedings, and referred two questions to the Court of Justice of the European Union for a preliminary ruling.

Referring to the first question posited by the referring court, the Court of Justice stated that the national court, faced with adjudicating in a dispute between private persons, sought to ascertain whether the general principle prohibiting discrimination on grounds of age is to be interpreted as precluding national legislation, the issue in the proceedings before it being that an employee was by national law deprived of the right to a severance allowance whereas that employee was entitled to claim an old-age pension from the employer under a pension scheme which the employee joined before reaching the age of 50, regardless of whether the employee chose to remain on the employment market or take his retirement.

In its second question the referring court sought to ascertain, in essence, whether EU law is to be interpreted as permitting a national court seized of a dispute between private persons, where it is established that the relevant national legislation is at odds with the general principle prohibiting discrimination on grounds of age, to balance that principle against the principles of legal certainty and the protection of legitimate expectations and to conclude that the latter principle should take precedence over the former. In that context, the referring court was also uncertain whether, in carrying out the balancing exercise, it may or must take account of the fact that EU Member States are under a duty to compensate for the harm suffered by private persons as a result of the incorrect transposition of a directive, such as Directive 2000/78.

Decision

The Court of Justice decision, delivered on 19 April 2016, clarified that the general principle prohibiting discrimination on the ground of age, as given concrete expression by Council Directive 2000/78/EC of 27 November 2000 establishing a general framework for equal treatment in employment and occupation, must be interpreted as precluding, including in disputes between private persons, national legislation, such as that at issue in the proceedings before the referring court, which deprives an employee of entitlement to a severance allowance where the employee is entitled to claim an old-age pension from the employer under a pension scheme which the employee joined before reaching the age of 50, regardless of whether the employee chooses to remain on the employment market or take his retirement.

EU law is to be interpreted as meaning that a national court adjudicating in a dispute between private persons falling within the scope of Directive 2000/78 is required, when applying provisions of national law, to interpret those provisions in such a way that they apply in a manner that is consistent with the Directive or, if such an interpretation is not possible, to disapply, where necessary, any provision of national law that is contrary to the general principle prohibiting discrimination on grounds of age. Neither the principles of legal certainty and the protection of legitimate expectations nor the fact that it is possible for the private person who considers that he has been wronged by the application of a provision of national law that is at odds with EU law to bring proceedings to establish the liability of the Member State concerned for breach of EU law, can alter that obligation.

Law Applied

See Judgement.

JUDGEMENT

Question 2

[…]

22 In order to answer that [first] question, it is appropriate first of all to note that the source of the general principle prohibiting discrimination on grounds of age, as given concrete expression by Directive 2000/78, is to be found, as is clear from recitals 1 and 4 of the directive, in various international instruments and in the constitutional traditions common to the Member States (see judgements in *Mangold*, C144/04, EU:C:2005:709, paragraph 74, and *Kücükdeveci*, C555/07, EU:C:2010:21, paragraphs 20 and 21). It is also apparent from the Court's case-law that that principle, now enshrined in Article 21 of the Charter of Fundamental Rights of the European Union, must be regarded as a general principle of EU law (see judgements in *Mangold*, C144/04, EU:C:2005:709, paragraph 75, and *Kücükdeveci*, C555/07, EU:C:2010:21, paragraph 21).

23 It should then be noted that, as Directive 2000/78 does not itself lay down the general principle prohibiting discrimination on grounds of age but simply gives concrete expression to that principle in relation to employment and occupation, the scope of the protection conferred by the directive does not go beyond that afforded by that principle. The EU legislature intended by the adoption of the directive to establish a more precise framework to facilitate the practical implementation of the principle of equal treatment and, in particular, to specify various possible exceptions to that principle, circumscribing those exceptions by the use of a clearer definition of their scope.

24 Lastly, it should be added that, in order for it to be possible for the general principle prohibiting discrimination on grounds of age to be applicable to a situation such as that before the referring court, that

situation must also fall within the scope of the prohibition of discrimination laid down by Directive 2000/78.

25 It is sufficient to observe in that regard that, as the Court has previously held, by generally excluding a whole category of workers from entitlement to the severance allowance, Paragraph 2a(3) of the Law on salaried employees affects the conditions regarding the dismissal of those workers for the purposes of Article 3(1)(c) of Directive 2000/78 (judgement in *Ingeniørforeningen i Danmark*, C499/08, EU:C:2010:600, paragraph 21). It follows that the national legislation at issue in the main proceedings falls within the scope of EU law and, accordingly, within the scope of the general principle prohibiting discrimination on grounds of age.

26 In those circumstances and in the light of the fact that the Court has previously held that Articles 2 and 6(1) of Directive 2000/78 are to be interpreted as precluding national legislation, such as the legislation that is the subject of the present request for a preliminary ruling, pursuant to which workers who are eligible for an old-age pension from their employer under a pension scheme which they joined before attaining the age of 50 cannot, on that ground alone, claim a severance allowance aimed at assisting workers with more than 12 years of service in the undertaking in finding new employment (judgement in *Ingeniørforeningen i Danmark*, C499/08, EU:C:2010:600, paragraph 49), the same applies with regard to the fundamental principle of equal treatment, the general principle prohibiting discrimination on grounds of age being merely a specific expression of that principle.

27 In the light of the foregoing considerations, the answer to the first question is that the general principle prohibiting discrimination on grounds of age, as given concrete expression by Directive 2000/78, must be interpreted as precluding, including in disputes between private persons, national legislation, such as that at issue in the proceedings before the referring court, which deprives an employee of entitlement to a severance allowance where the employee is entitled to claim an old-age pension from the employer under a pension scheme which the employee joined before reaching the age of 50, regardless of whether the employee chooses to remain on the employment market or take his retirement.

Question 2

28 By its second question, the referring court seeks to ascertain, in essence, whether EU law is to be interpreted as permitting a national court seized of a dispute between private persons, where it is established that the relevant national legislation is at odds with the general principle prohibiting discrimination on grounds of age, to balance that principle against the

principles of legal certainty and the protection of legitimate expectations and to conclude that the latter principle should take precedence over the former. In that context, the referring court is also uncertain whether, in carrying out that balancing exercise, it may or must take account of the fact that the Member States are under a duty to compensate for the harm suffered by private persons as a result of the incorrect transposition of a directive, such as Directive 2000/78.

29 In the first place, it should be noted in that regard that, according to settled case-law, where national courts are called on to give judgement in proceedings between individuals in which it is apparent that the national legislation at issue is contrary to EU law, it is for those courts to provide the legal protection which individuals derive from the provisions of EU law and to ensure that those provisions are fully effective (see, to that effect, *Pfeiffer and Others*, C397/01 to C403/01, EU:C:2004:584, paragraph 111, and *Kücükdeveci*, C555/07, EU:C:2010:21, paragraph 45).

30 While it is true that, in relation to disputes between individuals, the Court has consistently held that a directive cannot of itself impose obligations on an individual and cannot therefore be relied upon as such against an individual (see, *inter alia*, judgements in *Marshall*, 152/84, EU:C:1986:84, paragraph 48; *Faccini Dori*, C91/92, EU:C:1994:292, paragraph 20; and *Pfeiffer and Others*, C397/01 to C403/01, EU:C:2004:584, paragraph 108), the fact nonetheless remains that the Court has also consistently held that the Member States' obligation arising from a directive to achieve the result envisaged by that directive and their duty to take all appropriate measures, whether general or particular, to ensure the fulfilment of that obligation are binding on all the authorities of the Member States, including, for matters within their jurisdiction, the courts (see, to that effect, *inter alia*, judgements in *von Colson and Kamann*, 14/83, EU:C:1984:153, paragraph 26, and *Kücükdeveci*, C555/07, EU:C:2010:21, paragraph 47).

31 It follows that, in applying national law, national courts called upon to interpret that law are required to consider the whole body of rules of law and to apply methods of interpretation that are recognised by those rules in order to interpret it, so far as possible, in the light of the wording and the purpose of the directive concerned in order to achieve the result sought by the directive and consequently comply with the third paragraph of Article 288 TFEU (see, *inter alia*, judgements in *Pfeiffer and Others*, C397/01 to C403/01, EU:C:2004:584, paragraphs 113 and 114, and *Kücükdeveci*, C555/07, EU:C:2010:21, paragraph 48).

32 It is true that the Court has stated that this principle of interpreting national law in conformity with EU law has certain limits. Thus, the

obligation for a national court to refer to EU law when interpreting and applying the relevant rules of domestic law is limited by general principles of law and cannot serve as the basis for an interpretation of national law *contra legem* (see judgements in *Impact*, C268/06, EU:C:2008:223, paragraph 100; *Dominguez*, C282/10, EU:C:2012:33, paragraph 25; and *Association de médiation sociale*, C176/12, EU:C:2014:2, paragraph 39).

33 It should be noted in that connection that the requirement to interpret national law in conformity with EU law entails the obligation for national courts to change its established case-law, where necessary, if it is based on an interpretation of national law that is incompatible with the objectives of a directive (see, to that effect, judgement in *Centrosteel*, C456/98, EU:C:2000:402, paragraph 17).

34 Accordingly, the national court cannot validly claim in the main proceedings that it is impossible for it to interpret the national provision at issue in a manner that is consistent with EU law by mere reason of the fact that it has consistently interpreted that provision in a manner that is incompatible with EU law.

35 That point having been made clear, it should be added that even if a national court seized of a dispute that calls into question the general principle prohibiting discrimination on grounds of age, as given concrete expression in Directive 2000/78, does in fact find it impossible to arrive at an interpretation of national law that is consistent with the directive, it is nonetheless under an obligation to provide, within the limits of its jurisdiction, the legal protection which individuals derive from EU law and to ensure the full effectiveness of that law, disapplying if need be any provision of national legislation contrary to that principle (judgement in *Kücükdeveci*, C555/07, EU:C:2010:21, paragraph 51).

36 Moreover, it is apparent from paragraph 47 of the judgement in *Association de médiation sociale* (C176/12, EU:C:2014:2) that the principle prohibiting discrimination on grounds of age confers on private persons an individual right which they may invoke as such and which, even in disputes between private persons, requires the national courts to disapply national provisions that do not comply with that principle.

37 Accordingly, in the present case, if it considers that it is impossible for it to interpret the national provision at issue in a manner that is consistent with EU law, the national court must disapply that provision.

38 In the second place, with regard to identifying the obligations deriving from the principle of the protection of legitimate expectations for a national court adjudicating in a dispute between private persons, it should be noted that a national court cannot rely on that principle in order

to continue to apply a rule of national law that is at odds with the general principle prohibiting discrimination on grounds of age, as laid down by Directive 2000/78.

39 Indeed, the application of the principle of the protection of legitimate expectations as contemplated by the referring court would, in practice, have the effect of limiting the temporal effects of the Court's interpretation because, as a result of that application, such an interpretation would not be applicable in the main proceedings.

40 According to settled case-law, the interpretation which the Court, in the exercise of the jurisdiction conferred upon it by Article 267 TFEU, gives to EU law clarifies and, where necessary, defines the meaning and scope of that law as it must be, or ought to have been, understood and applied from the time of its coming into force. It follows that, unless there are truly exceptional circumstances, which is not claimed to be the case here, EU law as thus interpreted must be applied by the courts even to legal relationships which arose and were established before the judgement ruling on the request for interpretation, provided that in other respects the conditions for bringing a dispute relating to the application of that law before the courts having jurisdiction are satisfied (see, *inter alia*, judgement in *Gmina Wrocław*, C276/14, EU:C:2015:635, paragraphs 44 and 45 and the case-law cited).

41 Moreover, the protection of legitimate expectations cannot, in any event, be relied on for the purpose of denying an individual who has brought proceedings culminating in the Court interpreting EU law as precluding the rule of national law at issue the benefit of that interpretation (see, to that effect, judgements in *Defrenne*, 43/75, EU:C:1976:56, paragraph 75, and *Barber*, C262/88, EU:C:1990:209, paragraphs 44 and 45).

42 With regard to the referring court's question mentioned in paragraph 19 above, it should be noted that the fact that it is possible for private persons with an individual right deriving from EU law, such as, in the present case, employees, to claim compensation where their rights are infringed by a breach of EU law attributable to a Member State (see, to that effect, judgements in *Francovich and Others*, C6/90 and C9/90, EU:C:1991:428, paragraph 33, and *Brasserie du pêcheur and Factortame*, C46/93 and C48/93, EU:C:1996:79, paragraph 20) cannot alter the obligation the national court is under to uphold the interpretation of national law that is consistent with Directive 2000/78 or, if such an interpretation is not possible, to disapply the national provision that is at odds with the general principle prohibiting discrimination on ground of age, as given concrete expression by that directive, or justify that court giving precedence, in

the dispute before it, to the protection of the legitimate expectations of a private person, namely in this case the employer, who has complied with national law.

43 In the light of all the foregoing, the answer to the second question is that EU law is to be interpreted as meaning that a national court adjudicating in a dispute between private persons falling within the scope of Directive 2000/78 is required, when applying provisions of national law, to interpret those provisions in such a way that they may be applied in a manner that is consistent with the directive or, if such an interpretation is not possible, to disapply, where necessary, any provision of national law that is contrary to the general principle prohibiting discrimination on grounds of age. Neither the principles of legal certainty and the protection of legitimate expectations nor the fact that it is possible for the private person who considers that he has been wronged by the application of a provision of national law that is at odds with EU law to bring proceedings to establish the liability of the Member State concerned for breach of EU law can alter that obligation.

[…]

[Source: Case C441/14 *Dansk Industri (DI), acting on behalf of Ajos A/S v. Estate of Karsten Eigil Rasmussen* delivered on 19 April 2016]

ANNOTATION

This Grand Chamber judgement of the Court of Justice of the European Union (CJEU) is of relevance both to EU labour law and non-discrimination law, especially age discrimination law, and to EU law in general and issues related to the EU Charter of Fundamental Rights, general principles of EU law and horizontal applicability.

An ageing population is a challenging and urgent European (and global) trend that brings increased costs for pensions, health care and elder care, and a risk of increasing intergenerational tension. The EU Active Ageing Policy aims to promote a healthy and active ageing population, increase the labour market participation of older workers (55+) and prolong working life. Furthermore, Article 25 of the EU Charter of Fundamental Rights establishes the rights of the elderly.

The Employment Equality Directive (2000/78/EC) introduced the ban on age discrimination (in relation to all ages) in secondary EU law.

The Employment Equality Directive bans discrimination on the grounds of religion or belief, disability, age or sexual orientation as regards employment and occupation. The Directive encompasses prohibitions on direct and indirect discrimination, harassment, and instruction to discriminate, as well as provisions on positive action and active measures, and a rule on a reversed burden of proof. EU law provides both for a general justification of age-related differential treatment and for some specific exemptions. According to Article 6(1), differences of treatment on grounds of age do not constitute discrimination if they are objectively and reasonably justified by a legitimate aim, including legitimate employment policy, labour market, and vocational training objectives, and if the means of achieving that aim are appropriate and necessary.

Since the adoption of the Employment Equality Directive there is a growing, and by now quite extensive, case law from the CJEU on age discrimination. Many of these cases have dealt with compulsory retirement and premature retirement, and the absolute majority of these cases has dealt with old-age discrimination. The CJEU seems to have developed different 'standards of justification' depending on the issue at hand. The most lenient standard is applied as regards more general systems of compulsory retirement, while a stricter standard is applied, for example, when it comes to compulsory retirement of specific professional groups, premature retirement, and collective dismissals. In principle, EU age discrimination law (through a large scope for justification of age-related differential treatment, specific exemptions and a broad margin of appreciation for Member States and social partners) enables direct and indirect age-related regulation. A comparative analysis of a number of EU Member States demonstrates that there is still a large number of directly and indirectly age-related labour law rules and practices as well as collective bargaining schemes in the areas of employment protection, compulsory retirement, recruitment and working conditions. This has received academic comment, for example in A. Numhauser-Henning and M. Rönnmar (eds), *Age Discrimination and Labour Law. Comparative and Conceptual Perspectives in the EU and Beyond* (Alphen aan den Rijn, Kluwer Law International 2015).

In the decision at hand, the CJEU confirms its reasoning and conclusion from the 2010 judgement in *Ingeniørforeningen i Danmark* as regards the age discriminatory character of the same Danish provision on severance payment at issue. The CJEU's conclusion thus applies both to the public and private sector of the labour market.

The CJEU also confirms its earlier case law in *Mangold* and *Kücükdeveci*, and states that the general principle prohibiting discrimination on grounds of age is a general principle of EU law that is given concrete expression in the Employment Equality Directive and is now also enshrined in Article 21 of the EU Charter of Fundamental Rights.

When it comes to the complex issue of the horizontal application (in disputes between private persons) of the EU Charter of Fundamental Rights and general principles of EU law, the CJEU also refers to, and confirms, its earlier case law in *Mangold* and *Kücükdeveci*. In addition, the CJEU concludes that in a dispute between private persons falling within the scope of the Employment Equality Directive a national court must interpret national provisions in conformity with EU law. (It is interesting to note in this context that Advocate General Bot, when delivering his Opinion on 25 November 2015, concluded that the existence of national case law which is inconsistent with Directive 2000/78 presents no obstacle to the national court's fulfillment of its obligation to interpret national law in conformity with EU law.) The CJEU makes it clear that if such interpretation is not possible, the national court must disapply, where necessary, any provision of national law that is contrary to the general principle prohibiting discrimination on grounds of age. This obligation of the national court is not altered by the principles of legal certainty or protection of legitimate expectations nor by the possibility for private persons to bring proceedings to establish damage liability of the Member State concerned for breach of EU law.

But the story of age discrimination does not end there. At the national level the Supreme Court controversially challenged the CJEU, and chose not to follow the preliminary ruling (*inter alia*, relying on the Act on Denmark's Accession to the EU). The Danish Supreme Court reversed the ruling of the Danish Maritime and Commercial Court. Further commentary can be perused in R. Nielsen and C. D. Tvarnø, "Danish Supreme Court Infringes the EU Treaties by Its Ruling in the *Ajos* Case", *Europarättslig tidskrift*, 2017, pages 303 to 326.

H.R. 1

COUNCIL OF EUROPE

European Court of Human Rights
Çam v. Turkey (Application no. 51500/08)

Article 14 of the European Convention for the Protection of Human Rights and Fundamental Freedoms and Article 2 of its Protocol No. 1 – interface of regional and U.N. norms – right to education and discrimination based on disability

HEADNOTES

Facts

Ms Çam, who is blind, took part in the entrance competition for the Turkish National Music Academy and was included in a published list of successful candidates. In the context of the enrolment procedure, a medical board of a hospital prepared a medical report finding that the applicant could receive education and instruction in the sections of the Music Academy where eyesight was unnecessary. The Director of the Music Academy subsequently wrote to the hospital, informing its Chief Medical Officer that none of the seven sections of the Music Academy could be deemed not to require eyesight. The Director of the Music Academy asked the Chief Medical Officer to prepare a fresh medical report taking account of the fact that no section of the Music Academy could be considered as not necessitating eyesight, and accordingly to specify whether or not the applicant was capable of being educated in the Music Academy. The Music Academy also rejected the applicant's request for enrolment. Acting in her name and on her behalf, the applicant's parents lodged a series of appeals in the administrative courts, which were finally dismissed by a judgement of 19 February issued by the Council of State. The applicant eventually entered the music department of another Turkish University.

Decision

The refusal to enrol the applicant in the National Music Academy was based solely on the fact that she was blind and the domestic authorities had at no stage considered the possibility that reasonable accommodation might have enabled her to be educated in that establishment. That being the case, the European Court of Human Rights considered that the applicant was denied the opportunity to study in the National Music Academy, without any objective and reasonable justification, solely on account of her visual disability. Therefore, there had been a violation of Article 14 of the Convention taken in conjunction with Article 2 of Protocol No. 1.

Law Applied

Article 14 (Prohibition of discrimination) of the European Convention for the Protection of Human Rights and Fundamental Freedoms and Article 2 (Right to education) of Protocol No. 1 to the Convention.

JUDGEMENT

[...]

2. The Court's assessment

a. General principles

52. As regards the right to education, the Court reiterates that it has already had occasion to point out that in a democratic society that right is indispensable to the furtherance of human rights and plays a fundamental role (see *Velyo Velev v. Bulgaria*, no. 16032/07, § 33, ECHR 2014 [extracts]). In that connection, while repeating that education is one of the most important public services in a modern State, the Court acknowledges that it is an activity that is complex to organise and expensive to run, whereas the resources that the authorities can devote to it are necessarily finite. It is also true that in deciding how to regulate access to education, a State must strike a balance between, on the one hand, the educational needs of those under its jurisdiction and, on the other, its limited capacity to accommodate them. However, the Court cannot overlook the fact that, unlike some other public services, education is a right that enjoys direct protection under the Convention (*ibid.*).

53. The Court reiterates that in interpreting and applying Article 2 of Protocol No. 1, account must also be taken of any relevant rules and principles of international law applicable in relations between the Contracting Parties and that the Convention should so far as possible be interpreted in harmony with other rules of international law of which it forms part (see *Catan and Others*, cited above, § 136). The provisions on the right to education set out in such instruments as the European Social Charter or the United Nations Convention on the Rights of Persons with Disabilities should therefore be taken into consideration. Lastly, the Court emphasises that the object and purpose of the Convention, as an instrument for the protection of individual human beings, requires that its provisions be interpreted and applied so as to make its safeguards practical and effective (*ibid.*).

54. As regards the prohibition of discrimination, the Court reiterates that discrimination means treating differently, without an objective and reasonable justification, persons in similar situations, and that "no objective and reasonable justification" means that the distinction in issue does not pursue a "legitimate aim" or that there is not a "reasonable relationship of proportionality between the means employed and the aim sought to be realised" (see *Sejdić and Finci*, cited above, § 42). However, Article 14 of the Convention does not prohibit a member State from treating groups differently in order to correct "factual inequalities" between them; indeed in certain circumstances a failure to attempt to correct inequality through different treatment may in itself give rise to a breach of the Article (see, among other authorities, *D.H. and Others v. the Czech Republic* [GC], no. 57325/00, § 175, ECHR 2007 IV). The Contracting State enjoys a margin of appreciation in assessing whether and to what extent differences in otherwise similar situations justify a different treatment (see *Vallianatos and Others v. Greece* [GC], nos. 29381/09 and 32684/09, § 76, ECHR 2013 ([extracts]).

b. Application of those principles to the present case

55. The Court considers that the possibly discriminatory treatment of the applicant is central to her complaint. It therefore takes the view that the case should be assessed first of all under Article 14 of the Convention in conjunction with Article 2 of Protocol No. 1 (see, for a similar approach, *Oršuš and Others v. Croatia* [GC], no. 15766/03, §§ 143-145, ECHR 2010). The Court reiterates that it has already held that the scope of Article 14 includes discrimination based on disability (see *Glor v. Switzerland*, no. 13444/04, § 80, ECHR 2009).

56. In the present case, the applicant submitted that the rejection of her application for enrolment in the Music Academy had been discriminatory because it had been based on her blindness. In that regard, the Court observes that various legislative provisions in force at the material time confirmed the right to education of children with disabilities, without discrimination. [...]

57. That being the case, the Court also notes that the conditions for enrolment in the Music Academy included the requirement to provide a medical certificate of physical fitness for receiving education in that establishment. Accordingly, the initial grounds for withholding access to education in the Music Academy from the applicant lay not in the law but in the Academy's regulations. In that connection the Court further notes from the defence case submitted to the domestic courts by the administration of Istanbul Technical University [...] that the Music Academy was unable to admit persons with any kind of disability.

58. In the instant case, therefore, the Court must ascertain whether, the State having decided to provide specialist musical education, access to such education could be withheld from a group of persons in particular because the discrimination includes cases where a person or group is treated, without proper justification, less favourably than another, even though the more favourable treatment is not called for by the Convention (see *Glor*, cited above, § 73).

59. Clearly, as the Government submitted [...], the regulations on enrolment in the Music Academy contained no provisions geared to excluding blind persons. It is also true that all applicants for enrolment in the Music Academy are required to provide a medical certificate concerning their physical fitness. Nevertheless, the Court cannot overlook the effects of such a requirement on persons such as the applicant who have a physical disability, having regard, in particular, to the manner in which the Academy in question interprets that requirement.

60. The Court observes that the applicant did indeed provide the administration of the Academy with a medical report on her physical fitness, albeit with one reservation concerning her blindness [...]. However, the Music Academy rejected that report, going so far as to demand amendments to it by the medical officer who had drawn it up [...]. Consequently, even though the Academy attempted to justify its refusal to enrol the applicant with her failure to comply with the requisite administrative formalities, and in particular the absence of a medical

report prepared by a fully equipped hospital, the Court considers, having regard to all the foregoing considerations and to the letter from the Director of the Music Academy to the Chief Medical Officer of Bakirköy Hospital [...], that there can be no doubt that the applicant's blindness was the sole reason for that refusal.

61. Moreover, in view of the ease with which the Music Academy secured the amendment of the medical report originally prepared by the Chief Medical Officer of Bakirköy Hospital [...], the Court holds that the applicant would in any event have been unable to meet the physical fitness requirement, since the definition of the latter was apparently left to the Academy's discretion. In that connection the Court also refers to the criticism voiced on that matter by the Governing Board of Istanbul Medical Association [...].

62. The Court observes that the Government justified the rules governing enrolment in the Music Academy first of all with the fact that the Academy was designed to admit only students with special talents [...]. Although the Court considers that the domestic authorities undeniably had a margin of appreciation in defining the qualities required of applicants to the Music Academy, that argument cannot stand up in the particular circumstances of the present case. If the Music Academy aims to provide education for specially gifted students, since the applicant had passed the entrance examination prior to any application for enrolment [...], she demonstrated that she possessed all the requisite qualities in that regard.

63. The Government then argued that at the material time the Music Academy had lacked appropriate infrastructures to admit students with disabilities.

64. The Court reiterates that the Convention is intended to guarantee rights that are practical and effective and not theoretical and illusory (see, among other authorities, *Del Río Prada v. Spain* [GC], no. 42750/09, § 88, ECHR 2013, and *Dvorski v. Croatia* [GC], no. 25703/11, § 82, 20 October 2015; see also paragraph 54 above). In the context of the present case, the Court also reiterates that it must have regard to the changing conditions of international and European law and respond, for example, to any emerging consensus as to the standards to be achieved (see, *mutatis mutandis*, *Konstantin Markin v. Russia* [GC], no. 30078/06, § 126, ECHR 2012 [extracts], and *Fabris v. France* [GC], no. 16574/08, § 56, ECHR 2013 [extracts]). In that connection, it notes the importance of the fundamental principles of universality and nondiscrimination in the exercise of the

right to education, which are enshrined in many international texts ([...] see *Catan and Others*, cited above, §§ 77-81). It further emphasises that those international instruments have recognised inclusive education as the most appropriate means of guaranteeing the aforementioned fundamental principles.

65. The Court considers that Article 14 of the Convention must be read in the light of the requirements of those texts regarding reasonable accommodation – understood as "necessary and appropriate modification and adjustments not imposing a disproportionate or undue burden, where needed in a particular case" – which persons with disabilities are entitled to expect in order to ensure "the enjoyment or exercise on an equal basis with others of all human rights and fundamental freedoms" (Article 2 of the Convention on the Rights of Persons with Disabilities [...]). Such reasonable accommodation helps to correct factual inequalities which are unjustified and therefore amount to discrimination (see paragraph 54 above).

66. The Court is not unaware that every child has his or her specific educational needs, and this applies particularly to children with disabilities. In the educational sphere, the Court acknowledges that reasonable accommodation may take a variety of forms, whether physical or non-physical, educational or organisational, in terms of the architectural accessibility of school buildings, teacher training, curricular adaptation or appropriate facilities. That being the case, the Court emphasises that it is not its task to define the resources to be implemented in order to meet the educational needs of children with disabilities. The national authorities, by reason of their direct and continuous contact with the vital forces of their countries, are in principle better placed than an international court to evaluate local needs and conditions in this respect.

67. However, the Court takes the view that it is important for the States to be particularly careful in making their choices in this sphere, having regard to the impact of the latter on children with disabilities, whose particular vulnerability cannot be overlooked. It consequently considers that discrimination on grounds of disability also covers refusal to make reasonable accommodation.

68. In the instant case, the Court notes from the case-file that the relevant domestic authorities at no stage attempted to identify the applicant's needs or to explain how her blindness could have impeded her access to a musical education. Nor did they ever consider physical adaptations in order to meet any special educational needs arising from the applicant's

blindness (cf. *McIntyre v. the United Kingdom*, no. 29046/95, Commission decision of 21 October 1998, not published). The Court can only note that since 1976 the Music Academy has made no attempt to adapt its teaching methods in order to make them accessible to blind children.

69. Having regard to all the foregoing considerations, the Court observes that the refusal to enrol the applicant in the Music Academy was based solely on the fact that she was blind and that the domestic authorities had at no stage considered the possibility that reasonable accommodation might have enabled her to be educated in that establishment. That being the case, the Court considers that the applicant was denied, without any objective and reasonable justification, an opportunity to study in the Music Academy, solely on account of her visual disability. It therefore finds that there has been a violation of Article 14 of the Convention taken in conjunction with Article 2 of Protocol No. 1.

[Source: European Court of Human Rights, Second Section, Case of *Çam v. Turkey*, Application no. 51500/08), Judgement of 23 February 2016]

ANNOTATION

In February 2013, the European Court of Human Rights had declared inadmissible an application brought by a disabled civil servant regarding lack of suitable toilet facilities (*Bayrakcı v. Turkey*). In that case, the Court accepted that Article 8 (right to private and family life) and Article 14 (prohibition of discrimination) of the European Convention for the Protection of Human Rights and Fundamental Freedoms were applicable to the case but the applicant had failed to exhaust available domestic remedies.

In *Glor v. Switzerland*, decided in 2015, the facts concerned an applicant who suffered from diabetes and was declared unfit for military service. However, the applicant was required to pay tax for not doing his military service. In this case, the Court, establishing for the first time that discrimination based on disability was prohibited under Article 14, held that there had been a violation of that Article in conjunction with Article 8 of the Convention.

In a case concerning access to higher education, *Ghergina v. Romania*, a student with a disability had complained that the lack of suitable facilities on the premises of his university were contrary, *inter alia*, to Article 2 of Protocol No. 1 and Article 14 of the Convention. The Grand

Chamber of the Court in 2015 declared the application inadmissible on the grounds that the applicant had not made use of the national legal system to seek to remedy of any violations of rights protected under the Convention.

The judgement in the case of *Çam v. Turkey* discussed here represents a noteworthy further development in the Court's evolving jurisprudence regarding discrimination against persons with disabilities under the Convention. This is the first time that the Court found a violation of Article 14 in connection with the access to higher education, which is protected under the provisions on the right to education set out in Article 2 of Protocol No. 1 to the Convention. Furthermore, this is the first time that the Court specifically established that "discrimination on grounds of disability also covers refusal to make reasonable accommodation" (paragraph 67 in the above extract of the judgement). In the present case, discrimination was found to have occurred because the "domestic authorities had at no stage considered the possibility that reasonable accommodation might have enabled [the applicant] to be educated in [the] establishment" concerned (paragraph 69).

Dealing with a set of relatively straightforward facts, the Court had an opportunity to integrate the concept of reasonable accommodation into its established test for assessing whether or not a case of discrimination was at hand. The Court built on its jurisprudence according to which the Convention does not prohibit a State Party from treating groups differently in order to correct "factual inequalities" between them and "indeed in certain circumstances a failure attempt to correct factual inequality through different treatment may in itself give rise to a breach" of Article 14. Referring to the European Social Charter and the UN Convention on the Rights of Persons with Disabilities, the European Court of Human Rights stressed that it must have regard to developments in international law and respond to any "emerging consensus as to the standards to be achieved" (paragraph 64). For the Court, reasonable accommodation as defined in Article 2 of the UN Convention "helps to correct factual inequalities which are unjustified and therefore amount to discrimination" (paragraph 65). While insisting on the need to ensure reasonable accommodation in the field of education, the Court also stressed that it was for the national authorities to take such measures based on an evaluation of local needs and conditions (paragraph 66).

As can be noted from the decision, there were laws in Turkey providing for the right to education of children with disabilities without discrimination. Also, the National Music Academy's regulations had no provisions explicitly geared to excluding blind persons, and medical certificates were required for all students. However, the Court found the manner in which these regulations were applied resulted in discrimination, along with the fact that no attempt was made to accommodate the special needs of the applicant. It is also interesting that in the course of the appeals process in the Turkish courts, a dissenting opinion of the President of the Administrative Court and the views of the State Prosecutor at the Council of State, had in fact argued that the decision of the National Music Academy was in violation of the Constitution and should be set aside. However, these arguments remained minority views (paragraphs 28 and 32 of the judgement, not included in the extract above).

The decision will have to be taken into account by any future applicant seeking redress against alleged discrimination based on disability in the context of training and education, as well as in employment and occupation. Cases involving a lack of reasonable accommodation in these fields clearly fall within the scope of the rights under Articles 8 and 14 of the Convention, as well as Article 2 of Protocol No. 1. While States Parties to the European Convention will have to ensure that their laws and policies are in line with the UN Convention on the Rights of Persons with Disabilities, and this is subject to monitoring by the Committee set up under that Convention, access to the European Court potentially offers an important remedy for persons with disabilities. The fact that the Court considered that Article 14 of the regional instrument had to be read in light of the requirements under Article 2 of the UN Convention is a promising development, although it remains to be seen whether the courts will eventually go as far as assessing the "reasonableness" of accommodation measures or whether this will be entirely left to the margin of appreciation of States Parties.

Pol. 1

POLAND

Supreme Court
The resolution of seven judges of 28 September 2016, III PZP 3/16

The claim for compensation for a discriminatory termination of an employment contract – age discrimination – time limits when lodging cases

HEADNOTES

Facts

Joanna M. had been employed at company V. since 1998. The company declared bankruptcy and was taken over by company M. As a result, under Article 23¹ of the Polish Labour Code (referred to below with the Polish initials: k.p.), the former enterprise was taken over along with its employees by the acquirer. Joanna M. continued to be employed as a production planning and settlement specialist. Besides her, two other women performed similar duties in the same department.

In January 2009 the enterprise experienced a fall in the number of orders and services, which resulted in financial trouble and necessary redundancies. Company M. decided to lay off some of its employees. As the layoffs were to be conducted for reasons directly involving the employer and in accordance with the provisions on collective layoff, company M. prepared the redundancy qualification criteria. These included: overall assessment of an employee's performance at work not related to the annual appraisal, the employee's aptitude for a given job, and his/her family circumstances.

Although Joanna M. was the longest-serving and the oldest employee in her department, she was selected for the layoff. The arguments against her further employment were, among others, inadequate skills in using the company's computer software and no knowledge of English (which was related to the company's operations in other than Polish markets, where the staff was required to communicate in at least one foreign language).

Eventually, Joanna M. was given a notice of termination of the employment contract under Article 10 of the Act of 13 March 2003 on special rules of termination of employment for reasons not attributable to employees. The grounds listed in the termination notice included the necessity of restructuring tasks and work schemes at the logistics department, which meant that the post of a production planning and settlement specialist became redundant.

The former employee lodged a complaint against the layoff at the labour court, yet she did not respect the time limit for bringing such an action. In accordance with the law applicable at the time, a complaint against the termination of an employment contract was to be lodged at the labour court within seven days of the letter of notice being served by the employer (under Article 264(1) k.p.; since 1 January 2017, the time limit has been extended to 21 days). Joanna M. lodged her complaint against the termination of employment almost a year after her employment contract was terminated. Therefore the court dismissed the complaint in a final and binding judgement. Joanna M. brought another claim against her former employer, this time demanding Polish Zloty 40,999 compensation due to, in her opinion, contravention of the principle of equal treatment in employment. She claimed that she was selected for the layoff because of her age (she was over 50) and by reason of her prior employment at the company V. She based her claim on Article 18^{3d} k.p., which provides for the right to compensation due to contravention of the principle of equal treatment in employment, and on Article 291(1) k.p., under which claims resulting from the employment relationship fall under the statute of limitation upon the lapse of three years since the day when such a claim became enforceable.

The courts of the first and second instance dismissed her claim. The courts of both instances found that the claim concerning discrimination when selecting employees for layoffs was inextricably linked to questioning the legitimacy of termination of the employment contract by the employer in line with Article 45(1) k.p. However, the complaint of the employee against the termination of her employment contract was dismissed in the final and binding judgement by reason of her failure to respect the seven-day time limit for bringing such action. Consequently, the courts considered it inadmissible to adjudicate the compensation claim alleging discriminatory termination of the employment contract.

The complainant filed a cassation appeal at the Supreme Court against the judgement of the court of second instance. The Supreme Court judges considering the appeal noted a legal issue in the case and decided to submit it for consideration by the full Court in extended composition. The issue was whether a prior complaint against termination of the employment contract (claiming damages due to wrongful termination of the employment contract under Article 45(1) k.p.) was a necessary precondition for adjudicating compensation to an employee under Article 18^{3d} k.p. in relation to discriminatory termination of employment. The former employee had already – without legal effect – appealed against the termination of employment. As mentioned above, under the Polish law the time limit for lodging a complaint against the termination of employment used to be set as seven days (since 1 January 2017, the time limit is 21 days) and it ran from the time of the serving of the employer's termination of employment notice on the employee (Article 264(1) k.p.). At the same time, other claims of employees, including those alleging discrimination, in principle fall under a three-year statute of limitations applicable from the day on which the claim has become enforceable. The adjudication in this case before the Supreme Court is therefore significant, as it determines the time limit for bringing an action in connection with discriminatory termination of an employment contract.

Decision

The Supreme Court ruled that an appeal by an employee against a lay off notice (being a filed claim for illegal termination of an employment contract under Article 45(1) k.p.) is not a pre-requisite to awarding compensation under Article 18^{3d} k.p. for a discriminatory reason for the termination of employment contract or a discriminatory reason when making dismissal choices.

Law Applied

Polish Labour Code
Article 18^{3d}
Any person in respect of whom the principle of equal treatment in employment is violated by an employer has the right to compensation equal at least to the amount of the statutory minimum wage, as defined in separate regulations.

Article 45
(1) If termination of an indefinite-term contract of employment is found to be unjustified or contrary to the applicable provisions governing the termination of contracts of employment with notice, the labour court may, on the basis of the employee's claim, declare the notice of termination

ineffective, and if the contract of employment has already been terminated, the labour court may order that the employee be reinstated under the previous terms and conditions or that compensation be awarded to that employee.

(2) The labour court may not consider the employee's claim to declare a notice of termination ineffective or to order reinstatement if this is deemed impossible or ungrounded; if this be the case, the labour court shall award compensation.

Article 264(1)

An appeal against termination of a contract of employment with notice shall be filed at a labour court within 7 days of the date of the notice of termination being served (since 1 January 2017, within 21 days)

Article 291(1)

Any claims arising from an employment relationship shall be subject to prescription 3 years after the date when a claim became enforceable.

JUDGEMENT

First of all, the Supreme Court noted that there was a discrepancy in the judicial practice in relation to the case being the subject of the legal issue addressed to the extended composition of the Supreme Court. Older judgements favoured the standpoint that non-compliance with the law (the wrongfulness) of the dismissal or termination of an employment contract by the employer can be proved by the employee exclusively by way of an action stipulated in Article 45 k.p. (a claim for adjudication of the employment contract termination as wrongful, and for reinstatement or compensation when re-inststement is not an option) brought within the time limit prescribed in Article 264 k.p. (i.e. within seven days, and since 1 January 2017 within 21 days). Therefore, having failed to bring such an action, the employee cannot quote wrongful termination of employment in any other proceedings as a circumstance for compensation claims. The final dismissal of the complaint against the termination of employment is binding in the subsequent claim for compensation instituted under Article 18[3d] k.p., which results from Article 365(1) and Article 366 of the Polish Code of Civil Procedure (referred to by its Polish initials: k.p.c.). However, more recent judgements present a different standpoint. In the judgement of 14 February 2013 (No. III PK 31/12), the Supreme Court found that the employee's complaint based on wrongful termination of an employment contract (under Article 45(1) in relation to Art. 264(1) k.p.) was not a necessary precondition for adjudicating compensation, as provided for in Article 18^{3d} k.p., due to the discriminatory reason of the contract termination.

In the resolution of seven judges of 28 September 2016, the Supreme Court resolved the doubts and conclusively decided that the complaint lodged by the employee against the termination of employment (claiming wrongful termination of the employment contract under Article 45(1) k.p.) was not a circumstance required to adjudicate on compensation provided for in Article 18^{3d} k.p. in relation to the discriminatory reason for the termination of employment or the discriminatory selection of an employee for dismissal. The Supreme Court assumed also that, in case of claims for damages provided for in Arts. 45 and 18^{3d} k.p., there was an aggregation of financial claims.

The justification laid down in the 2016 resolution contains an extensive discussion of the source of the stipulation in Article 18^{3d} k.p., the type and premises of compensatory liability for contravening the principle of equal treatment in employment and the different sorts of the resulting compensation due, as well as the nature of compensatory liability of the employer due to wrongful termination of an employment contract provided for in Article 45 and the following k.p. Articles of special attention are the passages in the Supreme Court's resolution that refer directly to the relationship between the procedure of claiming for damages under Article 18^{3d} k.p. and the procedure of complaining against the termination of an employment contract.

The Supreme Court pointed out that the legal provisions stipulating the principle of equal treatment of men and women in employment, and the principle of equal treatment in employment represent implementation of the EU equality Directives in Polish law, and as such they were introduced into the Labour Code on 1 January 2002 and on 1 January 2004, respectively, i.e. a number of years after the Labour Code itself had come into force. These provisions do not refer to the existing regulations concerning effects of wrongful termination of an employment relationship. Nor does the Labour Code contain provisions introducing a relationship between the complaint under Article 45(1) k.p. alleging illegal or wrongful termination of an employment contract and a claim provided for in Article 18^{3d} k.p., i.e. a claim for damages due to contravention of the principle of equal treatment in employment. Those are independent and separate claims that an employee is entitled to pursue as a result of different infringements of law committed by the employer.

The Supreme Court even described the situations as "two different types of wrongfulness". On the one hand, under Article 45(1) k.p. if the termination of an employment contract concluded for an unlimited term is illegal or contravenes the provisions on termination of employment contracts, the employee is entitled to lodge, depending on his/her choice, a restitution claim (for a declarartion of wrongful termination or for a reinstatement order) or a claim for compensation. On the other hand, the compensation under Article 18^{3d} k.p. may be sought by a person "with reference to whom the employer has breached the principle of equal treatment in employment", and its amount may not be lower than the minimum wage. As indicated by the Supreme Court, not every dismissal of an employee which is illegal or contrary to the regulations on termination of employment contracts is driven by prohibited reasons, and not every dismissal found to be legitimate means that there has been no discrimination against the employee who has been made redundant. The latter situation takes place, among other situations, when the employer has given several reasons for the termination of an employment contract, some of which do not have discriminatory features and at the same time are true, direct and sufficient to motivate the decision on the dismissal, while other reasons contravene the principle of equal treatment in employment. The dismissal of the claim provided for in Article 45(1) k.p. when the defendant proves that those non-discriminatory reasons are legitimate does not settle the matter of the employer's wrongful conduct in cases where the employer has contravened the principle of equal treatment in employment with respect to the employee, which is a premise for adjudicating compensation under Article 18^{3d} k.p.. Therefore, in the view of the Supreme Court, it is inadmissible to make the compensation claim based on the existence of discriminatory reasons subject to the timely lodging of a complaint against termination of an employment contract and to the outcome of court proceedings instituted as a result of such complaint.

Moreover, the Supreme Court indicated that, in the light of Article 18^{3b} (1) in relation to Article 18^{3a} k.p., discrimination in employment may take place at every stage of an employment relationship – at the commencement when it is established, in the course of and at termination of employment. If the admissibility of effective suing for damages in cases of discrimination when terminating an employment relationship depended on the action brought under Article 45(1) k.p. and its expected outcome for the employee, this would result in a differentiation between claims related to discrimination in employment. The successful suing for compensation due to discriminatory termination of employment would therefore be subject to supplementary conditions, which are not envisaged for persons claiming their rights in connection with discrimination at the commencement of or during an employment relationship. These conditions are burdensome not only due to the requirement of instituting court proceedings with respect to other claims (alleging wrongful termination of an employment relationship), especially if the employee is not interested in reinstatement, but also because of the short time limit for lodging such an action at court. The view that the claim for compensation based on discrimination at the termination of employment depends on already having effective court proceedings under Article 45 k.p., would mean that the employee would have only seven days in which to make a decision on whether to lodge such an action, while the employee who has been discriminated against when establishing an employment relationship or during employment would have three years in which to make such a decision.

As also emphasized by the Supreme Court, the seven-day time limit does not meet the requirement resulting from the EU law, of having an effective process for claiming damages in case of discrimination. In the Supreme Court's opinion, this shortcoming is because of the too short time limit and because of the nature of the event from which such time period runs, namely from an employer's serving of a written notice on termination of employment on the employee.

In view of the above considerations, the Supreme Court ruled that an earlier unsuccessful suing for damages in relation to an infringement of the law when terminating an employment relationship did not immediately result in the dismissal of the claim for compensation based on a violation of the prohibition on discrimination. If the employee is not awarded damages for wrongful termination of employment, for example if for formal reasons the court has dismissed his/her complaint, that employee may still claim for compensation due to discrimination, provided he/she proves that the inequality in treatment has in fact taken place. Moreover, the Supreme Court decided the aggregation of claims in cases where damages are claimed under Article 45 k.p. and under Article 18^{3d} k.p.. To be precise, if an employment contract has been terminated for discriminatory reasons, the employee may bring two separate claims, i.e. one for compensation based on a violation of the prohibition on discrimination and another due to infringement of the law when terminating an employment contract. As emphasized by the Supreme Court, in this respect the labour law provisions do not stipulate the maximum amount of possible compensation in case of the aggregation of claims. While the limit is defined for compensation due to wrongful termination of an employment contract (under Article 47^1 k.p., this amounts to the remuneration for a period from two weeks up to three months, however, it may not be lower than the remuneration for the notice period), the Polish regulations do not provide for a maximum amount of compensation in discrimination cases.

ANNOTATION

The resolution of seven judges of the Supreme Court dated 28 September 2016 is a departure from the commonly held view. The resolution dispels the doubts which so far have been occurring in both judicial practice and legal doctrine, and provides that employees do have a right to claim damages in case of a discriminatory reason for terminating employment (or when they suffered discrimination when layoff selections were being made) without the necessity of a prior lodging of a complaint against termination of an employment contract. Consequently, based on the resolution of the Supreme Court, employees may claim compensation based on discriminatory termination of employment within three years, and not 21 days (before 1 January 2017, this time frame was seven days).

The standpoint expressed in the Supreme Court's resolution deserves approval for several reasons. First, none of the Labour Code provisions, let alone other laws (for example the Code of Civil Procedure), introduces a relationship between a claim under Article 45(1) k.p. and a claim under Article 18^{3d} k.p. There are no legal grounds for treating the claim for compensation due to discrimination of an employee as supplementary to the claims stipulated under Article 45(1) k.p.. Both types of claims are provided for in the Labour Code as independent, separate and available to employees due to different breaches of law committed by an employer.

Their scope also varies. If the termination of an unlimited-term employment contract is illegal or infringes the provisions concerning terminating employment contracts, the employees – under Article 45(1) k.p. – are entitled to bring, depending on their choice, a restitution claim (for a declaration of wrongful termination or a reinstatement order) or a claim for compensation. Under Article 47(1) k.p., the compensation amounts to the remuneration for the period from two weeks up to three months, however it may not be lower than the remuneration for the period of notice. The claims resulting from Article 45(1) k.p. are aimed at punishment of only one precisely defined action of the employer (serving of the wrongful notice of termination of employment), and their objective is to reduce the financial effect of such a termination, which takes place in accordance with the rules defined in the provision. The compensation provided for in Article 18^{3d} k.p. may, in turn, be claimed by a person towards whom the employer has contravened the principle of equal treatment in employment. The contravention of that principle, under Article 18^{3d} k.p. in relation to Article 18^{3b} (1) k.p., gives rise to a right to compensation for the aggrieved party in the amount of not lower than the minimum remuneration for work (defined under separate provisions), unless the employer proves that it has been guided by objective reasons. Articles 18^{3a}-18^{3e} k.p., included under Chapter IIa of the Labour Code entitled "Equal treatment in employment", result from the implementation by the Polish legislator of the European Union Directives stipulating the principles of equality of treatment and of equal opportunities in employment as well as the prohibition on discrimination. Article 18^{3d} k.p. was envisaged as a separate basis for compensation based on a violation of the principle of equal treatment in employment, i.e. not only in relation to the discriminatory termination of an employment contract. The employee's right to such compensation is independent from other claims related to the employment relationship. The employee is entitled to as many claims as are provided by the law with respect to one event, unless there is a provision under which one claim excludes another. In this case being annotated, no such exclusion is applicable. It should be noted however that the entitlement to compensation by reason of discrimination is available to the employee also when there is no related damage. Article 18^{3d} k.p. does not limit the employer's liability to the damage caused to the employee's financial situation, but extends it also to personal damage and infringement of the employee's personal well-being, which is not covered by claims stipulated in Article 45(1) k.p.. Contrary to Article 45 k.p., Article 18^{3d} k.p. does not envisage any maximum limit for the amount of the compensation.

Secondly, the adoption of an adverse standpoint than the one presented in the Supreme Court's resolution would considerably limit the employer's liability for contravention of the principle of equal treatment in employment in situations involving termination of an employment contract by linking infringment of this principle only to the events when such termination gives grounds for the employee's claim under Article 45(1) k.p.. However, the termination of employment may be legitimate under Article 45(1) k.p. but the employer may still be required to pay the compensation due for discrimination under Article 18^{3d} k.p.. For instance, if the employer gives, as layoff reasons, the loss of the right to perform a job through the employee's own fault and the employee's attaining the retirement age, such termination may be legitimate for the first of the quoted reasons (this will result in dismissal of the employee's claim under Article 45(1) k.p.), yet the employee can still claim compensation under Article 18^{3d} k.p. (because the other reason is discriminatory).

Thirdly, the too short time limit for complaining against termination of employment, which runs from the employer's serving of the notice of contract termination, favours the standpoint adopted in the resolution of the Supreme Court. Under the law in force at the time when the resolution of the Supreme Court was issued, the employee had only seven days, after having been served the notice of contract termination, for filing his/her complaint in court (since 1 January 2017 the time limit has been extended and amounts to 21 days). The assumption that lodging of the employee's complaint against termination of employment (bringing claims under Article 45(1) k.p.) is the precondition for awarding the compensation stipulated in Article 18^{3d} k.p. based on a discriminatory reason behind the employment termination or a discriminatory reason being applied when selecting an employee for layoff would in fact amount to a fictitious court legal protection. Although the 21-day time limit is sufficient for claiming damages under Article 45 k.p., it is too short to bring claims in relation to contravention of the principle of equal treatment in employment, which concerns financial loss suffered by a person and non-pecuniary damages awarded to the employee. The results of the discriminatory termination of an employment contract as damages caused to a person may be revealed in the future as time passes. Moreover, making the effectiveness of discriminatory claims dependent on the 21-day period for lodging a complaint against the termination of employment does not allow the employee to make a reasonable assessment of whether he/she has been discriminated against. In other words, such a short time limit, running since the notice is served by the employer, may prove insufficient for determining whether the termination has been based on discriminatory reasons. In particular, this could arise in cases where the employer has written in the notice a circumstance of a non-discriminatory nature as the reason for termination of employment, while the actual discriminatory cause has not initially been disclosed. In other words, the disclosure of discrimination in employment may be difficult for the employee when indirect discrimination takes place. The reference to the legal and factual situation of another employee and making a comparison between "similar persons" (employees in the same circumstances) are often impossible to establish without taking specific steps, like conducting interviews among the staff, collecting information or evidence.

Fourthly, the claim for compensation due to unequal treatment in employment may be legitimate by reason of factual circumstances other than those referring to the discriminatory termination of employment or discriminatory criteria when making a selection of employees for layoffs. There are no rational reasons to support the 21-day time limit for claiming damages due to discriminatory causes of terminating employment, when for another discriminatory event the time limit is three years. The time limit for claiming compensation due to unequal treatment in employment should be the same, irrespective of what facts (circumstances, premises, assumptions) the complainant uses when lodging his/her claim for compensation.

In conclusion, this 2016 resolution of the Supreme Court is a significant decision in Polish judicial practice and merits full approval.

SPAIN

Supreme Court Social Chamber (acting as a General Chamber)
Decision of 25 October 2016, Appeal No 881/2016

Surrogate motherhood and right to maternity/paternity benefits

HEADNOTES

Facts

The plaintiff was a Spanish citizen who had two daughters, born in New Delhi, India using human assisted reproduction techniques (HART). He was the genetic father and the eggs came from the surrogate mother, a woman who under a contract of surrogate motherhood gestated the fertilized eggs resulting from artificial insemination in favour of the claimant. The two minors were registered in the Spanish Consulate as daughters of a Spanish citizen. The father agreed to exercise parental authority on his own after the biological mother´s renouncing according to Indian Law. He subsequently claimed maternity benefits before the Spanish Authorities and his application was rejected. Later he claimed maternity benefits before a Spanish Social Tribunal, and his claim was dismissed.

On appeal, the Higher Court of Justice of Catalonia (decision dated 15 September 2015) ruled in favour of his access to maternity benefits based on the following reasoning: a) the registration of the filiation in the Civil Registry can be assimilated to adoption or fostering; b) although the European Court of Justice considers the denial of maternity benefits in surrogacy cases not to be discriminatory, this does not prevent States from recognizing such rights under their internal legislation; c) access to maternity benefits cannot be denied under the Spanish Act on HART since this particular legal instrument does not regulate maternity benefits; d) the application of both the principle of the best interests of the child and the principle of equality of all children irrespective of birth obliges public authorities to interpret the legal provisions in favour of special relations between the father and the newborn; and e) application of social security legal norms regarding adoption and foster care can be extended to surrogacy (by legal analogy).

The Social Security Administration (National Institute of Social Security – INSS) filed an appeal for the unification of doctrine, claiming as the contradictory decision a Decision of the Higher Court of Justice of the Basque Country dated 13 May 2014 (Appeal No 749/2014) alleging that in that earlier case maternity benefits were denied to pregnant women in a case of surrogate motherhood. INSS also alleged infringements of European Union Directive 92/85/EEC of 19 October 1992 on the application of measures to encourage improvements in the occupational safety and health of pregnant workers, workers who have recently given birth or are breastfeeding, Article 133a of the General Social Security Act (currently renumbered as Article 177), and Article 48.4 of the Workers' Statute in relation to Article 10 of the Act on HART.

Decision

The Supreme Court's Decision of 25 October 2016 (File Procedure No 3818/2015) regarding a 'cassation review for unification of doctrine', rejects the INSS's appeal and confirms the previous judgement of the Social Chamber of the Higher Court of Justice of Catalonia (dated 15 September 2015), which recognized the right to maternity leave and benefits to the genetic father in case of surrogacy carried out abroad.

Law Applied

Spanish Constitution (27 December of 1978)
Article 39
1. Public authorities will ensure the social, economic and legal protection of the family.
2. Public authorities will also ensure the integral protection of children, equal before the law regardless of their filiation, as well as mothers, regardless of their marital status. The law will allow the investigation of paternity.

Civil Code
Article 6[…]
3. Acts contrary to mandatory and prohibitive rules are null and void, unless a different effect in the case of contravention is stated.

4. Acts carried out under the text of a rule that pursue an outcome prohibited by or contrary to the legal system shall be considered to have been executed in a fraudulent manner and shall not prevent the proper application of the rule –the avoidance of which has been attempted.

Act 14/2006 of 26 May 2006 on Human Assisted Reproduction Techniques (HART)

Article 10. Surrogate Gestation
1. The contract for which gestation is agreed by a woman who renounces her maternal filiation in favour of the contracting party or a third party, with or without price, shall be null and void.
2. The filiation of the children born by gestation of substitution will be determined by childbirth.
3. The possible action of claims of paternity with respect to the biological father, according to the general rules, is safeguarded.

General Social Security Act, Consolidated Text approved by Royal Legislative Decree 2/2015 of 23 October 2015. Chapter VI: Maternity

Article 177

For the purpose of maternity benefits, maternity, adoption, custody for adoption and foster care are considered protected situations, in accordance with the Civil Code or the civil laws of the Autonomous Communities that regulate it, provided that, in the latter case, their duration is not less than one year, during the leave periods that, for such situations, are enjoyed in accordance with the provisions of paragraphs 4, 5 and 6 of Article 48 of the consolidated text of the Workers' Statute and Article 49.a) and b) of Act 7/2007 dated 12 April on the Basic Statute of the Public Employee.

Royal Decree 295/2009 of 6 March 2009 that regulates the economic benefits of social security for maternity, paternity, risk during pregnancy and risk during breastfeeding.

Article 2.2: Those legal institutions declared by foreign judicial or administrative decisions, whose purpose and legal effects are those foreseen for adoption and fostering, irrespective of their denomination/naming, are considered legally equivalent to adoption and fostering.

JUDGEMENT

ANTECEDENTES DE HECHO
[…]
FUNDAMENTOS DE DERECHO

The issue to be solved is focused on the granting of maternity benefits in situations of surrogacy. In particular, when the applicant is the biological father and sole registering person, who signed a surrogacy contract alone.

The main arguments of the current decision are included in the following legal reasoning on which the judgement is based.

OCTAVO. – Doctrinas enfrentadas.

En el presente caso concurre de forma natural el presupuesto básico del recurso de casación para la unificación de doctrina (art. 219.1 LRJS): hay doctrinas contrapuestas respecto de un mismo problema. Antes de dar solución al debate interesa repasar los principales argumentos desplegados por ambas posiciones, todos ellos invocados en los escritos procesales que se han presentado o en las sentencias enfrentadas.

1. Denegación de las prestaciones.

La Entidad Gestora considera que las prestaciones reclamadas no pueden concederse y a tal efecto invoca diversos argumentos:

- Es consecuencia inesquivable de lo preceptuado por el art. 6, apartados 3 y 4 del Código Civil, el art. 23 de la Ley 20/2011, de 21 de julio, el art. 981 de la LEC y el art. 10 de la Ley 14/2006, de 26 de mayo.
- El art. 133 bis LGSS establece como situaciones protegidas por maternidad, la propia maternidad natural, la adopción y el acogimiento, tanto preadoptivo, como permanente o simple, pero no la maternidad por subrogación.
- […]
- El contrato de gestación por sustitución del que trae causa el derecho al permiso de maternidad, así como su correspondiente prestación, es plenamente nulo y fraudulento. La mera inscripción registral de la filiación no puede crear efectos constitutivos para una situación nula de pleno Derecho.
- La prestación económica por maternidad trata de proteger a la mujer trabajadora, siendo el interés del menor una consecuencia, pero no el principal bien protegido.

- La finalidad de la protección de la maternidad por parto no es equiparable con la de gestación por sustitución, porque la finalidad que se persigue con esta concreta protección es diferente: salud de la madre, antes y después del parto, además de la de su atención al nacido.

2. *Concesión de las prestaciones.*

Los argumentos que conducen a la concesión de las prestaciones asociadas a la maternidad, pese a haber surgido la misma por subrogación, pueden entresacarse de la sentencia recurrida y el escrito de impugnación. Son los siguientes:
- La finalidad de la prestación de maternidad está relacionada no solo con el descanso obligatorio y voluntario por el hecho del parto, sino . también con la atención o cuidado del menor.
- Es el interés superior del menor el que debe llevar a respetar su derecho a disfrutar plenamente de su vida familiar y privada ex art. 8 en relación con el 14 del Convenio Europeo de Derechos Humanos hecho en Roma el 4 de noviembre de 1950.
- Los principios informadores de nuestro Sistema legitiman un devengo fundamentado más en el prioritario interés del menor protegido que en el del progenitor al que la Norma no le reconoce la condición de tal.
- La condición de progenitor no se ostenta por ser sujeto que ha contribuido físicamente a dar a luz sino que viene otorgada porque así figura en el Registro Civil en su condición de sujeto que ha obtenido esa posición por virtud de una filiación conseguida mediante gestación por sustitución.
- Cabe la aplicación analógica de lo previsto para adopción o acogimiento, trasladándolo a los casos de maternidad subrogada.
- Los problemas sobre constancia registral del progenitor biológico no deben privar al menor de la atención, bienestar y cuidado que su persona merece y que constituye un elemento prioritario de la prestación por maternidad en nuestra legislación.
- Carece de sentido invocar la Ley 14/2006, de 26 de mayo (RCL 2006, 1071), pues no es una norma reguladora de la prestación, ni tiene por objeto condicionar la atención a los menores, cuestión ajena a la petición de prestación económica de la Seguridad social.

NOVENO.– Consideraciones específicas.
[…]
1. Acotación del problema.
   A) En modo alguno nos corresponde pronunciarnos sobre la filiación de los menores nacidos el 25 de septiembre de 2013 en Nueva Delhi. Mucho menos, acerca de si procede su inscripción el Registro español.
   […]
   B) Lo que se trata es de determinar si el padre biológico de dos niñas, gestadas mediante subrogación y a su instancia, tiene derecho al disfrute de las prestaciones asociadas a la maternidad.
   […]
2. Argumentos de la Sala.
Parte de los argumentos que conducen a considerar acertada la doctrina albergada en la STSJ Cataluña que se recurre ya han quedado expuestos en pasajes precedentes. Sin embargo, en este tramo conclusivo conviene compendiarlos y adicionar algún otro.
   A) El interés del menor y las prestaciones por "maternidad". El interés superior del menor no puede erigirse en principio a partir del cual los órganos jurisdiccionales alteren el contenido de las normas y eludan la sujeción al ordenamiento jurídico (art. 9.1 CE). Ahora bien, sí constituye un canon interpretativo de relevancia cuando debemos aplicar normas que lo han querido tener presente, como aquí sucede. En efecto, pese a sus orígenes y denominación, la protección que la Seguridad Social dispensa a la "maternidad" va mucho más allá del descanso asociado al alumbramiento. Así lo hemos dicho en ocasiones precedentes:
   […]
   No parece dudoso que para las dos menores nacidas en Nueva Delhi resulta conveniente que quien es y actúa como progenitor pueda estar a su cuidado al amparo de la situación protegida por la Seguridad Social (relevado de su actividad laboral, percibiendo prestaciones económicas). Si ello resulta posible, por tanto, debe accederse a lo pedido por el Sr. Rodríguez.
   B) Listado de situaciones protegidas parcialmente abierto. […]
   Actualmente el RD 295/2009, de 6 de marzo, regula las prestaciones económicas del sistema de la Seguridad Social por maternidad, paternidad, riesgo durante el embarazo y riesgo durante la lactancia natural. El primer párrafo de su artículo 2.2 reza así:

[…]
La relativa apertura del elenco de supuestos protegidos permite cierta flexibilidad interpretativa que antes no existía. Podría pensarse que la posición de los progenitores en los casos de maternidad subrogada es similar a la que, también como progenitores, ocupan aquéllos que se hallan en supuestos de adopción o acogimiento. Sin duda, en algunos casos puede ser así, mientras que en otros, como el presente, en que concurre la paternidad biológica de quien demanda las prestaciones, ese recurso interpretativo es solo adicional.

En todo caso, pugna con la lógica más primaria que se deniegue la prestación en los supuestos de gestación por sustitución cuando se reconocería *ex lege* si el solicitante se hubiera limitado a adoptar o a acoger a un menor, o a manifestar que lo ha engendrado junto con la madre.

C) Protección a un estado de necesidad real. Como queda expuesto, cuando la Sala Primera de este Tribunal niega la inscripción registral de los hijos habidos mediante maternidad subrogada lleva cuidado en atender las necesidades famil*iares* que hayan surgido *de facto*.

Para el TEDH uno de los puntos muy relevantes a considerar es el referido a la vida privada de las menores que están integradas en una unidad familiar, bien que sea como consecuencia de una maternidad subrogada que las leyes nacionales proscriben. Esa dimensión se recalca todavía más cuando uno de los miembros de la unidad familiar es quien engendró al niño.

A la luz de ello, cuando el padre (biológico, tras maternidad subrogada) es el único de los progenitores que materialmente está al cuidado de las menores la única forma de atender la situación de necesidad consiste en permitirle al acceso a las prestaciones. Unas prestaciones, obvio es, que están reconocidas por nuestras Leyes y que se han denegado como consecuencia de que la gestación deriva de un negocio jurídico nulo. Lo que estamos haciendo, en contra de lo que el escrito del recurso entiende, es interpretar las normas sobre prestaciones de maternidad no solo a la luz de la "realidad social del tiempo en que han de ser aplicadas, atendiendo fundamentalmente al espíritu y finalidad de aquella" (art. 3.1 CC) sino, muy especialmente, a la vista del tenor de otros preceptos. No se trata de violentar lo preceptuado por el legislador sino de aquilatar el alcance de sus previsiones, armonizando los diversos mandatos confluyentes. […]

D) Interpretación constitucional. Nuestro Derecho preconiza la nulidad del contrato de maternidad por subrogación. Al mismo tiempo, la LGSS contempla la protección de la maternidad y paternidad, sin mayores restricciones. No es que los bloques normativos estén enfrentados, sino que obedecen a lógicas diversas y también distinta es su aproximación el supuesto de hecho.

[...]

Por otro lado, el ordenamiento laboral no es ajeno al reconocimiento de efectos en casos de negocios jurídicos afectados de nulidad. Por ejemplo, cuando se reconoce el derecho al salario por el tiempo ya trabajador al amparo de un contrato que resultase nulo (art. 9.2 ET); se establece pensión de viudedad en determinados casos de nulidad matrimonial (art. 220.3 LGSS/2015); se acotan los efectos de la ausencia de permiso de trabajo (art. 36.5 LOEx 4/2005); se conceden ciertos efectos a los matrimonios poligámicos, etc.

En suma: que una Ley Civil prescriba la nulidad del contrato de maternidad por subrogación no elimina la situación de necesidad surgida por el nacimiento del menor y su inserción en determinado núcleo familiar; y tal situación de necesidad debe ser afrontada desde la perspectiva de las prestaciones de Seguridad Social procurando que esos hijos no vean mermados sus derechos. Y aquí nos encontramos con un contrato de maternidad por subrogación que es nulo pero que ha desplegado sus efectos, en particular los que interesan: inserción de las menores nacidas en el núcleo familiar de quien solicita las prestaciones por tal motivo.

El art. 39.3 CE obliga a los padres a prestar asistencia a los hijos habidos "dentro o fuera del matrimonio". En el supuesto que abordamos no cabe duda de que quien solicita las prestaciones es el padre (biológico, pero también registral) de las dos menores nacidas en La India y que resulta más acorde con ello permitirle la atención que las prestaciones económicas persiguen.

De igual modo, la "protección integral de los hijos, iguales éstos ante la ley con independencia de su filiación" (art. 39.2 CE), aconseja no adicionar causas de exclusión ignoradas por la LGSS al establecer sus prestaciones.

[...]

E) Paternidad biológica con maternidad subrogada. Los argumentos precedentes, a nuestro juicio contrarrestan suficientemente los desplegados por el INSS al denegar las prestaciones cuando media una maternidad por subrogación. Adicionalmente, cuando quien reclama las prestaciones es el padre biológico de las neonatas aumentan las razones para acceder a ello. Porque, al margen de la nulidad del negocio sobre gestación (el "alquiler" del "vientre") lo cierto es que estamos ante una realidad contemplada por la LGSS. Carece de sentido admitir la protección cuando nace un hijo fuera del matrimonio, o como consecuencia de una relación sexual esporádica, pero rechazarla en supuestos como el presente.

El art. 3.2 del RD 295/2009 contempla el fallecimiento de la madre biológica y, ante su ausencia y la supervivencia del menor, opta por transferir al padre (siendo compatible con el subsidio por paternidad) la prestación económica por maternidad. La renuncia que la madre biológica realiza a ejercer la patria potestad, al margen de la valoración jurídica que merezca, y su material ausencia del núcleo familiar ha conducido a que, de hecho, sea solo el Sr. Rodríguez quien está en condiciones de disfrutar el permiso por maternidad.

La misma solución se aplica al caso en que la madre sea trabajadora por cuenta propia y no tuviese derecho a prestaciones, por no hallarse incluida en el Régimen Especial de la Seguridad Social de Trabajadores por cuenta propia o Autónomos ni en una mutualidad de previsión social alternativa.

Es decir: la transferencia del derecho a prestaciones por maternidad en estos casos muestra a las claras la finalidad que se asigna a las mismas y concuerda con la interpretación analógica que se viene defendiendo, al no haber mediado conducta fraudulenta para obtener indebidamente prestaciones.

[...]

Recalquemos que estamos ante un supuesto particularmente cualificado en tanto la situación fáctica creada con la cesión o renuncia de derechos por la madre y el abandono de sus obligaciones como tal sitúa al demandante en posición de progenitor único. Desde la perspectiva *de facto* no cabe duda de que las menores conviven con quien es y aparece como su progenitor mientras que la madre biológica (y única que aparece con tal título registral) permanece deliberadamente ajena a ese núcleo. Por tanto, la situación de necesidad que las prestaciones de maternidad desean afrontar es evidente que concurre: las menores nacidas por gestación con sustitución forman un núcleo familiar con su padre, que desea prestar los cuidados parentales apropiados, como cualquier otro progenitor.

DÉCIMO.– resolución.

A [...]

1. El Convenio Europeo de Derechos Humanos y las SSTEDH 26 junio 2014 o 27 enero 2015 amparan el derecho a la inscripción de menores nacidos tras gestación por sustitución en ciertos casos pero no condicionan el derecho a la protección social. Además, el ordenamiento español posee cauces (adopción, investigación de la paternidad) para mitigar las consecuencias de la negativa a la inscripción registral.

2. De las diversas Directivas de la UE que influyen sobre el tema y de las SSTJUE de 18 marzo 2014 se desprende que la cuestión examinada es ajena a las mismas. No es discriminatorio (ni por razón de sexo, ni por discapacidad) rechazar el permiso por maternidad o las prestaciones asociadas en estos casos. Tampoco es exigible lo contrario desde la perspectiva de la seguridad y salud laborales. Tales conclusiones no impiden que el ordenamiento español abrace solución contraria, dado el carácter de *norma mínima* que poseen las Directivas.

3. La Sala Primera del Tribunal Supremo considera que las normas civiles españolas que declaran nulo el contrato de maternidad por subrogación impiden que pueda inscribirse como hijos de quienes han recurrido a esa técnica a los habidos en un tercer Estado, aunque exista resolución judicial (o equivalente) que así lo manifieste. Pero advierte que si los menores poseen relaciones familiares de facto Debe partirse de tal dato y permitir el desarrollo y la protección de esos vínculos.

4. La actual regulación legal (LGSS) y reglamentaria (RD 295/2009) omite la contemplación de estos supuestos pero no es tan cerrada como para impedir su interpretación en el sentido más favorable a los objetivos constitucionales de protección al menor, con independencia de su filiación, y de conciliación de vida familiar y laboral.

5. Existiendo una verdadera integración del menor en el núcleo familiar del padre subrogado, las prestaciones asociadas a la maternidad han de satisfacerse, salvo supuestos de fraude, previo cumplimiento de los requisitos generales de acceso a las mismas.

6. Cuando el solicitante de las prestaciones por maternidad, asociadas a una gestación por subrogación, es el padre biológico y registral de las menores existen poderosas razones adicionales para conceder aquéllas.

B) Todo lo anterior conduce a que, de acuerdo con el parecer del Ministerio Fiscal, consideremos ajustada a Derecho la doctrina sentada por la sentencia recurrida, desestimando el recurso interpuesto frente a la misma por la Administración de la Seguridad Social.

[Source: http://www.poderjudicial.es/search/indexAN.jsp; ROJ: STS 5375/2016 - ECLI:ES:TS:2016:5375]

ANNOTATION

All types of surrogacy are illegal in Spain, so those who want to work with a surrogate must go abroad.

The problem has arisen in relation to the filiation and registration of surrogate motherhood in the corresponding Spanish registers of minors born abroad, as well as whether or not in such situations the intended parents are entitled to labour and social security rights applicable to maternity.

The issue to be solved by the Supreme Court Social Chamber is focused on determining whether or not in such situations the intended parents are entitled to labour and social security rights applicable by law to maternity. In particular, in this case the issue arose when the applicant is the biological father and sole person registering the birth, who signed a surrogacy contract alone.

The solution has not been without contestation, and this decision and the later decision of 26 November 2016 have both generated a large debate even within the Chamber itself, giving rise to several dissenting votes within the majority positions.

1. Motherhood protected from the viewpoint of Spanish social security legislation and the legal gap concerning surrogacy

The social security system uses a mixed technique when it comes to configuring the protected situation. On the one hand, it states that the protected situations are maternity, adoption and fostering, but, on the other hand, it states that protection will be provided during periods of leave enjoyed in accordance with the provisions of labour and civil law.

The first case deserving protection by the social security legislation is the "biological maternity" of the working mother, without mentioning the 'surrogacy'. In the case of childbirth, the rights-holder is the working mother, who can enjoy the benefit entirely or share it with the other parent provided he/she is also a worker (the father or the female partner who has adopted the biological child of the other). The mother has to benefit from six weeks compulsory leave after delivery.

In the case of adoption or foster care the duration is the same as that in case of childbirth, but the leave can be taken interchangeably by both adopters or welcoming foster parents.

2. The legal situation of the father

According to Spanish legislation, in the case of childbirth, the working and biological father may only opt for full or partial maternity leave (compatible with paternity leave) and subsequent benefits in any of the situations provided for by law (Article 3 of Royal Decree 295/2009). These are: a) assignment/transfer of maternity rights from the mother to the father; or b) the mother´s death.

As a result, surrogacy is not explicitly included as a protected situation under the Spanish social security norms. The Social Security Act does not mention the assumption of the biological father who has agreed to paternity by means of the technique of surrogate gestation, with subsequent abandonment by the biological mother of the obligations towards the child.

Does this mean that surrogate maternity is outside the scope of protection of the rules of the social security law that regulates maternity benefits?

3. The legal position of the INSS

The National Institute of Social Security (INSS) has always been against the recognition of maternity benefits in the case of surrogacy. It does not matter if the petition comes from the intended or commissioning mother (who is not considered the mother according to Spanish law) or from a "single" intended father. The main argument put forward by the INSS is that surrogacy is prohibited, contrary to public order, and therefore null and void.

4. The judicial interpretation: the contradiction between Spanish civil and social jurisdictions

With regard to the filiation of a minor born under a contract of gestation and surogate registration, this issue was being resolved favourably by the

General Directorate of Public Registries and Notaries. But that Directorate took a 'Copernican turn' after the Supreme Court Civil Chamber Decision of 6 February 2014, which agreed to waive the entry in the Spanish Civil Registry of two children born in the State of California, by surrogacy, based on the foreign registration certificates in which two Spanish males married to each other appeared as 'Parents'.

4.1 Supreme Court Civil Chamber

In its decision of 6 February 2014, the Supreme Court Civil Chamber declared that the prohibition of the surrogacy contract does not only have effects for the actions that might occur in Spain, but also for cases carried out abroad, even if they are in countries where the legal system recognizes this practice of surrogacy.

Therefore the Court prevented the registration of foreign certificates concerning filiation between children born abroad under a surrogacy contract, and their intended parents. The result is that filiation in any case must be made in favour of the biological mother, without prejudice to the paternity with respect to the biological father.

According to the Supreme Court Decision of 6 February 2014, the prohibition by the Spanish rules of the surrogacy contract does not only have effects for the actions produced in Spain, but also for cases carried out abroad, even if they occur in countries that recognize these practices as legal.

However, the General Directorate of Registries and Notaries, following the pronouncements of the European Court of Human Rights (ECHR) in the *Mennesson* and *Labassee v. France* cases, continues to consider that the birth of a foreign national through the surrogate gestation technique can be registered in the Spanish Civil Registry in cases where there is a judicial decision emanating from the competent body stating the filiation of the newborn, as well as the free consent of the pregnant mother and the abandonment by the mother of the child. The General Directorate is of this opinion despite the reiteration of the position of the 1st Chamber of the Supreme Court in subsequent decisions.

4.2 Criteria established by the Supreme Court Social Chamber decisions of 2016

The Supreme Court found for the claimant so that he can have access to the maternity/paternity leave and benefits, basing its decision on the following grounds:
1. Nullity of the surrogacy contract does not imply that the child is deprived of his/her rights.

2. The best interest of the child must guide any decision that affects him or her.
3. Comprehensive protection of family and children, as well as non-discrimination, reasons. In particular, the existence of a family nucleus composed of the minor and the intended parents must be protected as well. Maternity leave and benefits are a suitable and appropriate means to do so.
4. Extension of the maternity leave and benefits established for adoption and foster care can apply to surrogacy.
5. According to this last argument, surrogacy must be protected since social security legislation considers those legal institutions duly declared by foreign judicial or administrative decisions equivalent to Spanish adoption and foster care as long as they have a purpose or effect similar to adoption or foster care. Surrogacy must be considered to be one of those institutions.

5. Conclusion

The prohibition of surrogacy in Spain does not prevent people to go abroad in order to have access to surrogate or gestational motherhood. That situation poses several problems. First, in relation to the filiation and registration of surrogate motherhood in the corresponding Spanish registers of minors born abroad, and secondly, to determine whether or not in such situations the intended parents are entitled to labour and social security rights that are applicable to maternity.

Appealing to the child's best interest, the social jurisprudence of the Supreme Court, that contradicts the civil jurisprudence of the same Court, recognizes the effectiveness of such practices, and even grants a maternity benefit to the intentional parents.

For this jurisdiction of the Court, the relationships between the new relatives and the minor also occur in cases of surrogacy, so that these situations must be duly protected, in the same way as adoption and foster care deserve protection, considering also that the social security legislation itself accepts situations juridically equivalent to adoption and/or fostering, if these legal institutions are declared by foreign judicial or administrative decisions whose purpose and legal effects are those foreseen for adoption or foster care. Such an assimilation can be extended to situations of surrogacy. For the Supreme Court, the content of the statutory provision of social security with respect to situations protected by maternity benefits, allows some interpretive flexibility, which, before its validity, did not exist. This means that the position of the parents in cases of surrogate maternity is similar to that occupied by persons, also as parents, who are in the situation of adoption or fostering. An additional support for this extended protection is that it goes against the illogical position where the benefit would be denied in cases of surrogated gestation where the applicant had legal documents that he had fathered the minor and that the mother has abandoned it, whereas the benefit would be granted *ex lege* if the applicant had limited himself to adopting or hosting a minor in foster care.

Swe. 1

SWEDEN

Labour Court
AD 2015 No. 74

*Temporary agency work – equal treatment principle
– interpretation of collective agreement*

HEADNOTES

Facts

This is a dispute relating to the pay provision of the temporary work agency collective agreement applied to blue-collar workers. Randstad Ltd – a member of the employer organization called The Swedish Staffing Agencies – is bound by that collective agreement. Randstad Ltd had been hiring out workers to Scania Ltd since 2012, and Scania Ltd applied a bonus system called SRB (Scania Result Bonus, consisting of two components: Direct Run and ´Rätt Från Mig´). A dispute arose over the question as to whether the bonus system formed part of the average wage level (GFL), which applied to comparable workers at Scania Ltd. The petitioner union (Federation IF Metall) argued that this was the case. The union contended that this was a performance wage system, and as such, was part of the GFL; it requested a declaratory judgement that would determine that SRB was part of the GFL. The employer parties rejected the claim. They argued that the bonus was something that Scania Ltd had unilaterally established, and that it had no relation to the productivity of a worker, but solely to the quality of the production (i.e. a profit sharing system). The bonus was therefore not to be considered as part of the GFL in the opinion of the employer parties.

Decision

The Labour Court adjudicated in favour of the employer parties and declared that the bonus did not form part of the payment relating to the average wage level (GFL).

Law Applied

The pertinent provision of the temporary work agency collective agreement, section 4(2) provides: "The hourly or monthly pay [for temporary agency workers] is equivalent to the average wage level (T + P) as applied to comparable workers at the user enterprise where T relates to the fixed hourly/monthly pay; and P means performance pay, piecework rate, wage incentive, bonus and commission […], which is calculated *post factum* according to an accounting period of not more than 3 months, and shall be based, if the local parties do not agree otherwise, on the latest known accounting period".

JUDGEMENT

"The dispute in this case concerns the question of whether the bonus system of Scania SRB, as far as Direct Run and ´Rätt från Mig´ [components] are concerned, shall form part of P relating to the average pay level (GFL) according to section 4(2) of the temporary agency work agreement during the period from 1 May 2012 until 31 December 2014. […]

Under the agreement it is required that the bonus has to be related to an accounting period of not more than 3 months. The trade union has alleged that the amount each worker has earned with respect to the bonus is shown each month and shall therefore forms part of the GFL. The fact that the bonus is summed up month after month, whereafter a final sum-up is performed after the end of the year, and that the sum is transferred to a foundation, is of no relevance according to the union.

The employer parties have alleged the following. The SRB is run on a yearly basis, and the bonus amount is accumulated and established in February the year after the qualification year. The bonus has thus an accounting period of one year and one month. The total sums are transferred to a profit sharing foundation that manages the funded money. The individual worker is given information about his/her share of the funded money, but cannot claim any benefits from the foundation until four years have passed from the date when the money was funded […].

The Labour Court makes the following assessment. [...]

The purpose of the stipulated three-month rule was to set a limit for each payment, calculated *post factum*, with respect to the determination of the GFL (average wage level). [...] The rule must thus be understood so that the outcome of P must be fixed and definitive within a three-month period in order to make it possible to account for the rate of the proper payment which is related to the same three-month period.

As indicated before, both Direct Run and 'Rätt Från Mig' [components] are shown every month. However, it has also been shown that the monthly sums are accumulated after the end of the year and in that respect there are certain ceiling rules regarding the bonus to be paid, which may imply that, if a ceiling limit has been reached, the already shown monthly sums are not accounted for. Furthermore, it has been said that the total amount of the bonus is carried over and managed by the foundation, and that an individual employee will be given the value of his/her share of the foundation after the end of the year, but the assembled sum of money will not be available for cashing out until four years have passed.

According to the Labour Court it is clear that one cannot calculate the amount of the bonus of Direct Run and 'Rätt Från Mig' as a fixed and definitive sum of money within a given three-month period. It is not until the final sum-up is performed after the end of the year, considering even the ceiling rules as indicated above, that it is possible to determine the real bonus for the entire calendar year.

Regarding the Direct Run and 'Rätt Från Mig' [components], under these circumstances, the SRB cannot be considered to have a calculation period of a maximum of 3 months, which is required for P to be included in the GFL in accordance with the provisions of section 4(2) of the temporary work agency collective agreement, which is why the trade union´s claim for a declaratory judgement on this point is dismissed by the Labour Court."

[Source: Labour Court Judgements 2015, published by the National Courts Administration, Stockholm 2016]

ANNOTATION

There have been three recent cases relating to the blue-collar temporary work agency collective agreement. The case reported on here is the latest one. All these cases refer to the equal treatment principle, which has been the backbone of this collective agreement since 2000 when it was concluded. It should be noted that as regards salaried employees, another agreement had been concluded between the social partners as far back as 1988. According to that agreement, temporary agency worker´s salary is set individually, and is not at all connected with the equal treatment principle.

The background to the Labour Court cases is as follows: in 2014 temporary workers in Sweden were covered by collective agreements with approximately 95% of the labour force of all temporary agency workers so covered. Approximately 1.4% of the entire workforce in Sweden are temporary agency workers. The largest temporary work agencies in 2017 include: Manpower, Randstad (which acquired Proffice in 2016), Adecco, Lernia Bemanning AB and Academic Work. They are all members of the employer organization called The Swedish Staffing Agencies. The very high coverage rate among temporary agency workers is probably linked to the special authorization process necessary to become a member of the employer organization, which has been mandatory since 2009, and which is governed by a board with the participation of both social partners. The aim is to improve the quality of activities in order to become and stay on as a member of the employer organization. It is a kind of 'eco-label'.

All the three cases refer to the interpretation of the agreement as applied to blue-collar workers and the disputed section 4(2). None of the cases refers to or is based on the concepts of pay, as laid down in the EU Directive 2008/104 on temporary agency work.

An account of the first two cases is necessary.

In Labour Court judgement 2009 No. 54, the issue referred to the guidelines set forth in the same section, providing that: "A comparable group refers to the organizational or clear vocational criteria of work at the user enterprise in order to create 'neutral wages' as a reference point for the temporary work agency's pay. In establishing the reference object, the proper worksite or area of activity will be treated as a unit". The Court had to decide a case when the user enterprise, a large Swedish building company (NCC), had no building workers employed at its two worksites in Gothenburg. It is to these two sites that a temporary work agency sent Polish building workers. The agency was an Irish company and a member of The Swedish Staffing Agencies. The Swedish Building Workers' Union claimed that the wages of the Polish workers were not in compliance with the collective agreement (the difference amounted to some 875,000 Swedish crowns across the two building projects). The Labour Court found that the wage level in that case should have been based on the wage level as applied to comparable groups of workers employed by the user enterprise in the Gothenburg region, since NCC had other building workers employed on sites there. According to the Court, to apply the agreement in this way was also in line with the purpose of the agreement, which was to secure that ´neutral wages´ should be applied by the temporary work agency. The Court thus adjudicated in favour of the Union, and awarded exemplary damages amounting to 350,000 Swedish crowns based on the breach of the collective agreement.

In this way, the Labour Court established a default rule in cases when temporary agency workers are sent to a user enterprise which does not have any workers employed at the workplace where the temporary workers have been assigned by the temporary work agency.

In a second earlier decision, Labour Court judgement 2009 No. 94, the issue was whether apprentices and so-called vacation trainees should form part of a comparable group of workers, together with the regular building workers employed by another big Swedish building company (Peab). The temporary work agency had included such labour in the comparable group, and, as a result of this inclusion, the equivalent pay level was much lower than the pay level applied to regular building workers. To start with, the Court found that this specific issue had not been discussed between the contracting parties when the temporary work agency's collective agreement came into force in 2000, or at any later date. Based on this information the Court concluded that there was no consensus among the contracting parties. The Court concluded that apprentices, and to a far lesser degree so-called vacation trainees, could not be included in the group of comparable building workers. So in this case as well, the Court had to design a default rule as a gap filler because the collective agreement itself gave no adequate guidance.

Apart from these earlier cases, it should be noted that Sweden has implemented Articles 5.1 (on the equal treatment principle), 5.2 (as regards pay for workers who have a permanent contract of employment) and 5.3 (collective agreements which respect the overall protection of temporary agency workers) of the EU Directive in its domestic legislation (noted in the Official Gazette 2012:854). However, no amendments to the collective agreements have been made with respect to the implementation of the EU Directive and, as noted above, the EU Directive was not relied on in the Labour Court judgement being commented on here.

As indicated also by the European Court of Justice case law involving temporary agency work (which is scant), situations in which a temporary work agency can be involved in a legal dispute are manifold.

The most contentious issue on the Swedish labour market has been the right to re-employment after a redundancy dismissal, as provided for in the Swedish Employment Protection Act, and the option for the employer to hire workers from a temporary work agency (see, in particular Labour Court judgements 2003 No. 4 – which was reported in ILLR volume 23 – and 2007 No. 72). After the negotiations between the social partners in 2010 and 2012 restrictions with respect to the use of temporary agency workers were included in the pertinent blue-collar collective agreements. No dispute on that particular issue has since been brought before the Swedish Labour Court.

PART TWO

BASIC RIGHTS PERTAINING TO LABOUR

ISRAEL

The National Labour Court
Koach LaOvdim Democratic Workers' Organization
v. Z.L.F. Industries Inc.
NLC 51407-07-15

Right to union organization – union recognized bargaining agent – union de-recognition – protected period of union recognition – employer's anti-union activities – penalty for employer anti-union activity

HEADNOTES

Facts

Koach LaOvdim Democratic Worker's Organization (the Union) is a trade union, which succeeded in organizing over a third of the plant workers at Z.L.F. Industries Inc. (the Employer). Under Israeli law a union whose members are at least a third of the workplace workers becomes the exclusive bargaining agent. Therefore, when the Union organized about 40 per cent of the Employer's workers it notified the Employer that it was the legal bargaining agent and was duly recognized. After the Union was recognized, the parties negotiated for over a year without reaching an agreement. The Union then declared a work dispute and four months later a one day strike. A month after that the Employer refused to continue negotiations, claiming that the Union was no longer the exclusive bargaining agent because it represented less than a third of the workforce since some workers had renounced Union membership.

The Union petitioned the Regional Labour Court (the Labour Court system's trial court) to order the Employer to continue negotiating. During the hearing, held shortly after the petition was filed, it was shown that a considerable number of workers had renounced their Union membership. The parties agreed that the Employer would not pressure workers to leave the Union, a Government Mediator would count the Union's membership cards and if the Union still represented more than the required third of the Employer's workforce, the parties would negotiate twice a week for at least six months. The card count showed that the Union represented only 31 per cent of the workers and, therefore, the Employer continued its refusal to negotiate.

The Union again filed a claim in the Regional Labour Court requesting an order affirming that it is the bargaining agent, compelling the Employer to continue negotiations and to desist from unlawful anti-union activities, and penalizing the Employer by making it pay the Union's damages for the previous anti-union activities.

A year later the Regional Labour Court handed down its judgment and held that the Employer had interfered with the workers' right to organize and had unlawfully refused to bargain. The Court compelled the Employer to continue bargaining another year from the date the judgment was handed down, at which time the situation would be evaluated again by the Court, which could give the Union still another year to negotiate, if the circumstances so warranted. The Court further held that during the negotiations the Employer was prohibited from pressuring the workers and even from communicating with them about the Union, thus extending the ban placed on Employers by the *Pelephone* judgment (*The New Histadrut General Labour Federation v. Pelephone Communications Ltd.*, 33 ILLR 355). Both parties appealed to the National Labour Court, (the Labour Court System's final appeal court).

Decision

Parts of both appeals were accepted and rejected. The National Labour Court held that even when there was only one union at the workplace, which had been recognized as the exclusive bargaining agent, under certain conditions the employer was entitled to question whether it represented the workers and refuse to continue negotiations.

Law Applied

See judgment.

JUDGMENT

The Judgment of The National Labour Court was handed down by Judge Segal Davidov-Motola, with the agreement of President Yigal Plitman, Judge Ilan Itach, and Public Representatives Members S. Tzafrir and Shlomo Neeman.

[…]

[24] […] Union representation under law is a cogent principle which grants a union exclusive status to sign a collective agreement determining working conditions when it represents the largest number of workers at a workplace and at least a third of them.

[…]

[28] The Regional Court set a period of "organizational stability" which has yet to be adopted in precedent and which prevented the Employer from questioning the Union's status after it was recognized and when there is not a competing union. Generally, collective relations assume that the union retains it representative status, without questioning its status. Such questioning in bad faith can undermine the union's representative status and be an incentive for employers to act this way […] it can also cause unrest at the workplace and both parties have a "win-win situation" interest in workplace stability. […] We note that after a union is recognized a period of stability is required so that both sides to the collective relationship can adjust to each other, and build confidence and cooperation, without the union feeling that every day its membership status was being tested. However, this does not mean that there is a fixed "organization stability" period or "estoppel" during which the employer is obligated to continue to negotiate with the recognized union as the bargaining agent, without the possibility of again raising the issue of whether it is still the bargaining agent, even though there have arisen legitimate doubts regarding its status. The recognition of an exclusive bargaining agent does not remain static indefinitely, and the period during which a union can rely on being the bargaining agent is determined by the entire situation, including: whether the union was active at the workplace following the notice that it was the bargaining representative; were there negotiations with the employer concerning working conditions; whether there were significant changes in the workforce so that the union does not have the necessary membership to be the bargaining representative. […] On the other hand, while negotiations are taking place an employer should not raise the

issue of whether the union is still the bargaining representative. It is an exception that an employer does so, when it acts in good faith and was not responsible for the changes which justify it questioning the union's representative status. [...]

[29] However, what we have said above does not necessarily mean there is a formal and set stability period or estoppel during which the employer will always be obligated to negotiate, without the opportunity to raise again the issue of the union's representative status when there is a justified basis to do so. In the Horn and Leibowitz judgment this Court said: "*The question how the status of a representative union can change is very serious and depends, among other things, on the need to balance between the importance of stability of union representation and the freedom of association*. Recognition of a union as the exclusive bargaining agent does not, therefore, exist forever [...]". [...] When the employer learns from workers' notifications that the union no longer represents them [...] it is entitled to demand that the union produce up-to-date data that it is still the bargaining representative. In this instance the Company did not prove that it had no part in the workers' renouncing their union membership or that it did not put direct or indirect pressure on the workers to do so. Therefore, the union membership renunciation will not be given effect and the Union remained their legal bargaining representative when the Employer questioned its status. The Company was, therefore, obligated to continue to negotiate with the Union and its refusal to do so was a violation of the freedom of association. [...]

[...]

[40] Another relevant principle relates to the initial stage of union organization at a workplace. [...] This situation places special importance on employers' actions to discourage initial union organization [...] which justifies special protection for workers who seek to obtain their right to join a union and organize their workplace. [...] It is important to emphasize that even after the employer recognizes the union and the relationship transfers from "pre-recognition" to "pre-collective agreement" and the parties are negotiating, the union's status is still fragile. [...] Employers should also be prevented from delaying the negotiations while they are at the same time acting to reduce the union's membership, so that they can claim the union is no longer the bargaining representative. [...]

[...]

[42] [...] in the Horn and Leibowitz judgment this Court noted:

"*there is a presumption, which can be contradicted, that if workers leave the union after the notification to the employer that it is the legal bargaining representative, the reason for workers' renouncing their union membership was illegal employer pressure.*"

[...]

[46] [...] When it became known to the Employer in this case, through good faith notifications of workers and not from the Employer's initiative that the Union no longer had representative status, and conditional on the Employer not being involved in the workers renouncing their union membership, we hold that the Employer was justified in demanding that the Union produce current data to prove its status.

[47] The Union refused to produce the data and instead filed a petition to the Regional Court. [...] When it was proven in court that 70 workers had renounced their Union membership [...] the burden of proof was on the Company to show that it was not involved in the workers renouncing their membership and did not pressure the workers directly or indirectly. The Regional Court held [...] that "*we are not convinced that anyone from the Company was not involved in the renouncing of Union membership*" [...] and, therefore, the Employer did not meet the required burden of proof. After it was proven that the Union was the representative union at the time when the Employer had demanded proof of its status, the Employer was obligated to negotiate at that stage, and refusing to do so was a violation of the freedom to organize collectively.

[48] In general, monetary compensation is not an adequate remedy for violations of freedom of association and, accordingly, there are additional remedies. Courts should give injunctions or positive orders to prevent or reduce the damage caused and enable the workers to achieve their aspirations to organize. [The Court continued to explain why it is not feasible in this situation to grant such an injunction or positive order.]

[49] [...] At this workplace, where there had been no collective activity or union involvement for a long time, it is not possible to restore and revive previous representative status. Therefore there was no basis for the Regional Court to rule that the Union, which represented less than a third of the workers will negotiate with the Employer. It was also not practical for this Court to compel the parties to negotiate for six months following our judgment. Therefore, we reject the Union's petition for an order compelling the Employer to negotiate, despite our holding that the Employer unlawfully violated the workers' freedom to organize collectively. [...]

[Source: NLC 51407-07-15]

ANNOTATION

This judgment raises a number of problems.

The trial court's judgment was handed down almost a year after the Union's petition had been filed and the National Labour Court's judgment about two and a half years after the Employer refused to negotiate. By the time the decisions were handed down the Employer had succeeded in undermining the Union's representative status, and it had no leverage at the bargaining table. Thus, by committing unlawful anti-union activity and delaying the negotiations, combined with the long Court hearings, the Employer succeeded in remaining a non-union workplace. This does not rule out the possibility that the Union made tactical and negotiating mistakes which contributed to its downfall, but is a negative labour relations lesson.

Under the trial court's order the Employer was obligated to negotiate until 31 December 2015. The National Labour Court's judgment was handed down on 7 October 2016. By the time the trial court's judgment was handed down the Union membership had disintegrated and when the National Labour Court handed down its judgment any collective negotiations would have been purely theoretical. Time is crucial in collective bargaining cases and when judgments are not handed down close to the time of the violation of the workers' rights to organize the passing of time in itself defeats their rights. To solve this problem courts in the past gave intermediate judgments or final judgments without reasons at the conclusion of a hearing and shortly thereafter gave the completed final judgment. This is the practice suggested by National Labour Court precedent in cases of injunctions regarding petitions against strikes and should also be done in petitions against unfair employer anti-union activity, such as refusal to negotiate or threatening union members. Therefore, because there was no intermediate decision handed down immediately after the Employer's unlawful interference and pressure on the workers to renounce their union membership, the Court hearing had become a method whereby the Employer could defeat the Union's attempt to organize the workplace and reach a collective agreement.

Another problematic aspect of this decision is that even though the Employer pressured workers to renounce their union membership, succeeded in weakening the Union by defeating a strike and unlawfully refused to negotiate, the Court refused to grant the Union any damages or other relief. This can be interpreted as encouraging employers to resist union attempts to consummate collective negotiations by signing an agreement.

The Court correctly cited the general principle that financial compensation is not the only remedy when an employer violates workers' rights to join a union and organize, and that further effective remedies are justified. However, when this Court concluded that the further remedies were not practical because the Union's presence at the workplace had disintegrated, it still could have used the remedy of monetary damages to compensate the Union and discourage other employers from committing similar anti-union activity.

Yet another problematic aspect of the decision is the confusion between recognized representative status and the obligation to bargain collectively. Once a union is recognized as the bargaining agent, after showing it represents over one third of the workplace employees, an employer is obligated to negotiate with the recognized union. This obligation is not conditional on the union being required to prove during the negotiations the number of members it represents. Union strength at the bargaining table and the ability to reach a reasonable collective agreement depends on the support of the workers at the workplace. However, when a union is negotiating its first collective agreement, the workers have just joined the union and worker support will often fluctuate. During negotiations a union can compromise and make concessions, which can reduce support among part of the workforce. Some types of workers at the workplace will be satisfied with their union's proposals and others less so. Employers' having the ability to question union status will discourage unions from being flexible. Workers are not used to union representation and the friction involved with their employer. Workers have not been convinced that the union can obtain substantial benefits for them. For this reason the Histadrut General Labour Federation does not even collect dues until an agreement is signed. Membership, therefore, is less relevant then workers' support for the union and willingness to take collective action if necessary. The employer should not be able to question a union's representative status during the negotiations, as happened in this case. If the union is constantly worried about losing support during negotiations it will balk at compromising, and reaching agreement will be difficult. Despite mentioning that the employer should not be able to question union status during negotiations, the Court allowed the Employer in this case to question the Union's status and even ruled that the Union was no longer the representative union.

The Union's petition was to obligate the Employer to negotiate, which is the obligation towards any recognized union. On the one hand, a good argument can be made for the Regional Labour Court's ruling to compel the Employer to negotiate, without regard to the fact that the Union represented only 31 per cent of the workers instead of 33 per cent. On the other hand, the relevance of the loss of the Union's members and, therefore, power at the bargaining table, is that the Union had little chance of convincing the Employer to reach a decent collective agreement. The National Labour Court decision, therefore, seems to have confused the issues of union status and the obligation to bargain collectively during which it could pressure the employer to compromise.

There is also a question as to the meaning of the Court's statement regarding the lack of collective union presence at the workplace. Does this mean there had been no strikes, or no meetings, or no visits by union representatives or that there are no members left? It seems to mean that with the passing of time the workers had lost interest in the Union. Can the Court make a distinction between a lack of worker interest in the Union and fear of being associated with it because of the Employer's pressure? What the Court could also have meant is that the Union's representatives ceased to visit the workplace. Does this signify that the plant is no longer organized? This presents questions about what period is necessary for the Court to rule a workplace as no longer organized. Also, if we have a workplace, which has been organized for a considerable period, with existing collective agreements and workers who belong to the union, can the Court rule that a lack of union presence at the workplace means that it is no longer the representative union? This is especially problematic since we are talking about an appeal court that did not hear evidence.

It is hoped that in future judgments the Court will clarify some of the issues raised in this case.

UNITED STATES OF AMERICA

Court of Appeals for the District of Columbia Circuit
Hyundai Am. Shipping Agency, Inc. v. NLRB

Employer handbook rules – interference with right to engage in concerted activity

HEADNOTES

Facts

The employer provided employees with a handbook setting forth work rules and guidance. Four rules were challenged on the ground that they interfered with the employees' protected right to engage in concerted activities. The challenged rules and guidance prohibited employees from discussing matters under investigation by the employer, limited the disclosure of information from the employer's electronic communication and information systems, prohibited activities other than work during working hours, and urged employees to make complaints to their immediate supervisors rather than to fellow employees.

The issue was: Is it an unfair labor practice for an employer to maintain rules or guidance that on its face may deter workers from sharing information respecting the terms and conditions of their work or work environment?

Decision

Three of the employer's rules broadly prohibited conduct that included activities for mutual aid and protection and, therefore, violated the National Labor Relations Act. Because the fourth rule was merely exhortatory, not prohibitory, it did not interfere with the protected right to engage in concerted activity.

Law Applied

National Labor Relations Act

Section 7 (29 U.S. Code § 157): "Employees shall have the right to [...] engage in [...] concerted activities for the purpose of [...] mutual aid or protection [...]."

Section 8(a) (29 U.S. Code § 158): [...] "It shall be an unfair labor practice for an employer – (1) to interfere with, restrain, or coerce employees in the exercise of the rights guaranteed in section 157 of this title [...]."

JUDGMENT

Before Henderson and Griffith, Circuit Judges, and Williams, Senior Circuit Judge.

Williams, Senior Circuit Judge:

We review an order of the National Labor Relations Board invalidating five rules in the employee handbook maintained by the Hyundai America Shipping Agency. [...]

The Board had found that Hyundai's maintenance of the five handbook rules violated [Section] 8(a)(1) of the National Labor Relations Act, which requires that employers not "interfere with, restrain, or coerce employees in the exercise of" their rights—enumerated in § 7—to form labor organizations, bargain collectively, and engage in similar concerted activities. 29 U.S.C. §§ 157, 158(a)(1). [...]

The case began with a charge by Sandra McCullough, a former Hyundai employee, alleging that Hyundai fired her "because she engaged in protected concerted activities," thus violating her § 7 rights. [...] This led to a complaint by the Board's General Counsel alleging not only that McCullough's dismissal violated the NLRA but also that Hyundai had unlawfully maintained five rules violating § 8(a)(1) on their face. The ALJ [Administrative Law Judge] found that Hyundai would have fired McCullough regardless of whether she had violated any of the challenged rules, and the Board affirmed. Hyundai America Shipping Agency, Inc. & Sandra L. McCullough, 357 N.L.R.B. No. 80 at *2 (August 26, 2011) ("Order"). So McCullough herself is out of the case. But the ALJ went on to find that all five rules violated § 7. The Board affirmed that conclusion as well, and Hyundai appealed. Our first task is to resolve whether the complaint's allegations against the five rules were properly before the

Board. As we'll explain below, we find that the Board had jurisdiction over the claims against four rules—ones that the complaint linked to the dismissal by asserting that Hyundai discharged McCullough because of her violations of those rules. Not so as to the fifth; as to it, the Board lacked jurisdiction because the General Counsel never alleged it to have played a causal role in the dismissal. As to the four rules properly before the Board, we enforce the Board's order as to three but reverse as to the fourth.

[...]

Merits. The four disputed rules [...] were: (1) a rule prohibiting employees from discussing matters under investigation by Hyundai ("investigative confidentiality rule" [...]); (2) a rule limiting the disclosure of information from Hyundai's electronic communication and information systems ("electronic communications rule") [...]; (3) a rule prohibiting activities other than work during working hours ("working hours rule") [...]; and (4) a provision urging employees to make complaints to their immediate supervisors rather than to fellow employees ("complaint provision") [...].

We address the four in that order. As usual, we accept the Board's findings of fact if they are supported by substantial evidence, 29 U.S.C. § 160(e), and we defer to the Board's reasonable interpretations of the National Labor Relations Act under *Chevron, U.S.A., Inc. v. Natural Resources Defense Council, Inc.*, 467 U.S. 837 [...] (1984), "which [...] means (within its domain) that a 'reasonable agency interpretation prevails.'" Northern Natural Gas Co. v. FERC, 700 F.3d 11, 14 (D.C. Cir. 2012) (quoting *Entergy Corp. v. Riverkeeper, Inc.*, 556 U.S. 208, 218 n.4 [...] (2009)).

To decide whether an employer's rule violates § 8(a)(1), the Board asks "whether the rule[] would reasonably tend to chill employees in the exercise of their statutory rights." *Guardsmark v. NLRB*, 475 F.3d 369, 374 (D.C. Cir. 2007) [...]. That inquiry requires the Board to determine, first, whether the rule restricts § 7 activity explicitly. If the rule does not do so—and none of these rules does—the Board asks next whether the rule (1) could be reasonably construed by employees to restrict § 7 activity, (2) was adopted in response to such activity, or (3) has been used to restrict such activity. *Id.* An affirmative answer to any of these three questions means that the employer can retain the rule only by showing an adequate justification.

There is no allegation that Hyundai's rules were promulgated in response to protected concerted activity, and the Board does not suggest that Hyundai applied them to restrict such activity. Rather, the Board found that the rules ran afoul of the first of the three tests, i.e., were facially invalid. The Board's reasoning is that, even in the absence of enforcement, "mere maintenance of a rule likely to chill Section 7 activity, whether explicitly or through reasonable interpretation, can amount to an unfair labor practice." *Id.* [...].

On review, we ask whether the Board reasonably concluded that "employees would reasonably construe [each rule] to prohibit Section 7 activity." *Cintas Corp. v. NLRB*, 482 F.3d 463, 468 (D.C. Cir. 2007) [...]. We accept the Board's conclusions with respect to all but the employee complaint provision.

Investigative confidentiality rule. The Board found, and Hyundai does not dispute, that Hyundai maintained an oral rule prohibiting employees from revealing information about matters under investigation. [...] Since this blanket confidentiality rule clearly limited employees' § 7 rights to discuss their employment, the question is whether Hyundai has presented a legitimate and substantial business justification for the rule, outweighing the adverse effect on the interests of employees. Desert Palace, Inc., 336 N.L.R.B. 271, 272 (2001); see also *Jeannette Corp. v. NLRB*, 532 F.2d 916, 918 (3d Cir. 1976).

Hyundai argues that federal and state anti-discrimination statutes and guidelines, which require confidentiality in many investigations, constitute a legitimate and substantial business justification for its rule. For example, Equal Employment Opportunity Commission guidelines suggest that information about sexual harassment allegations, as well as records related to investigations of those allegations, should be kept confidential. Enforcement Guidance on Vicarious Employer Liability for Unlawful Harassment by Supervisors, § V(C)(1) (915.002, June 18, 1999) [...].

We agree that the obligation to comply with such guidelines may often constitute a legitimate business justification for requiring confidentiality in the context of a particular investigation or particular types of investigations. But Hyundai has not shown that these concerns offer a legitimate business reason to ban discussions of all investigations, including ones unlikely to present these concerns. The Board therefore reasonably concluded that the rule was overbroad.

In enforcing the Board's order, we need not and do not endorse the ALJ's novel view that in order to demonstrate a legitimate and substantial justification for confidentiality, an employer must "determine whether in any give [sic] investigation witnesses need protection, evidence is in danger of being destroyed, testimony is in danger of being fabricated, and there is a need to prevent a cover up." Order, 2011 NLRB LEXIS

498, 2011 WL 4830117, at *27. Instead, we simply hold that Hyundai's confidentiality rule was so broad and undifferentiated that the Board reasonably concluded that Hyundai did not present a legitimate business justification for it.

Electronic communications rule. Hyundai's employee handbook included a rule describing limitations on the use of the company's electronic communications systems and concluding with the requirement that "employees should only disclose information or messages from theses [sic] systems to authorized persons." [...] The Board held that a reasonable employee could read this rule to prevent the sharing of any information exchanged on Hyundai's electronic communications network, thereby restricting employees' ability to share information about the terms and conditions of employment.

We note the somewhat academic nature of the dispute: both parties agree that the electronic communications rule cannot legally apply to information about terms and conditions of employment (absent adequate justification). There is therefore no substantive dispute over the scope of the employer's authority to maintain confidentiality. We hold that the Board's conclusion was a reasonable application of the existing case law. The disposition of this issue depends largely on whether the electronic communications rule is more analogous to the policy challenged in *Community Hospitals of Central California v. NLRB*, 335 F.3d 1079 (D.C. Cir. 2003), or to the rule at issue in *Cintas*, 482 F.3d at 465, 468-70. In *Community Hospitals*, 335 F.3d at 1089, we reversed the Board's order invalidating a handbook rule prohibiting "[r]elease or disclosure of confidential information concerning patients or employees," *id.* at 1088. We concluded that a reasonable employee would not interpret the rule to ban discussion of the terms of his or her own employment. In *Cintas*, 482 F.3d at 468-69, by contrast, this court enforced the Board's order invalidating a policy that protected "the confidentiality of any information concerning the company," *id.* at 465. We distinguished that policy from the rule in *Community Hospitals* on the ground that the latter expressly limited its prohibition to confidential information. *Id.* at 470.

Hyundai's rule, unlike the one we held lawful in *Community Hospitals*, is not limited by its terms to confidential information. A reasonable reader, however, might interpret the provision to apply only to such information, just as a reasonable reader of the rule in *Community Hospitals* would understand confidential information to exclude the terms and conditions of his or her own employment. *Community Hospitals*, 335 F.3d at 1089.

Since these two cases do not clearly dictate the result in this case, we defer to the Board's reasonable conclusion that *Cintas* controls and that the electronic communications rule is invalid.

Working hours rule. Hyundai's employee handbook included a rule allowing disciplinary action, including termination, for "[p]erforming activities other than Company work during working hours." [...] The Board invalidated this rule because it prohibited employees from engaging in union-related activities even during breaks. We have previously accepted the Board's distinction between "working time," which excludes breaks, and "working hours," describing the period from the beginning to the end of a shift, breaks and all. *United Servs. Auto. Ass'n v. NLRB*, 387 F.3d 908, 914 (D.C. Cir. 2004). Restrictions on union activity during working hours are presumptively invalid; similar restrictions during working time are not. *Id.* Applying this distinction, the Board reasonably concluded that Hyundai's rule restricted union activity during a work shift but outside of working time.

Complaint Provision. Hyundai's Employee Handbook included an employee conduct provision:

> Voice your complaints directly to your immediate superior or to Human Resources through our 'open door' policy. Complaining to your fellow employees will not resolve problems. Constructive complaints communicated through the appropriate channels may help improve the workplace for all.

[...] The ALJ concluded that this rule implicitly prohibited complaints protected by § 7.

We disagree. In *Guardsmark*, 475 F.3d at 376, we enforced the Board's order invalidating a rule banning workplace complaints because the rule prevented employees from complaining to customers or to other non-supervisor employees. In enforcing that order, however, we relied specifically on the rule's "mandatory language." *Id*; see also *SNE Enters., Inc.*, 347 N.L.R.B. 472, 492 (2006) (invalidating anti-complaint rule that led to dismissal of employee); *Kinder-Care Learning Centers*, 299 N.L.R.B. 1171 (1990) (invalidating policy that expressly prohibited complaints to customers and threatened disciplinary action for noncompliance).

Here, by contrast, the handbook urges employees to voice their complaints to their supervisors or to Human Resources, but the language is neither mandatory nor preclusive of alternatives: "Constructive complaints communicated through the appropriate channels may help improve the workplace for all" [...]. Moreover, the handbook does not prescribe penalties for complaints to fellow employees. A reasonable employee would not read the provision, with its exhortatory language and lack of penalties, to prohibit complaints protected by § 7.

[Source: 805 F.3d 309 (2015)]

ANNOTATION

The NLRB proceeding revealed that the employee, McCullough, who initiated this case asserting that she had been dismissed from employment because she complained about sexual harassment and the general treatment of employees, had been unlawfully interrogated about her protected concerted activity, and had violated rules in the employer's handbook that allegedly restricted the right of employees to engage in protected concerted activity. The NLRB found that the unfair labor practice hearing established that, among other things, McCullough had lied to management with respect to a refund request, had left threatening voice mails with several employees, unlawfully entered the apartment of two employees who were at work and telephoned them to say where she was, and made an inappropriate sexual comment to a co-worker, prompting the co-worker to file a complaint. Based on these findings, the Board ruled that the dismissal of McCullough was sufficiently justified by considerations independent of the challenged handbook rules. Nevertheless, although no remedy was available to McCullough, the Board addressed the issue of whether the employer was guilty of unfair labor practices in maintaining the challenged handbook rules.

A person filing an unfair labor practice charge need not show personal injury from the alleged unfair labor practice. Indeed, the person filing the unfair labor practice charge need not be an employee of the party being charged. Thus, to the extent that it found that the employer's handbook rules for its employees had the potential of discouraging lawful concerted activity for employee mutual aid or protection, the court enforced the NLRB's order that found an unfair labor practice and struck down the offending rules.

It should also be noted that the court's discussion did not address whether the potential discouraged concerted activity involved efforts to organize or support a labor organization. So long as the discouraged conduct is concerted and involves some form of employee mutual aid or protection, it is an unfair labor practice under the NLRA.

In another case decided during this term, a federal appellate court held that the National Labor Relations Act protects an employee's right to communicate to a manager about dissatisfaction with working conditions shared by others and that an employee handbook rule that inhibits employees from sharing information relating to the comparative pay and benefits of other employees, can be enforced only if shown to be necessitated by legitimate and substantial business justifications. The court also ruled that, in a workplace that has no union representation, if it is shown that a contributing factor in the decision to dismiss an employee was the employee's exercise of the right to share information about comparative pay and benefits of the work force and complain that some employees were treated unfairly, the employer has the burden of proof to show that it would have reached the same result even absent the protected activity of sharing that information and complaining about unfair treatment. *MCPc Inc. v. NLRB*, 813 F.3d 475 (3d Cir. 2016).

AUSTRIA

Supreme Court, 25 May 2016 9 ObA 117/15v

Lawful dismissal due to refusal to remove a full-face veil or an Islamic headscarf at the workplace – discrimination on ground of religion?

HEADNOTES

Facts

The plaintiff had been working at the defendant's notary office from 12 January 2009 until 15 July 2014. The employer gave notice of termination of the employment relationship on 11 April 2014. At the beginning, the plaintiff was working 30 hours per week, and then she worked at the notary office as a full time employee.

Already in 2005, the plaintiff had converted to Islam. The defendant knew about the plaintiff's creed from the start of the employment relationship, accepted it and allowed the plaintiff to pray regularly in a separate room. After a certain time, the plaintiff wanted to wear an Islamic headscarf not just during her prayers, but also on a daily basis. For this reason, in February 2010, she asked the defendant to allow her to wear the Islamic headscarf also during working hours, a request which the defendant rejected. As of October 2010, the plaintiff decided to wear the Islamic headscarf anyway. Later, she also started to wear an Islamic dress (abaya) during all working hours.

In the period from 25 April 2011 until 3 October 2011, the plaintiff, as well as other employees, had to interact directly with customers (making and receiving calls, working at the reception desk) and to act as a testamentary witness. At that time, just before her maternity leave and irrespective of the fact that she was wearing a headscarf, the plaintiff was assigned tasks involving direct interaction with customers for two to three half-days a week in addition to acting as a testamentary witness. The defendant did not ask her to remove the headscarf at any time while carrying out the given assignments.

After her maternity leave, the plaintiff worked 20 hours per week. From that moment onwards, the plaintiff's assignments involving direct interaction with customers became significantly fewer.

Due to a severe illness, the plaintiff was on sick leave from 31 July 2013. Thereafter, she decided to wear an Islamic face veil (niqab). After her return to work in December 2013, she declared that she would like to wear her niqab also during working hours. The defendant, however, claimed that wearing a face veil was not compatible with a job in a notary's office. A compromise, such as taking off the veil while talking to customers, could not be achieved since the plaintiff's office was constantly visible for customers. Furthermore, working in a separate room was not an option, because the plaintiff had to be able to communicate with her co-workers at all times. The notary wrote two emails to the plaintiff stating that wearing a face veil was not compatible with her job in a notary's office. The employee did not follow the employer's invitation to discuss the issue in person. Eventually, due to the fact that the employee did not want to follow the employer's instructions, not to wear a niqab, the defendant, on 11 April 2014, gave her notice of dismissal with the termination date specified as 15 July 2014.

The plaintiff requested compensation for non-material damage of €7,000. She argued that she had been subject to discrimination as regards the termination of her employment relationship and other working conditions based on her religious beliefs.

The defendant employer pleaded limitation of the claim for damages. Also, he argued that he had not discriminated against the plaintiff at any time and had not terminated the employment contract due to her religion since wearing a face veil was not part of exercising the Islamic creed. Additionally, according to Paragraph 7(2) of the Notary Regulation, a notary as someone who holds public office shall wear decent clothes.

The Labour Court agreed with the defendant. Parts of the underlying claim had become subject to the statute of limitations. Furthermore, the employer was entitled to introduce general rules concerning working conditions, such as regulations on clothing. No discrimination had taken place since the employer had never been opposed to the plaintiff's creed, but solely to her appearance. The defendant's request to dress "in a neutral way" had the same impact on every religion and, thus, no discrimination had taken place.

The Court of Appeal set aside the contested judgement and remitted the case to the original court of first instance (the Labour Court) for a new decision following supplementary proceedings. The Court of Appeal held that discrimination had taken place after the end of her parental leave. The employer did not prevent her from wearing the abaya after parental leave, but her working conditions were changed (reduction of client contact and the possibilities to act as a notarial witness). With regards to those changed working conditions, it decided that the plaintiff had been subject to direct discrimination based on her religious beliefs. However, the Court of Appeal did not qualify the dismissal as a discriminatory act based on religion. It found that the employer does not have to permit wearing an Islamic face veil since – pursuant to the jurisdiction of the European Court of Human Rights – it could affect an essential value, being the value of unhindered social interaction.

Cross-appeals were brought before the Austrian Supreme Court.

Decision

The Supreme Court held that the appeals of both parties were in part lawful and justified.

Law Applied

Gleichbehandlungsgesetz (GlBG/Equal Treatment Act)
Section 17
(1) No person shall be subject to direct or indirect discrimination on grounds of ethnic belonging, religion or belief, age or sexual orientation in employment, in particular as regards […] termination of employment. […]

Section 20
(1) A different treatment which is based on a characteristic related to any of the grounds referred to in § 17 of the Equal Treatment Act shall not constitute discrimination where, by reason of the nature of the particular occupational activities concerned or of the context in which they are carried out, such a characteristic constitutes a genuine and determining occupational requirement, provided that the objective is legitimate and the requirement is proportionate.

JUDGEMENT

The dismissal as an act of discrimination:

2.1 According to § 17(1) and (7) of the Equal Treatment Act [Gleichbehandlungsgesetz, GlBG] no person shall be subject to direct or indirect discrimination on grounds of religion or belief in employment, in particular with regard to termination of employment.

2.2. The term "religion" is defined neither by the Directive 2000/78 nor by the Austrian Equal Treatment Act.

2.3. The constitutional provision in Article 14(1) of the Fundamental Law of the General Rights of Citizens (Staatsgrundgesetz, StGG) 1867 provides that everyone has the right to freedom of belief and conscience. According to section 63(2) of the State Treaty of St. Germain, all inhabitants of Austria shall be entitled to the free exercise, whether public or private, of any creed, religion or belief, whose practices are not inconsistent with public order or public morals. Furthermore, everybody's right to freedom of thought, conscience and religion is laid down in Article 9(1) of the Convention for the Protection of Human Rights and Fundamental Freedoms (ECHR). This right includes freedom to change their religion or belief and freedom, either alone or in community with others and in public or private, to manifest their religion or belief, in worship, teaching, practice and observance.

2.4. The wearing of religious clothing falls under the scope of Article 9 of the ECHR. Pursuant to the jurisdiction of the European Court of Human Rights (ECtHR) wearing an Islamic headscarf "indicates allegiance to a particular faith […]. Such garments may even be said to constitute a 'powerful' religious symbol […]." (ECtHR 15 February 2001, *Dahlab v. Switzerland*, 42393/98).

2.5. The protection against discrimination embodied in § 17 (1) of the Equal Treatment Act also includes wearing religious clothing at the workplace due to the broad term "religion". Furthermore, wearing religious signs is also covered by the right to freedom of belief and conscious according to the ECtHR (15 January 2013, *Eweida v. United Kingdom*, 48420/10). The aim of anti-discrimination rights is to prevent any direct or indirect discrimination laid down by law. […]

3.1. Contrary to the legal opinion of the plaintiff, it is not relevant if the Qur'an enshrines wearing a face veil (ECtHR 15 January 2013, *Eweida v. United Kingdom*, 48420/10, recital 82). The key factor is whether wearing such an accessory as an expression of religious customs and as one's decision on a matter of conscience falls within the scope of Article 9 ECHR since it involves the actual practice of a specific faith. [...]

3.2. The legal assessment undertaken by the Court of Appeal considering unequal treatment due to the wearing of a headscarf a form of direct discrimination based on religion is accurate, because religious clothing cannot be seen as a "neutral distinction criterion". [...]

3.3. That is why, it has to be determined if a dismissal due to non-compliance with the employer's specific instruction to not wear a face veil at the workplace qualifies as one of the derogations provided for in § 20 of the Equal Treatment Act. [...]

4.1.1. A different treatment which is based on a characteristic related to any of the grounds referred to in § 17 of the Equal Treatment Act, for instance religion, shall not constitute discrimination where, by reason of the nature of the particular occupational activities concerned or of the context in which they are carried out, such a characteristic constitutes a genuine and determining occupational requirement, provided that the objective is legitimate and the requirement is proportionate (§ 20(1) of the Equal Treatment Act, Article 4(1) of Directive 2000/78).

4.1.2. Since non-discrimination is a main principle under EU Law (Article 21 of the Charter of Fundamental Rights of the European Union; Article 10 TFEU), only a few exceptions may be assumed within the scope of Article 4(1) of Directive 2000/78 and § 20(1) of the Equal Treatment Act respectively. For example, this is the case when a characteristic (such as religion or gender) constitutes a genuine occupational requirement for the job (RV [Austrian Governmental bill] 307 BlgNR 22. GP). Due to the provision's narrow concept, only those requirements are covered that are fundamental and vital for the performance of the activities concerned (see also Directive 2002/73/EC, recital 11). [...]

4.2. The first step is to determine whether not to wear a full-face veil constitutes a genuine and determining occupational requirement [...].

4.2.1. Despite the fact that the employer allows the wearing of both the abaya and the Islamic headscarf, his instruction not to wear a face veil interferes not only with the exercise of the employee's right to freedom of religion, but also, pursuant to § 16 of the General Civil Code (Allgemeines Bürgerliches Gesetzbuch, ABGB) and Article 8 of the ECHR, the employee's right to privacy (that is, the individual's appearance). These provisions constitute further reasons for justification. [...]

4.2.3. A blanket ban on the wearing of the full-face veil in public is disproportionate since less intrusive measures for identification purposes may be possible. However, the ECtHR stated that the impugned

French limitation is justified when looking at the ground rules of social communication within a society. A government may lay foundations for a society in respect of their way of living together and, thus, may consider the interaction between individuals to be adversely affected by people concealing their faces in public (ECtHR 1 July 2014, *S.A.S. v. France*, 43835/11).

4.2.4. Applying these principles to the present case, it has to be noted that there is no blanket ban on the wearing of the full-face veil in Austria. However, also within Austria it is an uncontested basic rule of interpersonal communication not to conceal one's face.

4.2.5. The Islamic face veil (niqab) – contrary to the Islamic headscarf (hijab) – covers the whole face except the eyes. Therefore, wearing a face veil may not only have an adverse effect on an open communication and social interaction in public, but also at the workplace. The same applies to the working environment at a notary office, as in the present case, regarding not only the interaction with customers, but also co-workers and the employer and results in an aggravated communication. However, an unimpaired communication and interaction is a crucial requirement for the plaintiff performing her contractual duties as an employee at a notary office. Due to the nature of the particular occupational activity concerned, the *Nichtverschleierung* (non-concealment) is an essential and vital occupational requirement. [...]

4.2.7. The employer's instruction not to wear a face veil at the workplace is within the scope of § 20(1) of the Equal Treatment Act, and therefore justified, since, as her employer, he may ensure the performance of his employees' duties under their contracts of employment. The compromise proposed by the defendant, such as taking off the veil while talking to customers, is not sufficient, since, as argued above, an unimpaired communication shall be ensured also with the co-workers and the employer. Additionally, taking off and putting on the veil might disturb the operating processes at the workplace.

4.2.8. Furthermore, the defendant's instruction constitutes an appropriate as well as necessary measure to achieve the intended purpose – ensuring the performance of the contractual duties through an unimpaired communication.

5. The plaintiff argued that such a prohibition also involves an indirect discrimination against women since, due to their religious background, only Muslim women are affected by such rules. However, in the present case it is not a question of whether a neutral policy discriminates a certain group – even though it may appear as such –, but rather of whether the

plaintiff had to follow an individual order of the employer regarding a certain dress code. The defendant employer did not dismiss the plaintiff due to non-compliance with a general and "neutral" rule, but non-compliance with an individual instruction.

6. With regard to the above-mentioned principles, it can be concluded that there has been neither a direct discrimination on grounds of religion nor an indirect discrimination on grounds of gender regarding the termination of the employment.

The possible discrimination regarding other working conditions:

[…] 4. The fact that the employee was wearing an Islamic headscarf and the abaya after parental leave led to a change of professional tasks, such as reduced assignments to interact with customers or act as a notary witness. […]

6.1. First, it has to be ascertained whether not wearing a headscarf is an essential and vital occupational requirement for an employee at a notary office and, therefore, falls within the scope of § 20(1) of the Equal Treatment Act. § 20(2) of the Equal Treatment Act, which deals with occupational activities within churches and other public or private organisations the ethos of which is based on religion, does not include employment at a notary office and, therefore, is not applicable in the present case.

[…] The Court of Appeal accurately ruled that the plaintiff had suffered a direct discrimination on ground of religion regarding general working conditions after her parental leave (March 22, 2013 until July 30, 2013, that is, during the time when she was wearing an Islamic headscarf) because the defendant had treated her less favourably than her colleagues (less contact with customers, rarely appointed as notary witness).

[Sources: Das Recht der Arbeit 2017 page 50 *Rebhahn* = juridikum 2016 page 420, *Smutny* = ecolex 2016 page 809 *Dullinger* = Zeitschrift für Arbeits-und Sozialrecht 2017 page 38 *Marhold*. Additionally, the decision is available on publicly accessible websites such as https://www.ris.bka.gv.at/Jus/ under its file number "9ObA117/15v"]

ANNOTATION

The present decision is remarkable in various ways: the Austrian Supreme Court decision was handed down almost one year before the European Court of Justice (ECJ) in the cases of *Bougnaoui* and *Achbita*; it deals with the niqab; and it sets out clear limits as to which religious behaviours must be accepted in the employment context.

1. Unlike in the ECJ cases, the employee was wearing a niqab, which is a full-face veil that reveals only the wearer's eyes. The Supreme Court's first step was to decide whether the constitutional freedom of religion also protects the wearing of religious signs such as clothes, hats, and necklaces because the understanding of this fundamental right also determines "religion" and "belief" in the sense of equal treatment rules on lower levels of law. Like the ECJ, the Supreme Court stated that not only the belief as such, the *forum internum*, but the *forum externum* as well, that is to say, manifestations of religious belief, are covered by the various sources of fundamental rights enshrining freedom of religion. Therefore, the right to free exercise of religion or belief also includes the wearing of religious clothing and insignia. This applies to Article 9 of the ECHR as well as to § 17 of the Austrian Equal Treatment Act, due to the broad understanding of the terms "religion" or "belief". As a consequence, principally, religious practice is protected at the workplace as well; the employer, and also the co-workers and the customers, must tolerate religion to a certain extent.

2. The Austrian Supreme Court based its decision mainly on § 20(1) of the Equal Treatment Act, which corresponds to Article 4(1) of EU Directive 2000/78. This provision allows unequal treatment on the ground of religion (or gender, ethnicity, etc.) where such a characteristic constitutes a genuine and determining occupational requirement. Moreover, the objective of the legal measure has to be legitimate and the requirement must be proportionate.

2.1. Based on their *telos*, these provisions must be interpreted in a narrow sense, meaning, firstly, only relating to characteristics of an employment that are absolutely necessary and reasonable for the performance of the work would not constitute any discrimination. For example, in the context of another field of equal treatment, this would apply to a job advertisement requesting a female psychologist for treatment of female victims of male violence.

2.2. On interpreting the phrase "genuine and determining occupational requirement", the Supreme Court referred to both fundamental rights and general principles of "living together". To begin with, the Court considered a general ban of the full-face veil disproportionate. Here, it also has to be mentioned that – apart from criminal proceedings – there existed no such general prohibition of wearing full-face veils in public at the time of the decision and, unlike in France, "laicism" or "secularism" is not laid down in the Austrian Constitution. Furthermore, the main goal of the Austrian Equal Treatment Act is to lay down a framework for combating discrimination on the grounds of religion or belief, with a view to giving effect to the principle of equal treatment. The Act provides equal treatment and protects employees from discrimination based on religion, gender and other grounds in the employment context. Again, this leads to the result that practising one's religion – at least to a certain extent – is permissible also at work and has to be tolerated.

3. The limits, or in other words the extent of tolerance, may be deduced from various provisions. For example, there are several exceptions applying to churches or religious groups which act as employers (see § 20(2) of the Equal Treatment Act). Other derogations exist in the field of health and safety rules, for example, the order to wear helmets on a construction site. Furthermore, there is the above-mentioned provision that allows for unequal treatment if religion constitutes a qualified occupational requirement. When does the latter apply?

3.1. In the present case, the employer is a notary whose official title is "notary public" in Austria. Notaries furnish legal advice, they determine the parties' will and authenticate documents, as well as exercise sovereign functions, for example when acting as public certifying officers. They may also draft private documents and represent parties in non-litigious matters in court and *vis-à-vis* government administration (for example, in matters related to the Register of Companies or the Land Register). The employees of notaries have many contacts with clients; their work includes talking to them, arranging dates or preparing drafts, often in co-operation with their colleagues and their employer. Sometimes, the notary's employees also carry out legal acts in a strict sense, for example when being an attesting witness in a last will.

3.2. Nevertheless, the Supreme Court did not use the public (that is, official or administrative) function of the defendant notary to argue against the wearing of the full-face veil. Unlike the ECtHR in cases such as *Eweida* or *S.A.S*, the Austrian Supreme Court did not refer to the "neutrality" of the State and its representatives. Especially in the area of public services, neutral appearance of the State's representatives is a specific requirement. Civil servants or employees of the State (not only members of the police, army and judiciary, but also employees in public schools and hospitals) have to give an impartial and unbiased impression when interacting with people. Consequently, the prohibition of wearing religious symbols is considered legitimate and appropriate there. This could have been applied to the employment relationship with a notary *public* who also – as mentioned above – sometimes acts on behalf of the courts.

The Supreme Court chose another way to justify the employer's order not to wear a full-face veil. Like the ECtHR in the *S.A.S* case, the Austrian

Supreme Court pointed out that an unimpaired communication and interaction is a crucial requirement for individuals, both in society and in the working environment. Mostly, at the workplace, communication between the employee and other persons is a major factor and part of the employment relationship, which includes the employer, the co-workers and the customers. Therefore, the religious signs must not in any way interfere with or disturb social interaction or communication that is usual with regard to the profession concerned.

3.3. But it is not only an "uncontested basic rule of communication" not to conceal one's face – as the Supreme Court put it. Moreover, although the Court did not explicitly refer to them, the rules and principles of contract law might be taken into account to define the extent of religious manifestation allowed at the workplace. According to common civil law, one party must be able to consider and realize the determinedness, the seriousness and the distinctiveness of the other party's declarations of intent (such as an offer or acceptance, but also when engaged in bargaining). In this context, the face is a significant element to identify the other party and to realize their intentions as well. Moreover, one might argue that many employees act on their employer's behalf and, therefore, their features must be visible – especially but not only for the customers with whom deals are made or contracts signed. In this sense, non-concealment may be considered an essential and determining occupational requirement in most cases of employment relationships. The identity and individuality of the person *vis-à-vis* must be obvious, comprehensible and recognizable. If an employee does not fulfill this condition, they do not carry out their contractual duties properly, which constitutes a legitimate ground for the ending the employment relationship.

4. The present decision implies another essential conclusion: wearing an abbaya or the Islamic headscarf does not lead to an impaired communication or interaction in the sense of the law, nor does it prevent the employee from performing their contractual duties. Taking into account also the current ECJ jurisprudence, at least according to the case of *Bougnaoui*, a religious sign that does not hide the identity or the intents of a person (for example, an Islamic headscarf) principally must be tolerated and accepted by the employer, the co-workers and also the customers (as regards exceptions, see above paragraphs 3 and 3.2). The employee wearing such symbols is protected by the Equal Treatment Act against discriminatory acts such as denial of making a contract or career promotion as well as relegation or reclassification in their work. More generally put, religious manifestations that do not hinder social interaction

or the fulfillment of the contractual duties usually arising from the work in question do not constitute a legitimate ground for being treated less favourably by the employer.

Consequently, in the present case, the Supreme Court imposed on the employer compensation for damages on the ground of discriminatory changes in the employee's working conditions. Due to her headscarf and the abaya, the employer transferred the employee to a workplace with less or no contacts with customers. But, as also the ECJ pointed out, the willingness of an employer to take account of the wishes of a customer no longer to have the services of an employee wearing an Islamic headscarf cannot be considered a genuine and determining occupational requirement. Dismissal or other unfavourable treatment of the employee solely on the ground of (assumed) customers' notions constitutes discrimination.

As elaborated in the above-mentioned decisions, both the ECJ and the Austrian Supreme Court are unanimous that mere wishes of customers cannot be considered a genuine and determining requirement. This corresponds with comparable jurisprudence on equal treatment in the field of gender issues: even determinedly entrepreneurial goals such as "helpdesks for women" or "men's tailor shop" as such would principally not suffice to refuse the employment of persons of the other sex; additional justification would be needed.

5. Apart from that, many aspects of "genuineness" and "determination" of the "occupational requirement" are still open to legal discussion; this applies especially to the meaning of the phrase "by reason of the nature of the particular occupational activities concerned". In particular, clarification is needed as to whether or not the employer's possibility to dispose of entrepreneurial aims and goals in their company has to be taken into account a little bit more. Principally, based on their occupational freedom (laid down in Article 16 of the Charter of Fundamental Rights of the European Union), the employer can – apart from limitations according to criminal law or common civil law – set the aims of their undertaking completely on their own, by which they also can influence the "nature" of their employees' occupations.

5.1 As for the discretion of the employer's dispositions concerning their employees' religious manifestations, the ECJ gave some explanation in the case of *Achbita*: the employer may establish internal rules laying down for all employees the obligation to wear "neutral apparel" (without any political or religious symbols). However, only if the internal rule is objectively justified by a legitimate aim, it does not constitute an indirect discrimination. Additionally, the entrepreneurial aim (here, the policy of neutrality) has to be pursued in a consistent and systematic manner towards all employees concerned. As an example for a legitimate aim that the undertaking wants to realize, the ECJ explicitly mentions "the pursuit by the employer, in its relations with its customers, of a policy of political, philosophical and religious neutrality". This part of the ECJ's decision gives an employer considerable room for manoeuvre, when and by establishing general rules in their business (for example, a code of conduct) prohibiting the wearing of all kind of religious or political symbols. In fact, in Austria, some employers tried to introduce such rules on a policy of neutrality in their businesses immediately after the ECJ had rendered its decision.

5.2. However, it must not be overlooked that the ECJ line in the cases to date also demands further requirements: the means of achieving the entrepreneurial aim must be appropriate and necessary. That is, on the one hand, it must be determined whether the prohibition of religious clothing or behaviour is limited to what is strictly necessary. For example, it has to be ascertained whether the discussed provision laying down neutral clothing actually has to cover all employees or only those who interact with customers. This could even imply the employer's obligation to offer posts not involving any visual contact with customers instead of dismissing employees who refuse to take off their religious clothing. On the other hand, the interests of the employer have to be taken into account as well. An employer should not suffer an additional (financial) burden, for example, by being obliged to organize their business in order to be able to create "extra" jobs, even for persons who cannot pursue the (legitimate) professional aim of the undertaking concerned. Thus, the restrictions on both sides' freedoms have to be evaluated and limited to what is strictly necessary.

6. The above analysis leads to the following summary and conclusions.

6.1. The Austrian Supreme Court held that the non-compliance with the employer's individual instruction not to wear a full-face veil (niqab) prevented the employee from carrying out their contractual duties and therefore justified a dismissal.

6.2. According to the ground rules of social communication within a society (of "living together") and also to common civil law principles, the identity and individuality of the person with whom one is dealing must be obvious, comprehensible and recognizable.

6.3. On the contrary, a religious manifestation that does not hinder social interaction or the fulfillment of the contractual duties usually arising from the work concerned does not constitute a legitimate ground for being treated less favourably by the employer.

6.4. General provisions for all employees in a business laying down the pursuit of a policy of neutrality may realize a legitimate, entrepreneurial aim, but this alone cannot justify the prohibition of wearing religious (or political and other) symbols in all cases. Additionally, the aim of the enterprise must be appropriate and necessary. Therefore, the restrictions on both sides' freedoms have to be weighed carefully and limited to what is strictly necessary.

Fr. 1

FRANCE

Supreme Court, Labour Division
Mr Jean-François X… v. Mr Serge Y… et alia
1 June 2016

*Occupational health and safety – employers' safety obligations –
psychological harassment of employees – employer's liability –
grounds for exemption*

HEADNOTES

Facts

Mr Jean-François X… was hired by the Finimétal Company in 1997 as a radiator assembly line worker. He claims that he was subjected to psychological harassment by his immediate superior in 2011. On 22 March 2011 he lodged a case before the Employment Tribunal, as a first instance labour court, seeking an order rescinding his employment contract with fault assigned to the Finimétal Company, represented by Mr Serge Y…, and sentencing his employer to pay compensation for breach of contract and damages for psychological harassment/bullying. At that time, Mr Jean-François X… was out on sick leave. Following two reinstatement visits with the occupational physician on 5 and 21 July 2011, which concluded that he was unfit for his current job but fit to work in a similar position in a different working environment, Mr X… was dismissed by letter sent 27 December 2011 on grounds of lack of physical fitness and the impossibility of redeployment.

The Employment Tribunal rejected the employee's claim, finding that the employer "had successfully implemented numerous measures to put an end to the psychological harassment, and no serious breach of contract could be imputed to it on such grounds." Mr Jean-François X… appealed this decision to the Appeal Court at Douai. In a ruling pronounced on

20 December 2013, the Appeal Court dismissed the employee's claim for psychological harassment, pointing out in particular that the employer had amended its internal regulations to include a procedure for reporting psychological harassment, had undertaken an internal investigation into the facts of the case as soon as it became aware of the employee's personal conflict with his immediate supervisor, and had organized a mediation meeting with the occupational physician, the human resources director, and three members of the CHSCT (Health, Safety and Working Conditions Committee). During this meeting, the employer took the decision to organize a three-month mediation mission between the two employees concerned, to be facilitated by the human resources director.

Mr Jean-François X... subsequently brought an appeal against the ruling pronounced by the Appeal Court of Douai before the Labour Division of the Supreme Court. In his appeal, the employee cited the fact that employers have a "safety performance obligation" with regard to the protection of their employees' health and safety, and that if their employees' health is prejudiced during the term of their employment contract, employers have accordingly failed to satisfy this obligation, even if they did take measures intended to end such prejudice. By deciding that the employer had not committed any violation because it was able to prove that it had taken measures necessary to prevent acts of psychological harassment and had then taken remedial action, the Appeal Court would seem to have failed to draw the proper legal conclusions resulting from its own findings, and violated the provisions of article L. 4121-1 of the Labour Code.

Decision

The Supreme Court overturned and declared void the 20 December 2013 ruling of the Appeal Court of Douai.

Law Applied

– Article L. 1152-1 of the French Labour Code: "No employee shall be subject to repeated acts of psychological harassment with the objective or effect of degrading his or her working conditions in a manner tending to violate his or her rights and dignity, impact his or her physical and mental health, or compromise his or her professional future."

- Article L. 4121-1 of the French Labour Code: "Employers shall take the necessary measures to ensure workers' physical and mental safety and protection. These measures shall include:

1. Measures to prevent occupational risks;
2. Information and training activities;
3. The establishment of an appropriate organization and resources.

Employers shall ensure that such measures are appropriate in the light of changing circumstances and tend to improve the current situations."

– Article L. 4121-2 of the French Labor Code: "Employers shall implement the measures set forth in article L. 4121-1 based on the following general principles of prevention:

1. Prevent risks;
2. Assess such risks as cannot be prevented;
3. Combat risks at their source;
4. Adapt the work to the worker, in particular with regard to the design of workstations and the choice of working equipment and working and production methods, in particular with a view to limiting monotonous work and machine-paced work, and reduce health impacts;
5. Stay abreast of technological progress;
6. Replace hazardous factors with non-hazardous or less hazardous factors;
7. Plan for prevention by integrating technology, work organization, working conditions, labour relations, and the influence of environmental factors, in particular the risks related to psychological harassment as defined in Article L. 1152-1, into a coherent whole;
8. Implement collective protective measures, giving them priority over individual protective measures;
9. Give appropriate instructions to workers."

JUDGEMENT

The Supreme Court, Labour Division, recalls in a statement of principle that "the employer who, being informed of the existence of acts likely to constitute psychological harassment, takes immediate measures to put an end to them, and can prove that all the preventive measures provided for under articles L. 4121-1 and L. 4121-2 of the Labour Code are in place, shall not be considered to be in violation of the legal obligation to take the necessary measures to ensure the safety and protect the physical and mental health of workers, particularly as regards psychological harassment." It did not agree with the Appeal Court of Douai as it was not apparent in its findings "that the employer had taken all the preventive measures discussed in articles L. 4121-1 and L. 4121-2 of the Labour Code, or in particular that it had implemented the proper informational and training measures to prevent the occurrence of acts of psychological harassment, (...) and the employer had therefore violated the above-mentioned legislation."

[*Source*: Supreme Court, Labour Division, Ruling no. 1068 of 1 June 2016, in appeal no. 14-19.702, as published in the Supreme Court Bulletin]

ANNOTATION

This is an important case from the Labour Division of the Supreme Court, which overturned the ruling pronounced by the Appeal Court rejecting the employer's liability in a situation of alleged psychological harassment. We must not fail to recognize the meaning and significance of the recent ruling. For nearly fifteen years, jurisprudential recognition of the "safety performance obligation" incumbent upon employers has led to the near-automatic imposition of employer liability, even in the absence of any fault on the employer's part. The ruling of the Labour Division of the Supreme Court on 1 June 2016 is indeed a reversal in regard to psychological harassment, although it is simply a legal transposition of the jurisprudential reorientation already carried out in terms of psychological risk. This ruling marks the end of the absolutist understanding of the safety performance obligation. Exemption from employer liability has now become a real possibility. It will however likely prove a delicate matter if judges have a high standard of proof for employers to demonstrate their implementation of preventive measures against psychological harassment in the workplace.

As commentators have pointed out, the employer's safety obligation, "originating in law no. 91-1414 of 31 December 1991 transposing European Directive 89/391 of 12 June 1989 into domestic legislation... has had a tormented history" (J. Mouly, "*L'assouplissement de l'obligation de sécurité en matière de harcèlement moral*" [*Relaxation of the Safety Obligation with regard to Psychological Harassment*], La Semaine Juridique, Ed. G no. 28, 2016, p. 822), particularly after the rulings pronounced by the Supreme Court on 28 February 2002 concerning workers exposed to asbestos risks (Cf. *not*. A. Lyon-Caen, *Une révolution dans le droit des accidents du travail* [*A Revolution in Workers' Compensation Law*], Cass. soc. 28 February 2002, Droit Social 2002, p. 445; R. Vatinet, "En marge des *affaires de l'amiante: l'obligation de sécurité du salarié"* [On the Occasion of the Asbestos Cases: the Employee Safety Obligation], Droit Social 2002, p. 533). Reference to the safety obligation has thus allowed judges to redefine the notion of gross negligence authorizing the granting of supplementary compensation to employees who suffer workplace accidents. It is presented as a "performance obligation," which was first contractual in nature, and is today an obligation of legal origin based on article L. 4121-1 of the Labour Code. The concept of the safety obligation adopted at that time holds employers to be in breach based solely on a finding of damages and the materialization of a risk. The reinforcement of this employer obligation is part of a reparation-oriented approach, exempting employees from the burden of proof regarding employer fault.

This new concept was subsequently applied to disputes concerning not only industrial accidents and occupational diseases, but also cases dealing with breaches of employment contracts. In 2006 the Labour Division of the Supreme Court pointed out, *inter alia*, that employers have a safety performance obligation as regards their protection of employee health and safety in the workplace, particularly concerning psychological harassment, adding that "the absence of fault on the employers' part does not exempt them from liability" (*Cass. soc., 29 June 2006, Bull. V 2006, no. 223*). Building on the rule as expressed, the Supreme Court in 2010 drew all the necessary conclusions, establishing the principle that "employers bound to a safety performance obligation with regard to the protection of their workers' health and safety fail to comply with that obligation when an employee is subject to acts of psychological or sexual harassment in the workplace by another employee, even if the employer has taken measures intended to put an end to such acts" (*Cass. soc., 3 February 2010, Bull. V 2010, no. 30*).

This jurisprudence was strongly criticized in the writings of some jurists, where it was reproached for applying a solution derived from reparation-oriented reasoning to situations bound by a different rationale. The primary criticism concerned the "counter-productive" nature of such a jurisprudential approach: since employers would not be permitted to seek to exonerate themselves by citing their efforts to prevent risk, they could be discouraged from taking any such measures and this could lead to inaction (S. Fantoni-Quinton and P.-Y. Verkindt, "*Obligation de sécurité en matière de santé au travail. À l'impossible l'employeur est tenu ?*" [The occupational safety obligation. Are employers being required to do the impossible?], Droit Social 2013, p. 229). There is some merit to this argument, even if it may appear to be "excessive, since it is also conceivable that employers implementing effective risk prevention policies in the workplace would thus significantly reduce the probability that such risks would materialize" (J. Mouly, *op. cit*).

The Labour Division of the Supreme Court was nevertheless not unsympathetic to the argument when hearing a case in 2015 concerning a former steward with the company "Air France" who had been present in New York on 11 September 2001. He had been struggling with depression since 2006, and had complained, after even more time had passed, that his employer had failed to take the necessary preventive measures to protect him from psychological disorders associated with the terrorist attack of 2001. The case may appear somewhat ridiculous, but it did in fact contribute to changes in the safety obligation system. The Labour Division of the Supreme Court ultimately held in 2015 that "employers who can provide proof that they have taken all the measures provided for under articles L. 4121-1 and L. 4121-2 of the Labour Code shall not be considered to be in violation of the legal obligation to take the necessary measures to ensure the safety and protect the physical and mental health of workers." (*Cass. soc., 25 November 2015, Bull. V 2016, no. 2121*). From that time on, the materialization of a risk was no longer automatically synonymous with an employer's failure to comply with its safety obligation. It became necessary to include a check to verify whether or not measures to prevent the occurrence of such risks had been taken upstream. As has rightly been stated by commentators, the Supreme Court accordingly substituted a prevention-oriented approach for a reparation-oriented approach (G. and L.-F. Pignarre, "*La prévention : pierre angulaire ou/et maillon faible de l'obligation de santé et de sécurité au travail de l'employeur ?*" [Prevention: a cornerstone and/or a weak link in employer health and safety obligations?] *Revue de droit du travail, 2016, p. 151*).

Going back to a formulation very similar to its ruling in the "Air France" case of 25 November 2015, the Supreme Court stated in its ruling of 1 June 2016 that "the employer who, being informed of the existence of acts likely to constitute psychological harassment, takes immediate measures to put an end to them, and can prove that all the preventive measures provided for under articles L. 4121-1 and L. 4121-2 of the Labour Code are in place, shall not be considered to be in violation of the legal obligation to take the necessary measures to ensure the safety and protect the physical and mental health of workers, particularly as regards psychological harassment." In other words, the solution adopted in 2015 with regard to "psychological disorders" has been extended to cases of psychological harassment; employers may now be exempted from liability for psychological harassment when the same has occurred in the workplace, but consideration must be given to the condition(s) in which it occurs. In particular, the mere fact that the employer may have taken all the immediate measures necessary to put an end to the psychological harassment and may have effectively put an end to it, while necessary, is not in itself sufficient. The employer also needs to have taken all the preventive measures referred to in articles L. 4121-1 and L. 4121-2 of the Labour Code, and in particular needs to have (previously) implemented information and training measures to prevent the occurrence of acts of psychological harassment. That is furthermore the reason why the ruling pronounced on 1 June 2016 overturned the decision of the Appeal Court, which had rejected the employee's claim on grounds that the employer had introduced a reporting procedure for psychological harassment into its internal regulations, implementing it in order to put an end to the harassment. It did not follow from those findings alone that the employer had taken all the preventive measures referred to in articles L. 4121-1 and L. 4121-2 of the Labour Code.

A finding of violence or psychological harassment in the workplace only permits a "presumption" of the employer's failure to comply with its safety obligation. But the employer can now reverse that presumption by establishing that it has in fact complied with its "risk prevention obligation" by implementing appropriate measures. Undoubtedly, "the Regulating Court has been realistic here in its effort to reconcile the ideal with what is possible" (J. Mouly, *op. cit.*). This would be a "strong sign of the maturity of jurisprudence with regard to the performance obligation" (*Harcèlement moral : retour à l'équilibre [Psychological harassment: a return to balance]* Interview with P.-Y. Verkindt, *SSL 2016, no. 1727, p. 11*). Certainly, the new jurisprudence is more in line with the spirit of the 1989 European Directive, from which the Court of Justice of the European Union never intended to deduce an "absolute performance obligation" (CJEU, 14 June 2007, Aff. *C-127/05: JurisData no. 2007-008225 ; JCP G 2007, act. 300*).

That being so, the real scope of the jurisprudential reversal that has occurred will only be appreciated in light of the kinds of requirements judges will impose on employers claiming that they had implemented sufficient preventive measures. It is here that the whole question of the future ambit of the employers' safety obligation will be worked out. In a later judgement, pronounced only a few days after the one commented upon here (*Cass. soc., 8 June 2016, no. 14-13.418*), the Supreme Court ruled that "judges have the sovereign discretion to assess whether the employee has submitted sufficient evidence to justify a presumption of harassment, and whether the employer has proved that the alleged acts are entirely unrelated to harassment." The latter statement of principle is a manifestation of the Supreme Court's abandonment of psychological harassment verification testing. However, the future "jurisprudence of trial judges" will be built in a specific context, as the Supreme Court made clear in this case, maintaining that "it is up to the judge to examine all the evidence presented by the employee, taking account of any medical documents that may be presented, and make a determination as to whether the materially established facts of the case taken as a whole permit a presumption of psychological harassment within the meaning of Article L. 1152-1 of the Labour Code; if so, it is up to the judge to make a determination as to whether the employer has proved that the acts referred to do not in fact constitute such harassment, and that its decisions were justified on objective grounds entirely unrelated to any harassment." The density of the French legislative framework for psychological harassment, coupled with the directives given to trial judges by the Supreme Court, should ensure that this transfer of powers to the trial courts will not excessively modify the rules currently in force (D. Chenu, "*Le nouveau droit prétorien du harcèlement moral au travail*" *[The new case law on workplace psychological harassment]*, La Semaine Juridique Entreprises et Affaires, no. 30-34, 2016, p. 1452).

The fact remains that by giving primacy to the sphere of prevention with regard to psychological harassment, the Labour Division of the Supreme Court may well contribute to limiting effective reparation, at least in large corporations. They have resources available to them, particularly in terms of legal and human resources management that small and medium-sized enterprises do not have. These resources will often permit them to achieve exemption from all liability in cases of psychological harassment by providing evidence of real investments in preventive measures, except of course in cases of management harassment.

By making psychological harassment increasingly a matter of workplace mental health protection, French jurisprudence would seem to be distancing itself from an approach to the problem based on discrimination. But the idea of discrimination is central to the definition of psychological harassment established by the European Directive 2000/78/EC of 27 November 2000 establishing a general framework for equal treatment in employment and occupation. Employers certainly do have an obligation of prevention when it comes to ensuring occupational health and safety. But it must be remembered that psychological and sexual harassment constitute acts of discrimination, and they must be punished as such.

SP. 3

SPAIN

Supreme Court Social Chamber
Decision of 3 May 2016

Dismissal of sick employee – discrimination – disability – Directive 2000/78

HEADNOTES

Facts

An employee was injured in a car accident when on her way to work. As a result of the accident, she was absent from work on paid sick leave for about four weeks. During the leave, the employee was dismissed. The employee challenged the dismissal on grounds that it was based on discrimination. The Labour Court No. 33 of Barcelona found the dismissal void, ordering the reinstatement of the employee and the payment of €10,000 for moral damages. The Superior Court of Catalonia revoked that decision, finding the dismissal only unfair – not void. It ordered the employer to choose between reinstatement and severance compensation (in an amount of €2,084). An appeal was lodged with the Social Chamber of the Supreme Court.

Decision

The Social Chamber of the Supreme Court confirmed the ruling of the Superior Court of Catalonia.

Law Applied

Spanish Constitution
Article 14.
Spaniards are equal before the law and may not in any way be discriminated against on account of birth, race, sex, religion, opinion or any other personal or social condition or circumstance.

JUDGEMENT

[...]
FUNDAMENTOS DE DERECHO [...]
TERCERO.
1. El recurrente alega infracción de la jurisprudencia, citando la STJUE de 11 de abril de 2013, C 337/2011, "Caso Ring ", STC 62/2008, de 26 de mayo y STS, Sala Cuarta de 29 de enero de 2001, recurso 1566/2000.

En esencia alega que considera atentatorio a la dignidad personal y cabalmente discriminatorio el despido de la recurrente, por el único hecho de encontrarse en situación de incapacidad temporal.

2. El TC en sentencia 62/2008, de 26 de mayo, en la que examinó si debía calificarse de nulo, por discriminatorio, el despido de un trabajador que, con anterioridad a ser contratado había sufrido múltiples episodios de IT, relacionados con su profesión habitual de oficial de 1ª albañil, en empresa de construcción, contiene el siguiente razonamiento:

"5. Como ha señalado con reiteración este Tribunal al analizar el art. 14 CE, dicho precepto, además de recoger en su primer inciso una cláusula general de igualdad de todos los españoles ante la ley, contiene en el segundo la prohibición de una serie de motivos de discriminación. Esta referencia expresa a concretas razones de discriminación representa una explícita interdicción de determinadas diferencias históricamente muy arraigadas y que han situado, tanto por la acción de los poderes públicos como por la práctica social, a sectores de la población en posiciones no sólo desventajosas, sino contrarias a la dignidad de la persona que reconoce el art. 10.1 CE (por todas, SSTC 128/1987, de 16 de julio (RTC 1987, 128) , FJ 5 ; 166/1988, de 26 de septiembre (RTC 1988, 166) , FJ 2 ; 145/1991, de 1 de julio (RTC 1991, 145) , FJ 2 ; 17/2003, de 30 de enero (RTC 2003, 17) , FJ 3 ; 161/2004, de 4 de octubre (RTC 2004, 161) , FJ 3 ; 182/2005, de 4 de julio (RTC 2005, 182) , FJ 4 ; 41/2006, de 13 de febrero (RTC 2006, 41) , FJ 6 , o 3/2007, de 15 de enero (RTC 2007, 3) , FJ 2). Por ello, bien con carácter general en relación con el listado de los motivos o razones de discriminación expresamente prohibidos por el art. 14 CE , bien en relación con alguno de ellos en particular, hemos venido declarando la ilegitimidad constitucional de los tratamientos peyorativos en los que operan como factores determinantes los motivos o razones de discriminación que dicho precepto prohíbe, al tratarse de características expresamente excluidas como causas de discriminación por el art. 14 CE (STC 39/2002, de 14 de febrero (RTC 2002, 39) , FJ 4, y las que en ella se citan).

A diferencia de los casos que habitualmente ha abordado nuestra jurisprudencia, relativos por lo común a factores de discriminación expresamente citados en el art. 14 CE o, aun no recogidos de forma expresa, históricamente reconocibles de modo palmario como tales en la realidad social y jurídica (como la orientación sexual, STC 41/2006, de 13 de febrero), en esta ocasión se cuestiona la posible discriminación por causa de un factor no listado en el precepto constitucional, cual es el estado de salud del trabajador; en concreto, la existencia de una enfermedad crónica que se discute si resulta o no incapacitante para la actividad profesional del trabajador. Se hace por ello preciso determinar si dicha causa puede o no subsumirse en la cláusula genérica de ese precepto constitucional ("cualquier otra condición o circunstancia personal o social"), teniendo en cuenta que, como se sabe, no existe en el art. 14 CE una intención tipificadora cerrada (SSTC 75/1983, de 3 de agosto (RTC 1983, 75) , FJ 3 ; 31/1984, de 7 de marzo (RTC 1984, 31) , FJ 10 ; y 37/2004, de 11 de marzo (RTC 2004, 37) , FJ 3).

Para ello debemos partir de la consideración de que, como es patente, no todo criterio de diferenciación, ni todo motivo empleado como soporte de decisiones causantes de un perjuicio, puede entenderse incluido sin más en la prohibición de discriminación del art. 14 CE , pues, como indica acertadamente la Sentencia de suplicación citando jurisprudencia del Tribunal Supremo, en ese caso la prohibición de discriminación se confundiría con el principio de igualdad de trato afirmado de forma absoluta. De ahí que, para determinar si un criterio de diferenciación no expresamente listado en el art. 14 CE debe entenderse incluido en la cláusula genérica de prohibición de discriminación por razón de "cualquier otra condición o circunstancia personal o social", resulte necesario analizar la razonabilidad del criterio, teniendo en cuenta que lo que caracteriza a la prohibición de discriminación, frente al principio genérico de igualdad, es la naturaleza particularmente odiosa del criterio de diferenciación utilizado, que convierte en elemento de segregación, cuando no de persecución, un rasgo o una condición personal innata o una opción elemental que expresa el ejercicio de las libertades más básicas, resultando así un comportamiento radicalmente contrario a la dignidad de la persona y a los derechos inviolables que le son inherentes (art. 10 CE).

Así como los motivos de discriminación citados expresamente en el art. 14 CE implican un juicio de irrazonabilidad de la diferenciación establecido ya ex Constitutione, tal juicio deberá ser realizado inexcusablemente en cada caso en el análisis concreto del alcance discriminatorio de la multiplicidad de condiciones o circunstancias personales o sociales que pueden ser eventualmente tomadas en consideración como factor de diferenciación, y ello no ya para apreciar la posibilidad de que uno de tales motivos pueda ser utilizado excepcionalmente como criterio de diferenciación jurídica sin afectar a la prohibición de discriminación, como ha admitido este Tribunal en el caso de los expresamente identificados en la Constitución (así, en relación con el sexo, entre otras, SSTC 103/1983, de 22 de noviembre (RTC 1983, 103) , FJ 6 ; 128/1987, de 26 de julio, FJ 7 ; 229/1992, de 14 de diciembre (RTC 1992, 229) , FJ 2 ; 126/1997, de 3 de julio (RTC 1997, 126) , FJ 8; y en relación con la raza, STC 13/2001, de 29 de enero (RTC 2001, 13) , FJ 8), sino para la determinación misma de si la diferenciación considerada debe ser analizada desde la prohibición de discriminación del art. 14 CE , en la medida en que responda a un criterio de intrínseca inadmisibilidad constitucional análoga a la de los allí contemplados, o con la perspectiva del principio genérico de igualdad, principio que, como es sabido, resulta en el ámbito de las relaciones laborales matizado por "la eficacia del principio de la autonomía de la voluntad que, si bien aparece fuertemente limitado en el Derecho del trabajo, por virtud, entre otros factores, precisamente del principio de igualdad, subsiste en el terreno de la relación laboral" (STC 197/2000, de 24 de julio (RTC 2000, 197) , FJ 5).

6. Pues bien, no cabe duda de que el estado de salud del trabajador o, más propiamente, su enfermedad, pueden, en determinadas circunstancias, constituir un factor de discriminación análogo a los expresamente contemplados en el art. 14 CE , encuadrable en la cláusula genérica de las otras circunstancias o condiciones personales o sociales contemplada en el mismo. Ciñéndonos al ámbito de las decisiones de contratación o de despido que se corresponde con el objeto de la presente demanda de amparo, así ocurrirá singularmente, como apuntan las resoluciones ahora recurridas basándose en jurisprudencia previa de la Sala de lo Social del Tribunal Supremo, cuando el factor enfermedad sea tomado en consideración como un elemento de segregación basado en la mera existencia de la enfermedad en sí misma considerada o en la estigmatización como persona enferma de quien la padece, al margen de cualquier consideración que permita poner en relación dicha circunstancia con la aptitud del trabajador para desarrollar el contenido de la prestación laboral objeto del contrato."

La sentencia concluye declarando que el despido no ha de ser calificado de nulo, con el siguiente razonamiento:

"No es éste, sin embargo, el supuesto aquí analizado, en el que la valoración probatoria efectuada por los órganos judiciales ha puesto inequívocamente de manifiesto que en la decisión extintiva el factor enfermedad ha sido tenido en cuenta con la perspectiva estrictamente funcional de su efecto incapacitante para el trabajo. Por decirlo de otra manera, la empresa no ha despedido al trabajador por estar enfermo, ni por ningún prejuicio excluyente relacionado con su enfermedad, sino por considerar que dicha enfermedad le incapacita para desarrollar su trabajo, hasta el punto de que, según afirma, de haber conocido dicha circunstancia con anterioridad a la contratación no habría procedido a efectuarla."

3. La sentencia de esta Sala de 27 de enero de 2009 (RJ 2009, 1048) , recurso 602/2008 , ha examinado el supuesto en el que se procede al despido de un trabajador alegando falta de rendimiento, cuando la causa real eran las situaciones de IT que venía presentando, concluyendo la sentencia que la enfermedad no es equiparable a discapacidad, a efectos de discriminación, por lo que el despido ha de ser calificado de improcedente y no nulo. Contiene el siguiente razonamiento:

"Como dice nuestra sentencia de 29 de enero de 2001 (RJ 2001, 2069) , la cláusula final del art. 14 CE no comprende cualquier tipo de condición o circunstancia de los individuos o de los grupos sociales, "pues en ese caso la prohibición de discriminación se confundiría con el principio de igualdad de trato afirmado de forma absoluta". Los factores de diferenciación comprendidos en ella son aquellas condiciones o circunstancias que "históricamente han estado ligadas a formas de opresión o de segregación de determinados grupos de personas". En los términos de STC 166/1988 (RTC 1988, 16) , se trata de "determinadas diferenciaciones históricamente muy arraigadas" que han situado a "sectores de la población en posiciones no sólo desventajosas, sino abiertamente contrarias a la dignidad de la persona que reconoce el art. 10 CE."

Esta concepción de la discriminación, en la que coinciden como se ha visto la jurisprudencia constitucional y la jurisprudencia ordinaria, no debe ser sustituida por la expresada en la sentencia recurrida, donde se omite la referencia a los móviles específicos de la conducta discriminatoria. Así, pues, manteniendo la premisa de que el derecho fundamental a no ser discriminado ha de guardar relación con criterios históricos de opresión o segregación, debemos reiterar aquí que la enfermedad "en sentido genérico", "desde una perspectiva estrictamente funcional de incapacidad para el trabajo", no puede ser considerada en principio como un motivo o "factor discriminatorio" en el ámbito del contrato de trabajo (STS 29-1-2001 (RJ 2010, 2069) , citada). Se trata, por una parte, de una contingencia inherente a la condición humana y no específica de un grupo o colectivo de personas o de trabajadores. Se trata, además, de una situación cuyo acaecimiento puede determinar, cuando se produce con frecuencia inusitada, que "el mantenimiento del contrato de trabajo no se considere rentable por parte de la empresa" (STS 29-1-2001 (RJ 2001, 2069) , citada). De ahí que, si el empresario decide despedir al trabajador afectado, podría ciertamente incurrir en conducta ilícita, si no demuestra la concurrencia de la causa de despido prevista en el art. 52.d) ET (RCL 1995, 997) , pero no en una actuación viciada de nulidad radical por discriminación.

Sólo en determinados supuestos, por ejemplo el de enfermedades derivadas del embarazo que están ligadas a la condición de mujer, puede el despido por enfermedad o baja médica ser calificado como despido discriminatorio, viciado de nulidad. Pero se trata, en realidad, como ha declarado recientemente el Tribunal Constitucional (STC 17/2007 (RTC 2007, 17)), de un supuesto particular de despido discriminatorio por razón de sexo, en cuanto que la decisión o práctica de la empresa de dar por terminado el contrato de trabajo por motivo concerniente al estado de gestación sólo puede afectar a las mujeres, situándolas en posición de desventaja con respecto a los hombres.

Tampoco es posible considerar el despido por enfermedad sin más cualificaciones como despido acreedor a la declaración de nulidad por violación de otros "derechos fundamentales o libertades públicas del trabajador" (art. 55.5ET y 108.2 LPL (RCL 1995, 1144 y 1563)) distintos del derecho a no ser discriminado. En el presente pleito este argumento ha sido utilizado en la sentencia de instancia, insinuándose también en la definición genérica y extensiva de discriminación que utiliza la sentencia recurrida. El derecho constitucional señalado al efecto por la sentencia de instancia es el "derecho a la protección de la salud" reconocido en el art. 43.1 CE . Pero, sin entrar ahora en si el contenido de la protección de la salud puede alcanzar a conductas empresariales potestativas o de configuración jurídica como la enjuiciada en este caso, lo cierto es que, siguiendo la propia sistemática de la norma constitucional, el derecho mencionado no está comprendido en la categoría de los "derechos fundamentales y libertades públicas" (Sección 1ª del Capítulo II del Título primero) a la que se refieren los preceptos legales mencionados sobre nulidad del despido. El art. 43.1 CE está situado en el Capítulo III del Título I de la Constitución, donde se enuncian los "principios rectores del orden social y económico", a los que se asigna una función normativa distinta a la de los derechos fundamentales, en cuanto que dichos principios, sin perjuicio de desempeñar la función de información del ordenamiento que les es propia, han de ser alegados y aplicados por medio de las normas legales de desarrollo.

Así lo dice literalmente el art. 53.3 CE ("El reconocimiento, el respeto y la protección de los principios reconocidos en el Capítulo III, informarán la legislación positiva, la práctica judicial y la actuación de los poderes públicos. Sólo podrán ser alegados ante la jurisdicción ordinaria de acuerdo con lo que dispongan las leyes que los desarrollen").

En fin, cuanto se ha dicho en este fundamento y en el anterior respecto de las enfermedades o bajas médicas individualmente consideradas del trabajador demandante en el presente litigio, no queda desvirtuado por la coincidencia en el tiempo de su despido con despidos por enfermedad de otros trabajadores. Como ya hemos apuntado en el análisis del tema de la contradicción, en cada proceso individual de despido habrá que considerar, y en su caso se habrá considerado, cuál o cuáles hayan sido los factores tenidos en cuenta por la empresa, y a la vista de ellos se habrá adoptado la resolución correspondiente. Pues bien, en el presente caso no se ha acreditado que el móvil del despido haya sido otro que la inevitable repercusión negativa en el rendimiento laboral de las enfermedades o bajas médicas del trabajador, un móvil que en esta litis determina la ilicitud e improcedencia del despido pero no la nulidad del mismo por discriminación o lesión de derechos fundamentales.

QUINTO.

Después de rechazarse en la sentencia transcrita la existencia de discriminación en el sentido en que lo entendió la sentencia recurrida, se ocupa aquélla en dar respuesta a los argumentos utilizados en la segunda línea de argumentación de la tesis de la nulidad del despido por enfermedad, que fue, tal y como se dijo al relatar la forma y los razonamientos que se contiene en la sentencia de instancia, la equiparación de la enfermedad a la discapacidad.

En nuestra anterior sentencia (AS 2011, 1803) rechazamos esa equiparación. En principio hay que decir que, efectivamente, esa condición personal de discapacidad se ha convertido en causa legal de discriminación a partir de la entrada en vigor de la Ley 62/2003 (RCL 2003, 3093; RCL 2004, 5 y 892), que ha dado nueva redacción al art. 4.2.c), párrafo 2º ET ("Los trabajadores ... en la relación de trabajo ...

tampoco podrán ser discriminados por razón de discapacidad, siempre que se hallasen en condiciones de aptitud para desempeñar el trabajo o empleo de que se trate"). Pero, ni en el lenguaje ordinario ni en el lenguaje técnico de la ley, los conceptos de enfermedad y discapacidad son coincidentes o equiparables.

Y así se rechaza esa equiparación afirmando que la enfermedad, sin adjetivos o cualificaciones adicionales, es una situación contingente de mera alteración de la salud, que puede y suele afectar por más o menos tiempo a la capacidad de trabajo del afectado. Como es de experiencia común, el colectivo de trabajadores enfermos en un lugar o momento determinados es un grupo de los llamados efímeros o de composición variable en el tiempo. La discapacidad es, en cambio, una situación permanente de minusvalía física, psíquica o sensorial, que altera de manera permanente las condiciones de vida de la persona discapacitada. En concreto, en el ordenamiento español la discapacidad es considerada como un 'estatus' que se reconoce oficialmente mediante una determinada declaración administrativa, la cual tiene validez por tiempo indefinido.

Parece claro, a la vista de las indicaciones anteriores, que las razones que justifican la tutela legal antidiscriminatoria de los discapacitados en el ámbito de las relaciones de trabajo no concurren en las personas afectadas por enfermedades o dolencias simples. Estos enfermos necesitan curarse lo mejor y a la mayor brevedad posible. Los discapacitados o aquejados de una minusvalía permanente, que constituyen por ello un grupo o colectivo de personas de composición estable, tienen en cambio, como miembros de tal grupo o colectividad, unos objetivos y unas necesidades particulares de integración laboral y social que no se dan en las restantes dolencias o enfermedades.

Como ha recordado STS 22-11-2007 (RJ 2008, 1183) (citada) la diferencia sustancial en el alcance de los conceptos de enfermedad y discapacidad ha sido apreciada también por el Tribunal de Justicia de la Comunidad Europea en sentencia de 11 de julio de 2006 (TJCE 2006, 192) (asunto *Chacón Navas*), en una cuestión prejudicial planteada por el Juzgado de lo Social num. 33 de Madrid. De acuerdo con esta sentencia, la Directiva comunitaria 2000/78 (LCEur 2000, 3383) excluye la 'equiparación' de ambos conceptos, correspondiendo la discapacidad a supuestos en que 'la participación en la vida profesional se ve obstaculizada durante un largo período', por lo que 'una persona que ha sido despedida por su empresario exclusivamente a causa de una enfermedad no está incluida en el marco general establecido por la Directiva 2000/78 (LCEur 2000, 3383)'. A ello se añade que 'ninguna disposición del Tratado CE contiene una prohibición de la discriminación por motivos de enfermedad' y que 'no cabe deducir que el ámbito de aplicación de la Directiva 2000/78 deba ampliarse por analogía a otros tipos de discriminación además de las basadas en los motivos enumerados con carácter exhaustivo en el artículo 1 de la propia Directiva' (discapacidad, edad, religión o creencia, orientación sexual).

Por su parte la sentencia de 12 de julio de 2012 (RJ 2012, 9598), recurso 2789/2011 contiene el siguiente razonamiento:

"El desistimiento empresarial del contrato de trabajo durante el período de prueba producido a raíz de accidente de trabajo sufrido por el trabajador no constituye de entrada discriminación del trabajador ni vulneración de sus derechos fundamentales. Tanto esta Sala de lo Social como el propio Tribunal Constitucional han declarado en numerosas ocasiones que la mera enfermedad ni figura entre los factores de discriminación enunciados en el artículo 14 CE, ni puede ser incluida tampoco en la cláusula final genérica de dicho artículo (" cualquier otra condición o circunstancia personal o social"), limitada a aquellos otros posibles factores discriminatorios que hayan comportado o puedan comportar marginación social para un determinado grupo de personas (entre otras, STS 29-1- 2001 (RJ 2001, 2069) , rec. 1566/2000 y STS 11-12- 2007 (RJ 2008, 2884) , rec. 4355/2006). No parece dudoso que la misma conclusión ha de imponerse respecto de las dolencias (o enfermedades en sentido amplio) que tienen su origen en lesiones derivadas de accidente de trabajo, y que hayan dado lugar a una situación de incapacidad temporal."

4. Aplicando la anterior doctrina al supuesto examinado, procede la desestimación del recurso formulado.

En el supuesto ahora sometido a la consideración de la Sala no nos encontramos ante un despido discriminatorio por causa de enfermedad. La recurrente sufrió un accidente de tráfico el 1 de marzo de que le provocó un "latigazo cervical", iniciando IT en la misma fecha, siendo despedida el 11 de marzo de 2013 -cuando aún se encontraba en situación de IT- siendo despedidas ese mismo día otras cuatro trabajadoras, de un total de nueve adscritas al mismo servicio de la actora "campaña Planeta", que también se encontraban en IT, a fin de posibilitar su sustitución y garantizar la productividad y continuidad del servicio.

Por lo tanto, no nos encontramos en el supuesto en el que el factor enfermedad es tomado en consideración como un elemento de segregación basado en la mera existencia de la enfermedad en sí misma considerada, o en la estigmatización como persona enferma de quien la padece, al margen de cualquier consideración que permita poner en relación dicha circunstancia con la aptitud del trabajador para desarrollar el contenido de la prestación laboral objeto del contrato sino, al contrario, la empresa ha tenido en cuenta que la trabajadora y sus otras compañeras en la misma situación de IT no eran aptas para desarrollar su trabajo, por lo que procedió a despedirlas, a fin de que pudieran ser sustituidas por otras personas y garantizar así la productividad y la continuidad del servicio. No es la mera existencia de la enfermedad la causa del despido, sino la incidencia de la misma en la productividad y en la continuidad del servicio.

En consecuencia, al no existir un factor de discriminación en el despido de la recurrente, ni estar encuadrado en los supuestos que el ET califica como despidos nulos, el mismo ha de merecer la calificación de despido improcedente.

CUARTO.

1. Resta por examinar si la STJUE de 11 de abril de 2013 (TJCE 2013, 122), C-acumulados 335/11 y 337/11 ha introducido alguna modificación relevante en la doctrina hasta ahora mantenida por el referido Tribunal, en especial en el asunto Chacón Navas, al que se hace referencia en la precitada sentencia de esta Sala de 27 de enero de 2009 (RJ 2009, 1048), recurso 602/2008.

2. La STJUE de 11 de julio de 2006 (TJCE 2006, 192), asunto Chacón Navas, C-13/05, resolvió una cuestión prejudicial planteada por el Juzgado nº. 33 de los de Barcelona, en el seno de un litigio entablado por la Sra. Sandra contra la Sociedad Eurest Colectividades SA., por despido.

Los hechos a considerar son los siguientes:

Doña. Sandra trabajaba para la empresa Eurest Colectividades S.A., iniciando situación de IT el 14 de octubre de 2003 por enfermedad, existiendo informe de los servicios públicos de salud de que no estaba en condiciones de reanudar su actividad a corto plazo. El 28 de mayo de 2004 la empresa despidió a la actora sin especificar motivo alguno reconociendo la improcedencia del despido.

La sentencia contiene el siguiente razonamiento:

"41. A tenor de su artículo 1, la Directiva 2000/78 (LCEur 2000, 3383) tiene por objeto establecer un marco general para luchar, en el ámbito del empleo y la ocupación, contra la discriminación por cualquiera de los motivos mencionados en dicho artículo, entre los que figura la discapacidad.

42. Habida cuenta del mencionado objetivo, el concepto de "discapacidad" a efectos de la Directiva 2000/78 debe ser objeto, de conformidad con los criterios recordados en el apartado 40 anterior, de una interpretación autónoma y uniforme.

43. La finalidad de la Directiva 2000/78 es combatir determinados tipos de discriminación en el ámbito del empleo y de la ocupación. En este contexto, debe entenderse que el concepto de "discapacidad" se refiere a una limitación derivada de dolencias físicas, mentales o psíquicas y que suponga un obstáculo para que la persona de que se trate participe en la vida profesional.

44. Ahora bien, al utilizar en el artículo 1 de la mencionada Directiva el concepto de "discapacidad", el legislador escogió deliberadamente un término que difiere del de "enfermedad". Así pues, es preciso excluir la equiparación pura y simple de ambos conceptos."

La sentencia concluye:

1) "Una persona que haya sido despedida por su empresario exclusivamente a causa de una enfermedad no está incluida en el marco general establecido por la Directiva 2000/78/CE (LCEur 2000, 3383) del Consejo, de 27 de noviembre de 2000, relativa al establecimiento de un marco general para la igualdad de trato en el empleo y la ocupación, para luchar contra la discriminación por motivos de discapacidad.

2) La prohibición, en materia de despido, de la discriminación por motivos de discapacidad, recogida en los artículos 2, apartado 1, y 3, apartado 1, letra c), de la Directiva 2000/78, se opone a un despido por motivos de discapacidad que, habida cuenta de la obligación de realizar los ajustes razonables para las personas con discapacidad, no se justifique por el hecho de que la persona en cuestión no sea competente o no esté capacitada o disponible para desempeñar las tareas fundamentales del puesto de que se trate.

3) La enfermedad en cuanto tal no puede considerarse un motivo que venga a añadirse a aquellos otros motivos en relación con los cuales la Directiva 2000/78 prohíbe toda discriminación."

3. Resta por examinar si la STJUE de 11 de abril de 2013 (TJCE 2013, 122), C-acumulados 335/11 y 337/11, que resolvió sendas cuestiones prejudiciales planteadas por Dinamarca en el seno de dos litigios por despido, ha introducido alguna modificación respecto a lo establecido en el asunto Chacón Navas, que tenga incidencia en la resolución del asunto ahora examinado.

Los hechos a considerar son los siguientes: La sra. Aurelia fue contratada por una empresa en 1996 y desde el 6 de junio de 2005 hasta el 24 de noviembre de 2005 estuvo de baja por dolores permanentes en la región lumbar, para los que no hay tratamiento, siendo despedida el 24 de noviembre de 2005. La sra. Encarna fue contratada por una empresa en 1998, habiendo sufrido un accidente de tráfico el 19 de diciembre de 2003, a resultas del cual sufrió "latigazo cervical", permaneciendo tres semanas de baja, iniciando una nueva baja el 10 de enero de 2005, siendo despedida el 21 de abril de 2005.

La sentencia razona lo siguiente: "Con carácter preliminar, debe señalarse que, según se desprende de su artículo 1, la Directiva 2000/78 tiene por objeto establecer un marco general para luchar, en el ámbito del empleo y la ocupación, contra la discriminación por cualquiera de los motivos mencionados en dicho articulo, entre los que figura la discapacidad (véase la sentencia *Chacón Navas*, antes citada, apartado 41). Conforme a su articulo 3, apartado 1, letra c), esta Directiva se aplica, dentro del limite de las competencias conferidas a la Unión Europea, a todas las personas, en relación con, entre otras, las condiciones de despido.

Es preciso recordar que el concepto de "discapacidad" no se define en la propia Directiva 2000/78. De este modo, el Tribunal de Justicia declaró, en el apartado 43 de la sentencia *Chacón Navas*, antes citada, que debe entenderse que dicho concepto se refiere a una limitación derivada de dolencias físicas, mentales o psíquicas y que suponga un obstáculo para que la persona de que se trate participe en la vida profesional.

Por su parte, la Convención de la ONU, ratificada por la Unión Europea mediante Decisión de 26 de noviembre de 2009, es decir, después de que se dictara la sentencia *Chacón Navas*, antes citada, reconoce en su considerando e) que "la discapacidad es un concepto que evoluciona y que resulta de la interacción entre las personas con deficiencias y las barreras debidas a la actitud y al entorno que evitan su participación plena y efectiva en la sociedad, en igualdad de condiciones con las demás". Así el artículo 1, párrafo segundo, de esta Convención dispone que son personas con discapacidad aquellas "que tengan deficiencias físicas, mentales, intelectuales o sensoriales a largo plazo que, al interactuar con diversas barreras, puedan impedir su participación plena y efectiva en la sociedad, en igualdad de condiciones con las demás."

Habida cuenta de las consideraciones mencionadas en los apartados 28 a 32 de la presente sentencia, el concepto de "discapacidad" debe entenderse en el sentido de que se refiere a una limitación, derivada en particular de dolencias físicas, mentales o psíquicas que, al interactuar con diversas barreras, puede impedir la participación plena y efectiva de la persona de que se trate en la vida profesional en igualdad de condiciones con los demás trabajadores.

Concluye:

"El concepto de 'discapacidad' a que se refiere la Directiva 2000/78/CE del Consejo, de 27 de noviembre de 2000, relativa al establecimiento de un marco general para la igualdad de trato en el empleo y la ocupación, debe interpretarse en el sentido de que comprende una condición causada por una enfermedad diagnosticada médicamente como curable o incurable, cuando esta enfermedad acarrea una limitación, derivada en particular de dolencias físicas, mentales o psíquicas que, al interactuar con diversas barreras, puede impedir la participación plena y efectiva de la persona de que se trate en la vida profesional en igualdad de condiciones con los demás trabajadores, y si esta limitación es de larga duración. La naturaleza de las medidas que el empleador ha de adoptar no es determinante para considerar que al estado de salud de una persona le es aplicable este concepto.

La Directiva 2000/78 debe interpretarse en el sentido de que se opone a una disposición nacional que establece que un empleador puede poner fin a un contrato de trabajo con un preaviso abreviado si el trabajador discapacitado de que se trate ha estado de baja por enfermedad, manteniendo su remuneración, durante 120 días en los últimos doce meses, cuando esas bajas son consecuencia de su discapacidad, salvo si tal disposición, al tiempo que persigue un objeto legítimo, no excede de lo necesario para alcanzarlo, circunstancia que corresponde apreciar al órgano jurisdiccional remitente."

4. A la vista del concepto de discapacidad recogido en la Directiva no cabe sino concluir que no procede calificar de discapacidad la situación de la recurrente, que permaneció diez días de baja antes de que la empresa procediera a su despido, habiendo finalizado la IT, que había iniciado el 1 de marzo de 2013, por alta médica el 28 de marzo de 2013, sin que pueda entenderse que dicha enfermedad le ha acarreado una limitación, derivada de dolencias físicas, mentales o psíquicas que, al interactuar con diversas barreras, pueda impedir su participación en la vida profesional en igualdad de condiciones con los demás trabajadores. El despido de la recurrente no es el de una trabajadora discapacitada, ni su IT deriva de la situación de discapacidad, por lo que no resulta de aplicación la declaración contenida en el último párrafo de la STJUE parcialmente transcrita.

ANNOTATION

A good understanding of this case – and other cases decided in the last few years by the Spanish Supreme Court and by the European Court of Justice, such as *Daouidi* (C-395/15) – requires account to be taken of an important distinction made in Spanish domestic law between unfair dismissal and void dismissal. A dismissal is fair only if the employer follows the legal procedure and has a good cause /legitimate reason for the dismissal. If the good cause does not exist or if the legal procedure is not properly followed, the dismissal will ordinarily be considered unfair. Unfairness entails the obligation of the employer of either reinstating the employee who had been unfairly dismissed or paying her the severance compensation established by law (currently at 33 days of salary per year worked, although for periods worked before 12 February 2012, the formula is 45 days of salary per year worked). Since the option is open to the employer, many employers choose to pay compensation rather than to reinstate. In order to avoid legal proceedings after dismissal, employers usually admit that the dismissal is unfair and immediately pay the severance compensation calculated according to the statutory formula. Obviously, this means that when the employee has little seniority and her salary is low, the compensation may be almost insignificant. This is what happened in the case annotated here, in which the compensation was only €2,000.

The practical outcome of this legal framework is that many employers are able to dismiss employees at a very low cost, even though they do not have a legal cause for dismissal. The law does not offer additional protection unless the true reason for dismissal is discrimination or retaliation, or unless the dismissal violates in some way a constitutional fundamental right, or unless the employee enjoys a special statutory protection (employee representative, employee on parental leave, pregnant employee, etc.).

One of the many cases in which employers prefer dismissal over retaining the employee is when the latter becomes sick. During sickness, no matter its cause (professional or not), employees are entitled to sickness benefits, which are largely paid by social security; however, a small fraction of the cost is borne by the employer (for example, the employer must pay the benefit during a set number of days, the employer must continue paying social security taxes during the sickness leave, many employers have to pay extra benefits pursuant to collective agreements that are in force). In order to avoid these extra costs, some companies apply a policy of dismissing sick employees. As explained above, the only general remedy available in most cases is a somewhat modest monetary compensation, which is usually paid upfront by the employer without any need to initiate legal proceedings before a court.

This situation has been considered unsatisfactory by a number of lawyers, judges and scholars. Some of them have argued that dismissing a sick employee constitutes a violation of fundamental human rights, including human dignity, the right to life and physical and moral integrity, and even the right to health. The Supreme Court has established in a number of decisions that sickness is not a social or personal circumstance in the sense protected by Article 14 of the Spanish Constitution. This Article prohibits discrimination on grounds of birth, race, sex, religion, opinion or any other personal or social condition or circumstance. The Constitutional Court has stated in a number of cases that the phrase "any other personal or social condition or circumstance" must be construed in such a way that not every criterion of differentiation can be automatically included under the discrimination ban. What causes a given condition or circumstance to become included among the grounds of discrimination under Article 14 is the particularly hideous nature of the criterion of differentiation. This particularly hideous nature means that the criterion of differentiation is based on an essential characteristic of the person or on a fundamental choice of theirs in the exercise of basic liberties and rights. Hence, sickness is not considered among the prohibited grounds of discrimination, unless the particular sickness is associated with historical or traditional segregation or persecution, which is quite exceptional.

Since sickness is not among the protected conditions under Article 14 of the Constitution, some lawyers and scholars have tried to protect dismissed workers by alleging discrimination on grounds of disability. Disability is a well established protected category, both under domestic and international (European) law. Importantly, European Union Directive 2000/78 prohibits discrimination on the grounds of disability. With this legal support, some Spanish courts have questioned the validity of Spanish case law before the European Court of Justice (ECJ).

In an important decision on this subject (*Chacón Navas*, C-13/05), the ECJ ruled that "by using the concept of 'disability' in Article 1 of that Directive, the legislature deliberately chose a term which differs from 'sickness'. The two concepts cannot therefore simply be treated as being the same". The Court also considered that "the concept [of disability] must be understood as referring to a limitation which results in particular from physical, mental or psychological impairments and which hinders the participation of the person concerned in professional life" (*Chacón Navas*, C-13/05, and *HK Danmark*, C-335/11). In its latest decision on this subject (*Daouidi*, C-395/15), the ECJ recalled that "the concept of 'disability' within the meaning of Directive 2000/78 must be understood as referring to a limitation which results in particular from long-term physical, mental or psychological impairments which, in interaction with various barriers, may hinder the full and effective participation of the person concerned in professional life on an equal basis with other workers". Thus, long-term impairments resulting from long-term sickness could be considered disability.

In the particular case annotated here, the illness process of the employee was effectively short-term (only a few days), which made it easier for the Supreme Court to reach the conclusion that the dismissal could not be considered discriminatory and void. However, in other cases recently decided in Spain, illness progressing over several months have been considered amounting to a "disability" in the sense defined by EU Directive 2000/78 and, hence, are being considered discriminatory and void.

The question hinges, therefore, upon a fact which is highly contentious in practical terms: whether or not a given illness process is short-term or long-term. In order to discover the evidence which makes it possible to find that such a limitation is long-term, the ECJ in *Daouidi* ruled that the domestic court or agency must include "the fact that, at the time of the allegedly discriminatory act, the incapacity of the person concerned does not display a clearly defined prognosis as regards short-term progress or the fact that that incapacity is likely to be significantly prolonged before that person has recovered". It should be clear, therefore, that a sickness process in which the prognosis is full recovery in a few months' time is not a disability in the sense discussed here. By contrast, if the prognosis is not full recovery or if the likely recovery is going to be attained over the course of years, the sickness must be considered a disability for discrimination purposes and also for classifying the dismissal as void (with the mandatory remedy of reinstatement).

PART THREE

MANPOWER

# AUSTRIA

Supreme Court, 29 November 2016, 9 ObA 53/16h

Wage dumping through temporary work of an Austrian employee in Germany – applicability of the German minimum wage law

HEADNOTES

Facts

The plaintiff worked for the defendant from 16 November 2013 until 6 February 2015, as a rental car driver in full-time employment (173 hours per month). The plaintiff's salary amounted to €1,207.11 gross per month (€6.98 gross per hour). The collective bargaining agreement for the sector of trade and industry of passenger transports applied to the employment relationship. The employer belongs to the sub-section "car-rental trade" and offers airport transfers in particular. The business headquarters are located in the city of Salzburg, from where also the plaintiff started his daily work regularly by picking up the vehicle and ended it by returning the car. The plaintiff mainly picked up passengers in and around Salzburg to take them to the airport in Munich and *vice versa*. Between passenger transports, the plaintiff could use his time as he wished and got paid €6.98 per hour gross for this time as well. Occasionally, the plaintiff had to work at the airport counter in Munich. In January 2016, the plaintiff worked 50 hours and 52 minutes in Germany.

The plaintiff requested the payment of outstanding salaries, based on the German Minimum Wage Act (Deutsches Mindestlohngesetz, MiLoG). The defendant denied the claim and the applicability of the German Act to an Austrian employment relationship.

The Labour Court denied the plaintiff's claim and held that Austrian labour law applies to the employment relationship under Article 8 of Regulation (EC) No 593/2008 of the European Parliament and of the Council on the law applicable to contractual obligations (Rome I).

The Court of Appeal denied the plaintiff's appeal. The plaintiff requested the revision of the judgement, upholding his claim.

Decision

The Supreme Court held that the appeal was not justified.

Law Applied

Deutsches Mindestlohngesetz (MiLoG, German Minimum Wage Law)
Section 1 Minimum Wage

(1) Each employee is entitled to payment of remuneration by their employer of at least the amount of the minimum wage.

(2) As of 1 January 2015, the amount of the minimum wage shall be €8.50 gross per hour.

[…].

Section 20 Duties of the Employer to Pay Minimum Wages

Employers who operate branches, businesses or other professional establishments in Germany or abroad are obliged to pay any of their workers employed in Germany a remuneration of at least the amount of the minimum wage, in accordance with section 1(2) […].

JUDGEMENT

1. Regulation (EC) No 593/2008 of the European Parliament and of the Council dated 17 June 2008 on the law applicable to contractual obligations (Rome I) applies to the present employment contract, which was concluded on 16 December 2009. According to Article 8 para. 2 of the Regulation, an employment contract shall be governed by the law of the country in which or, failing that, from which the employee habitually carries out their work in performance of the contract. The country where the work is habitually carried out shall not be deemed to have changed if the employee is temporarily employed in another country. Since the parties did not choose a specific national legislation and the work assignments in Germany took place only temporarily (Rome I, Recital 36; Judgement of 15 March 2011, *Koelzsch*, C-29/10, ECLI:EU:C:2011:151, paras. 49 *et seq.*), Austrian labour law generally applies, which was not disputed by the plaintiff. The plaintiff did not refer to the application of Directive 96/71/EC concerning the posting of workers in the framework of the provision of services (the Posting of Workers Directive) and to the coherent application of section 20 of the German Minimum Wage Law to the employment relationship. The plaintiff did not argue, in particular, that it might be a case of posting a worker under the terms of the Posting of Workers Directive.

2. This said, it is questionable whether sections 1 and 20 *et seq.* of the German Minimum Wage Law can be considered overriding mandatory provisions within the meaning of Article 9 of the Rome I Regulation which would apply to the employment relationship in question. "Overriding mandatory rules" are provisions the respect for which is regarded as crucial by a country for safeguarding its political, social or economic organization to such an extent that they are applicable to any situation falling within their scope, irrespective of the law otherwise applicable to the contract under Rome I. According to Austrian jurisprudence and literature, such mandatory provisions – whether under public or private law […] – still apply, even if the workplace is only temporary, due to their crucial nature […].

3. Pursuant to section 20 of the German Minimum Wage Law, employers with branches, agencies or other establishments in Germany or abroad are obliged to pay workers employed by them in Germany a remuneration of no less than the amount of the minimum wage, in accordance with section 1(2) of the German Minimum Wage Law. Beginning with 1 January 2015 the minimum wage was €8.50 per hour; on 1 January 2017, it amounted to €8.84 per hour.

4. However, even by qualifying these provisions as overriding mandatory provisions, which, besides, would be consistent with Austrian and German doctrine, the plaintiff could not succeed.

5.1. According to Article 9 para. 3 of the Rome I Regulation, direct application of overriding mandatory provisions within the meaning of Article 9(1) *leg cit* requires that these mandatory provisions have been given effect, in so far as those overriding mandatory provisions would render the performance of the contract unlawful. "Giving effect" not only includes the application of possible legal sanctions (nullity, voidability) laid down in the law of the country where the contract is being enforced, but that such a provision can be considered as an obstacle to performance […].

5.2. Considering whether or not to give effect to provisions, their nature and purpose, and the legal consequences of their application or non-application have to be taken into account (Article 9 para. 3 sentence 2 of the Rome I Regulation). This enables the national judge to ascertain the relevance […] of the foreign overriding mandatory provision. […]

5.3. The intent of the German legislator was to protect workers against unreasonably low wages when introducing a nationwide minimum wage. Such a provision would prevent competition between undertakings through wage dumping at the employees' costs, but, at the same time, promote competition between who is offering better products and services.

Moreover, a lacking minimum wage could also affect the social security systems, because entrepreneurs might not provide a living wage and, therefore, workers would rely on additional social benefits to secure their livelihoods. Consequently, the minimum wage would also ensure the financial stability of the social security system.

The German minimum wage shall apply to workers who mainly, not only temporarily, carry out their work in Germany. This is because the workers concerned are affected by the German cost of living. However, the plaintiff who only worked in Germany occasionally did not argue that he was affected by the German cost of living, nor that the Austrian salary would be inappropriate in comparison with the German minimum wage. Furthermore, taking into account that, according to the applicable Austrian collective bargaining agreement, the plaintiff is entitled to a 13th salary (Christmas pay) as well as a 14th salary (vacation benefit), unlike employees in Germany, there is no imminent risk of wage dumping by the Austrian employer. Considering these additional payments, the plaintiff's hourly wage amounts to €8.14 gross ([€1,207.11 x 14 : 12] : 173). Consequently, the difference between the German minimum wage (€8.50 gross) and his hourly wage amounts to €0.36. [...] As to the discussed case, the other goal of the German minimum wage laws, to protect the stability of the German social security systems, is of no importance, either.

5.4. The consequences for an Austrian employer, on the other hand, are severe. If an employer entrusts a worker with a task in Germany occasionally, as in the case present, they would be restricted by reporting and documentation requirements pursuant to sections 16 and 17 of the German Minimum Wage Law. Observing these provisions, any kind of an employee's spontaneous, professional activities, such as an airport shuttle from Salzburg to Munich Airport after a customer's call, would become actually impossible, because – with a few exemptions – employers are obliged to give notice on the employee's name, beginning and end of the employment, the workplace etc. of the intended professional activities, in advance. [...]

6. Under these circumstances – that is, when weighing the consequences for the employer and those for the employee (see above, 5.3 and 5.4) – it is justified not to give effect to the provisions of the German Minimum Wage Law, according to Article 9 para. 3 sentence 2 of the Rome I Regulation. Consequently, sections 1 and 20 of the German Minimum Wage Law cannot apply to the employment relationship at issue. Pursuant to Article 8 para. 2 of the Rome I Regulation, the minimum wage level applicable to

the plaintiff's employment contract shall be determined, as prescribed by Austrian law.

[Source: The decision is available on publicly accessible websites such as https://www.ris.bka.gv.at/Jus/ under its file number *9 ObA 53/16h*]

ANNOTATION

The decision at issue is of interest regarding the following aspects: The Austrian Supreme Court interpreted Article 9 of the Rome I Regulation on "overriding mandatory provisions" and gave its clarification as regards the requirements for giving effect to such rules. From a substantive point of view, the Court had to deal with the question whether an Austrian citizen working for an Austrian company, mostly in Austria, would be entitled to the higher German minimum wage. In other words, the Court had to decide whether there had been "wage dumping" through applying the Austrian wage rules, whereas, regularly, countries such as Austria are used to claiming the applicably of their rules, in order to prevent wage dumping by applying other countries' wages rules.

1. In the present case, despite some work in Germany, primarily Austrian labour law applies. Based on the rules dealing with cases of cross-border impact, the law chosen by the parties governs an individual employment contract. This choice can be made expressly or can be clearly demonstrated by the terms of the contract or even the circumstances of the case. The plaintiff did not dispute the primary applicability of the Austrian laws, nor did he argue, in particular, that it might be a case falling under the terms of the Posting of Workers Directive of the European Union. As regards individual employment contracts, work carried out in another country shall be regarded as temporary if the employee is expected to resume working in the country of origin after carrying out their tasks abroad. Moreover, the country where the work was habitually and mostly carried out was indeed Austria. However, the employee claimed to be entitled to the German minimum wage as regards the (temporary) time he worked in Germany, which amounted to about 50 hours out of 173 hours per month.

One of the employee's arguments is the wording of section 20 of the German Minimum Wage Act, which prescribes the minimum wage for any work carried out within Germany, regardless of duration or sector, or whether the employer's site is in Germany or abroad. This international aspect is held to be the actual aim of section 20 *leg cit*. Any performance of work in Germany, even short-time, is covered, according to some German doctrine.

2. Due to the undisputed applicability of Austrian labour law, the Supreme Court examined whether sections 1 and 20 of the German Minimum Wage Act might be qualified as "overriding mandatory provisions" in the sense of the Rome I Regulation. If so, these rules – that is, another country's provisions – would apply, regardless of the two parties' choice and so forth.

Regularly, by way of interpretation, it has to be ascertained whether or not a provision is one of an "overriding mandatory" nature. According to the legal definition in Article 9 para. 1 of the Rome I Regulation, a provision that is regarded as crucial by a country for safeguarding its public interests, such as its political, social or economic organization, constitutes an overriding mandatory provision. At first, referring to the Austrian and German doctrine, the Supreme Court considered the German minimum wage rules as overriding mandatory provisions (see para. 4. of the judgement).

3. However, the Supreme Court then focused on para. 3 of Article 9 of the Regulation, laying down that in considering whether to give effect to those provisions regard shall be had to their nature and purpose and to the consequences of their application or non-application.

3.1. Therefore, to begin with, the Supreme Court took into account the goals of the German lawmaker, and examined in which way they affect the circumstances of the case at hand. The Court concluded that the non-application of German minimum wages rules would neither affect the German Social Security System adversely, because the Austrian employee would not claim any social benefits increasing his income, nor have impacts on the employee who was not faced with (higher) German costs of living.

3.2. Furthermore, the Supreme Court's argument was that the German lawmaker's intent was to prevent "unreasonable" wage dumping by workers from neighbouring countries, with no or a lower (national) minimum wage, the occurrence of which the Court denied in the case at issue. In Austria, to date, there is no statutory minimum wage. Nevertheless, about 95 per cent of all employees are covered by binding minimum wages, which arise from (sectoral) collective bargaining of the social partners. Additionally, the employees are granted the so-called 13th and 14th month salaries, which leads to actual minimum wages mostly amounting to the German levels, and in many sectors being even higher. As a result, the Austrian Supreme Court considered a difference in wages of €0.36 per hour "not unreasonable".

Moreover, one might approve of this approach when comparing the minimum wages of several European countries that do not even amount to €3.00 per hour, such as in Germany's neighbouring countries, Poland or the Czech Republic. Besides, as elaborated in the *International Labour Law Reports*, Volume 34, page 245, the Administrative Court has ruled on the Austrian Anti Wage and Social Dumping Act of 2011, finding that incorrect rates ranging from €0.77 for two hours up to €20.81 for 52.5 hours would be considered only "minor" wage dumping. Therefore, as regards the circumstances of the employment relationship being commented on here, the non-application of the German wage laws did not amount to a denial of their nature and purpose.

3.3. In the eyes of the Austrian Supreme Court, on the other hand, the consequences of the application of German rules would impose an unbearable hardship on Austrian employers: they would be obliged to report and document all employment relationships with cross-border impact (also) to the German authorities, in advance.

3.4. Ascertaining the nature and purpose of the laws and considering the consequences of their (non-)application for both parties, as prescribed in Article 9 para. 3 of the Rome I Regulation, the Supreme Court denied "giving effect" to the German minimum wage rules. This leads to the result that the minimum wage level applicable to the plaintiff's employment contract shall be determined as prescribed by Austrian law.

Bel. 1

BELGIUM

Labour Court Brussels, Summary Proceedings
28 January 2016, GR n° 2015/CB/14

Transfer of a business or part of a business – retention of employment relationship with entity taking over business – competence of court in summary proceedings

HEADNOTES

Facts

The employer company (E) is active in the communication business. Mr C and Mr T are part of its personnel. Company S is active in the delivery of services to companies and public companies in, among other things, the area of IT and telecommunications. T is a communication agency.

EDCC stands for the Europe Direct Contact Centre. It is the European information hub that allows citizens and companies to obtain, in the language of their choice, answers to their questions for general information on the activities and politics of the European Union. This information service that belongs to the European Commission (DG Communication) uses external contractors for delivering services. A call for tenders was launched for such service providers, and E won the tender in 2007 and again in 2011. The functioning of the information centre was entrusted to E by the European Commission from 2008 to 2015. In 2015 a new tender was launched. This time S and T won the tender. As from 1 February 2016 they are assuring the functioning of the EDCC services instead of E. In July 2015 this decision had been communicated to the companies concerned.

On 8 July 2015 E commenced a collective dismissal procedure within its company, which it suspended on 9 July 2015. On 3 August E wrote to S and to T informing them that, in application of the Collective Bargaining Agreement n° 32*bis,* all the employees of its EDCC division would by functioning of the law be transferred to S and T as of 1 February 2016.

S replied on 10 August 2015 indicating that it considered that the situation could not be seen as transfer of a business, so that one was not dealing with an automatic transfer of the personnel and that neither itself nor T had the intention of assuming the personnel of E. By registered letter dated 28 August 2015 E's counsel demanded that S and T would confirm prior to 15 September 2015 that they would take over the entire personnel of the EDCC division of E on 1 February 2016. On 15 September 2015, the legal representatives of S and T informed E that their clients could not reply positively to this demand.

On 25 September this procedure was started by a writ of summons for Summary Proceedings. A procedure on the merits was also started on 15 October 2015.

Decision

The Labour Court in Summary Proceedings refuses to oblige a service provider to take over the personnel of the old service provider that lost the tender, prior to the transfer of services actually taking place, indicating that this would surpass the powers of the Court acting in Summary Proceedings. The fact that the request was lodged in the framework of an alleged transfer of a business does not make a difference.

Law Applied

Collective Bargaining Agreement n° 32*bis* of 7 June 1985 with respect to the acquired rights of workers in case of change of their employer as a result of a transfer of undertaking by agreement, and to regulating the rights of workers taken over in the framework of a take-over of assets following bankruptcy, rendered generally binding by Royal Decree of 25 July 1985, Official Gazette 9 August 1985 (modified subsequently).

Article 584 of the Code of Civil Procedure.

JUDGEMENT

[...]
2. With respect to the grounds on which the demands are based
2.1 Urgency
The condition of urgency is satisfied.
This decision is based on the following reasoning:

2.1.1. Principles

The Court in Summary Proceedings only intervenes in case of urgency, in application of article 584 (2) of the Code of Civil Procedure.

Urgency is required as a basis for the competency of the Court in Summary Proceedings, but also to consider whether the request is well founded.

If urgency is invoked in the document with which the proceedings are started, then the Court is competent to deal with the matter.

The reality of the urgency that is invoked by the plaintiff is a condition of the demand being grounded in Summary Proceedings. If the urgency is not present then the claim is to be declared unfounded.

There is an urgency as soon as the fear of harm of a certain seriousness or even serious inconveniences make an immediate decision desirable. The urgency is assessed in the light of the imminent or pending damage, the length of a possible substantive procedure, the attitude of the parties and their interests.

The urgency in case of Summary Proceedings is to be appreciated at the moment the judge makes their decision.

2.1.2. Application of the principles to this case

In this case the urgency has been invoked in the document that started the proceedings. The competence of the judge in Summary Proceedings is not seriously contested.

The discussion by S and T deals with the urgency as a condition for the demands to be grounded.

It is as of 1 February 2016 that E will no longer be in charge of the functioning of the information centre EDCC, a task that will from then on be left to S and T, by decision of the European Commission. The present proceedings try to provisionally regulate the fate of the contracts of employment of the workers dedicated to, according to E, its EDCC division.

The European Commission's decision was announced to the parties in July 2015. It is certain that a substantive procedure on the merits, before the French speaking employment tribunal of Brussels, would not allow a decision on the fate of the employment contracts to be obtained before 1 February 2016.

S and T state that E and its staff members C, M and R created the urgency themselves because they were insufficiently forward-looking and did not take the necessary precautions.

The contract between E and the European Commission could have been renewed, like it had been in 2011. E cannot therefore be blamed for not having served its personnel with a notice that would come to an end at the end of the contract.

It cannot be blamed for having tried for a couple of weeks to convince S and T to take over the staff, before starting the court action on 25 September 2015.

The urgency of the request has therefore been established.

2.2. The summary proceeding and the limits of the court's power

The measures that are demanded are more than provisional matters and exceed the powers of the Court.

This decision is grounded on the following reasoning:

2.2.1. The principles with respect to provisional measures

In accordance with article 584 (2) of the Code of Civil Procedure, the Court in Summary Proceedings decides 'provisionally'. Article 1039 of the Code of Civil Procedure holds that 'orders on interim measures do not adversely affect the final outcome on the merits.'

The notion of provisional in the framework of a summary proceeding is interpreted in case law and doctrine in the sense that the interim or provisional nature of the court's intervention prohibits it to order measures that would definitively and irreparably infringe the rights of the parties. In other words, the court in summary proceedings cannot come to a declaration of the rights of the parties, nor come to a final resolution of the legal situation of the parties.

2.2.2 The limits of the powers of the Court with respect to the employment contract

In the current state of the law, it is very widely accepted that judges cannot oblige a party to enter into a contract of employment. The principle of the autonomy of the will of the parties, in contract matters, prohibits this.

This principle is also the basis of the power of each of the parties to end the employment contract. Each party to the employment contract is recognized to have the ability to put an end to it at any time, without any formalities and without having an obligation to give the reasons. If this termination is contrary to any legal provision and/or implies a fault, the party is exposed to having to pay an indemnity, but the effectiveness of his or her decision is not put in doubt: the contract is irreversibly terminated.

There are no exceptions to this principle in the case of a transfer of a business. There is certainly Collective Bargaining Agreement n° 32*bis* to implement European Directive 2001/23 that foresees, for cases in which it applies, that the rights and obligations flowing from the employment contracts in force at the time of the transfer for the transferring employer, are, by the mere fact of the transfer, transferred to the transferee. The employment contracts of the transferred workers are by law transferred from the transferor to the transferee without the agreement of either being required. Furthermore, it is forbidden, both for the transferee and for the transferor, to terminate employment contracts because of the transfer.

In any case, if one of the employers is not respecting its obligations, either by firing workers because of the transfer, or if the transferee refuses to employ the personnel, neither the Directive nor the collective bargaining agreement grant the power to the Court to prohibit the termination, nor to order that a worker be hired. The sanctioning of not living up to its obligations, under Belgian law, is done through damages.

2.2.3 Application of the principles to this case

The plaintiffs [including Company E] demand the Court in Summary Proceedings to hold that the legal operation constitutes a transfer of a business and consequently to direct S and T to employ the personnel affected to its EDCC division. They are therefore asking the Court to pronounce itself on the rights and obligations of the parties, which would exceed the limits of the 'provisional' nature [of rulings in Summary Proceedings].

Furthermore, what is requested exceeds the powers of the Court, the limits of which are explained above.

In fact the demand is in reality asking to have S and T condemned to become the employers of the workers concerned. However, the Court does not have the power to oblige a party to conclude an employment contract.

The plaintiffs hold, with reason, that the change of employer occurs automatically in furtherance of the Collective Bargaining Agreement n° 32*bis*, in such a manner that S and T according to them would automatically become the employers of the workers, as of 1 February 2016.

From that perspective, however, the first part of the demand is without logic as the transfer would be automatic once the conditions applying to a transfer of a business had been satisfied. In the event that the judge finds that these conditions have been fulfilled, the limits of the 'provisional' are exceeded.

Furthermore, if one considers that the workers automatically become members of the personnel of S and T on 1 February 2016 by application of the Collective Bargaining Agreement, the fact remains that those two companies have expressed their formal wish not to engage these workers. Case law analyses this as a termination of the employment contract by the transferee. The true purpose of the plaintiffs' claim is rather to prohibit S and T, transferees by definition, to terminate the employment contracts. From that perspective, the demand overruns the limits of the judge's power.

The demand therefore must be declared unfounded.

ANNOTATION

The Acquired Rights Directive of 12 March 2001 (2001/23/EC, on the approximation of the laws of the Member States relating to the safeguarding of the employees' rights in the event of a transfer of undertakings, businesses or parts of an undertaking or business) was implemented in Belgian law through an inter-industry wide collective bargaining agreement (CBA n° 32*bis*) concluded in the National Labour Council. It was rendered generally binding by Royal Decree. This means that the implementing measure is applicable to the entire private sector.

It is difficult in practice to determine whether a succession of service providers is to be seen as an application of the Acquired Rights Directive and CBA n° 32*bis*. The determination has to be made looking at all the specific circumstances of each case. The European Court of Justice has addressed this issue many times before. Belgian courts faithfully follow the jurisprudence from the European Court of Justice.

Quite often it will remain very unclear prior to any kind of judgement to know whether a certain transaction will be covered by CBA n° 32*bis*. Nevertheless the issue of whether or not the Acquired Rights Directive and CBA n° 32*bis* apply is of the utmost importance for all the workers concerned who are working in the business or in the part of the business that is being transferred. If CBA n° 32*bis* applies, the workers will have a right and obligation to transfer to the new service provider, acting as transferee. While the Directive, according to the case law of the European Court of Justice, implies only a right to transfer, Belgian courts have read CBA n° 32*bis* to include an obligation to transfer together with the business that is being transferred. This means conversely that the individual in a case of transfer of a business covered by CBA n° 32*bis* cannot refuse to transfer with the business. In a situation where a worker would refuse to transfer then he or she would be considered resigning from employment with the transferee. Since the employee who is refusing to transfer will not serve the transferee, per definition, with the appropriate term of notice, that worker may have to pay severance in lieu of notice to the transferee, based on the reasoning that this amounts to an improper termination of his or her employment contract.

When confronted with a situation like the one in the case being commented on, employees will quite often not know for sure whether the transactions are covered by CBA n° 32*bis* or not. Furthermore, when dealing with a personnel intensive business (as opposed to capital intensive business), the outcome of the question whether the Directive and CBA n° 32*bis* apply will largely depend on the answer to the question whether a substantial part of the workers, in numbers or expertise, transfer together with the activity.

In such businesses, those who won the tender for the new services provision contract will quite often argue that the transaction is not covered by the Directive and CBA n° 32*bis*. If on the one hand that argument is held to be correct, they can use either their own staff already in service or hire new and cheaper and maybe more competent new staff. If, on the other hand, CBA n° 32*bis* does apply, all employees belonging to the part of the business that is being transferred have the right to transfer together with the activity. Furthermore, they would transfer with all the rights they have at the moment of the transfer. They are equally protected against dismissal for reasons of the transfer.

While it is uncertain whether the Directive and CBA n° 32*bis* apply when service providers succeed one another, some sectors of industry in which contract changes are quite frequent have made some sector-level collective bargaining agreements in which the succeeding company has to at least offer contracts of employment to a percentage of the workers who were employed on the contract activity that was lost by the prior provider. This is for instance the case in the cleaning sector, where cleaning contracts are often awarded for a limited period of time. The same is true in the security sector.

The collective bargaining agreement of the cleaning sector tries to limit the effect of loosing cleaning contracts and hence having to go through, for instance, a collective dismissal procedure if the personnel related to the contract would not be transferring to the new service provider. The collective bargaining agreement seems to be a good incentive for the parties not to even discuss the applicability of the Acquired Rights Directive and CBA n° 32*bis*. Of course the applicability of the sector-level CBA cannot, as such, exclude the application of CBA n° 32*bis*, for instance if invoked by an employee of the transferor (who looses a contract), in a situation where the transferee rehires a substantial part of the former service provider's work force, but not all the employees. Those 'left behind' could on the basis of CBA n° 32*bis* still try to claim the CBA to be applicable, and hence to claim a right to be transferred (or receive severance pay in lieu).

Workers and their representatives are quite often caught in the middle between the transferor who wants the relevant work force to transfer together with the activity, and the transferee who may prefer hiring new cheaper workers or performing the contract with its own workers.

In the case at hand the same story seems to have developed. The transferor who lost the contract starts the procedure for a collective dismissal of the workers performing in the division that lost its activity to a competitor. The transferor immediately suspends the procedure, arguing that it was dealing with a transfer of the division, meaning an automatic transfer of the employment contracts to the new service providers (who had won the contract). Not surprisingly the new service providers do not agree with the old provider's point of view. They do not consider the transaction to fall within the scope of CBA n° 32*bis*.

In order to provide some clarity both for itself and its workers the first service provider started a court case asking the Court in Summary Proceedings basically to enjoin the new service providers to take over the employees, awaiting the outcome of a substantive court case on the merits.

In a 2011 case the Labour Court of Brussels (Summary Proceedings GR n° 2011/CB/17) had considered itself competent to deal with the issue and to impose on the new service provider an obligation to put the workers concerned on its pay roll. The Court stated that it considered that the obligation resulting from its judgement was not the same as forcing a new service provider to enter into an employment contract with a number of workers.

The present annotated 2016 case decides differently. It is hard to see how an effective transfer of the employees to a new employer could not be seen as a definite judgement on the rights of all involved, whereas summary judgements are not supposed to deliver a final determination of the rights of those involved in the case.

This means that, in the absence of a new service provider accepting the employment of the workers concerned, these workers will always have to argue *post factum*, following the transfer of the activity for which they were performing, and following the refusal by the new service provider to provide them with work. Once the new service provider refuses them work, the situation would be considered tantamount to firing the workers, at least if the deal in question proves to fall within the scope of the Acquired Rights Directive and CBA n° 32*bis*. In such a case the workers could sue for an indemnity in lieu of notice. They could equally try to argue that the termination of their employment contracts in violation of CBA n° 32*bis* should be considered as manifestly unreasonable in the sense of CBA n° 109, which imposes an obligation on employers (as of 1 April 2014) not to dismiss workers unless there are grounds related to either the ability or the behaviour of the worker concerned, or to the necessities of the functioning of the company. A manifestly unreasonable termination may be punished with an order to pay an indemnity of between 3 and 17 weeks' pay.

Jap. 1

JAPAN

Supreme Court (Second Petty Bench)
19 February 2016

Validity of employees' consent to changes to their retirement benefits as prescribed in work rules

HEADNOTES

Facts

The appellants had been employed by Credit Cooperative A. Credit Cooperative A was merged into Credit Cooperative B, the appellee, on 14 January 2003 (referred to below as the 2003 Merger). This merger was made in order to prevent the failure of Credit Cooperative A. Credit Cooperative B changed its name to its current one (Yamanashi Credit Cooperative) at the time of another merger with three other local credit cooperatives on 16 February 2004 (referred to as the 2004 Merger). The appellee succeeded to the appellants' labour contracts in place of Credit Cooperative A through the 2003 Merger.

On the one hand, the appellants claimed retirement benefits based on Credit Cooperative A's Rules for Retirement Benefits (the Former Rules). On the other hand, the appellee contends that new Rules for Retirement Benefits (the New Rules), which entered into force upon the 2003 Merger, should apply on the basis that they had been agreed between the appellants and appellee.

The New Rules were adopted on 19 December 2002 by the Joint Council, which consisted of the directors of both Credit Cooperative A and Credit Cooperative B. The contents of the New Rules were as follows. On the one hand, they made two changes to the Former Rules namely (i) the calculation of retirement benefits that previously had been based on a 'payment multiplier' and 'monthly salary' (i.e. the final salary at the time of retirement), had the latter reduced to 'one-half of the monthly salary' and (ii) the 'payment multiplier' would be fixed according to the length of service and the type of retirement (ordinary retirement due to reaching the retirement age or voluntary retirement) and this multiplier was capped at 55.5 under the New Rules, although there had been no such cap under the Former Rules. On the other hand, parts of the Former Rules were maintained. An additional old-age pension under an old national pension scheme, which was calculated into an actuarial present value, was then to be deducted from the amount of the retirement benefits (called the Inclusive Method). In contrast, this deduction had not applied to the appellee's employees before the 2003 Merger. The amount of lump-sum payment corporate pension insurance refunded to the Credit Cooperative A's employees as a result of the 2003 Merger was also to be deducted. Consequently retirement benefits to be paid under the New Rules became considerably smaller than the payment that would have been paid under the Former Rules.

Regarding the agreements between the appellee and the appellants, at the Credit Cooperative A's meeting with employees on 13 December 2002, a month before the 2003 Merger, a draft consent form was distributed to each employee. This draft provided that the level of retirement benefits given to the then Credit Cooperative A's employees would be the same as the employees who had been employed by the appellee. An explanation was also given regarding the changes (i) and (ii) mentioned above. Following this meeting, a schedule of retirement benefits was shown to the eight appellants, who were in managerial positions at Credit Cooperative A at that time. Retirement benefits in the schedule were calculated on the basis of 'ordinary retirement'.

On 20 December 2002, Credit Cooperative A's twenty managerial employees including the appellants were requested to sign the consent form which included information regarding the changes (i) and (ii). They were told at the time that the 2003 Merger would fail if they did not consent to it. All of these managerial employees signed the form. On the same day, a collective agreement involving these changes was signed by the president of a union, of which all Cooperative A's employees were members.

At the time of the 2004 Merger, further changes were made: (a) retirement benefits in compensation for the length of service before the 2004 Merger would be based on the coefficient for voluntary retirement; (b) retirement benefits in compensation for the length of service after the

2004 Merger would be governed by a new different retirement benefit plan; and (c) these latter retirement benefits would not be paid to employees who retire voluntarily before the new retirement benefit plan was adopted.

In this instance, these changes were announced verbally to employees. Around 2 February 2004, the branch managers read aloud to the employees of their respective divisions the description of the changes, and then the branch managers and the employees of the respective divisions (including the appellants) signed their names in the column entitled 'Names of Persons Who Consent to Work under the New Working Conditions' in a document.

Among the appellants, seven appellants, who retired after the new retirement benefit plan came into force on 1 April 2009, received retirement benefits in compensation for the length of service after the 2004 Merger. However, as a result of changes made at the time of 2003 Merger and 2004 Merger, they received no retirement benefits in compensation for the length of service before the 2004 Merger. The amount of old national pension and corporate pension to be deducted was larger than the amount of retirement benefits obtained by multiplying one-half of the monthly salary by the years of service and the coefficient for voluntary retirement. Furthermore, in the case of five persons, who retired before 2009, no retirement benefits were to be paid because their retirement preceded the adoption of the new retirement benefit plan.

The Kofu District Court dismissed all of the appellants' claims, holding that collective agreements regarding the changes at the time of the 2003 Merger were binding on those employees, who were union members; that the appellants, who were in managerial positions, had validly consented to the changes; that all the appellants had consented to the changes made at the time of the 2004 Merger (Judgement of 6 September 2012). This decision was upheld by the Tokyo High Court (Judgment of 29 August 2013).

Decision

The Supreme Court quashed the High Court's decision because it failed to take into account matters such as the content of the information provided to the employees, and it made its determination without fully examining whether reasonable grounds existed for finding that the employees had signed of their own free will. The case was remanded to the High Court for further examination.

Law Applied

Labour Standards Act

Article 2(1). Working conditions shall be determined by both employees and employers on an equal basis.

Labour Contracts Act

Article 3(1). A labour contract is to be concluded or changed between an employee and an employer by agreement on an equal basis.

Article 8. An employee and an employer may, by agreement, change any working conditions that constitute the contents of a labour contract.

Article 9. An Employer may not change any of the working conditions that constitute the contents of a labour contract in a manner disadvantageous to an employee by changing the work rules, unless an agreement to do so has been reached with the employee; provided, however, that this does not apply to the cases set forth in the following Article.

JUDGEMENT

1. Working conditions may be changed by an individual agreement between an employee and an employer, and it is construed that the same applies where work rules are also revised to reflect these changes (see Articles 8 and 9 of the Labour Contracts Act). However, where changes to working conditions are related to wages and retirement benefits, even if an employee performs an act by which he/she accepts such changes, careful determination should be made as to whether or not the employee has consented to the changes. This is because an employee is in the position where he/she is hired by the employer and subject to the employer's orders and has only a limited ability to gather information based on which he/she can make his/her own decision. Such determination should be made not only by considering whether the employee has performed an act by which he/she accepts the changes, but also from the perspective of whether reasonable grounds exist for finding that the employee has performed the act of his/her own free will, and in order to consider this latter point, it is necessary to take into account factors such as the content and degree of any resulting disadvantages, the circumstances and the manner regarding the performance of the employee's act and the content of the information or explanation provided to the employee.

2. From this standpoint, we examine whether the appellants, who were in managerial positions, consented to the changes at the time of 2003 Merger. The appellants, who were in managerial positions, received an explanation that their consent to the changes to the Former Rules was required to achieve the 2003 Merger in order to avoid the failure of Credit Cooperative A, and they then signed the consent form. In the draft consent form, it was stated that the same level of payment as that for those who had been employed by the appellee since before the 2003 Merger would be guaranteed. However, according to the payment standards under the relevant terms of the New Rules, the retirement benefits would be one-half of or smaller than the conventional total amount, while deducting both the amount of employee pension benefit and corporate pension refunds from the amount of retirement benefits. In addition, the coefficient for voluntary retirement was used to calculate the retirement benefits in compensation for the length of service before the 2004 Merger. Consequently, it was very likely that no retirement benefits would be paid, and that, contrary to what was stated in the above-mentioned draft consent form, payment rules were extremely imbalanced when compared with those applicable to the persons who had been employed by the appellee since before the 2004 Merger, persons who did not adopt the Inclusive Method.

The appellants are not deemed to have been provided with the necessary and sufficient information for considering and deciding by themselves whether to consent to the changes if they were only provided with the information and explanation concerning matters such as the necessity of the changes, but rather they should have been provided with additional information and explanations concerning the content and degree of the specific disadvantages, such as the likelihood that no retirement benefits would be paid in the case of voluntary retirement and that the outcome would be extremely imbalanced when compared with the payment standards applicable to the persons who had been employees of the appellee since before the 2004 Merger.

However, the lower court determined that the appellants consented to the changes, based on the grounds that they knew, from the schedule of retirement benefits, the amount of retirement benefits as well as the calculation method. When so issuing its determination, the lower court did not fully consider such matters as the content of the disadvantages and the circumstances leading up to the signatures.

Thus, with regard to whether or not the appellants consented to the changes, the lower court did not fully examine the issue from the perspective of whether reasonable grounds exist for finding that these appellants had signed the consent form of their own free will.

In order to determine whether or not the appellants consented to the changes at the time of the 2004 Merger, the issue is whether or not their signing is deemed to be their giving consent. As in the case of the 2003 Merger, the lower court, without fully examining the case from the perspective stated in paragraph 1 above, determined that the appellants had given consent immediately from their signing.

As explained above, the determination by the lower court involves a violation of laws and regulations that apparently affects the judgement.

[Source: Case No. (ju) 2595 of 2013, decided on 19 February 2016: Minshu Vol. 70, No. 2]

ANNOTATION

The terms of contracts cannot be changed without the consent of both parties to the contracts. This principle has the following exceptions in cases of labour contracts. First, collective agreements changing the terms and conditions of employment unfavourably can have a binding effect on employees who join trade unions which conclude such agreements, whether or not individual employees have given their consent to the changes (Article 16 of the Labour Union Act). However, collective agreements would not be the vehicle used to effect a change of working conditions across the board as they have binding force in principle only on their members – non-union members are not bound by collective agreements. That is why work rules are needed as a second means of making changes to working conditions. Work rules, which employers can establish unilaterally, can validly change the terms and conditions of employment unfavourably, where these changes were reasonable and announced to the employees working in that establishment. This doctrine of work rules was first made by case law. Academic discussion occurred about whether and how this should be supported. One argument supporting this approach said, with regard to labour contracts, changes of terms and conditions would be unavoidably needed by possible changes of circumstances, considering the continuing character of labour contracts. Even in such situations, employers are not allowed to resort to economic dismissals immediately, as such dismissals would be considered an abusive exercise of dismissal rights (Article 16 of the Labour Contracts Act of 2007).

The Labour Contracts Act of 2007 subsequently codified this doctrine. It now finds its basis in Article 10 of the statute. According to this provision, when an employer changes the working conditions by changing the work rules, if the employer 'announces' to the employee the changed work rules, and if the change to the work rules is reasonable, the working conditions shall be in accordance with such changed work rules. Reasonableness depends on various facts of each case. Consideration is given to the extent of the disadvantage to be incurred by the employees, the need for changing the working conditions, the appropriateness of the changed work rules, the situation of negotiations with a labour union or the like, or any other circumstances pertaining to the change to the work rules (Article 10).

An important issue raised in the case at hand was as to whether, in cases where an individual employee has given consent to such changes to the work rules, should such consent be acknowledged as valid and, if so, then the examination of the change's reasonableness should be omitted. The position supporting this is based on the principle of agreement laid down in Article 8, which stipulates that working conditions can be changed by agreement between an employee and an employer. This principle also can be seen in Article 9, which provides that an employer may not change any of the working conditions by changing the work rules 'unless an agreement to do so has been reached with the employee' (the binding effects of work rules explained above are provided for as exceptions to this principle). This could mean on the one hand that, with an employee's consent to the change in working conditions, the conditions as provided by work rules are considered valid, whether or not reasonableness can be seen in the changes (the agreement-based approach). On the other hand, academics argued that examination of reasonableness is still necessary even in cases where employees gave their consent to the changes. In this decision, the Supreme Court supported the agreement-based approach by citing Articles 8 and 9 of the Labour Contracts Act of 2007.

However, the Supreme Court also held that it should examine whether employees accepted the changes 'of their own free will'. Even from the point of view of the agreement-based approach, it was argued that careful examination should be given as to whether or not agreements were validly reached between an employer and an employee. It can be said that the Supreme Court also brought the academic discussion into this case.

According to the Supreme Court, the factors to be taken into consideration in deciding employees' free will are: "the content and degree of disadvantage; the circumstances and the manner regarding the performance of the employee's act of acceptance; and the content of the information or explanation provided to the employee, etc." In remanding the case to the High Court, the Supreme Court stressed that sufficient information, such as the likelihood that no retirement benefits would be paid to some employees, was not given to the employees.

Questions may arise as to whether the legal issue here is procedural or substantive. If procedural, even in cases where the degree of disadvantage is considerable, communication of full information would be enough to acknowledge employees' consent as valid. If substantive, in cases where the degree of disadvantage is considerable, communication of full information would not be enough for a determination that the employees' consent was valid.

At issue is also what can be included in Court's wording "etc." when listing evidentiary factors. For instance, should the courts examine whether sufficient time was given to the employees to examine the changes before acceptance? These and other questions will be resolved with further development of academic discussion and accumulation of court cases in the future.

It is to be noted that this case involved another legal issue, namely whether collective agreements concluded to change the Former Rules at the time of the 2003 Merger were binding on the appellants, who were members of a union organized by Credit Cooperative A's employees. The part of the decision concerning this issue is omitted in this annotation due to space limitations.

Nor. 1

NORWAY

Supreme Court
Rt. 2015 p. 1332

Business reorganization – redundancy – dismissal – scope of circle of employees to be considered for selection

HEADNOTES

Facts

Gresvig Detaljhandel AS (Gresvig) is a sports equipment company with retail outlets across Norway, in a fiercely competitive market. In the years 2009 to 2013 the company undertook considerable reorganization and downsizing, closing down 19 stores through 2012 and a further 14 stores in 2013. Altogether, 225 employees were made redundant.

In 2009, Gresvig acquired a smaller company, Agderbyen Sport AS, with sports equipment stores in two counties in the southern part of Norway. That company also had a self-contained department tasked with the sale of goods directly to sports clubs and businesses, independent of the retail business. That department was operated by one employee only, John Doe, from an office in the city of Kristiansand. The department was continued after Gresvig's acquisition of Agderbyen Sport, under the name of Intersport Profil, still with John Doe as the single employee handling that particular business activity. Intersport Profil's turnover decreased from NOK 6 million in 2009 to some NOK 2 million in 2011, and the department ran at a loss every year from 2010.

In March 2013 in a meeting with Gresvig's management, John Doe was informed that the company was considering closing down the Intersport Profil department for financial reasons, as part of a long-term strategy to improve the company's competitiveness. Gresvig subsequently resolved to go ahead with the closure. Consequently John Doe was given notice of dismissal on 11 April 2013, and was at the same time offered a – lower paid – position as sales staff in a retail outlet in a nearby city. He turned down that offer. Somewhat later John Doe applied for a position as shop manager of an outlet in Kristiansand; however, he was considered not to be qualified for that position.

After the expiry of the period of notice, in November 2013, John Doe filed for compensation for unfair dismissal, arguing, in particular, that the selection for dismissal should have been considered with reference not merely to his Intersport Profil place of work but on a more extensive basis including other employees in positions for which he was qualified. In that context he alleged that Gresvig had failed to offer him "other suitable work" and to honour his preferential right, when having been dismissed on grounds of redundancy, to a "new appointment at the same undertaking" to positions for which he was qualified.

The Kristiansand District Court found in favour of John Doe. However, the Court of Appeal held that Gresvig was not liable.

Decision

On appeal to the Supreme Court the matter of a "preferential right" to a new appointment was disallowed; hence the case was confined to the issue of unfair dismissal. At the outset, the scope of selections when considering employees for dismissal comprises the legal entity, its activities and employees, as a whole. The Supreme Court, in line with previous case law, held that in redundancy situations it may nonetheless be admissible to confine the scope of activity, and thus the circle of employees, to be taken into account. Comprehensively discussing factors to be considered in this regard, the Supreme Court found that in view of the particular circumstances of the case at hand, the dismissal of John Doe was not unfair within the meaning of the applicable statutory dismissal protection.

Law Applied

Act of 17 June 2005 No. 63 relating to the working environment, working hours and employment protection, etc. (Working Environment Act/WEA)

Section 15-7. Protection against unfair dismissal

(1) Employees may not be dismissed unless this is objectively justified on the basis of circumstances relating to the undertaking, the employer or the employee.

(2) Dismissal due to curtailed operations or rationalization measures

is not objectively justified if the employer has other suitable work in the undertaking to offer the employee. When deciding whether a dismissal is objectively justified by curtailed operations or rationalization measures, the needs of the undertaking shall be weighed against the disadvantage caused by the dismissal for the individual employee.

[Section 14-2. Preferential right to a new appointment
Para 1. Not quoted as it was not at issue before the Supreme Court]

JUDGEMENT

Mr Justice ENDRESEN for a unanimous Court gave the following opinion:
(34) [Quoting Section 15-7 of the WEA]
(35) The dismissal was based on circumstances relating to the undertaking. It is not in dispute that there were adequate economic grounds for closing the Intersport Profil department and that doing so entailed redundancy. I take this as a basis. The issue is whether there was just cause for dismissing John Doe, in particular whether he could only have been dismissed if that were objectively justified subsequent to a comprehensive assessment also including other employees in positions for which John Doe was qualified. It has not been argued that such an assessment was made.

(36) It was company practice to use each individual department as the unit delimiting the circle of employees to take into account with regard to the selection of who should be dismissed, considering this, under the circumstances, to be objectively justified. In the present case, concerning the closing down of the Intersport Profil department it is decisive whether the application of a principle of this kind is in conformity with the fairness requirement [of 'objective justification'] of Section 15-7 of the WEA. John Doe is not required to prove that a more comprehensive assessment would have resulted in another employee being dismissed instead of him. Unless it were evident that such a comprehensive assessment would have resulted in John Doe nonetheless being dismissed, the missing assessment must in itself suffice to hold that the dismissal should be considered null and void.

(37) [...] Consequently, it is decisive whether there was just cause to limit the scope for selection to the [Intersport Profil] department.

(38) Even though the point of departure is that the company as a whole defines the scope of the circle of employees to be included in selection assessments, it is established in [Supreme Court] case law that this may

be departed from on grounds of just cause [if "objectively justified"]. See decisions Rt. 1986 p. 879 and Rt. 1992 p. 776, that highlight the factors that may justify using a smaller circle for selection than using the company as a whole.

(39)–(41) [Case law citations]

(42) Those two decisions should be regarded as exemplifying relevant factors, not as laying down minimum requirements or delimiting such factors as may be relevant to the assessment. Whether there is just cause for limiting the circle for selection must be decided in each individual case, and a wide range of factors may be taken into account in the justification assessment. It may easily, in particular in larger companies, give rise to considerable practical problems if selection were to be based on the company as a whole. Furthermore, it is a legitimate objective for a company to retain requisite competencies, and securing continued operations is a fundamental consideration. A selection process that might not be unreasonably demanding as a once-only exercise could be considerably more of a strain if the need to adapt is recurrent. That could easily lead to apprehension and a sense of instability, which may entail very negative consequences for the company. It is also evident that a company's financial situation and business challenges may be of considerable importance.

(43) On the one hand, inasmuch as the point of departure pursuant to the WEA is the company as a whole, weighty considerations are therefore required to depart from this premise. On the other hand, the Act cannot be held to require procedures that are unreasonably burdensome on companies and that would also be conducive to undermining the safety of remaining employees.

(44) In the present case it is a natural starting point that, in the event of downsizing, the company has stuck to using the individual store as the basis for the purpose of settling on a circle for lay-off selection, and likewise if closing down a store. This has been a consistent practice since 2009, involving a great number of employees.

[…]

(46) It is clear that an established practice under the circumstances must be accorded considerable weight, not least when the limitation of the circle for selection is based on criteria that as a rule indicate that the limitation is justified. Against this background I shall point to circumstances that in this case imply that the established practice is within the bounds ensuing from case law concerning the use of selection circles of limited extent.

(47) Here, it is a natural point of departure that the company

concerned has about 2000 employees in some 100 stores spread over a vast geographical area. [...] Which stores should be included in a possible wider circle for selection is, at least in many cases, not obvious.

(48) The individual employee is, essentially, working in the department at which he or she is hired, and which is its primary point of connection to the company.

(49) Also, it is not a matter of one single case of reorganization and downsizing, but of continuous adjustment to market developments and competitiveness.

(50) Moreover, recurring processes involving a large number of employees would make heavy demands on management resources, which would be particularly serious when the company is in a process of reorganization with a view to securing a basis for continued operations.

(51) Gresvig's financial situation was in a precarious state during the period concerned. [...] Its cash-flow problems were strained to the extent that fresh funding was required to enable its continued operations.

(52) Thus in my view, when considering the weight the company's established practice is to be accorded, it must be taken as a basis that limiting the circle for selection to each individual department is consistent with considerations that normally imply that such limitation is justified.

[...]

(54) In my opinion, there is no foundation for precluding in principle that a department with one single employee may be a circle for selection. When a department is closed down and the employees in that department are dismissed it is precisely the point that there is no consolidated assessment including employees with similar positions in other departments. Applying this principle to the single employee in a department does not imply treating him less favourably than employees in a larger department that constitutes the circle for selection if being closed down.

[...]

(56) Moreover, as a consequence of the established practice of limiting the circle for selection to the individual store that is closed down, in any case as a matter of principle, John Doe has been exempt from being involved in dismissal assessments in cases of other departments being closed down. Avoiding differential treatment is in itself a relevant consideration.

[...]

(58) On this basis I find that there was just cause to limit the circle for selection also in the case of closing down the Intersport Profil department.

(59) It remains for me to consider whether a balancing of interests as regards the needs of the undertaking and the disadvantage caused by the dismissal for John Doe may result in holding the dismissal not to be based on just cause. In my opinion that is not the case. At the time of dismissal John Doe was 55 years of age with ten years of seniority. However, in the present context neither his age nor his seniority can be accorded considerable weight. He was offered an alternative job. Even if this involved considerably less pay, the offer nonetheless conformed to the requirement of "other suitable work" pursuant to section 15-7, second paragraph, as there were no available positions more equal to his previous job. The job offer was given in the same meeting in which he received notice of dismissal from his position at Intersport Profil. That being so, it is of no consequence that he was informed of the dismissal before the job offer was put to him.

(60) It is not contested that the downsizing was objectively justified on the basis of circumstances relating to the undertaking. Then, when it was legitimate for the employer to limit the circle for selection to the department concerned it is merely in extraordinary circumstances that the balancing of interests might be to the employee's advantage. Such extraordinary circumstances are clearly not present in the case at hand.

[Source: *Norsk Retstidende* 2015, p. 1332]

ANNOTATION

The above decision is illustrative of characteristic features of dismissal law pertaining to redundancy situations, explicitly as well as implicitly. It is commonplace that downsizing gives rise to issues around the selection of which employees to be laid off. One of the issues frequently involved is settling on the scope of circle of employees to be considered for selection, in short, the circle for selection. Thus the decision relates to a recurrent theme. It is exceptional primarily on the specific facts of the case, but is nonetheless important more generally by reinforcing and adding to the considerations to be made.

One starting point to be noted is that on its wording the provision in Section 15-7, second paragraph, of the WEA does not apply to selection among those employees that are to be taken into account. The obligation on the employer to offer "other suitable work" pertains to the individual employee concerned. So does the second limb of the provision, on the balancing of interests, applying to the 'vertical' relationship between the interests of the undertaking and those of the individual employee. The selection among employees involved is in principle another matter. It is however established in case law that selections also must be "objectively justified", and that the factors to be taken into account in the 'vertical' assessment are equally relevant to the 'horizontal' selections that need to be made. The seminal decision in this regard is that of the Supreme Court in Rt. 1986 p. 879, referred to in the present case (in paragraph 38). In that decision the Court held that several considerations would have to be taken into account, such as qualifications, age, seniority, and also evident social and humane considerations. Thus the statutory provision is construed to imply a form of 'social selection' (*Sozialauswahl*), albeit of limited reach. It must be added that depending on the circumstances the needs of the undertaking essentially will prevail; this is amply illustrated by the 1986 decision as well as that in Rt. 1992 p. 776, also referred to in paragraph 38, and indeed by the present case.

A next point of departure is that the frame of reference for the application of section 15-7 of the WEA and consequentially for possible selections is the legal entity as a whole, that is to say, all of its departments and spheres of activity, as the case may be. This is explicitly reaffirmed by the Supreme Court in this decision being commented on, in paragraphs 38 and 43 of the judgement. The reference in paragraph 43 to "weighty considerations" is not much more than a stepping stone. The salient point is that the legal entity as the frame of reference may be departed from, and hence, what is crucial in the first place is on what grounds.

In this regard the Court, in paragraphs 42 and following, essentially follows the line of reasoning first developed in the 1992 decision referred to. In short, the size of the undertaking as a whole, the number and geographical distribution of units or departments, possible specialization of tasks and qualifications needed, and practical complications involved if using the company as a whole as a frame of reference are weighty considerations. So is the company's financial situation, implying more latitude the more critical that situation may be. However, it is a novel element in the equation to accord "considerable weight" to an established practice within the company, as expressed in paragraph 46 of the judgement. The seeming reservation "under the circumstances" is not restricted to this particular case. The follow-up wording "not least ..." clearly demonstrates that this is a normative statement of general reach, and an intended one, it is safe to say. However, seen in a context of recurring cases of downsizing the concrete factors highlighted in paragraphs 47, 49 to 51, and 55, tie in with the general points of departure set out in paragraph 42 of the judgement.

Yet the observation on 'equal treatment' adds a new twist (paragraph 56). What is notably missing is any reference to the importance of interaction with elected trade union representatives in the company and possible consensus arrived at in the process of information and consultation on the issues involved. Normally, this is a factor of considerable weight. However, in this particular case no collective agreement applied and hence there were no elected union representatives to be concretely involved.

Another point to be noted in this context is the Court's statement, in paragraph 48, on "the primary point of connection" of an employee being the department in which he or she was hired, presuming that to be where his or her work essentially is performed. That is a tenuous argument, easily failing in view of employment contract practices by which hiring is for work in the company as a whole or a wider range of workplaces, enabling the employer to shift an employee from one place of work to another. If such is the case it is a fair guess, however, that it will not matter significantly.

The fundamental point to appreciate is that the overall approach employed by the Supreme Court effectively amounts to splitting the comprehensive assessment of justification of an individual dismissal into two. Notably, when first assessing whether the employer is justified in limiting the circle for selection, considerations pertaining to the individual employee or, as the case may be, employees do not enter into the equation. The conclusion in principle rests solely on efficiency and expediency considerations relating to the undertaking. This is amply illustrated by the case at hand. Allowing the employer to limit the 'circle for selection' to a one-employee unit simply exhausts the matter of selection. It would be the same in the case of closing down a unit with two or more employees, which, incidentally, was the situation in the decision in Rt. 1992 p. 776. In practical terms, the 'horizontal' process of selection among a number of employees is sidelined.

One important implication is that the employer's obligation to offer "other suitable work in the undertaking" if possible is fundamentally limited. It obviously does not extend to positions already filled by others; that would effectively entail setting aside the otherwise justified limitation of the circle for selection. However, if a vacant position exists for which the employee concerned may be qualified, such a position must be offered.

What remains, then, is the balancing of interests pursuant to the second limb of the second paragraph of section 15-7 of the WEA. That is already at the outset an uphill battle for the employee. As emphasized by the Supreme Court, once a limitation of the circle for selection is held to be justified it is only "in extraordinary circumstances" that the employee may gain the upper hand (paragraph 60). Moreover, this is emphatically illustrated by paragraph 59 of the decision, in particular by dismissing John Doe's age and seniority as not having significant weight. In an ordinary 'horizontal' selection assessment both the age and the seniority at the levels in question would be factors of considerable weight, for the selection among employees as well as for the interlinked 'vertical' balancing of interests. The fact that John Doe had turned down an offer of an alternative job held to be "suitable" within the meaning of section 15-7 evidently did not speak in his favour. However, this was not pointed out by the Court as decisive in itself.

On this point, the "extraordinary circumstances" criterion in its generality remains the bottom line, but an elusive one. Likewise, the Supreme Court's considerations on justification for limiting the circle for selection suggest its position but remain fairly open-ended. In sum, the door is not closed on either count; the issues are certain to reappear in future case law, potentially, then, to be further clarified and refined.

PART FOUR

INDIVIDUAL EMPLOYMENT RELATIONSHIP

G.B. 1

GREAT BRITAIN

Court of Appeal
Windle v. Secretary of State for Justice [2016] EWCA Civ 459

*Employment status – mutuality of obligation
– casual and intermittent workers*

HEADNOTES

Facts

The facts and appellate history of this case were set out in paragraphs 1 to 5 of the judgement of Underhill LJ, and can be summarised as follows. Dr Z. Windle and Mr F. Arada (W&A), the original claimants in these proceedings, were professional interpreters working for Her Majesty's Courts and Tribunals Service (HMCTS), on a 'case-by-case basis'. They were, respectively, of Czech and Algerian origin, and although they also performed similar assignments for other public bodies, translation work for HMCTS constituted an important share of their income, with Mr Arada spending, according to the facts reported at paragraph 38 of the EAT judgement, about 80% of his working time for the Tribunals Service and the remainder for the Magistrates' Court and the Crown Prosecution Service (CPS).

The contractual arrangements between HMCTS and W&A suggested that the Tribunal Service was under no obligation to offer them work, nor were they under any obligation to accept it when offered. They were paid for work done, with no provision for holiday pay, sick pay or pension. They considered themselves self-employed and were so treated for tax purposes.

In 2012 each of the claimants brought proceedings against the Ministry of Justice (MoJ) in the Employment Tribunal complaining of racial discrimination contrary to Part 5 of the Equality Act 2010, which prohibits discrimination against persons in 'employment', as defined under section 83(2)(a) of the Act. In essence their claims were that in various specific respects their terms were less generous than those accorded to British Sign Language interpreters, and that they could establish this comparison in the first place, as their work relationship with HMCTS fell within the personal scope of application of the Equality Act 2010, which for the relevant part is defined as applying to 'employment under a contract of employment, a contract of apprenticeship or a contract personally to do work' (section 83(2)(a)).

The MoJ took a preliminary point that the W&A were not its employees within the meaning of the 2010 Act. The two claims were listed together before an Employment Tribunal (ET) for that issue to be determined. By a reserved judgement dated 3 April 2013, the Employment Tribunal decided the issue in the MoJ's favour and dismissed the claims. The claimants appealed and by a judgement dated 3 July 2014 the Employment Appeal Tribunal (EAT, HH Judge Peter Clark presiding) allowed their appeals and remitted the claims to the ET. A critical passage in the EAT decision was contained in paragraph 54 of Judge Clark's decision, where the employer's counsel argument that 'a lack of mutuality between engagements was relevant not only to the contract of employment question but also the separate question of employment under a contract personally to do work' was rejected, in favour of the alternative view that 'lack of mutuality is relevant to the former and not to the latter'.

The Secretary of State appealed against the EAT decision to the Court of Appeal.

Decision

The appeal was allowed. A crucial element in the Court of Appeal's decision was contained in paragraph 23 of Underhill LJ's judgement, rejecting the suggestion that lack of mutuality of obligation between separate engagements could undermine the contractual and employment nature of the engagements themselves, during the period that the work is actually being done. In Underhill LJ's own words:

> "23. I do not accept that submission. I accept of course that the ultimate question must be the nature of the relationship during the period that the work is being done. But it does not follow that the absence of mutuality of obligation outside that period may not influence, or shed light on, the character of the relationship within it. It seems to me a matter of common sense and common experience

that the fact that a person supplying services is only doing so on an assignment-by-assignment basis may tend to indicate a degree of independence, or lack of subordination, in the relationship while at work which is incompatible with employee status even in the extended sense. Of course it will not always do so, nor did the ET so suggest. Its relevance will depend on the particular facts of the case; but to exclude consideration of it in limine runs counter to the repeated message of the authorities that it is necessary to consider all the circumstances."

Law Applied

The claim and the appeal were brought in respect of breaches of the Equality Act 2010, but as that Act implements and consolidates a number of European Union (EU) equality law directives, that are interpreted by the Court of Justice of the European Union (CJEU) and whose judgements are supreme and, often, directly applicable in domestic law, the Court of Appeal judgement elaborates on a number of EU concepts and CJEU precedents, as well as on domestic case law.

In his judgement Underhill LJ summarises the key provisions informing this area of employment discrimination law in the following terms:

> "7. Part 5 of the Equality Act, as I have said, prohibits discrimination against "employees": see section 39. Section 83(2) defines "employment", so far as relevant for present purposes, as:
>
>> "(a) employment under a contract of employment, a contract of apprenticeship or a contract personally to do work; [...]".
>
> Section 83(4) provides that a reference to an employee is to be read with sub-section (2). The same language appears in the predecessor legislation.
>
> 8. Section 83(2)(a) identifies three kinds of contract. The first – "a contract of employment" – means a contract of service. The Claimants accept that they were not employed under such a contract. It is their case that they were employed under the third kind of contract listed, namely "a contract personally to do work". The best explanation of what that phrase refers to appears in *Bates van Winkelhof v. Clyde & Co.* [2014] UKSC 32, [2014] 1 WLR 2047. In that case the Supreme Court was concerned with whether the claimant was a "worker" within the meaning of section 230(3) of the Employment Rights Act 1996, but Lady Hale, who delivered the majority judgement, reviewed the field more widely. Limb (b) of section

230(3) refers to employment under

> "... any other contract ... whereby the individual undertakes to do or perform personally any work or services for another party to the contract whose status is not by virtue of the contract that of a client or customer of any profession or business undertaking carried on by the individual".

Lady Hale pointed out, at para. 25 [...], that that formulation distinguished between two kinds of self-employed people:

> "One kind are people who carry on a profession or a business undertaking on their own account and enter into contracts with clients or customers to provide work or services for them. The arbitrators in Hashwani v. Jivraj (London Court of International Arbitration intervening) [2011] 1 WLR 1872 were people of that kind. The other kind are self-employed people who provide their services as part of a profession or business undertaking carried on by someone else. The general medical practitioner in Hospital Medical Group Ltd v. Westwood [2012] EWCA Civ 1005; [2013] ICR 415, who also provided his services as a hair restoration surgeon to a company offering hair restoration services to the public, was a person of that kind and thus a 'worker' within the meaning of section 230(3)(b) of the 1996 Act".

She then, at paras. 31-32, went on to observe that the same distinction was recognised for the purpose of discrimination law, even though section 83(2)(a) of the 2010 Act does not contain anything equivalent to the elaborate words of exception in the second half of section 230(3)(b). She said:

> "31. As already seen, employment law distinguishes between three types of people: those employed under a contract of employment; those self-employed people who are in business on their own account and undertake work for their clients or customers; and an intermediate class of workers who are self-employed but do not fall within the second class. Discrimination law, on the other hand, while it includes a contract 'personally to do work' within its definition of employment (see, now, Equality Act 2010, s 83(2)) does not include an express exception for those in business on their account who work for their clients or customers. But a similar qualification has been introduced by a different route.
>
> 32. In *Allonby v. Accrington and Rossendale College* (Case C-256/01) [2004] ICR 1328: [2004] ECR–I873 the European Court of Justice was concerned with whether a college lecturer who was ostensibly

self-employed could nevertheless be a 'worker' for the purpose of an equal pay claim. The Court held at para. 67, following *Lawrie-Blum v. Land Baden-Wurttemberg* (Case C-66/85) [1987] ICR 483; [1986] ECR 2121: that 'there must be considered as a worker a person who, for a certain period of time, performs services for and under the direction of another person in return for which he receives remuneration'. However, such people were to be distinguished from 'independent providers of services who are not in a relationship of subordination with the person who receives the services' (para. 68). The concept of subordination was there introduced in order to distinguish the intermediate category from people who were dealing with clients or customers on their own account. It was used for the same purpose in the discrimination case of *Jivraj v. Hashwani.* [2011] 1 WLR 1872".

9. As Lady Hale there acknowledged, the qualification on the apparently broad scope of the phrase "a contract personally to do work" had in fact already been recognised in the decision of the Supreme Court in *Hashwani v. Jivraj* [2011] UKSC 40, [2011] 1 WLR 1872, although the discussion is less explicit. In that case the issue was whether an arbitrator was an employee for the purpose of the Employment Equality (Religion or Belief) Regulations 2003, which had an identical definition. Lord Clarke, with whose judgement the other members of the Supreme Court agreed, emphasized that it was not enough that the putative employee should be a party to a contract personally to do work: he or she must be "employed under" such a contract (see para. 36, at p. 1887 B-C).

10. It has become common to refer to persons employed under contracts falling within the terms of section 230(3)(b) of the 1996 Act as "limb (b) workers". Because, inconveniently, the 2010 Act uses different language, it is inapt to refer to employees of the third kind listed under section 83(2)(a) by the same label. I will refer to them as "employees in the extended sense".

11. As to how the distinction is to be made between the two kinds of self-employment – that is, between employees in the extended sense and the "truly self-employed", as it is sometimes put – in *Hashwani* Lord Clarke said, at para. 34 (p. 1886 E-G):

"...The essential questions ... are ... those identified in paras 67 and 68 of *Allonby* [2004] ICR 1328, namely whether, on the one hand, the person concerned performs services for and under the direction of another person in return for which he or she receives remuneration or, on the other hand, he or she is an independent provider of services who is not in a relationship of subordination with the person who receives the services. Those are broad questions which depend upon the circumstances of the particular case. They depend upon a detailed consideration of the relationship between the parties ... The answer will depend upon an analysis of the substance of the matter having regard to all the circumstances of the case".

12. It will be seen that both Lady Hale in *Bates van Winkelhof* and Lord Clarke in *Hashwani* refer to the decision of the ECJ in *Allonby v. Accrington & Rossendale College* (Case C-256/01) [2004] ICR 1328. This concerned an equal pay claim by part-time lecturers at a further education college, who had initially been employed by the college but had been made redundant and required to offer their services through an agency. One of the issues was whether the claimants were "workers" within the meaning of article 141 of the EU Treaty. At paras. 64-72 (pp. 1359–60) the Court said this:

> "64. The term 'worker' within the meaning of article 141(1) EC is not expressly defined in the EC Treaty. It is therefore necessary, in order to determine its meaning, to apply the generally recognised principles of interpretation, having regard to its context and to the objectives of the Treaty.
>
> 65. According to article 2 EC, the Community is to have as its task to promote, among other things, equality between men and women. Article 141(1) EC constitutes a specific expression of the principle of equality for men and women, which forms part of the fundamental principles protected by the Community legal order: see, to that effect, *Deutsche Post AG v. Sievers* (Cases C-270 and 271/97) [2000] ECR I-929, 952, para. 57. As the court held in *Defrenne v. Sabena* (Case 43/75) [1976] ICR 547, 566, para. 12, the principle of equal pay forms part of the foundations of the Community.
>
> 66. Accordingly, the term "worker" used in article 141(1) EC cannot be defined by reference to the legislation of the member states but has a Community meaning. Moreover, it cannot be interpreted restrictively.
>
> 67. For the purposes of that provision, there must be considered as a worker a person who, for a certain period of time, performs services for and under the direction of another person in return for which he receives remuneration: see, in relation to free movement of workers, in particular *Lawrie-Blum v. Land Baden-Württemberg* (Case 66/85) [1987] ICR 483, 488, para. 17, and *Martínez Sala*, para. 32.

68. Pursuant to the first paragraph of article 141(2) EC, for the purpose of that article, 'pay' means the ordinary basic or minimum wage or salary and any other consideration, whether in cash or in kind, which the worker receives directly or indirectly, in respect of his employment, from his employer. It is clear from that definition that the authors of the Treaty did not intend that the term 'worker', within the meaning of article 141(1) EC, should include independent providers of services who are not in a relationship of subordination with the person who receives the services (see also, in the context of free movement of workers, *Meeusen v. Hoofddirectie van de Informatie Beheer Groep* (Case C-337/97) [1999] ECR I-3289, 3311, para. 15).

69. The question whether such a relationship exists must be answered in each particular case having regard to all the factors and circumstances by which the relationship between the parties is characterised.

70. Provided that a person is a worker within the meaning of article 141(1) EC, the nature of his legal relationship with the other party to the employment relationship is of no consequence in regard to the application of that article: see, in the context of free movement of workers, *Bettray v. Staatssecretaris van Justitie* (Case 344/87) [1989] ECR 1621, 1645, para. 16, and *Raulin v. Minister van Onderwijs en Wetenschappen* (Case C-357/89) [1992] ECR I-1027, 1059, para. 10".

13. Both Lord Clarke in *Hashwani* and the ECJ in *Allonby* refer to a "relationship of subordination". In *Bates van Winkelhof* Lady Hale warned against treating the presence or absence of "subordination" as the infallible touchstone for distinguishing between the two kinds of self-employed worker under section 230(3): see para. 39 (pp. 2058–9). That term was, however, used by the ET in this case (loyally applying *Hashwani*) and neither party criticises it for doing so. I will occasionally use it myself, though bearing in mind Lady Hale's caveat.

14. One other part of the legal background which it is necessary to refer to is the concept of mutuality of obligation. The position is most lucidly stated by Elias LJ in *Quashie v. Stringfellows Restaurant Ltd* [2012] EWCA Civ 1735, [2013] IRLR 99, at paras. 10-12 (pp. 102–3), as follows:

"10. An issue that arises in this case is the significance of mutuality of obligation in the employment contract. Every bilateral contract requires mutual obligations; they constitute the consideration from each party necessary to create the contract. Typically an employment contract will be for a fixed or indefinite duration, and one of the obligations will be to keep the relationship in place until it is lawfully severed, usually by termination on notice. But there are some circumstances where a worker works intermittently for the employer, perhaps as and when work is available. There is in principle no reason why the worker should not be employed under a contract of employment for each separate engagement, even if of short duration, as a number of authorities have confirmed: see the decisions of the Court of Appeal in *Meechan v. Secretary of State for Employment* [1997] IRLR 353 and *Cornwall County Council v. Prater* [2006] IRLR 362.

11. Where the employee working on discrete separate engagements needs to establish a particular period of continuous employment in order to be entitled to certain rights, it will usually be necessary to show that the contract of employment continues between engagements. (Exceptionally the employee can establish continuity even during periods when no contract of employment is in place by relying on certain statutory rules found in section 212 of the Employment Rights Act.)

12. In order for the contract to remain in force, it is necessary to show that there is at least what has been termed "an irreducible minimum of obligation", either express or implied, which continues during the breaks in work engagements: see the judgement of Stephenson LJ in *Nethermere (St Neots) v. Gardiner* [1984] ICR 612, 623, approved by Lord Irvine of Lairg in *Carmichael v. National Power plc* [1999] ICR 1226, 1230. Where this occurs, these contracts are often referred to as "global" or "umbrella" contracts because they are overarching contracts punctuated by periods of work. However, whilst the fact that there is no umbrella contract does not preclude the worker being employed under a contract of employment when actually carrying out an engagement, the fact that a worker only works casually and intermittently for an employer may, depending on the facts, justify an inference that when he or she does work it is to provide services as an independent contractor rather than as an employee [...]. This was the way in which the employment tribunal analysed the employment status of casual wine waiters in *O'Kelly v. Trusthouse Forte plc* [1983] ICR 728, and the Court of Appeal held that it was a cogent analysis, consistent with the evidence, which the Employment Appeal Tribunal had been wrong to reverse.""

JUDGEMENT

Underhill LJ, with whom Jackson LJ and Lindblom LJ agreed, delivered the following judgement.
[…]

21. The single question on this appeal is whether the EAT was right to find that the ET had misdirected itself by treating the absence of an umbrella contract as a relevant factor in the assessment of the Claimants' employment status.

22. The principal submission of Mr Humphreys in seeking to uphold the decision of the EAT was that in determining whether a claimant is an employee in the extended sense the essential question is to what extent he or she is acting "under direction", or is in a "subordinate" position, while at work. As he put it in his skeleton argument:

> "This will require an enquiry, founded on the contract, into the scope of that direction and the extent of any limitation on the putative employee's independence in that context. The absence of mutuality of obligation between engagement can add nothing to that enquiry […]".

23. I do not accept that submission. I accept of course that the ultimate question must be the nature of the relationship during the period that the work is being done. But it does not follow that the absence of mutuality of obligation outside that period may not influence, or shed light on, the character of the relationship within it. It seems to me a matter of common sense and common experience that the fact that a person supplying services is only doing so on an assignment-by-assignment basis may tend to indicate a degree of independence, or lack of subordination, in the relationship while at work which is incompatible with employee status even in the extended sense. Of course it will not always do so, nor did the ET so suggest. Its relevance will depend on the particular facts of the case; but to exclude consideration of it *in limine* runs counter to the repeated message of the authorities that it is necessary to consider all the circumstances.

24. That would be my view even without any reference to *Quashie*. But I do not in fact think that what Elias LJ said in the passage which I have italicised can properly be disregarded on the basis that the issue in that case was whether the claimant was employed under a contract of service. The underlying point is the same. The factors relevant in assessing whether a claimant is employed under a contract of service are not

essentially different from those relevant in assessing whether he or she is an employee in the extended sense, though (if I may borrow the language of my own judgement in *Byrne Bros (Formwork) Ltd v. Baird* [2002] ICR 667: see para. 17(5), at p. 678 H), in considering the latter question the boundary is pushed further in the putative employee's favour – or, to put it another way, the passmark is lower. I would add for completeness that I do not think that Judge Clark's point that continuity of employment is not an issue in Equality Act cases (see para. 19 above) affects the analysis. The question is whether the claimant is an employee at all; and it was that which was the issue in *Quashie*.

25. Mr Humphreys attempted to draw support from para. 72 of the judgement of the ECJ in *Allonby* (see para. 12 above), in which the Court said that the fact that the lecturers in that case had no obligation to accept an assignment "is of no consequence in that context [viz. in the context of deciding how much independence they enjoyed while at work]". But the paragraph starts by making clear that the Court is concerned with the particular case before it ("in the case of teachers who … [etc.]"), and I do not think that what is said there can be elevated into universal proposition: indeed Mr Humphreys accepted as much in his oral submissions. It is clear from the Opinion of the Advocate-General that the claimants continued to work very much as they had when they were employees (see para. 46, at p. 1341 F); and they were evidently not being engaged on a lecture-by-lecture basis.

26. Mr Humphreys also submitted that it was wrong in principle that a person who would otherwise satisfy the criteria to be treated as an employee during a particular engagement should fall out of protection only because there was no "umbrella contract"; and, by the same token, that where there were two people who were in substantially the same position at work but one of them was working on a casual basis and one was not it was wrong in principle that they should not enjoy the same protection. But that is an Aunt Sally. The absence of an umbrella contract is relevant only if and to the extent that it contributes to the conclusion that the claimant is not in fact in a "subordinate" relationship characteristic of an employee – in which case he or she will not be in the same position as their comparator. Whether that is so in any particular case will depend on the circumstances of that case.

27. For those reasons I do not believe that the ET misdirected itself, as the EAT held. I would allow the appeal and restore the decision of the ET to dismiss the claims.'

ANNOTATION

Windle is an important decision of the English Court of Appeal for restating the law on the personal scope of application of UK equality and employment protection legislation. Lord Justice Underhill, giving the lead judgement, reinforced a number of established common law doctrines that have arguably construed the personal scope of application of English employment law and equality law in a particularly narrow way. The particular common law doctrine on which Lord Justice Underhill elaborates is the doctrine known as 'mutuality of obligation'. For the past three decades the doctrine has been deployed in numerous decisions, including House of Lords and Supreme Court judgements (see, most notably *Carmichael v. National Power plc* [1999] UKHL 47) to argue that the absence of a contractually relevant – and often also a contractually evidenced – mutual commitment for future performance between the parties to a contract for work or services, inevitably denied the possibility for that contract to be a contract of employment, or even a 'worker contract' as per the concept of 'worker' arising from section 230(3)(b) of the Employment Rights Act (ERA) of 1996. Even where such contracts could, on the facts of the case, be construed as contracts of service or employment, the absence of a mutual commitment for these contracts to be performed on a regular and continuous basis could defeat the attempt to tie them together under a single 'umbrella contract', a necessary step to assist employees seeking protection against unfair dismissal that is subject to a qualifying period of two years.

In recent years, and in particular since the 2011 Supreme Court decision in *Jivraj v. Hashwani* [2011] UKSC 40, the problems arising from a narrow construction of the personal scope of application of domestic employment legislation have been further exacerbated by the emergence of an equally restrictive and narrow reading of the personal scope of application of UK anti-discrimination law. This is particularly problematic in view of an ostensibly broader definition of the personal scope of application of the Equality Act 2010 (and of the EU directives it implements) to a broader conception of employed person defined, as noted above, as somebody working 'under a contract of employment, a contract of apprenticeship or a *contract personally to do work*' (section 83(2)(a) of the Equality Act 2010, emphasis added).

In *Jivraj* this provision was read as requiring the presence of a relationship of subordination between the working person and the employer, for the anti-discrimination law to apply (see paragraph 36 of the judgement in *Jivraj*, and its emphasis on the words 'employment under a contract'). While this gloss on the scope of UK (and EU) equality law was, in our view, indirectly and *ob iter* questioned by the subsequent Supreme Court judgement by Lady Hale in *Bates van Winkelhof v. Clyde & Co LLP* [2014] UKSC 32, *Windle* clearly reaffirms the position expressed in Jivraj and further reinforces this by also suggesting that the absence of mutuality between assignments can also be used to 'shed light on' the character of the relationship within it (paragraph 23). So the absence of mutuality between intermittent contracts (that *in abstracto* could still be classified as contracts of employment or contracts for personal work) could be used to infer that these contracts are either contracts for self-employment not covered by anti-discrimination law, as per *Jivraj*, or as being non-contractual at all. In short, this case shows that an ongoing contractual relationship between several assignments is not a necessary requirement to prove employment status, but its absence can be an indication for there being none.

A more detailed analysis of the decision by the Court of Appeal in *Windle* can be found at: H. Dhorajiwala, '*Secretary of State for Justice v. Windle*: The Expanding Frontiers of Mutuality of Obligation?' (2017) 46 Industrial Law Journal 268-278.

ITALY

Court of Cassation
Labour Division
Decision no. 8068 of 21 April 2016

Agency work – sham labour intermediation – posting

HEADNOTES

Facts

An employee, who had been recruited by a company on a fixed-term contract, lodged a complaint asserting that she had worked from the beginning solely for another company, which, however, belonged to the same group. She sought to have established the existence of sham labour intermediation (which was and still is prohibited by Italian law), thereby claiming the existence of a permanent subordinate employment relationship with the company that had actually made use of her services.

The Court of first instance rejected the complaint, holding that the worker had not been a victim of a sham contract, but rather that she had been posted from one company to another. The Court of Appeal upheld the Court's decision.

The employee appealed to the Court of Cassation to have this decision overturned.

Decision

The Court of Cassation rejected her appeal.

Law Applied

Act no. 1369 of 1960
Article 1

1. An enterprise is prohibited from contracting out or subcontracting out, or assigning out in any other form whatsoever, including to cooperatives, the performance of services through the use of employees recruited and remunerated by the contractor or by any intermediary, whatever the nature of the work or service. The enterprise is likewise prohibited from contracting to intermediaries, be they employees, third parties or companies, including cooperatives, work to be performed at piece rate by workers recruited and remunerated by such intermediaries.

The contracting out of work shall include any form of contract work or subcontract work, including the performance of services, where the contractor uses capital, machinery and equipment supplied by the user enterprise, even when a sum is paid to the user enterprise for their use.

The provisions of the previous sections shall also apply to state-owned companies as well as public bodies, even if managed autonomously, without prejudice to the provisions of Article 8 below.

Workers, employed in breach of the prohibitions laid down by this Article, shall be considered, for all intents and purposes, employees of the user enterprise that actually used their services.

Legislative Decree no. 276 of 2003
Article 27

1. When agency work is performed outside the limits and conditions laid down by Articles 20 and 21, section 1, letters a), b), c), d) and e), a worker may make a complaint to a court, on the basis of Article 414 of the Italian Code of Civil Procedure, by means of an action which may be brought only against the user, requesting that an employment relationship be declared to exist between the worker and the user, with effect from the beginning of the supply/the agency work period.

2. All payments made under section 1 by the agency in the form of remuneration or social security contributions shall release the organization which actually made use of the service from payment of the sums due up to the amounts actually paid. All acts undertaken by the agency to establish or manage the relationship, for the period during which the agency work was performed, shall be considered to have been performed by the organization that actually made use of the services.

3. For the purposes of determining the reasons pursuant to sections 3 and 4 of Article 20, which allow agency work, judicial scrutiny, in compliance with the general principles of Italian law, shall be limited solely to determining the existence of reasons justifying it and may not be extended to determining the technical, organizational or production grounds and reasons, which fall to the user enterprise.

Article 30

1. The event of posting occurs when an employer, to satisfy its own interests, temporarily places one or more workers at the disposal of a third party for the performance of a given service.

4 ter. In the event that the posting of employees occurs between companies that have signed an enterprise network agreement, which is valid pursuant to Decree law no. 5 of 10 February 2009, converted, with amendments, by Act no. 33 of 9 April 2009, the interest of the service provider shall arise automatically by virtue of the presence of the network, without prejudice to the provisions regarding mobility of workers pursuant to Article 2103 of the Italian Civil Code. In addition, the same enterprises may have joint employership of workers recruited through rules established by virtue of the presence of the network itself.

JUDGEMENT

(omissis)

More specifically, and with reference to the first ground (infringement and wrongful application of Act no. 1369, Article 1), it should be considered that, even accounting for the presence of a separate legal entity, each member of the group of enterprises has an interest in contributing, also through the posting of its employees, to the creation of common production and organizational facilities, which are consistent with the goals of efficiency and functionality of the group itself. They share a convergence of economic interests, which includes the goal of reducing management costs now or in the future.

Indeed, it is clear that the interest of the service provider cannot be separated from that of the group of which the provider is an economically integrated part, and is in fact directly connected and functional to the realization of the latter.

Objective confirmation of the above considerations can be found in the legal changes made in the field of the posting of workers, and, in particular, in the introduction – through Legislative Decree no. 76 of 28 June 2013, converted as amended by Act no. 99 of 9 August 2013, of Article 30, section 4 ter which states in the first part (the second concerns "co-employership", i.e. the joint hiring of the same employee) that "if the posting of staff occurs between companies that have signed an enterprise network agreement which is valid pursuant to Legislative Decree no. 5 of 10 February 2009, converted, with amendments, by Act no. 33 of 9 April 2009, the interest of the service provider arises automatically by virtue of the presence of the network, without prejudice to the provisions regarding the mobility of workers pursuant to Article 2103 of the Italian Civil Code".

(omissis) It is significant that the provision in question connects the interest to the key fact of the presence of the network i.e. to the fact – which is at one and the same time legal and economic – of a functioning enterprise network agreement, through which a number of enterprises collaborate in conducting their enterprises in the pursuit of common objectives related to innovation and competitiveness.

Nevertheless, it is evident that such an agreement has, on the one hand, joint economic objectives which certainly make them similar to those that underlie the entrepreneurial rationale of a group of businesses and, on the other hand, do not establish closer relations than those which determine, pursuant to Article 2359 of the Italian Civil Code, the control or association of enterprises.

Within the framework set out above, which seems to be the only one that fits the peculiarity of varied and complex forms of production, the impugned decision is undoubtedly correct since it is based on the uncontested premise that both the service provider and the service user are part of the same group. It shows exactly the synergetic nature of organizational action to create one centre to manage the employees of the companies belonging to it. It also shows that the posting of the appellant served "a common need to rationalize and economize the service".

Nor can we share the appellant's argument that even the fact of the temporary time period, which is essential for the posting to be lawful, had been taken for granted by the impugned decision (and by the court of first instance), but had, in reality, not been fully demonstrated by the respondent.

Indeed, given that the appellant's case falls within the long-standing line of decisions, which melds the concept of "temporariness" and "non-permanence", Cass. decision no. 23933 of 25 November 2010, it specifically noted that the temporary nature of the posting does not require that the worker perform work for a different legal entity "for a pre-established length from the beginning, nor that it be of varying length or that it take place at the time of the worker's recruitment, or that it continue for the entire length of the employment relationship, but only that the length of the posting corresponds to that of the employer's interest that its employee perform work on behalf of a third party".

The preceding observations also lead us to conclude that the second ground of appeal, which claims a flaw in the reasoning, is unfounded.

And in truth the Court of first instance did sufficiently and correctly reason the decisive point, namely the lawfulness of the posting, as the fact which derogates from the prohibition of labour intermediation, putting the actual interest of the employer to order the posting of B. to Aurelia 80 on the same level as demonstrated by witness accounts and the factual situation (in other words, the emergence in the case in point of a group of enterprises). Nor did the Court of first instance neglect to evaluate the fact that the appellant was responsible for duties regarding staff of the latter company, identifying them as "internal ways of distributing work" and rightly regarding it to be immaterial "in a unified organization of activity".

ANNOTATION

Italian law has prohibited and continues to prohibit sham intermediation of work, which occurs when one of the parties to the employment relationship is not the end user of the service. This prohibition does not only apply in the case of agency work, which is undertaken by enterprises authorised under Articles 4 and 5 of Legislative Decree no. 276 of 2003.

This raises the question of whether the temporary "posting" from one employer to another, which is relatively normal among enterprise groups, does or does not constitute labour intermediation.

The limits on posting were initially laid down by case law, and later by the legislature through Article 30 of Legislative Decree no. 276 of 2003, which is also at the basis of the decision being commented on here. The law in question lays down two prerequisites: the temporary nature of the posting (in other words that it is not permanent); and that the service provider has an interest in its employee performing work for the service user.

The interesting aspect of this decision is that, while it takes into account current forms of production, which are varied and complex, it identifies the existence *per se* of an interest of the service provider in cases when it belongs to the same group of enterprises. Indeed – observes the Court – the interest of the service provider cannot be separated from that of the group of which it is an economically integral part: each member of the group of enterprises has a contributing interest, also through the posting of its employees, in the establishment of common production and organisational units, also with a view to reducing management costs now or in the future.

This decision is important because it adopts an unusual perspective in Italian case law and legal commentary, while rejecting a rigid position.

AUSTRALIA

Fair Work Commission
Four Yearly Review of Modern Awards – Penalty Rates

*Modern awards – minimum standards – safety net –
penalty rates in retail and hospitality sectors*

HEADNOTES

Facts

The Fair Work Commission (FWC) is an independent statutory tribunal established under Part 5-1 of the Fair Work Act 2009 (FW Act) with responsibility under Part 2-3 of the FW Act to make, vary and revoke 'modern awards'.

Modern awards are statutory instruments establishing minimum terms and conditions of engagement for employees in particular occupations and industries. There are presently 110 modern awards, which cover the majority of occupations and industries within the Australian labour market.

Along with the 'National Employment Standards' enshrined in Part 2-2 of the FW Act (which predominately relate to leave entitlements), modern awards constitute a safety net of wages and conditions for the vast majority of Australian employees who are covered by the Act.

An employee to whom a relevant award applies must receive as a minimum the terms and conditions within that modern award (FW Act section 45). Furthermore, any enterprise agreement negotiated between employees and their employer must leave the employees 'better off overall' than they would be under the relevant modern award (FW Act sections 186(2)(d) and 193).

Given the centrality of the modern award system to the safety net of employment conditions in Australia, the FWC is required to review all modern awards every four years (FW Act section 156). The current four-yearly review is the first conducted since the FW Act was enacted. It commenced on 5 February 2014, and has covered a wide range of technical and substantive issues within the modern award system.

In the review the FWC must apply the 'modern awards objective' in FW Act section 134. This requires the FWC to ensure that modern awards, together with the National Employment Standards, provide a fair and relevant minimum safety net of terms and conditions. There are a range of factors that must be considered in making this assessment, including *inter alia* 'the need to provide additional remuneration for employees working overtime; or employees working unsocial, irregular or unpredictable hours; or employees working on weekends or public holidays; or employees working shifts' (FW Act section 134(da)).

The present decision involves the review of penalty rates providing for increased remuneration for work performed on Saturdays, Sundays and public holidays in six modern awards: *Fast Food Industry Award 2010, General Retail Industry Award 2010, Hospitality Industry (General) Award 2010, Pharmacy Industry Award 2010, Registered and Licensed Clubs Award 2010*, and *Restaurant Industry Award 2010*. Penalty rates for work on Saturdays, Sundays or public holidays provide for employees to be paid for work on those days at between 125 per cent to 225 per cent of the base rate of pay. The actual rate received depends on the modern award applied and whether the employee is engaged on a permanent or casual basis.

Employer groups sought reductions to the penalty rates applicable to work performed on Saturdays, Sundays and public holidays across all of the relevant awards. The changes were resisted by unions and their employee members.

The proceedings involved 39 days of hearings, and the FWC received in addition to submissions from the parties (those covered by the relevant awards) almost 6,000 contributions from the public, Members of Parliament and State governments, unions, student organizations, community groups, small businesses, churches and industry groups. The FCW heard expert evidence from 143 lay and expert witnesses and commissioned its own research into industry profiles and changing patterns of work, including the increased rates of work on weekends and public holidays.

Decision

The Full Bench of the FWC determined to leave Saturday penalty rates in the relevant awards unchanged. Penalty rates for Sunday and public holiday engagements were proportionately reduced in four modern awards: *Fast Food Industry Award 2010, General Retail Industry Award 2010, Hospitality Industry (General) Award 2010*, and *Pharmacy Industry Award 2010.* The reductions varied but were generally 25 percentage points to 50 percentage points (where % is measured in respect of the increase against the standard rate of pay).

Law Applied

Fair Work Act 2009

Section 134 The modern awards objective

[...]

(1) The FWC must ensure that modern awards, together with the National Employment Standards, provide a fair and relevant minimum safety net of terms and conditions, taking into account: [...]

    (da) the need to provide additional remuneration for:

        (i) employees working overtime; or

        (ii) employees working unsocial, irregular or unpredictable hours; or

        (iii) employees working on weekends or public holidays; or

        (iv) employees working shifts; and

  (e) the principle of equal remuneration for work of equal or comparable value; and

  (f) the likely impact of any exercise of modern award powers on business, including on productivity, employment costs and the regulatory burden; and

  (g) the need to ensure a simple, easy to understand, stable and sustainable modern award system for Australia that avoids unnecessary overlap of modern awards; and

  (h) the likely impact of any exercise of modern award powers on employment growth, inflation and the sustainability, performance and competitiveness of the national economy.

This is the *modern awards objective.*

Section 156 Four yearly reviews of modern awards to be conducted
Timing of 4 yearly reviews

(1) The FWC must conduct a *4 yearly review of modern awards* starting as soon as practicable after each 4th anniversary of the commencement of this Part.

What has to be done in a 4 yearly review?

(2) In a 4 yearly review of modern awards, the FWC:

    (a) must review all modern awards; and

(b) may make:
  (i) one or more determinations varying modern awards; and
  (ii) one or more modern awards; and
  (iii) one or more determinations revoking modern awards; and
(c) must not review, or make a determination to vary, a default fund term of a modern award.

JUDGEMENT

[Fair Work Commission, Full Bench: Ross, J (President), Catanzariti, VP, Asbury, DP, Hampton, C and Lee, C]

2. The Decision: An Overview

2.1 The Legislative context and proposed changes in penalty rates

[34] Section 156 of the FW Act provides that the Commission must conduct a 4 yearly review of modern awards (the Review). Subsection 156(2) deals with what must be done in the Review and provides that the Commission must review all modern awards and may, among other things, make determinations varying modern awards.

[35] This decision deals with the review of the weekend and public holiday penalty rates and some related matters, in a number of Hospitality and Retail awards.

[36] The Commission's task in the Review is to decide whether a particular modern award achieves the modern awards objective. If it does not then it is to be varied such that it only includes terms that are 'necessary to achieve the modern awards objective' (s.138).

[37] The modern awards objective in s.134(1) of the FW Act is central to the Review. The modern awards objective is to 'ensure that modern awards, together with the National Employment Standards (NES) provide a *fair* and *relevant* minimum safety net of terms and conditions', taking into account the particular considerations identified in sections 134(1)(a) to (h). Fairness in this context is to be assessed from the perspective of the employees and employers covered by the modern award in question. 'Relevant' is intended to convey that a modern award should be suited to contemporary circumstances. We deal with the relevant legislative provisions in more detail in Chapter 3.

[38] Historically, industrial tribunals have expressed the rationale for penalty rates in terms of both the need to compensate employees

for working outside 'normal hours' (the compensatory element) and to deter employers from scheduling work outside 'normal' hours (the deterrence element).

[39] Having regard to more recent authority, the terms of the modern awards objective, and the scheme of the FW Act, we have concluded that deterrence is no longer a relevant consideration in the setting of weekend and public holiday penalty rates. We accept that the imposition of a penalty rate may have the *effect* of deterring employers from scheduling work at specified times or on certain days, but that is a consequence of the imposition of an additional payment for working at such times or on such days, it is not the *objective* of those additional payments. Compensating employees for the disutility associated with working on weekends and public holidays is a primary consideration in the setting of weekend and public holiday penalty rates.

[40] We note that the Productivity Commission has expressed a different view in respect of public holiday penalty rates:

> '... by definition, genuine public holidays are intended to serve a special community role and, as such, there are strong grounds to limit the expectation that they are for working. In that sense, the original concept of deterrence continues to have relevance'.

[41] We accept that public holidays, by their nature, are intended 'to serve a special community role' and that the expectation (and practice) is that the vast majority of employees do not work on public holidays. But these features do not support the adoption of deterrence as an objective in setting public holiday penalty rates. However, these features are relevant to determining the amount of compensation to be provided to employees who work on public holidays, given the additional disutility associated with working on a day when the vast majority of other employees are enjoying a day of leisure.

[42] A central contention advanced by the Shop, Distributive and Allied Employees Association (SDA) and United Voice in these proceedings is that before the Commission can vary a modern award in the Review, it must first be satisfied that since the making of the modern award there has been a material change in circumstances pertaining to the operation or effect of the award such that the modern award is no longer meeting the modern awards objective (the 'material change in circumstances test'). If adopted the proposed test would require the proponent of a variation to establish that there has been a material change in circumstances since the modern award was made. The proposed 'material change in circumstances' test

seeks to place a constraint on the discretion conferred by s.156 which is not warranted by the terms of this section or the relevant statutory context and purpose. There is no such express or implied requirement in s.156.

[43] We reject the proposition advanced by the Unions. The adoption of the proposed 'material change in circumstances test' would obfuscate the Commission's primary task in the Review, determining whether the modern award achieves the modern awards objective. To adopt such a test would add words into s.156 in circumstances where it is not necessary to do so in order to achieve the legislative purpose. For completeness we record our agreement with the point advanced by the Australian Industry Group (Ai Group) [...] that the variation of a modern award may be warranted if it was established that there was a 'material change in circumstances' since the modern award was made, but the establishment of such a change is not a condition precedent to the variation of a modern award in the Review.

[44] As mentioned, the modern awards objective is central to the Review. In determining whether an award achieves the modern awards objective the Commission must take into account a range of considerations, including those set out in s.134(1)(da). Relevantly, s.134(1)(da)(iii) requires that we take into account the 'need to provide additional remuneration' for 'employees working on weekends or public holidays'.

[45] An assessment of 'the need to provide additional remuneration' to employees working in the circumstances identified requires a consideration of a range of matters, including:

> (i) the impact of working at such times or on such days on the employees concerned (i.e. the extent of the disutility);

> (ii) the terms of the relevant modern award, in particular whether it already compensates employees for working at such times or on such days (e.g. through 'loaded' minimum rates or the payment of an industry allowance which is intended to compensate employees for the requirement to work at such times or on such days); and

> (iii) the extent to which working at such times or on such days is a feature of the industry regulated by the particular modern award.

[46] Assessing the extent of the disutility of working at such times or on such days (issue (i) above) includes an assessment of the impact of such work on employee health and work-life balance, taking into account the preferences of the employees for working at those times.

[47] Section 134(1)(da) speaks of the 'need to provide additional remuneration' for employees performing work in the circumstances

mentioned. We note that the minority in the *Restaurants 2014 Penalty Rates decision* made the following observation about s.134(1)(da): '...the objective requires additional remuneration for working on weekends'.

[48] To the extent that the above passage suggests that s.134(1)(da) '*requires* additional remuneration for working on weekends', we respectfully disagree. We acknowledge that the provision speaks of 'the *need* for additional remuneration' and that such language suggests that additional remuneration is required for employees working in the circumstances identified in paragraphs 134(1)(da)(i) to (iv). But the expression must be construed in context and the context tells against the proposition that s.134(1)(da) *requires* that each modern award must provide additional remuneration for working in the identified circumstances.

[49] The various employer parties have sought reductions in Sunday and public holiday penalty rates. These claims are summarised in Tables 1 and 74. There were also some claims to vary the penalty payments for early/late night work in some awards.

[50] Generally speaking, no changes are sought in relation to Saturday penalty rates.

[51] We have reviewed the Saturday penalty rates in 4 of the 6 modern awards before us and (subject to the observations at [65] and [66]) we are satisfied that the existing Saturday penalty rates achieve the modern awards objective – they provide a fair and relevant minimum safety net. [...]

[52] Variations to modern awards must be justified on their merits. The extent of the merit argument required will depend on the circumstances. Significant changes where merit is reasonably contestable should be supported by an analysis of the relevant legislative provisions and, where feasible, probative evidence.

[53] We have decided that the existing Sunday penalty rates in 4 of the modern awards before us (the *Hospitality, Fast Food, Retail and Pharmacy Awards*) do not achieve the modern awards objective, as they do not provide a fair and relevant minimum safety net.

[54] Except in the *Fast Food Award* (for the reasons set out at [1394]–[1397]), we do not propose to reduce the Sunday penalty rates to the same level as the Saturday penalty rates. As we mention shortly, for many workers Sunday work has a higher level of disutility than Saturday work, though the extent of the disutility is much less than in times past. In this regard we also note that it is implicit in the claims advanced by most of the employer interests that they accept the proposition that the disutility associated with Sunday work is *higher* than the disutility associated with

Saturday work. If this was not the case then they would have proposed that the penalty rates for Sunday and Saturday work be the same, but they did not.

[55] The reductions in Sunday penalty rates we have determined are set out below:

		Sunday Penalty Rate
Hospitality Award	Full & part time employees	175% → 150%
	Casual employees	no change
Fast Food Award	Level 1 employees only	150% → 125%
	Full & part time employees	175% → 150%
	Casual employees	no change
Retail Award	Full & part time employees	200% → 150%
	Casual employees	200% → 175%
Pharmacy Award*	Full & part time employees	200% → 150%
	Casual employees	225% → 175%

* 7.00 am – 9.00 pm only

[56] In relation to the *Fast Food Industry Award 2010*, for reasons associated with the preferences of the relevant employees and the limited impact of Sunday work upon those employees (see Chapter 7.5), we have decided to reduce the Sunday penalty rate, for level 1 employees from 150 per cent to 125 per cent (for full-time and part-time employees) and from 175 per cent to 150 per cent (for casual employees). We do not propose to change the Sunday penalty rate for Level 2 and 3 employees.

[57] The differential treatment of Level 1 versus Level 2 and 3 employees is on the basis that Level 2 and 3 employees experience a higher level of disutility associated with Sunday work than that experienced by level 1 employees. The evidence supports the retention of the current Sunday penalty rate for level 2 and 3 employees. In this context we note that level 2 and 3 employees are, generally speaking, regarded as 'career' employees with the major chains whereas casual and part-time crew members (level 1 employees) are usually regarded as 'non-career' employees. [...]

[61] We have also decided to reduce the public holiday penalty rates in the *Hospitality and Retail Awards* (except for the *Clubs Award*, for the reasons set out at [1915]).

[62] We also conclude that the two-tiered approach to public holiday penalty rates advanced by the Hospitality Employers lacks merit. The

distinction sought to be drawn between those public holidays expressly mentioned in s.115(1)(a) and the other days declared or prescribed by or under a law of a State or Territory as a public holiday (s.115(1)(b)), is illusory. In that regard we concur with the views expressed in the *1994 Public Holidays Test Case decisions* and the *Modern Awards Review 2012 – Public Holidays decision*, that, in essence, the number and standardisation of public holidays across Australia is primarily an issue for the Commonwealth, State and Territory legislatures.

[63] The effect of our decision in respect of public holiday penalty rates is shown (in marked up format) in Table 2 below.

Table 2

	Public holiday penalty rates (%)	
	Full & part-time	*Casual*
Hospitality Award (cl. 32)	~~250~~ 225	~~275~~ 250
Restaurant Award (cl. 34)	~~250~~ 225	250
Clubs Award (cl. 29)	250	250
Retail Award (cl. 29)	~~250~~ 225	~~275/250~~ 250
Fast Food Award (cl.30)	~~250~~ 225	~~275~~ 250
Pharmacy Award (cl. 31)	~~250~~ 225	~~275~~ 250

[64] The changes we propose to make to Sunday and public holiday penalty rates will result in greater consistency in penalty rate settings in the *Hospitality and Retail Awards*.

[65] In each of the Sunday and public holiday penalty rates we have fixed we have adopted what the *Productivity Commission Inquiry Report: Workplace Relations Framework* (PC Final Report) describes as the 'default approach' to setting the appropriate rate for casual employees (see [333]–[338]). Under this approach the rate of pay for casual employees is always 25 percentage points above the rate of pay for non-casual employees. Hence if the Sunday penalty rate for full-time and part-time employees is 150 per cent, the Sunday rate for casuals will be 150 + 25 = 175 per cent.

[66] We note that the approach we have adopted may have implications for the rate paid to casuals for Saturday work under the *Retail Award*. We refer to that issue at [1716]–[1720]. It may also result in a shift from casual to part-time employment in respect of those employed in the modern awards which we propose to vary.

[67] The decision to reduce Sunday and public holiday penalty rates in these awards is based on our conclusions with respect to the common evidence (see Chapter 6) and our assessment of the evidence in relation to each of these particular awards (see Chapters 7.2, 7.5, 8.2 and 8.3).

[68] In Chapter 6 we consider the 'common evidence' adduced in these proceedings and deal with the incidence and effects of weekend work and the employment effects of reducing penalty rates. The following propositions emerge from the common evidence before us:

> 1. There is a disutility associated with weekend work, above that applicable to work performed from Monday to Friday. Generally speaking, for many workers Sunday work has a higher level of disutility than Saturday work, though the extent of the disutility is much less than in times past.

> 2. We agree with the assessment in the PC Final Report that there are likely to be some positive employment effects from a reduction in penalty rates, though it is difficult to quantify the precise effect. Any potential positive employment effects from a reduction in penalty rates are likely to be reduced due to substitution and other effects.

[69] As to proposition 1 above, we are aware that our conclusion is different to that in the PC Final Report. However, in the proceedings before us we have had the opportunity to consider evidence not available to the Productivity Commission, such as the Pezzullo Weekend Work Report, the Rose Report and the Sands Report in addition to a substantial amount of lay employer and employee evidence. None of the above reports concluded that the activities conducted on, and attitudes towards, Saturdays and Sundays were identical.

[70] As to proposition 2, the Hospitality and Retail Employers' lay evidence supports the proposition that the current level of Sunday penalty rates has led employers to reduce labour costs associated with Sunday trading by imposing a number of operational limitations, such as:
- restricting trading hours;
- lowering staff levels; and
- restrictions on the type and range of services provided.

[71] The Hospitality and Retail Employers' lay evidence also supports the proposition that a reduction in penalty rates is likely to lead to:
- increased trading hours on Sundays and public holidays;
- a reduction in the hours worked by some owner operations;
- an increase in the level and range of services offered on Sundays and public holidays; and
- an increase in overall hours worked.

[72] We do not suggest that these changes will apply uniformly across all hospitality and retail businesses. The actual impact of a reduction in Sunday penalty rates will depend on the circumstances applying to individual businesses.

[73] As to public holiday penalty rates, we note that the disutility of working on public holidays is greater than the disutility of working on Sundays (which in turn is greater than Saturday work). The notion of relative disutility supports a proportionate approach to the fixation of weekend and public holiday penalty rates. In determining the appropriate penalty rate for public holiday work we have had regard to the level of Sunday penalty rates in the *Hospitality and Retail Awards* (after applying the decisions we have made to reduce those rates).

[74] We also note that the disutility in relation to public holidays has been ameliorated somewhat by the introduction of the statutory right to refuse to work on such days, on reasonable grounds. Contrary to ABI's submission, we would not characterise s.114(3) of the FW Act as making public holiday work 'voluntary' (it is a limited right to refuse to work, on reasonable grounds), but it is still a significant contextual matter which was not taken into account when the existing 250 per cent penalty was set.

[75] In addition, public holiday work is more common in the Hospitality and Retail sectors and, on the evidence before us, reducing the public holiday penalty rate will increase employment and have a number of positive effects on business.

[76] It is important to appreciate that the conclusions we have reached in relation to the weekend and public holiday penalty rates in the *Hospitality and Retail Awards* is largely based on the circumstances relating to these particular awards. The Hospitality and Retail sectors have a number of characteristics which distinguish them from other industries.

[77] The distinguishing characteristics of the Hospitality and Retail sectors are alluded to in the PC Final Report, where it explains the rationale for focusing on the 'HERRC' (hospitality, entertainment, retail, restaurants and cafes) industries.

> '... the appropriate *level* for regulated penalty rates for weekend work – particularly on Sundays in a number of discretionary consumer service industries – has become a highly contested and controversial issue. The industries of greatest concern are hospitality, entertainment, retail, restaurants and cafes (HERRC). These are industries where consumer expectations of access to services has expanded over time so that the costs of penalty rates affect consumer amenity in ways they did not when penalty rates were first introduced. Such industries are also important

sources of entry-level jobs for, among others, relatively unskilled casual employees and young people (particularly students) needing flexible working arrangements. The provision of discretionary, and therefore demand responsive, services on weekends is less frequent in most other industries, which is a key (but not only) rationale for a focus of concerns on the HERRC industries. It is notable that the FWC is currently also considering appropriate penalty rates in awards, and that their focus almost exactly matches the group of industries that the Productivity Commission has identified as the most relevant'.

[78] The data on weekend work show that workers in the Retail and Hospitality sectors are more likely to work on weekends than workers in other industries. [...]

[80] Data on the characteristics of employees in these industries presented in Chapters 7.1 and 8.1 show that they are more likely to be female, younger (under 25 years), work part-time hours, be employed on a casual basis and be award reliant than employees in other industries. Employees in these industries are also more likely to be low paid.

[81] Given the distinguishing characteristics of the Hospitality and Retail sectors, the decisions we have made in respect of the *Hospitality and Retail Awards* provide no warrant for the variation of penalty rates in other modern awards. Each case must be determined on its merits. We note the views expressed in the PC Final Report in this regard:

> 'There is no case for common penalty rates across all industries. The Commission is not recommending a reduction in the Sunday penalty rates beyond HERRC. Regulated penalty rates as currently constructed for essential services and many other industries are justifiable. The original justifications have not altered materially: they align with working arrangements that often involve rotating shifts across the whole week, are not likely to reduce service availability meaningfully, are commensurate with the skills of the employees, and are unlikely to lead to job losses'.

[Source: [2017] FWCFB 1001 issued 23 February 2017 (all footnotes omitted)]

ANNOTATION

Under the system of industrial relations that operated in Australia through most of the twentieth century, the employment conditions of workers were predominantly set by awards created through processes of conciliation and arbitration of industrial disputes. While collective bargaining did occur, it was largely in the shadow of the conciliation and arbitration system.

Commonly major industrial reform for workers (and employers) was achieved through 'test cases'. Disputes would be brought before the Australian Industrial Relations Commission (AIRC, the forerunner of the FWC) for resolution through arbitration. Where major changes were awarded by the AIRC in resolution of a dispute, subsequently these would be introduced into other awards so that the gains would be shared by all workers covered by the system.

With the shift to enterprise bargaining in Australia in the 1990's, the role of the award system changed from the establishment of wages and conditions for workers to the setting of minimum terms and conditions – against which parties were encouraged to engage in bargaining. A more dramatic change occurred in 2006 when the *Workplace Relations Amendment (Work Choices) Act, 2005*, removed the power of the AIRC to conciliate and arbitrate industrial disputes, and essentially froze the award system in time.

In 2008 the AIRC was directed by the recently elected Australian Labor Party Government to 'modernise' the award system. The thousands of awards which were created through the processes of dispute resolution were to be consolidated into a smaller set of short, stream-lined 'modern awards' setting minimum terms and conditions for workers in the form of a safety net. Over the course of 2009, the AIRC consolidated the awards, producing 110 modern awards that came into effect on 1 January 2010. While the awards retained the flavour of the old award system, they were statutory instruments. Review of these instruments is no longer a process intrinsically connected to the parties covered by the awards – instead, they are reviewed according to a statutory timetable (with more limited processes for party initiated review).

The 4 yearly review of modern awards has provided the FWC with the opportunity to identify and correct a range of problems that emerged in the modern award system after it first took effect. This is unsurprising given that the AIRC had only around 12 months to consolidate thousands of awards into just 110. The process of review has been lengthy – having commenced in 2012 and still being underway in 2017.

The decision commented on here is one aspect of the whole review process. The actual decision itself (the decision summary is extracted here) is 551 pages long and contains lengthy economic analysis.

Penalty rates payable to workers engaged in weekend and public holiday work are a long-standing feature of the Australian award system. They were originally introduced both to 'deter' the engagement of workers on weekends and public holidays, and to 'compensate' workers for having to work when others were not so obliged. However, the decision explores the changing nature of work, and society, such that it should no longer be considered appropriate for penalty rates to act as a 'deterrent'. Business and consumer expectations with respect to the availability of goods and services on weekends and public holidays have shifted dramatically.

Instead of 'deterrence', weekend and public holiday work is viewed through the prism of 'disutility' to the worker concerned – and the disutility associated with working on these days is seen as hierarchical with Saturday work attracting the least disutility, followed by Sunday and finally public holidays. Furthermore, there is acknowledgement in the decision that high Sunday and public holiday penalty rates may act as a deterrent to employing workers on those days, with small business operators in particular choosing not to open, or to operate their businesses with fewer employees engaged.

The decision to reduce penalty rates on Sundays and public holidays in industries with high rates of weekend work recognises the profound shift in the working patterns and consumption habits of Australians. It also acknowledges the emergence of a more secular society. However, it will also leave many workers worse off as the financial benefits of working on Sundays and public holidays are reduced.

The decision has been highly controversial with employer groups and the federal Government supporting the changes, and the union movement and the Australian Labor Party in opposition seeking to either overturn or ameliorate the effect of the decision.

POLAND

Supreme Court
Judgement of 17 November 2016, II PK 227/15

The concept of drivers' flat rate for overnight subsistence allowance in international transport

HEADNOTES

Facts

K.G, W.P, M.G, K.M. and S.A. (plaintiffs) were employed in N. sp. z o.o. (a limited liability company) (defendant) as drivers in international transport. Remuneration-related issues for employees of N. sp. z o.o. were governed by consecutive remuneration schemes. Since 1 September 2006 international drivers in N. sp. z o.o. had been entitled to "allowances" for each day spent in official travel. The amount of the allowance for travelling abroad was €40 per each full day, which was consistent with the level established in the Ordinance of 19 December 2002 issued by the Minister of Labour and Social Policy on the amount and conditions of determining receivables, to which the employees of local government units financed by the State budget are entitled on account of official travel outside the country.

On 1 April 2010 a new remuneration scheme was introduced in N. sp. z o.o. with effect from 15 April. Subsequent to that date the amount of allowance was reduced to €38, in which it was clarified that €13 was intended to cover the cost of meals and €25 to cover other social costs. The new remuneration scheme defined the allowance as the amount supposed to cover all increased costs of living while travelling abroad. Under the new remuneration scheme for the time spent on official travel employees were entitled to the allowances set out in the Ordinance for State-budget sector employees – meaning a daily subsistence allowance and a flat rate for overnight subsistence allowance. The only exception was that drivers who had lorries equipped with the right place to sleep were not entitled to the flat rate for overnight subsistence allowance if they did not sleep in a room in a hotel or hostel. Since 1 January 2011 – under an agreement between trade unions and the management of N. Sp. z o.o. signed to end a collective labour dispute – the amount of the allowances was increased to €41 per day, of which €14 were to cover the cost of meals and €27 were to cover other social costs. Since 1 March 2012 – under an agreement subsequent to the above-mentioned one – the amount of the allowances was increased again to €42.

The fleet of the defendant's vehicles consisted of Renault lorries, in which the cabins were adjusted to accommodate two drivers, equipped with 2 beds each being two meters long and one meter wide, with air-conditioning in working order while driving, and heating and ventilation working while stationary. The cabins were around 170 cm high and furnished with shelves for clothes and food. In the cabin there was the possibility to have a small fridge or TV. The defendant did not equip the lorries with bed linen, but paid the drivers a monthly equivalent for washing and cleaning agents.

Within the litigious period, the plaintiffs undertook travel to several EU countries. Each of them was travelling alone (called one-driver travels) and the travel lasted around three weeks each. The plaintiffs slept in the cabins of their lorries usually at petrol stations, car-parks or places indicated by the defendant, which was agreed on when they entered into employment. Rarely did the drivers sleep behind the client's company. The choice of the place for sleeping was dependent on the working time of the driver. The plaintiffs did not take any hotel, motel or hostel rooms, and they did not have any receipts for the costs of overnight stays. During the stays at petrol stations, car-parks and the defendant's places, the plaintiffs used the sanitary facilities available at those places. Most often the charge for parking – which was refunded by the defendant – included shower and toilet facilities and the social minimum.

In its judgement the Regional Court rejected K.G, W.P, M.G, K.M. and S.A.'s claim for payment of the flat rate for the overnight subsistence allowance and ordered the plaintiffs to pay the costs of proceedings. The Court established that the plaintiffs had known and accepted the fact that the €40 per diem (subsequently changed to 38, then 41, then 42 Euros) was to reimburse all the expenses connected with their travel – including costs of accommodation. The Court noted that the plaintiffs accepted the practice of sleeping in the cabin of the lorry and followed it without exceptions and without questioning. Within the whole period of employment the plaintiffs had always stayed in the cabin of the lorry at night time and had never claimed a flat rate for overnight subsistence allowance.

The plaintiffs lodged an appeal against the Regional Court's judgement with the Court of Appeal, which dismissed that appeal. The Court of Appeal shared the reasoning given by the court of the first instance and stressed that the aim of paying allowances to international drivers was not to provide extra benefits, but to reimburse the additional costs and expenses connected with their business travel. Pay provisions in N. sp. z o.o. regulated the allowances payable to drivers as reimbursement of the costs of overnight stay, which were not explicitly named flat rates for overnight subsistence allowance but were to achieve the same goal. All the drivers (including the plaintiffs) received those allowances. In the view of the Court of Appeal the plaintiffs were not entitled to higher allowances because the sum that they were paid reimbursed all the additional costs they had borne during business travel.

The plaintiffs lodged a cassation appeal against the judgement of the Regional Court to the Supreme Court. The plaintiffs requested the Supreme Court to quash the impugned judgement and to allow their claim in full, or to quash the impugned judgement and remit the case to the Regional Court. In the complaint the plaintiffs questioned the correctness of not applying the Ordinance of 19 December 2002 of the Minister of Labour and Social Policy on the amount and conditions of determining receivables, to which the employees of local government units financed by the State budget are entitled on account of official travel outside the country, in situations where the plaintiffs slept abroad and the employer did not provide them with free overnight accommodation. Apart from this, the plaintiffs argued that the remuneration scheme of 15 April 2010 had not entered into force as the condition of terminating the terms and conditions of work and pay with notice had not been satisfied.

Decision

The Supreme Court quashed the impugned judgement in part where it needed analysis to determine if the temporary decrease of the equivalent of allowances and flat rates for overnight accommodation below €40 to €38 had been legitimate. It therefore remitted the case in this part to the District Court and dismissed the remainder of the cassation appeal. As for the quashed part of the judgement, the Supreme Court ruled that the conditions of a remuneration scheme, which are less favourable for employees than previous ones shall take effect by the method of termination with notice of the previous conditions of a contract of employment or any other instrument that constitutes the basis of an employment relationship. As for the part of the lower court's judgement that was dismissed, the Supreme Court ruled that moderating the level of a flat rate for the overnight subsistence allowance for international transport drivers is legitimate on account of the social equipment installed in the lorry cabin but in such a proportionate manner so that the higher the standard of the cabin amenities, the lower the allowance.

Law Applied

Polish Labour Code

Article 77^2

(1) An employer who employs at least 20 persons as employees who are not covered by any single-employer or multi-employer collective labour agreement that defines the rules of remuneration for work and other work-related benefits to the extent and in a manner that may be used as a basis for determination of the individual terms and conditions of their contracts of employment, shall determine the terms and conditions of remuneration for work in a remuneration scheme.

(2) In the remuneration scheme, the employer may also define other work-related benefits and the rules for granting those benefits.

(3) The remuneration scheme shall remain in effect until employees are covered by a single-employer or multi-employer collective labour agreement that defines the rules of remuneration for work and other work-related benefits to the extent and in a manner that may be used as a basis for determination of the individual terms and conditions of their contracts of employment.

(4) The remuneration scheme is determined by the employer. If a trade union is active in the employer's establishment, the employer shall agree the remuneration scheme with the trade union.

(5) The provisions of [...] Article 241^{13} [...] shall apply accordingly to a remuneration scheme.

(6) The remuneration scheme shall come into effect two weeks after the date of its announcement to the employees, in accordance with the standard procedure adopted by the employer.

Article 241^{13}

(1) As of the effective date of an agreement, the more favourable terms and conditions thereof shall replace, by operation of law, the terms and conditions of a contract of employment or any other instrument which constitutes a basis of an employment relationship, arising from the previously applicable provisions of labour law.

(2) Those terms and conditions of an agreement, which are less favourable for employees shall take effect by way of termination with notice of the previous terms and conditions of a contract of employment or any other instrument that constitutes the basis of an employment relationship. When the previous terms and conditions of a contract of employment or any other instrument that constitutes the basis of an employment relationship are terminated with notice, the provisions that introduce restrictions on the termination of its terms and conditions shall not apply.

Article 77^{5}

(1) An employee who performs work assigned by the employer away from the location of the employer's registered office, or away from the permanent workplace, is entitled to reimbursement of any expenses related to business travel.

(2) The competent minister in charge of labour shall define, by way of a regulation, the amount and terms of determination of payments due to an employee of the budgetary unit of the State or the local authorities in relation to business travel in Poland and abroad. The regulation shall in particular define the amount of travel allowances, considering the time of travel, and in the case of foreign business travel also the currency in which travel allowances will be paid and an accommodation limit per country, as well as the terms and conditions of reimbursement of the cost of travel, accommodation and other expenses.

(3) The terms and conditions of payment of business travel allowances to an employee of an employer other than an employee of the budgetary unit of the State or the local authorities shall be defined in a collective labour agreement or a remuneration scheme, or in a contract of employment if the employer is not covered by any collective labour agreement or is under no obligation to adopt a remuneration scheme.

(4) The amount of per diem travel allowances for business travel in Poland and abroad defined in a collective labour agreement, remuneration scheme, or contract of employment, cannot be lower than the amount of per diem travel allowances for business travel in Poland defined for employees of the budgetary unit of the State or the local authorities.

(5) If a collective labour agreement, remuneration scheme or contract of employment contains no provisions determining the terms and conditions of payment of business travel allowances, an employee is entitled to business travel allowances in accordance with the provisions defined by way of a regulation of the competent minister in charge of labour.

JUDGEMENT

The Supreme Court first stated that the terms and conditions of the remuneration scheme, which are less favourable for employees than previous ones shall take effect by way of termination with notice of the previous terms and conditions of a contract of employment or any other instrument that constitutes the basis of an employment relationship. Changing the conditions of employment to the disadvantage of the plaintiffs by decreasing the level of allowances paid to international drivers from €40 to €38 per diem needs individual terminations with notice or the making of clear individual agreements with each of the employees. Neither the possibility of familiarizing themselves with the text of a changed remuneration scheme nor "being aware of the content of the employment relationship between the drivers and their employer" meant that the employer had obtained the plaintiffs' acceptance of the changed conditions of employment. Obtaining consent for less favourable conditions of employment from employees cannot be presumed *per facta concludentia* if established facts oppose this conclusion.

Secondly the Supreme Court stressed that it is legitimate to determine one overall flat rate to reimburse all increased costs and expenses while on business travel if it is known by both parties of the agreement that the flat rate is an overall one. The fact that in the remuneration scheme introduced on 1 April 2010 it was clearly stated that within the total sum of €38 Euro, €13 were to cover the cost of meals and €25 to cover other social costs, proved that paying one overall flat rate to reimburse all the costs was a rule practised in the enterprise. This understanding of allowances was confirmed also in the agreements made by N. Sp. z o.o. with the trade unions active in the employer's establishment when negotiating to end the collective labour disputes. In those agreements the overall sum of €38 (later changed to 41 and 42 Euros) was divided into increased costs of meals and other increased social costs which preserved the previous practice in the enterprise; this proved both the plaintiffs' knowledge and acceptance of the fact that the allowance was to reimburse all the costs and expenses connected with business travel.

Separately the Supreme Court discussed the level of the allowance. The plaintiffs claimed that, in any case, they were entitled to the flat rate for overnight subsistence allowance at the level of the minimum established in the Ordinance of 19 December 2002 of the Minister of Labour and Social Policy – which was €30 per each night during international transport instead of €25 or €28, which they were paid on the basis of the employer's consecutive remuneration schemes. The Supreme Court did not share the plaintiffs' view and ruled that this claim was not legitimate. According to the Supreme Court, providing lorry drivers with a decent place to sleep in a professionally equipped lorry cabin – if the driver sleeps in the cabin and does not rent a hotel or hostel room – must influence the level of the flat rate for overnight subsistence allowance. Although providing lorry drivers with a decent place to sleep in the lorry cabin does not constitute providing free accommodation by an employer, it must be taken into consideration while deciding the level of allowance on condition that the driver has the possibility of using sanitary facilities at the stationary place. Professionally adjusted lorry cabins with the possibility to use sanitary facilities available in car-parks, transport bases or petrol stations provides international drivers who lead professionally mobile lives with the social and living minimum similar to the standard of camping. The argument that usually entrepreneurs invest huge sums of money buying and using new lorries with professionally equipped cabins must be taken into consideration when deciding the level of the flat rate for the overnight subsistence allowance for drivers. Although the flat rate for the overnight subsistence allowance is generally not dependent on bearing the costs at the level of the flat rate, nevertheless the level of equivalents being paid on the basis of collective labour agreements, remuneration schemes or individual agreements may and ought to take into consideration certain, especially innovative, standards that are ensured by the employer in order to give lorry drivers the possibility of comfortable sleep in the lorry cabin while staying in the car-parks adjusted to overnight stays. As the Supreme Court held, the higher the standard of the cabin the lower the allowance for the driver. This way the allowance paid to drivers using lorries with well-equipped cabins could be lower than that paid by an employer who has not invested in the equipment and amenities.

ANNOTATION

The judgement of the Supreme Court dated 17 November 2016 closes a whole set of Polish judgements connected with allowances for drivers in international transport. Although these judgements were not unanimous and the arguments put forward by the Court did not always coincide, one may say that a jurisdictional line had been established, and the judgement dated 17 November 2016 subsumes the latest and most average attitude of the Supreme Court towards the matter. The judgement dispels the doubts which had arisen in the judicial practice and legal doctrine and decides that moderating the level of a flat rate for the overnight subsistence allowance for international transport drivers is legitimate, due to the social equipment installed in the lorry cabin in such a proportionate manner so that the higher the standard of the cabin amenities, the lower the allowance.

Analysing earlier jurisprudence of the Supreme Court it must be noted that on 12 June 2014 the Supreme Court – in a resolution issued by the full Court of seven judges – ruled that providing lorry drivers with a place to sleep in the lorry cabin does not constitute providing free accommodation within the meaning of Article 9(4) of the Ordinance of 19 December 2002 of the Minister of Labour and Social Policy. Article 9(4) of the Ordinance lays on the employer the obligation to provide drivers in international transport with free accommodation. As a result the employee is entitled to reimbursement of the costs of the overnight stay under conditions and at the level established by the Ordinance or other – more advantageous – provisions established in employment contract, collective labour agreement or other labour law frameworks (II PZP 1/14). That 2014 resolution strengthened the previously predominant jurisdictional approach, but nevertheless was thoroughly criticized in the doctrine of law debates (although there were some critiques supporting the view of the Supreme Court). The argument that lay behind that 2014 resolution was that in the 21st century no employer should gain advantages from insisting on having its employees sleep in the cabin of the lorry instead of renting a hotel or hostel room while on business travel. At the same time there were a few judgements of the Supreme Court in which it was established that equipping the car with the place to sleep, if it is used by the driver at night, excludes the possibility of claiming any compensation for the lack of the hotel or hostel room (for example, the Supreme Court judgement of 4 June 2013, II PK 296/12). Underlying this judgement was the reasoning that in the regulations concerning the working time of drivers, the daily uninterrupted rest period was set at 11 hours as a minimum and this time could be used in the car if it was parked in a car-park and equipped with a place to sleep. Regulations concerning the working time of drivers do not demand any additional conditions bearing in mind that the work of drivers depends on constant driving and staying in places chosen by the driver after finishing of the driving time.

This annotated Supreme Court judgement dated 17 November 2016 seems to be a kind of compromise between the above-mentioned previous approaches of the Supreme Court. On the one hand, the Court stresses that providing lorry drivers with the place to sleep in the lorry cabin does not constitute providing free accommodation, which means the driver is still entitled to reimbursement of the costs of accommodation in the form of a flat rate; but on the other hand, the Court states that the level of this flat rate may depend on the standard of the cabin. The Supreme Court's view here deserves approval for several reasons.

First and foremost it strikes a good balance between two very important but partly contradictory interests – of an employee to rest in a properly suitable place and of an employer to reduce the costs of transport. Secondly, it reflects the reality that drivers do not rent hotel or hostel rooms, but of their own choice opt for the cabin as the place to sleep treating amount for the overnight subsistence allowance as a supplement to their remuneration rather than as a reimbursement of costs. Linking the level of the allowance to the standard of the cabin encourages employers to invest in equipment, which allows the drivers to rest in improved social conditions. In practice such an attitude improves the standard of the drivers' rest period rather than obliging employers to pay the drivers for hotel rooms, which the drivers do not use. The previous attitude had led to the abuses in which the social standard of rest periods of the drivers was poorer and the reimbursement did not serve the purpose for which it had been introduced.

De lege ferenda it must be stressed that the subject examined in this judgement needs legislative intervention. Along with the technical improvements and innovations regarding international transport driving there should be legislative changes; the law should reflect the current state of affairs. The link decided by the Supreme Court in this judgement, according to which moderating the level of the flat rate for the overnight subsistence allowance for drivers in international transport is legitimate on account of the social equipment in the lorry cabin so that the higher the standard of the cabin amenities, the lower the allowance, should become a rule and be introduced in labour law regulations so as to eliminate any doubts that may arise in this area. Until the time such a regulation is introduced, this Supreme Court judgement should be used by courts to deal with similar cases. Because of the arguments described above, this judgement must be perceived as a significant decision in Polish judicial practice.

GERMANY

Federal Labour Court
Decision of 10 May 2016 – 9 AZR 347/15

Occupational health and safety – tobacco smoke-free workplace

HEADNOTES

Facts

The non-smoking plaintiff worked as one of 120 croupiers in a casino. The casino was divided into separate non-smoking and smoking sections. The smoking section was equipped with a negative pressure generating ventilation system, which kept smoke from escaping that smoking section. The employer assigned its employees to both sections on an equal treatment basis, except those employees who could provide the employer with a medical certificate stating that they would be required to stay clear from second-hand smoke. According to his duty-roster, the employee had to work an average of two shifts of between six and ten hours each per week in the smoking section of the casino. The plaintiff demanded from his employer to be assigned to work in tobacco smoke-free rooms only, even though he could not provide a medical certificate that stated such a requirement. The employer refused to assign the employee according to his wishes, even if such assignment would have been feasible due to the sufficient amount of smoking croupiers. All three instances dismissed the plaintiff's suit.

Decision

An employer has to protect its employees against the health hazards caused by second-hand smoke only insofar as the character of the establishment and the kind of work allows for that protection. This might lead to a mere obligation to minimize the exposure to second-hand smoke instead of a complete elimination of the exposure.

Law Applied

Grundgesetz – Constitution (GG)
Article 2(2)

Every person shall have the right to life and physical integrity. Freedom of the person shall be inviolable. These rights may be interfered with only pursuant to a law.

Article 12(1)

All Germans shall have the right freely to choose their occupation or profession, their place of work and their place of training. The practice of an occupation or profession may be regulated by or pursuant to a law.

Buergerliches Gesetzbuch (Civil Code – BGB)
Section 618(1)

The person entitled to services must furnish and maintain premises, devices and equipment that he must provide for performance of the services in such a way and must arrange services that must be undertaken on his order or under his supervision in such a way that the person obliged to perform services is protected against danger to life and limb to the extent that the nature of the services permits.

Arbeitsstättenverordnung (Workplaces Ordinance – ArbStättV)
Section 5

(1) The employer has to take the measures required to efficiently protect non-smoking employees from the health hazards of tobacco smoke. Insofar as necessary, the employer has to enact a ban on smoking either in general or restricted to certain areas of the workplace.

(2) In the arranging and operating of workplaces open to the public, the employer has to take technical or organizational measures corresponding to the character of the establishment and the kind of work to protect non-smoking employees according to subsection 1.

Hessisches Nichtraucherschutzgesetz (Non-smoker Protection Act of the State of Hesse – NRauchSchG HE)
Section 2

The ban on smoking according to Section 1 Para. 1 No. 11 does not apply 5. […] to casinos within the meaning of the Act on Casinos in the State of Hesse of 15 November 2007.

JUDGEMENT

[...] Die Klage ist unbegründet. Der Kläger hat gemäß § 618 Abs. 1 BGB iVm § 5 ArbStättV keinen Anspruch auf Zuweisung eines tabakrauchfreien Arbeitsplatzes.

1. § 618 Abs. 1 BGB wird durch § 5 ArbStättV konkretisiert. Gemäß § 5 Abs. 1 ArbStättV hat der Arbeitgeber die erforderlichen Maßnahmen zu treffen, damit die nicht rauchenden Beschäftigten in Arbeitsstätten wirksam vor den Gesundheitsgefahren durch Tabakrauch geschützt sind. Entgegen der Auffassung der Revision kann der Anspruch nicht isoliert aus der Fürsorgepflicht des Arbeitgebers hergeleitet werden. § 618 BGB konkretisiert iVm den öffentlich-rechtlichen Arbeitsschutznormen den Inhalt der Fürsorgepflichten, die dem Arbeitgeber im Hinblick auf die Sicherheit und das Leben der Arbeitnehmer obliegen. Den Vorschriften des technischen Arbeitsschutzes kommt eine Doppelwirkung zu, wenn ihre Schutzpflichten über § 618 Abs. 1 BGB in das Arbeitsvertragsrecht transformiert werden [...].

2. Der Kläger ist ein nicht rauchender Beschäftigter iSv. § 5 Abs. 1 Satz 1 ArbStättV und unterliegt somit dem persönlichen Schutzbereich des § 5 ArbStättV.

3. Der Kläger hat grundsätzlich Anspruch darauf, vor den Gesundheitsgefahren durch Tabakrauch geschützt zu werden. Das Landesarbeitsgericht hat zu Unrecht angenommen, der Kläger habe weder Tatsachen vorgetragen, die auf die Intensität der Belastung durch Tabakrauch schließen lassen, noch habe er dargetan, von welchen allgemeinen oder konkreten Gesundheitsgefahren durch Passivrauchen er ausgeht. Ein nicht rauchender Beschäftigter muss nicht darlegen, dass ein Raucherarbeitsplatz seine Gesundheit durch Passivrauchen gefährdet. [...].

a) Bereits nach dem Wortlaut des § 5 Abs. 1 Satz 1 ArbStättV müssen die nicht rauchenden Beschäftigten wirksam vor den Gesundheitsgefahren durch Tabakrauch geschützt werden. Der Gesetzgeber ist damit davon ausgegangen, dass Tabakrauch zwangsläufig die Gesundheit gefährdet.

b) Dies wird durch das Gesetzgebungsverfahren bestätigt. Es war Ziel des Gesetzgebers, die bestehenden Rechtsunsicherheiten zu beseitigen. Diese könnten sich vor allem daraus ergeben, dass in jedem Einzelfall festgestellt werden müsste, ob das Passivrauchen nach Konzentration und zeitlicher Belastung zu einer Gesundheitsgefährdung führt. Nach dem Inhalt der Debatte im Bundestag wurde es als untragbar angesehen, dass der Einzelne nachweisen müsse, inwieweit er durch die Einflüsse des Rauchens gesundheitlich geschädigt werde. Gerade diese Situation sei Grund für die Gesetzesinitiative gewesen [...]. Zudem sollte die Präzisierung der ArbStättV den neuen wissenschaftlichen Erkenntnissen Rechnung tragen, die grundsätzlich von einer krebserzeugenden Wirkung des Passivrauchens ausgingen [...]. Der Gesetzgeber wollte deshalb das Passivrauchen generell als gesundheitsgefährdend ansehen. [...].

c) Diese Auslegung wird durch den mittlerweile aufgehobenen § 32 ArbStättV [...] bestätigt. Dieser verlangte für Erholungsräume geeignete Maßnahmen zum Schutz der Nichtraucher vor Belästigungen durch Tabakrauch. Die Aufhebung dieser Vorschrift wurde damit begründet, die bisherige Nichtraucherschutzregelung sei inhaltlich in § 3a ArbStättV idF vom 27. September 2002 (nunmehr § 5 ArbStättV) enthalten. Damit schützt § 5 ArbStättV vor jeder Form des Passivrauchens. Im Übrigen wurde § 5 Abs. 1 Satz 2 ArbStättV zur Umsetzung der Tabakrahmenkonvention der Weltgesundheitsorganisation (WHO) eingefügt [...]. Nach Art. 8 Abs. 1 der Tabakrahmenkonvention erkennen die Vertragsparteien an, dass wissenschaftliche Untersuchungen eindeutig bewiesen haben, dass Passivrauchen Tod, Krankheit und Invalidität verursache. Deshalb folgt auch aus Art. 2 Abs. 2 GG eine staatliche Schutzpflicht vor dem Passivrauchen [...].

d) Diese Auslegung führt entgegen der Auffassung des Landesarbeitsgerichts dazu, dass der Arbeitgeber nach § 5 Abs. 1 ArbStättV verpflichtet ist, Maßnahmen zu ergreifen, die dazu führen, dass keine Tabakrauchemissionen im Aufenthaltsbereich des nicht rauchenden Beschäftigten nachweisbar oder wahrnehmbar sind [...]. Die Beklagte hat nicht behauptet, dass dieser Effekt durch die Klimatisierung sowie Be- und Entlüftung der Raucherzone erreicht wird. Sie hat lediglich gemeint, durch die installierte Anlage werde die Luftverunreinigung durch Tabakrauch auf ein Minimum verringert. Dies reicht nicht. Objektiv erforderlich iSv § 5 Abs. 1 ArbStättV wären Maßnahmen, die eine tabakrauchfreie Atemluft in der Arbeitsstätte gewährleisten. Dazu dürfte keinerlei Tabakrauch wahrnehmbar sein [...].

4. Der Anspruch des Klägers wird jedoch gemäß § 5 Abs. 2 ArbStättV eingeschränkt. Danach hat der Arbeitgeber in Arbeitsstätten mit Publikumsverkehr Schutzmaßnahmen nach § 5 Abs. 1 ArbStättV nur insoweit zu treffen, als die Natur des Betriebs und die Art der Beschäftigung es zulassen.

a) Das Landesarbeitsgericht hat zu Unrecht angenommen, § 5 Abs. 2 ArbStättV sei nicht anwendbar. Denn die Beklagte habe sich nicht darauf berufen, dass mit dem Spiel in Spielbanken untrennbar die Gefahr durch tabakrauchende Gäste verbunden sei.

aa) Die Anwendung von § 5 Abs. 2 ArbStättV folgt bereits aus den tatsächlichen Feststellungen des Landesarbeitsgerichts. Danach arbeitet der Kläger in einer Arbeitsstätte mit Publikumsverkehr. Die Art der Beschäftigung schränkt die Schutzpflicht des Arbeitgebers gemäß § 5 Abs. 2 ArbStättV ein, wenn die Tätigkeit des Arbeitnehmers im Einzelfall zwingend mit dem Kontakt zu rauchendem Publikum verbunden ist. Das sind Arbeitsstätten, zu denen Außenstehende - wie zB Kunden und Gäste - Zugang haben und in denen diese Personengruppen üblicherweise aufgrund der Verkehrsanschauung auch rauchen [...].

bb) Diese Voraussetzungen sind zumindest für den Raucherbereich der Spielbank der Beklagten erfüllt. Dort haben die Besucher Zugang und dürfen rauchen. Die Beklagte macht in ihrer Spielbank von der Ausnahmeregelung in § 2 Abs. 5 Nr. 5 des Hessischen Nichtraucherschutzgesetzes (HessNRSG) Gebrauch, die das Rauchen in Spielbanken ermöglicht. Damit haben die dort arbeitenden Beschäftigten zwangsläufig Kontakt zu rauchenden Gästen.

b) Die weiteren Voraussetzungen des § 5 Abs. 2 ArbStättV sind erfüllt.

aa) Wegen des Schutzes der Natur des Betriebs kann der Arbeitnehmer keine nichtraucherschützenden Maßnahmen verlangen, die zu einer Veränderung oder einem faktischen Verbot der rechtmäßigen unternehmerischen Betätigung führen würden [...]. Die Natur des Betriebs lässt Schutzmaßnahmen für die nicht rauchenden Beschäftigten in Raucherräumen von Einrichtungen mit Publikumsverkehr nur eingeschränkt zu [...]. Bei der Prüfung, welche Schutzmaßnahmen erforderlich und dem Arbeitgeber zumutbar sind, ist eine Abwägung zwischen der unternehmerischen Betätigungsfreiheit gemäß Art. 12 Abs. 1 GG und der Schutzpflicht aus Art. 2 Abs. 2 Satz 1 GG [...]. vorzunehmen. Das kann zur Folge haben, dass unter Umständen die unternehmerische Betätigung zu beschränken ist, wenn dem Recht des Arbeitnehmers auf körperliche Unversehrtheit gemäß Art. 2 Abs. 2 Satz 1 GG der Vorrang einzuräumen ist. Deshalb ist die gerichtliche Überprüfung nicht darauf beschränkt, ob die unternehmerische Entscheidung zur Ausübung seiner erlaubten Tätigkeit offenbar unsachlich oder willkürlich ist [...].

bb) Von der Beklagten kann nicht verlangt werden, für die gesamte Spielbank ein Rauchverbot auszusprechen. Ein Rauchverbot würde den unternehmerischen Tätigkeitsbereich verändern, da die Beklagte von der Erlaubnis gemäß § 2 Abs. 5 Nr. 5 HessNRSG in zulässiger Weise Gebrauch gemacht hat [...]. Im Rahmen der Abwägung zwischen körperlicher

Unversehrtheit des Arbeitnehmers nach Art. 2 Abs. 2 Satz 1 GG und der unternehmerischen Betätigungsfreiheit des Arbeitgebers gemäß Art. 12 Abs. 1 GG ist der Arbeitgeber gehalten, Maßnahmen zu ergreifen, die die gesundheitlichen Belastungen des Arbeitnehmers möglichst weitgehend minimieren. § 5 Abs. 2 ArbStättV enthält unter Abwägung der widerstreitenden Grundrechte ein Minimierungsgebot. Der Arbeitgeber ist gehalten, an die besondere Situation angepasste und unter Umständen weniger aufwendige Schutzmaßnahmen zu ergreifen [...].

c) Grundsätzlich hat der Arbeitgeber einen gerichtlich nur eingeschränkt überprüfbaren Gestaltungsspielraum bei der Wahl der zur Minimierung oder Vermeidung von Gesundheitsgefahren zu treffenden Maßnahmen. Neben technischen und organisatorischen Maßnahmen kann der Arbeitgeber unter Umständen auch verpflichtet sein, sein Direktions- und Weisungsrecht gemäß § 106 GewO, § 315 BGB auszuüben [...].

aa) Das Landesarbeitsgericht hat angenommen, die Beklagte habe ausreichende Maßnahmen getroffen. Sie habe getrennte Raucher- und Nichtraucherbereiche eingerichtet. Deshalb würden die Croupiers nunmehr zeitlich deutlich überwiegend im Nichtraucherraum eingesetzt. Weniger als ein Drittel ihrer Arbeitszeit müssten sie, von Krankheitsvertretungen abgesehen, im Raucherraum arbeiten. Zudem sei die Beklagte bemüht, die Belastung durch Tabakrauch durch das Betreiben einer Be- und Entlüftungsanlage und einer Klimaanlage im Raucherbereich gering zu halten. [...].

bb) Die Beklagte ist mit diesen Maßnahmen ihrer Pflicht zur Minimierung der Gesundheitsbelastung durch Passivrauchen gemäß § 5 Abs. 2 ArbStättV nachgekommen. Sie hat einen größeren Nichtraucherbereich geschaffen und die Belastung durch die Tätigkeit im Raucherbereich zeitlich verringert. Darüber hinaus hat sie im kleineren Raucherraum technische Maßnahmen zur Luftverbesserung umgesetzt. Weiter gehende Maßnahmen hat auch der Kläger nicht aufgezeigt. Der Verhängung eines absoluten Rauchverbots im gesamten Betrieb stehen die Natur des Betriebs und die Art der Beschäftigung entgegen. Der Kläger beruft sich ohne Erfolg darauf, die Beklagte könne seinen Anspruch erfüllen, indem sie ausschließlich Beschäftigte im Raucherraum einsetze, die sich hierzu freiwillig bereit erklären würden. Dem steht schon entgegen, dass § 5 ArbStättV alle nicht rauchenden Beschäftigten vor den objektiven Gesundheitsgefahren durch Passivrauchen schützt. Dieser Schutz gilt unabhängig vom Willen der Beschäftigten. Dass das

Dienstleistungsangebot der Beklagten auch aufrechtzuerhalten wäre, wenn ausschließlich bei der Arbeit rauchende Beschäftigte, die dem Schutzbereich des § 5 ArbStättV nicht unterfallen, im Raucherraum eingesetzt würden, hat der Kläger nicht behauptet. Dazu genügt es auch nicht vorzutragen, es gebe rauchende Beschäftigte. § 5 ArbStättV schützt nicht nur Nichtraucher, sondern auch rauchende Beschäftigte, die nicht an ihrem Arbeitsplatz rauchen. Nur Beschäftigte, die bei der Arbeit rauchen, sind nicht schutzbedürftig [...].

ANNOTATION

1. *A non-smoking employee is not required to argue and prove that second-hand smoke is hazardous to his health*

The Federal Labour Court emphasized, that – in accordance with the World Health Organization Framework Convention on Tobacco Control – the German legislator assumed the inevitable hazardous nature of tobacco smoke on human health. Accordingly, the Court made it clear that a non-smoking employee would not be required to argue and prove that second-hand smoke is hazardous to his or her health. Also, the Court pointed out, that section 5(1) of the Workplaces Ordinance had been enacted in order to translate the World Health Organization Framework Convention on Tobacco Control into national law aiming at protection against any kind of second-hand smoke. This objective requires the employer to adopt measures to avoid tobacco smoke emissions within the working place of non-smoking employees. The Court accordingly left no room for the lower instance courts' requirement that the plaintiff demonstrate the intensity of his exposure to second-hand smoke and the general or precise health hazards involved.

2. *Overvaluation of the significance of the character of the establishment and the kind of work*

However, the Court was of the opinion that the afore-mentioned protection of non-smoking employees could be restricted by the character and the kind of work in casinos in the German State of Hesse, according to section 5(2) of the Workplaces Ordinance. The Court deduced this particular restriction by virtue of the provisions of section 2 of the Non-smoker Protection Act of the State of Hesse, which exempts casinos within the meaning of the Act on Casinos of the State of Hesse from the ban on smoking. Astonishingly, this exemption does not apply to other kinds of gambling facilities.

This is problematic. Just because a State regulation tries to stipulate an exemption from a federal regulation on employee protection in the field of casinos, such a regulation does not automatically constitute a reasoning establishing the specific characteristic of or the kind of work in casinos, let alone create an effective exemption.

First, employee protection is a subject of the concurrent legislative power, concerning which the federal States have the power to legislate as long as and to the extent that the Federal jurisdiction has not exercised its legislative power by enacting legislation. In the case at hand, the Federation had exercised its legislative power by enacting the Workplaces Ordinance. Accordingly there was no room for a conflicting State legislative enactment. Such conflicting legislative action is void and therefore not adequate to create an exemption that would deviate from the federal law on the subject.

Second, specific characteristics of or the kind of work within the meaning of section 5(2) of the Workplaces Ordinance are determined by factual considerations, not by legal definitions, especially not those purportedly set out in a subordinate law. A mere exemption from the ban of smoking in a – subordinate – State regulation does not constitute an inevitable business need of casinos to allow smoking by their customers. Such an inevitable business need would only exist in cases where a casino would face massive, existence-threatening disaffection by its customers only due to no-smoking policy. An additional weakness in this case is that this exemption applies only to casinos which fulfill the requirements of the Act on Casinos of the State of Hesse, namely those premises being licensed by the State of Hesse. However, the State of Hesse does not license casinos based on the hazard they pose to the health and safety of their employees, but rather based on fiscal considerations. This leads to the absurd result that employees of illegal, non-licensed gambling halls benefit from stricter health protection than those working in State licensed casinos.

Third, the Court did not appropriately balance the constitutional provisions of the employee and the employer. While an employee's health is protected by the constitutional right to physical integrity, the employer's business needs are protected by the constitutional rights to the freedom of occupation and the right of property. By simply asserting that the protection of non-smoking employees could be restricted by the character and the kind of work in a special type of casinos in the State of Hesse, the Court assumes that it would be inevitable for the economic existence of casinos to allow their customers to smoke. However, there is no evidence for such an assumption. It is unknown whether any recreational facility had been obliged to cease its business activities merely because it lost customers by prohibiting them from smoking at a time of increasing, legal, non-smoker protection. Only if a smoking ban could be proven to lead to a factual prohibition on running a casino, would there be room for trade-offs in the health protection of the employees involved. However, even in such a theoretical case, the employer would have to act proportionately. For instance the employer could assign employees who smoked to work in smoking sections of the premises prior to assigning non-smoking employees to perform such work.

3. *Comment*

At first sight, the decision of the Federal Labour Court is an achievement since it emphasizes the precedence of international law on employee health and safety protection compared to national law, by pointing out that non-smoking employees are not required to argue and prove that second-hand smoke is hazardous to their health when lodging complaints. However, the decision of the Court is inconsequential and poorly reasoned. The Court not only deducts a business need for exposing employees to second-hand smoke derived from a subordinate and inconsistent State-level regulation, but also the Court fails to balance appropriately the conflicting constitutional provisions involved. By these weaknesses the Court virtually abolishes the achievement it made in the first place.

CANADA

Supreme Court of Canada
Wilson v. Atomic Energy of Canada Limited
2016 SCC 29, [2016] 1 S.C.R. 770

Unjust dismissal – statutory protection – non-unionized workers – scope of protection under statute as compared to common law

HEADNOTES

Facts

W worked as an Administrator for his employer for four and a half years until his dismissal in November 2009. He had a clean disciplinary record. He filed an "Unjust Dismissal" complaint, claiming that his dismissal was in reprisal for having filed a complaint of improper procurement practices on the part of his employer. In response to a request from an inspector for the reasons for W's dismissal, the employer said he was "terminated on a non-cause basis and had been provided a generous dismissal package". A labour adjudicator was appointed to hear the complaint. The employer sought a preliminary ruling on whether a dismissal without cause together with a sizeable severance package meant that the dismissal was a just one. The adjudicator concluded that an employer could not resort to severance payments, however generous, to avoid a determination under the Labour Code about whether the dismissal was unjust. Because the employer did not rely on any cause to fire him, W's complaint was allowed. The employer appealed. The Application Judge found this decision to be unreasonable because, in his view, nothing in Part III of the Code precluded employers from dismissing non-unionized employees on a without cause basis. The Federal Court of Appeal agreed. The case went on appeal to the Supreme Court of Canada.

Decision

The Supreme Court allowed the appeal, and the decision of the labour adjudicator at first instance was affirmed. The text, the context, the statements of the Minister of Labour when the legislation was introduced, and the views of the overwhelming majority of arbitrators and labour law scholars, confirm that the entire purpose of the statutory scheme was to ensure that non-unionized federal employees would be entitled to protection from being dismissed without cause under Part III of the Code. The alternative approach of severance pay in lieu falls outside the range of "possible, acceptable outcomes which are defensible in respect of the facts and law" because it completely undermines this purpose by permitting employers, at their option, to deprive employees of the full remedial package Parliament created for them. The adjudicator's decision was, therefore, reasonable.

Law Applied

Canada Labour Code R.S.C. 1985, c. L 2, Part III s.240.

JUDGEMENT

[Only the majority judgement written by Abella J and supported by six of the nine members of the Supreme Court is excerpted here. A dissenting judgement by three members of the Court is not included. In addition, the portion of the judgement dealing with the administrative law issue of the "standard of judicial review" of administrative decisions, namely was the decision of the adjudicator to be reviewed on a standard of "correctness" or a standard of "reasonableness" (the answer is "reasonableness") is also omitted. Only the portion of the majority judgement dealing with the proper approach to statutory protection against unjust dismissal is annotated.]

Abella J:

At common law, a non-unionized employee could be dismissed without reasons if he or she was given reasonable notice or pay in lieu. The issue in this appeal is whether Parliament's intention behind amendments to the Canada Labour Code in 1978 was to offer an alternative statutory scheme consisting of expansive protections much like those available to employees covered by a collective agreement. In my respectful view, like almost all of the hundreds of adjudicators who have interpreted the scheme, I believe that is exactly what Parliament's intention was.

Background

[2] In 1971, Parliament passed amendments to the Canada Labour Code setting out the notice requirements for firing non-unionized employees who had worked for three or more consecutive months. The amendments also stipulated a minimal rate of severance pay for those who had worked for 12 months. Employees dismissed for just cause are not entitled to either notice or severance pay.

[3] More fundamental reforms were enacted in 1978, when the Code was again amended by adding a series of provisions to Part III under the heading "Unjust Dismissal". They are found at ss. 240 to 246. This Unjust Dismissal scheme applies to non-unionized employees who have completed 12 consecutive months of continuous employment. Any such employee who has been dismissed has 90 days to make a complaint in writing to an inspector if the employee considers the dismissal to be unjust (s. 240).

[4] A dismissed employee or an inspector can ask the employer for a written statement setting out the reasons for the dismissal. The employer must then provide the statement within 15 days (s. 241(1)).

[5] An inspector is required to try to immediately settle the complaint (s. 241(2)). If the complaint cannot be settled within a reasonable time, the inspector can, at the request of the dismissed employee, refer the matter to the Minister (s. 241(3)), who may appoint an adjudicator to hear the complaint (s. 242(1)). The report of an inspector acts as a screening mechanism to prevent complaints which are frivolous, vexatious or clearly unmeritorious from proceeding to adjudication: Harry W. Arthurs, *Fairness at Work: Federal Labour Standards for the 21st Century* (2006), at pp. 179-80 (Arthurs Report).

[6] The mandate of the adjudicator is to determine whether the dismissal was unjust (s. 242(3)). If it was, the adjudicator has broad authority to grant an appropriate remedy (s. 242(4)), including requiring the employer to

> (a) pay the person compensation not exceeding the amount of money that is equivalent to the remuneration that would, but for the dismissal, have been paid by the employer to the person;
>
> (b) reinstate the person in his employ; and
>
> (c) do any other like thing that it is equitable to require the employer to do in order to remedy or counteract any consequence of the dismissal.

[7] No complaint can be considered by an adjudicator if the employee was laid off because of lack of work or the discontinuance of a function (s. 242(3.1)(a)).

[...]

[39] [...] The issue here is whether the Adjudicator's interpretation of ss. 240 to 246 of the Code was reasonable. The text, the context, the statements of the Minister when the legislation was introduced, and the views of the overwhelming majority of arbitrators and labour law scholars, confirm that the entire purpose of the statutory scheme was to ensure that non-unionized federal employees would be entitled to protection from being dismissed without cause under Part III of the Code. The alternative approach of severance pay in lieu falls outside the range of "possible, acceptable outcomes which are defensible in respect of the facts and law" because it completely undermines this purpose by permitting employers, at their option, to deprive employees of the full remedial package Parliament created for them. The rights of employees should be based on what Parliament intended, not on the idiosyncratic view of the individual employer or adjudicator.

[40] Adjudicator Schiff's decision was, therefore, reasonable.

[41] As previously noted, Parliament passed amendments to the Code in 1971 which included provisions setting out the minimum remuneration owed to an employee whose employment had been terminated if that employee worked for a threshold number of consecutive months and was not dismissed for just cause. These provisions are now found in ss. 230(1) and 235(1) of the Code, both in Part III. The enactment of these provisions neither codified nor extinguished the common law; instead, it offered an alternative to going to court by setting out minimum entitlements for dismissed employees who wanted to avoid the expense and uncertainty of civil litigation: Arthurs Report, at pp. 172-74.

[42] In 1978, Parliament further amended the Code and established the Unjust Dismissal scheme, currently found in ss. 240 to 246 in Part III of the Code. The central question in this case is what effect the 1978 amendments had on the rights of non-unionized employees whose employment had been terminated. When the provisions were introduced, the then Minister of Labour, the Hon. John Munro, said:

It is our hope that [the amendments] will give at least to the unorganized workers some of the minimum standards which have been won by the organized workers and which are now embodied in their collective agreements. We are not alleging for one moment that they match the standards set out in collective agreements, but we provide here a minimum standard. [...]

(House of Commons Debates, vol. II, 3rd Sess., 30th Parl., December 13, 1977, at p. 1831.)

[43] He explained the purpose of the new "Unjust Dismissal" provisions to the Standing Committee on Labour, Manpower and Immigration in March 1978 as follows:

The intent of this provision is to provide employees not represented by a union, including managers and professionals, with the right to appeal against arbitrary dismissal – protection the government believes to be a fundamental right of workers and already a part of all collective agreements.

(House of Commons, Minutes of Proceedings and Evidence of the Standing Committee on Labour, Manpower and Immigration, Respecting Bill C-8, An Act to amend the Canada Labour Code, No. 11, 3rd Sess., 30th Parl., March 16, 1978, at p. 46.)

[44] The references in this statement to the right of employees to "fundamental" protection from arbitrary dismissal and to the fact that such protection was "already a part of all collective agreements", make it difficult, with respect, to draw any inference other than that Parliament intended to expand the dismissal rights of non-unionized federal employees in a way that, if not identically, then certainly analogously matched those held by unionized employees.

[45] Parliament's intentions were also on display when, the previous August, the Minister acknowledged that while the terminology of "just" and "unjust" was, on its face, ambiguous, the extensive arbitral jurisprudence from organized labour would illuminate the way forward for non-unionized federal employees who were dismissed:

I realize that the terms "just" or "unjust" are sometimes difficult to define. However, we have a vast body of arbitral jurisprudence on dismissals in the organized sector. They contain precedents that will enable arbitrators to determine whether a firing is warranted or not. Each case has to be decided according to its circumstances, but the application of the principles of fairness and common sense have established pretty clearly what constitutes just or unjust dismissal.

(The Hon. John Munro, "A better deal for Canada's unorganized workers" (1977), 77 The Labour Gazette 347, at p. 349.)

[46] And this, in fact, is how the new provisions have been interpreted by labour law scholars and almost all the adjudicators appointed to apply them, namely, that the purpose of the 1978 provisions in ss. 240 to 246 was to offer a statutory alternative to the common law of dismissals and to conceptually align the protections from unjust dismissals for non-unionized federal employees with those available to unionized employees:

Geoffrey England, "Unjust Dismissal in the Federal Jurisdiction: The First Three Years" (1982), 12 Man. L.J. 9, at p. 10; Innis Christie, Employment Law in Canada (2nd ed. 1993), at p. 669; Arthurs Report, at p. 172.

[47] The effect of the 1978 amendments was to limit the applicability of the notice requirements in s. 230(1) and the minimum severance provisions in s. 235(1) to circumstances that fell outside the Unjust Dismissal provisions. The notice and severance pay requirements under ss. 230(1) and 235(1), for example, apply to managers, those who are laid off due to lack of work or discontinuance of a function, and, in the case of s. 230(1), employees who have worked for the employer for more than 3 consecutive months but less than 12 months. In other words, ss. 230(1) and 235(1) are not an alternative to the Unjust Dismissal provisions in ss. 240 to 246, they apply only to those who do not or cannot avail themselves of those provisions: Redlon Agencies, at paras. 38-39; *Wolf Lake First Nation v. Young* (1997), 130 F.T.R. 115, at para. 50.

[48] The soundness of the consensus among adjudicators interpreting the Unjust Dismissal provisions was confirmed in Prof. Arthurs' 2006 report on Part III of the Code, commissioned by the then Minister of Labour. In preparing his report, Prof. Arthurs established a 16-person Commission Secretariat, consulted two advisory panels (one consisting of impartial experts and the other of labour and management representatives), held two academic round tables engaging 38 participants from almost 20 universities as well as industry groups, and consulted 23 independent research studies conducted by leading Canadian and foreign experts. Nine additional studies were provided by Commission staff on topics such as comparisons between Part III and labour standards legislation across Canada and in other countries. The Commission heard from 171 groups and individuals at public hearings and received over 154 briefs and other submissions. The Commission also met with labour, management and community-based organizations, and labour standards administrators and practitioners.

[49] After this extensive review of Part III of the Code and its application, Prof. Arthurs confirmed that the goal of the new "Unjust Dismissal" provisions was meant to give "unorganized workers protection against unjust dismissal somewhat comparable to that enjoyed by unionized workers under collective agreements" (p. 172 [...]):

> [...] over the years the adjudication system has not only remedied many of the procedural shortcomings of civil litigation, it has significantly modified the old civil and common law doctrines governing wrongful dismissal.

> [...] Adjudicators, borrowing extensively from the jurisprudence developed over the years by arbitrators in unionized workplaces, have built up their own distinctive doctrines that confer on unorganized federal workers quite extensive substantive and procedural protections. [...] [T]his has coincided with, and arguably hastened, the adoption of progressive attitudes and practices in the field of workplace discipline, many of which were also advocated by human resource and industrial relations professionals as a matter of best practice. [p. 178]

(See also Gilles Trudeau, "Is Reinstatement a Remedy Suitable to At-Will Employees?" (1991), 30 Indus. Rel. 302, at pp. 312-13.)

[50] The new Code regime was also a cost-effective alternative to the civil court system for dismissed employees to obtain meaningful remedies which are far more expansive than those available at common law. As Prof. Arthurs observed:

> At common [...] law, employers who wish to reconfigure or reduce their workforce for business reasons are obliged to give "reasonable" notice to employees they intend to dismiss, unless the contract of employment provides otherwise. Of course, as with other protections supposedly enjoyed by workers under the general law, this one has always been difficult to enforce. Nonetheless, it remains the law today, and Part III does nothing to change it. What Part III does do is establish a different, more accessible procedure under which workers confronting discharge for business or economic reasons can claim notice and compensation without having to sue.
>
> [...]
>
> In effect, then, one great merit [...] is that it overcomes the main deficiencies of civil litigation. It provides effective remedies and it removes cost barriers to access to justice. It thereby translates a universally accepted principle – that no one should be dismissed without just cause – into a practical reality. Part III can therefore be understood as an exercise in the reform of civil justice. [pp. 172-73 and 177]

[51] The most significant arbitral tutor for the new provisions came from the way the jurisprudence defined "Unjust Dismissal". It is true, as the Federal Court of Appeal noted, that the word "unjust" is a familiar one in the legal profession's tool kit and has a generic, even iconic role. In the collective bargaining context, however, it has a specific and well understood – and no less iconic – meaning: that employees covered by collective agreements are protected from Unjust Dismissals and can only be dismissed for "just cause". This includes an onus on employers to give reasons showing why the dismissal is justified, and carries with it a wide remedial package including reinstatement and progressive discipline.

As in the 1978 provisions, there is no Unjust Dismissal protection in the case of layoffs or discontinuance of a job.

[52] Notably, adjudicators did not interpret their mandate as requiring the automatic application of the arbitral jurisprudence or any remedies. Instead, while they "have drawn heavily" from it, they also "modified it in order to reflect the differences at play in the non-unionized environment": Christie, at p. 688.

[53] The decision which continues to be the accepted theoretical template, was the 1979 decision of Prof. George W. Adams in *Roberts v. Bank of Nova Scotia* (1979), 1 L.A.C. (3d) 259 (Can.). It helps illuminate what is generally understood by the terms "just cause" and "Unjust Dismissal":

> I am of the view that when Parliament used the notion of "unjustness" in framing [ss. 240 to 246], it had in mind the right that most organized employees have under collective agreements – the right to be dismissed only for "just cause". I am of this view because the common law standard is simply "cause" for dismissal whereas "unjust" denotes a much more qualitative approach to dismissal cases. Indeed, in the context of modern labour relations, the term has a well-understood content – a common law of the shop if you will: see Cox, "Reflections Upon Labour Arbitration", 72 Harv. L. Rev. 1482 (1958) at p. 1492. But having said that, I do not deny that the statute is silent on a whole host of important considerations that will, in any particular case, affect the precise meaning to be given to "justness". [pp. 264-65]

[54] He concluded that Parliament must also have had the concept of progressive discipline in mind (Roberts, at pp. 265-66). This concept generally requires employers seeking to justify the dismissal to demonstrate that they have made the employee aware of performance problems, worked with the employee to rectify them, and imposed "a graduated repertoire of sanctions before resorting to the ultimate sanction of dismissal": Arthurs Report, at p. 96; Christie, at pp. 690-91.

[55] Prof. Adams explained why he thought progressive discipline was incorporated into the scheme:

> Under a collective agreement, arbitrators have adopted the concept of progressive discipline, subject to specific provisions under the collective agreement to the contrary. [...] Parliament must have had this basic concept in mind when it enacted the instant provision because it is the very essence of "justness" in any labour relations sense. [...] [M]ore fundamentally, it would be my view that on the enactment of [ss. 240 to 246] all employers subject to this new provision were accorded the powers

to meet the requirements of progressive discipline. With the greatest of respect, [a] more technical and contrary interpretation [...] would simply frustrate and squander the purpose of this legislation. [Citations omitted.] (Roberts, at pp. 265-66)

[56] But he also noted that adjudicators should be mindful of the varying employment contexts under the Code, so that the arbitral jurisprudence is not rigidly applied:

> However, this does not mean that Adjudicators should import the law of the collective agreement in discipline cases unthinkingly and without modification. They should be extremely sensitive to the varying employment contexts subject to this new provision of the Code, many of which may not fit comfortably within the "industrial" discipline model. In such cases appropriate modifications can be made as required. Thus, I must ask whether the use of suspensions in the banking industry ought not to be required. (Roberts, at p. 266)

[57] Ultimately Prof. Adams concluded that while the dismissal in the case before him was unjust, he did not consider reinstatement to be an appropriate remedy in the circumstances. Instead, he awarded Ms. Roberts the equivalent of five months' wages.

[58] What turned out to be the consensus interpretation of the new provisions as reflected in the *Roberts* decision, was also the interpretation accepted by Prof. Gordon Simmons in a report commissioned by Labour Canada to explain the provisions:

> For some guidance as to what constitutes just or unjust dismissal we can turn to nearly three decades of dismissal decisions pursuant to collective agreements. There are no hard and fast rules as each situation must be determined according to the particular circumstances of each case. However, the arbitral jurisprudence which has been developed can act as a guide to what have traditionally been regarded as sufficient or insufficient grounds for just dismissal. (C. Gordon Simmons, *Meaning of Dismissal: The Meaning of Dismissals Under Division V.7 of Part III of the Canada Labour Code* (1979), at p. 1)

[59] Until 1994, when Adjudicator T. W. Wakeling broke away in *Knopp v. Westcan Bulk Transport Ltd.*, [1994] C.L.A.D. No. 172 (QL), the adjudicative path was clear that an employee could only be dismissed for just cause as that term was understood in the collective bargaining context. Adjudicator Wakeling's revisionism led him to conclude that the common law approach applied, and that if the employer has satisfied the requirements in ss. 230(1) and 235(1) of the Code or according to the

common law, whichever amount is higher, the dismissal would not be unjust. His is the interpretation accepted by the Federal Court of Appeal in this case.

[60] Out of the over 1,740 adjudications and decisions since the Unjust Dismissal scheme was enacted, my colleagues have identified only 28 decisions that are said to have followed the Wakeling approach: Reagan Ruslim, "Unjust Dismissal Under the Canada Labour Code: New Law, Old Statute" (2014), 5:2 U.W.O. J. Leg. Stud. 3 (online), at p. 28. Of these 28 decisions, 10 were rendered after this case was decided at the Federal Court and are therefore not relevant to determining the degree of "discord" amongst adjudicators before this case was heard: *Sharma v. Maple Star Transport Ltd.*, 2015 CanLII 43356; *G & R Contracting Ltd. and Sandhu, Re*, 2015 CarswellNat 7465 (WL Can.); *Pare v. Corus Entertainment Inc.*, [2015] C.L.A.D. No. 103 (QL); *Madill v. Spruce Hollow Heavy Haul Ltd.*, [2015] C.L.A.D. No. 114 (QL); *Swanson and Qualicum First Nation, Re* (2015), 26 C.C.E.L. (4th) 139; *O'Brien v. Mushuau Innu First Nation*, 2015 CanLII 20942; *Newman v. Northern Thunderbird Air Inc.*, [2014] C.L.A.D. No. 248 (QL); *Taypotat v. Muscowpetung First Nation*, [2014] C.L.A.D. No. 53 (QL); *Payne and Bank of Montreal, Re* (2014), 16 C.C.E.L. (4th) 114; and *Sharma and Beacon Transit Lines Inc., Re*, 2013 CarswellNat 4148 (WL Can.).

[61] That leaves 18 cases that have applied the Wakeling approach. Three of them were decided by Adjudicator Wakeling himself. In other words, the "disagreement [that] has persisted for at least two decades" referred to by my colleagues consists of, at most, 18 cases out of over 1,700 (para. 74). What we have here is a drop in the bucket which is being elevated to a jurisprudential parting of the waters.

[62] Even AECL concedes in its factum that "[t]he majority of adjudicators have held that employees may only be dismissed for just cause". This consensus is hardly surprising given the unchallenged goals of the Unjust Dismissal scheme and their incompatibility with what is available under the common law.

[63] In fact, the foundational premise of the common law scheme – that there is a right to dismiss on reasonable notice without cause or reasons – has been completely replaced under the Code by a regime requiring reasons for dismissal. In addition, the galaxy of discretionary remedies, including, most notably, reinstatement, as well as the open-ended equitable relief available under s. 242(4)(c), are also utterly inconsistent with the right to dismiss without cause. If an employer can continue to dismiss without cause under the Code simply by providing adequate severance

pay, there is virtually no role for the plurality of remedies available to the adjudicator under ss. 240 to 245.

[64] It is true that under s. 246, dismissed employees may choose to pursue their common law remedy of reasonable notice or pay in lieu in the civil courts instead of availing themselves of the dismissal provisions and remedies in the Code. But if they choose to pursue their rights under the Unjust Dismissal provisions of the Code, only those provisions apply. As Prof. Arthurs observed in his Report:

> [...] the two types of proceedings differ most importantly in other respects. The first relates to remedies. If successful in a civil action, an employee is entitled to damages equivalent to whatever compensation he or she would have received if the employment contract had been allowed to run its natural course – that is, for whatever period of notice would have been "reasonable." If an employer has been unfair or high-handed in carrying out the discharge, the employee may be awarded additional damages. By contrast, if successful before an Adjudicator under Part III, an employee is entitled both to reinstatement and to compensation, not only for the duration of the notice period, but for all losses attributable to the discharge. These are potentially more extensive and expensive remedies than those a court might award. [... p. 177.]

[65] It is worth noting that the Code's scheme, which was enacted in 1978, was preceded by similar Unjust Dismissal protection in Nova Scotia in 1975, and followed by a similar scheme in Quebec in 1979. Unlike other provinces, the Nova Scotia and Quebec schemes display significant structural similarities to the federal statute. They apply only after an employee has completed a certain period of service and do not apply in cases of termination for economic reasons or layoffs. Like the federal scheme, the two provincial ones have been consistently applied as prohibiting dismissals without cause, and grant a wide range of remedies such as reinstatement and compensation.

[66] It seems to me to be significant that in *Syndicat de la fonction publique du Québec v. Quebec (Attorney General)*, [2010] 2 S.C.R. 61, interpreting the Unjust Dismissal provision in the Quebec Act, this Court concluded that "[a]lthough procedural in form", the provision creates "a substantive labour standard" (para. 10). It would be untenable not to apply the same approach to the Unjust Dismissal provision in the federal Code, and instead to characterize the provision as a mere procedural mechanism.

[67] The remedies newly available in 1978 to non-unionized employees reflect those generally available in the collective bargaining context. And this, as Minister Munro stated, is what Parliament intended. To infer instead

that Parliament intended to maintain the common law under the Code regime, creates an anomalous legal environment in which the protections given to employees by statute – reasons, reinstatement, equitable relief – can be superseded by the common law right of employers to dismiss whomever they want for whatever reason they want so long as they give reasonable notice or pay in lieu. This somersaults our understanding of the relationship between the common law and statutes, especially in dealing with employment protections, by assuming the continuity of a more restrictive common law regime notwithstanding the legislative enactment of benefit-granting provisions to the contrary: *Machtinger v. HOJ Industries Ltd.*, [1992] 1 S.C.R. 986, at p. 1003; *Rizzo & Rizzo Shoes Ltd.* (Re), [1998] 1 S.C.R. 27, at para. 36.

[68] AECL's argument that employment can be terminated without cause so long as minimum notice or compensation is given, on the other hand, would have the effect of rendering many of the Unjust Dismissal remedies meaningless or redundant. The requirement to provide reasons for dismissal under s. 241(1), for example, would be redundant. And, if an employee were ordered to be reinstated under s. 242(4)(b), it could well turn out to be a meaningless remedy if the employer could simply dismiss that employee again by giving notice and severance pay. These consequences result in statutory incoherence. Only by interpreting ss. 240 to 246 as representing a displacement of the employer's ability at common law to fire an employee without reasons if reasonable notice is given, does the scheme and its remedial package make sense.

[69] That is how the 1978 provisions have been almost universally applied, including – reasonably – by the Adjudicator hearing Mr. Wilson's complaint. It is an outcome that is anchored in parliamentary intention, statutory language, arbitral jurisprudence, and labour relations practice. To decide otherwise would fundamentally undermine Parliament's remedial purpose. I would allow the appeal with costs throughout and restore the decision of the Adjudicator.

ANNOTATION

This is a simple case of statutory interpretation and the result is widely recognized in Canada as clear and correct. But it should never have required the attention of the Supreme Court of Canada. This is so for the following reasons.

The result is correct, useful, and conforms to the very clear and consensus view which had prevailed until the decision of the Federal Court of Appeal, here overturned. Indeed, until that decision there was no real legal doubt at all among Canadian labour lawyers, adjudicators, and academics about the correct approach to this statute, and the nature and point of its effort to reform the common law of dismissal. This is a case of the Supreme Court having to correct a very surprising and unnecessary error in the court below.

How this error came to be committed will remain something of a mystery. This is because the holding below, that an employer can avoid a determination of unjust dismissal by offering no reason at all for the dismissal, is very hard for Canadian labour lawyers to intellectually digest. So hard, because for decades the statutory system in question had operated on a completely different understanding – that the key to the statutory reform at issue in this case was precisely the abolition of the pre-existing common law rules regarding dismissal. The key common law rule abolished was that an employer could dismiss an employee for any reason, or no reason, so long as the employer compensated the employee (by providing a sum of money calculated by estimating what a period of "reasonable notice" would be in the circumstances). The point of the statute can only be understood against the background of the common law it was meant to reform. The central common law rule here abolished is just this rule that no reason for dismissal is required. The statute demands a reason. That is the fundamental point.

Then the statute demands that the reason be a just one in the circumstances. It then provides for an adjudicator to make that judgement call. The statute also alters another common law rule – that of "no reinstatement". Of course that remedial rule fitted hand in glove with the other parts of the common law picture – no rule against dismissal itself (for any reason), but only against dismissal without compensation. It is only when you introduce the requirement of a just reasons that the possibility of the reinstatement remedy exists because it is no longer the case that the employee right is merely to be compensated but, rather, the right not to be dismissed without a good reason. The fact that this alteration had already been made in collective agreements governing organized workers in Canada, and that the statute was clearly bringing the same reform to the unrepresented workers, only adds to the mystery of how Federal Court of Appeal went off the rails.

Thus the most important and insightful passage in the judgement being commented on here is to be found in paragraph 63 of Justice Abella's judgement: "In fact, the foundational premise of the common law scheme – that there is a right to dismiss on reasonable notice without cause or reasons – has been completely replaced under the Code by a regime requiring reasons for dismissal. In addition, the galaxy of discretionary remedies, including, most notably, reinstatement, as well as the open-ended equitable relief available under s. 242(4) (c), are also utterly inconsistent with the right to dismiss without cause. If an employer can continue to dismiss without cause under the Code simply by providing adequate severance pay, there is virtually no role for the plurality of remedies available to the adjudicator under ss. 240 to 245". Canadian labour law is in Justice Abella's debt once again. But it is to be regretted that the time and energy of the Court, not to mention the limited resources of a single unrepresented worker, had to be exhausted in order to arrive where we had been all along.

IRELAND

The Employment Appeals Tribunal
Gregory Crowe v. An Post

Dismissal – criminal conviction – offence committed outside workplace – whether sufficient nexus between offence and employment – whether dismissal fair and reasonable

HEADNOTES

Facts

The claimant was a postman who, while on long-term sick leave, was convicted of the sale and supply of drugs (€2,500 worth of cocaine) and was sentenced to a nine month suspended prison term. This came to the employer company's attention through a newspaper article which reported the sentencing. The claimant was suspended on pay and, following an investigation and an internal appeal, he was dismissed on grounds of gross misconduct. The claimant then brought a claim of unfair dismissal before the Employment Appeals Tribunal.

Decision

The claim failed. If a dismissal for out-of-work conduct is to be fair, there must be a genuine connection between that conduct and the employment such that it leads to a breach of trust and/or causes reputational damage to the employer. In this case, the claimant's conduct destroyed the relationship of trust and caused reputational damage.

Law Applied

Unfair Dismissals Act 1977
Section 6
(1) Subject to the provisions of this section, the dismissal of an employee shall be deemed, for the purposes of this Act, to be an unfair dismissal unless, having regard to all the circumstances, there were substantial grounds justifying the dismissal
(4) Without prejudice to the generality of subsection (1) of this section, the dismissal of an employee shall be deemed, for the purposes of this Act, not to be an unfair dismissal, if it results wholly or mainly from one or more of the following:
[...] (b) the conduct of the employee, [...].

JUDGEMENT

The determination of the Employment Appeals Tribunal (Chair: Tom Ryan) was delivered on 26 January 2016 stating:
[…]
There is considerable uncertainty as to whether an employee's conviction for a crime committed outside the workplace would entitle the employer to dismiss the employee. In such circumstances the employer would argue that the bond of trust had broken down. The matter is not that straightforward. The basic principle is that usually an employer's jurisdiction over misconduct of the employee ends at the company gate. A dismissal for misconduct outside the workplace can only be justified where there is sufficient connection between the crime committed and the employee's work, in such a way that would render the employee unsuitable or capable of damaging the employer's reputation. The guiding principle in cases involving misconduct outside the workplace is that the employer must be able to show a connection between the misconduct and the company's operational requirements.

As a general rule, the employer has no right to institute disciplinary proceedings unless it can be demonstrated that it has some legitimate interest in the conduct of the employee. An interest would normally exist where there is some nexus between the employee's conduct and the employer's business. The employer has to demonstrate that it has a legitimate interest in the crime committed to the extent that the misconduct is disruptive to business, employee relations or affects the reputation of the company. The test is: has the out-of-work conduct of the employee impacted adversely, or is capable of impacting adversely, on the employer's business? If it has, then the employer has the right to institute disciplinary proceedings. Whether this gives the employer the right to impose sanctions, up to and including dismissal, will depend on the particular circumstances of each case. No two cases are the same and each case must be decided on its own particular merits. Because of this it is extremely difficult to have consistency of approach.

The Tribunal's attention was drawn to *Moore v. Tesco Ireland Ltd* UD 2924/2011 where the claimant was held to be unfairly dismissed and awarded €11,500 compensation, even though the claimant had been convicted of sale and supply of drugs. The Tribunal distinguishes *Moore* from the case before it, in that in *Moore* there was no publication in newspapers of the conviction, whereas in the instant case there was prominent publication of the conviction. (The Tribunal is not saying that if there is no publication an employer cannot dismiss an employee. Neither is it saying that if there is publication that the employer is automatically entitled to dismiss an employee.) The Tribunal in *Moore* also held that the employer had not given sufficient consideration to alternative sanctions. The Tribunal also reminds itself that no two cases are the same and each case must be decided on its own particular merits.

In summary if a dismissal for out-of-work conduct is to be fair there must be a genuine connection between the employee's offence and the employment. That connection must be such that:

- it leads to a breach of trust and/or causes reputational and/or other damage to the company;
- the employee's offence makes the employee unsuitable to continue in the job – for example if an employee is convicted of theft and his job involved dealing with cash then this could well be sufficient grounds for dismissal;
- the employee's offence causes the employer to genuinely lose trust and confidence in the employee;
- the employee's behaviour risks bringing the employer's name into ill repute;
- dismissal is more likely to be fair if the conviction is reported in the press – for example in *Post Office v. Liddiard* [2001] EWCA Civ 940 the dismissal of a postman whose conviction for hooliganism at a football match in France was reported in the press in a "name and shame" campaign was held to have brought the company into disrepute and was held to be a fair dismissal.

The Tribunal is satisfied that the claimant's conduct had destroyed the relationship of trust. The claimant (as postman) held a position of great trust. He was responsible for delivering mail, some of which may be registered mail containing money. A reasonable employer would also be concerned that the claimant might be forced into distribution of drugs (which his position as postman provided ideal cover for), given that he was convicted for having drugs for sale or supply. The Tribunal is fully satisfied that there is a connection or nexus between the claimant's criminal conviction and his employment. Such a conviction inevitably led to a breach of trust, caused reputational damage, and led to the claimant's dismissal which the Tribunal holds is fair and reasonable having regard to all the circumstances.

Accordingly the claimant's claim fails.

[Source: UD 1153/2014; [2016] E.L.R. 93]

ANNOTATION

This case demonstrates the difficulty employers face when confronted with a situation, which has come to their attention through the media, of an employee who has been convicted of a criminal offence relating to conduct outside employment but who has been given a non-custodial sentence. The Employment Appeals Tribunal has consistently held that a claimant's contract of employment is frustrated on receipt of a prison sentence: see *Gallagher v. Eircom Ltd* UD 953/2004.

The Unfair Dismissals Acts 1977 to 2015 require that an employer must show that there were substantial grounds, such as competence, capability or conduct, justifying the decision to dismiss. This requirement involves the employer not just demonstrating that there was substantial evidence to justify the decision, but also that there was substantial justification for the sanction of dismissal. The standard of review adopted by the Employment Appeals Tribunal, and endorsed by the High Court (see *Bank of Ireland v. Reilly* 35 I.L.L.R. 301), is to consider against the facts what a reasonable employer, in the employer's position and circumstances, would have done and decided and to set this up as the standard against which the employer's actions and decision should be judged.

"Conduct" is not restricted to an act at work, or at the place of work; nor does the behaviour have to be connected with the employee's work. It is sufficient that, in some respect, it affects the employee, or would be likely to affect the employee, when doing his or her work.

Consequently, where an employee is convicted of a criminal offence and does not receive a custodial sentence, the employer may be entitled to dismiss. A blanket policy of dismissal upon conviction of an offence unconnected with employment will not be upheld. Each case has to be decided on its own facts and own merits. As *Moore* and *Crowe* demonstrate, all such cases are very fact specific. The critical test is whether the claimant's criminal conduct is such as to render him or her unsuitable for employment with the employer. Factors such as the nature of the offence and the employee's position, the nature of the employer's business, and the reaction of clients, customers and/or fellow employees will all be central to the decision.

IRELAND

The Workplace Relations Commission
Senelisiwe Buthelezi
v.
Coy Dlamini, Thobeka Dlamini and the Republic of South Africa

Diplomatic immunity – complaint of discriminatory dismissal – embassy staff – vicarious liability

HEADNOTES

Facts

The complainant, a South African national, was employed by Coy Dlamini (CD) and Thobeka Dlamini (TD) (the latter being a counsellor in the South African Embassy) as a housekeeper/childminder in their private residence in Dublin. The contract of employment was entered into in South Africa with wages being paid in South African rand. The complainant was dismissed by CD and TD in July 2013 and she instituted proceedings pursuant to the Employment Equality Act 1998 with what is now the Workplace Relations Commission.

The Republic of South Africa made a preliminary application that the complaint be dismissed on the basis that it had no contractual relationship with the complainant and that it was not vicariously liable for the actions of CD or TD both of whom enjoyed diplomatic immunity.

Decision

The Workplace Relations Commission had no jurisdiction to hear the complaint. The Republic of South Africa was not vicariously liable for the actions of CD and TD with whom the complainant had a private contractual relationship. CD and TD enjoyed diplomatic immunity as the latter was an accredited diplomatic agent and the former was accredited as a family member.

Law Applied

Vienna Convention on Diplomatic Relations 1961
Article 30

(1) A diplomatic agent shall enjoy immunity from the criminal jurisdiction of the receiving state. He shall also enjoy immunity from its civil and administrative jurisdiction, except in the case of:

[...] (c) An action relating to any professional or commercial activity exercised by the diplomatic agent in the receiving state outside of his official functions.

Article 37

(1) The members of the family of a diplomatic agent forming part of his household shall, if they are not nationals of the receiving state, enjoy the privileges and immunities specified in Articles 29 to 36.

Diplomatic Relations and Immunities Act 1967
Section 5

(1) The provisions of the Vienna Convention on Diplomatic Relations done at Vienna on the 18th April 1961, as set out in the First Schedule to this Act, shall have the force of law in the State.

JUDGEMENT

An Adjudication Officer of the Workplace Relations Commission (Niamh O'Carroll Kelly BL) delivered her decision on 19 July 2016 stating: [...]

Does the complainant have *locus standi* to bring the within claim against the Republic of South Africa?

It is clear from the submissions and the documentation submitted that the complainant's contract of employment was with the first and second respondents. It is clear that there is no nexus between the complainant, the contract and the third named respondent. I am satisfied that the Republic of South Africa, in circumstances where a private contractual arrangement was entered into between the complainant and the first and second named respondents, is not and never could be vicariously liable for the actions of those respondents.

Accordingly, I find that the complainant does not have *locus standi* to bring a claim against the Republic of South Africa and therefore I have no jurisdiction to hear that matter.

Does the [Commission] have jurisdiction to hear the claim as against the first and second respondents?

[The Adjudication Officer then referred to the provisions of the Vienna Convention and the 1967 Act set out above and continued]

I fully accept that over the passage of time the generally recognised principle of absolute state immunity has been eroded. A more restrictive principle now exists. However, any deviation from the principle must be carefully considered. The leading case in this jurisdiction in relation to the matter is the Supreme Court decision in *Canada v. Employment Appeals Tribunal* [1992] 2 I.R. 484 (the *Government of Canada* case).

> (a) *Into which category does the complainant's claim fall, public or private?*
> The employment of a 'domestic worker/child-minder' is clearly not a commercial contract in the ordinary sense of the word. It is a normal private contract of service.
>
> (b) *Is the contract of service for the commercial purposes of the foreign mission?*
> It is clear from the facts of this case that it is not.
>
> (c) *Do the facts of the matter bring it within the exceptions set out in the Convention?*
> None of the exceptions as set out in Article 31(1)(a) to (c) are applicable to the within case.

The complainant seeks to differentiate the within case from that of the *Government of Canada* case. In that regard it is stated that the nature of the complainant's role was separate from that of the diplomats and did not overlap with the diplomat's government's public business organisation and interests in any way, unlike the chauffeur's role. The complainant argues that Case C-154/11, *Mahamdia v. People's Democratic Republic of Algeria* [2013] I.C.R.1 is relevant to her situation. I find, having considered the full text of the case, that it mainly relates to the interpretation of Council Regulation 44/2001. However, it is clear from it that under German law, employment contracts of the type in this case do fall within the jurisdiction of the German courts where the employee has not carried out, for the state by which he or she is employed, activities forming part of the sovereign functions of the state. Whilst this case may have some persuasive value I am not bound by it unlike the *Government of Canada* case.

The complainant further relies on *Cudak v. Lithuania* (2010) 51 E.H.R.R. 418 wherein a Lithuanian national employed as a secretary at the Polish Embassy in Vilnius brought an action for compensation in the Lithuanian courts following her dismissal. The Republic of Poland had claimed immunity from jurisdiction, which had resulted in the Lithuanian courts declining jurisdiction. The applicant claimed a violation of her right of access to a court and the [European Court of Human Rights] ECtHR found a violation of Article 6(1) of the ECHR. The ECtHR noted that the application of absolute state immunity has clearly been eroded. The ECtHR undertook an extensive review of the principles of international law in relation to the principles of sovereign immunity and held that the 1991 Draft Articles of the International Law Commission and the United Nations Convention on Jurisdictional Immunities of States and their Property 2004 codified the principles of customary international law. The judgement continues by considering the nature of the employment of the applicant.

> "The court observes in particular that the applicant was a switchboard operator at the Polish Embassy whose main duties were: recording international conversations, typing, sending and receiving faxes, photocopying documents, providing information and assisting with the organisation of certain events. Neither the Lithuanian Supreme Court nor the respondent government have shown how these duties could objectively have been related to the sovereign interests of the Polish government. Whilst the schedule to the employment contract stated that the applicant could have been called upon to do other work at the request of the head of mission, it does not appear from the case file – nor have the government provided any details in this connection – that she actually performed any functions related to the exercise of sovereignty by the Polish state.
>
> In conclusion, by upholding in the present case an objection based on state immunity and by declining jurisdiction to hear the applicant's claim, the Lithuanian courts, in failing to preserve a reasonable relationship of proportionality, overstepped their margin of appreciation and thus impaired the very essence of the applicant's right of access to a court."

This case involved primarily the right of access to the courts. Unlike the within case, the applicant in *Cudak* was a Lithuanian national, working in Lithuania albeit for the Polish embassy, with a contract of employment stating that she was bound by the law of Lithuania. On that basis the case must be distinguished from the within case.

The complainant, who is South African, was employed by the first and second named respondents who are South African, under a contract of employment whose terms and conditions of employment are governed by the law of South Africa. Her remuneration was in the currency of South Africa, the rand. Her place of work was at the private residence of the first and second named respondents in Ireland.

It is clear from the complete reading of this case and all of the submissions made during the course of the preliminary hearing that I cannot deviate from the findings in the *Government of Canada* case and must interpret those findings in line with our Constitution and the Vienna Convention. In doing so I find that I do not have jurisdiction to hear this matter and that the complainant if she wishes to enforce her rights must do so in the Republic of South Africa.

[Source: DEC-E2106-105: [2017] E.L.R. 24]

ANNOTATION

The *Government of Canada* case, which the Adjudication Officer felt bound to follow, concerned a claim made by a chauffeur in the former employment of the Canadian Embassy in Dublin. He referred a complaint of unfair dismissal to the Employment Appeals Tribunal. The Government of Canada objected, stating that the Tribunal had no jurisdiction to hear the complaint because it was a sovereign authority and immune from suit in a foreign court or tribunal. The Tribunal nevertheless heard the complaint and awarded compensation. The Government of Canada sought a judicial review, to which the former chauffeur was a notice party, and the determination of the Tribunal was quashed by the Supreme Court.

Hederman J dealt with the matter as follows:

> "The service with which this case is concerned is one related to the exercise of the diplomatic functions of the Ambassador in that the notice party's work was that of driving the Canadian Ambassador's motor car which was provided for the assistance of the Ambassador in the performance of his duties. I am satisfied that this falls within the area of sovereign immunity envisaged and adopted by the Constitution. For the purpose of this case it is unnecessary to express any view upon the extent to which the doctrine of sovereign immunity may have been modified or limited in respect of commercial activities conducted or undertaken by a foreign sovereign."

McCarthy J made similar observations:

"The employment of an embassy chauffeur is not within a trading or commercial area of activity – is it within the sphere of governmental or sovereign activity? Is there some other category, neither commercial nor governmental, in which the embassy may be engaged? A contract of employment or contract of service is not, in that context, a commercial transaction nor is contract cleaning or contract car hire unless such be for the commercial purposes of the foreign mission. Whatever the implications may be in domestic law, whatever the rights might, at first sight, arise in respect of the Unfair Dismissals Act, unless it can be shown that there is a conflict with some private constitutional right, that matter is entirely governed by whatever are established to be the generally recognised principles of international law. There is no indication, whatever, that such principles recognise any exception in litigation or like procedures concerning the employment or non-employment of a member of the embassy domestic staff."

O'Flaherty J was of a similar view:

"The employment of a chauffeur at the Canadian Embassy is clearly not a commercial contract in the ordinary sense of the word; it is a contract of service. Is it any different to having the heating system in the embassy repaired? (*cf. Claim against the Empire of Iran* (1963) 45 I.L.R. 57). I believe it is. I think once one approaches the embassy gates one must do so on an amber light. Prima facie anything to do with the embassy is within the public domain of the government in question. It may be that this presumption can be rebutted as happened in the *Empire of Iran* case. I believe that the element of trust and confidentiality that is reposed in the driver of an embassy car creates a bond with his employer that has the effect of involving him in the employing government's public business organisation and interests. Accordingly, I hold that the doctrine of restrictive state immunity applies to this case."

In *Buthelezi*, however, the complainant was clearly not an employee of the Republic of South Africa. Unlike *Cudak*, where the employee was a Lithuanian national whose contract was governed by Lithuanian law, the complainant in this case was a South African national whose contract with CD and TD was governed by South African law.

The *Government of Canada* case has, more recently, been applied by the Employment Appeals Tribunal. In *Greene v. Government of the United States of America* UD 289/2014, the Tribunal held that the complainant (a former security guard at the US Embassy) had been recruited to perform particular functions in the exercise of governmental authority. Accordingly the Tribunal held that the doctrine of "Restrictive State Immunity" applied and that it had no jurisdiction to hear his unfair dismissal complaint.

ITALY

Court of Cassation
Labour Division
Decision no. 24157 of 26 November 2015
Agrigento Industrial Development Consortium
v. C.S.

*Dismissal – public sector employment – Art. 18 of Act no. 300/1970
– Amendment Act no. 92/2012 – applicability*

Facts

A consortium dismissed an employee on disciplinary grounds. The disciplinary procedure was initiated, investigated and concluded by just one member of the disciplinary procedures office, the body responsible for disciplinary action in the public sector under Italian law. The Court of Cassation ruled that this did not amount to a mere procedural flaw, but was an infringement of an imperative norm. As a result, it held that the employee was entitled to reinstatement pursuant to section one of Article 18 of Act no. 300 of 1970, as amended by Act no. 92 of 2012, rather than a compensatory award for damages.

Decision

The Court of Cassation rejected the employer's appeal.

Law Applied

Act no. 300 of 20 May 1970
Article 18, section 1

The court, in ruling that a dismissal is not well-founded on discriminatory grounds pursuant to Article 3 of Act no. 108 of 11 May 1990, or that notice of dismissal was issued at the time of marriage under Article 35 of the Equal Opportunities Code, in respect of Legislative Decree no. 198 of 11 April 2006, or in violation of the prohibitions of dismissal under sections 1, 6, 7 and 9 of Article 54 of the consolidated law protecting and supporting maternity and paternity, pursuant to Legislative Decree no. 151

of 26 March 2001, and subsequent amendments, or in other cases where it is null and void by law, or due to an unlawful ground pursuant to Article 1345 of the Italian Civil Code, orders the employer, be it an enterprise or other organization, to reinstate the employee, whatever the formally stated reason and whatever the number of workers in the enterprise. This provision shall also apply to senior managers. Following the reinstatement order, the employment relationship shall be considered terminated in the event that the employee does not resume service within 30 days of the date of the employer's invitation to do so, except in cases in which the employee has requested compensation in lieu of reinstatement pursuant to section three of this Article. The provisions of this Article shall also apply to dismissals found to be invalid because they were notified orally.

Act no. 92 of 28 June 2012
Article 1, sections 7 and 8

In respect of all matters not specifically referred to herein, the provisions of this Act shall constitute the general principles and criteria for the regulation of employment contracts of public sector employees pursuant to section 2 of Article 1 of Legislative Decree no. 165 of 30 March 2001, and subsequent amendments, in compliance with the provisions of Article 2, section 2, of the same Legislative Decree. The provisions stated in Article 3 of the same Legislative Decree shall apply.

For the purposes of the application of section 7 the Minister for Public Administration and Simplification, after consulting with the more representative employee trade union organizations in the public administration, shall identify and determine, also by means of enactments, the areas, modes and pace of harmonization regarding public administration employees.

Legislative Decree no. 165 of 30 March 2001
Article 51, section 2

Act no. 300 of 20 May 1970, and subsequent amendments, shall apply to all parts of the public administration irrespective of the number of employees.

Article 55, section 1

The provisions of this Article and of the following Articles up to Article 55-octies, form imperative norms, pursuant to and by virtue of Articles 1339 and 1419, section two, of the Italian Civil Code, and shall apply to employment relationships in respect of Article 2, section 2, in the public administration under Article 1, section 2 thereof.

Article 55-bis, section 4

Each administration, on the basis of its regulations, shall identify the competent office for disciplinary procedures pursuant to section 1, sentence two. This office shall state the allegation of misconduct to the employee, shall call a meeting with the employee to state his/her case, shall investigate and conclude the proceedings pursuant to section 2, but, if the penalty to be applied is greater than those laid down in section 1, sentence one, then terms double those set out therein shall apply, save for its suspension pursuant to Article 55-ter. The final date for presenting the allegation shall begin on the date that the documents are sent pursuant to section 3 or, alternatively, the date on which the office was notified of the misconduct, while the initial date for the completion of the proceedings shall in any case be the date on which notice of the misconduct is first given, even if this occurs on the part of the manager of the unit in which the employee works. Failure to comply with the terms stated in this section shall lead, in the case of the administration, to the cancellation of the disciplinary action and, in the case of the employee, to relinquishing his/her right to state his/her case.

JUDGEMENT

(omissis)

Pursuant to Legislative Decree no. 165 of 2001, Article 55-bis, section 4, each public administration, in accordance with its regulations, identifies the competent office for disciplinary procedures. This is an imperative norm. And as such it is expressly set out in the preceding Article 55, section 1.

Both parties as well as the impugned decision concur that the Consortium's office for disciplinary procedures is made up of a three-member collegial body.

The Court of first instance acknowledged – and this is also not in dispute – that the entire disciplinary proceedings against the counter-appellant were initiated, investigated and concluded (and the final report sent to the Special Commissioner) by just one member of the office for disciplinary procedures, namely Ms *(omissis)*.

Contrary to the opinion of the Court of first instance, the Consortium claims that there was no infringement of the law in view of the fact that it was a subdivision of a collegial body.

Even if we were to accept that this collegial body was not a full collegial body and that, therefore, it need not necessarily function with the presence of all its members, it must nevertheless be noted that in no case, may a subdivision of a collegial body function through just one of its members. This would make it equivalent to a single-member body, in breach of the Consortium's internal rules, which always require a collegial body for disciplinary procedures.

With regard to this, we can only concur with the case law of the *Consiglio di Stato* (cf. decision no. 140 of 16.3.76), which has deemed that a collegial body must necessarily be made up of a number of members and cannot be transformed into a single-person body, insofar as such a body completely disregards the rationale of administrative efficiency underlying the adoption of a collegial system.

This has resulted in the infringement, in the case in question, of the imperative norm consisting of Legislative Decree no. 165 of 2001, Article 55-bis, section 4, thereby making – due to this fact alone – the dismissal on disciplinary grounds that it gives rise to null and void.

Nor can such a conclusion be countered by the argument that Legislative Decree no. 165 of 2001, Article 55-bis, section 2, final sentence, states that "failure to comply with the terms stated in this section shall lead, in the case of the administration, to the cancellation of the disciplinary action and, in the case of the employee, to relinquishing his/her right to state his/her case".

In truth, the fact that this law envisages a certain remedy (cancellation of the disciplinary action) due to infringement of the terms established in the same section does not imply that the infringement of the subsequent section 4 must not be punished with its annulment, given that any infringement of imperative norms always results in annulment "unless the law provides otherwise" (Article 1418, section 1of Italian Civil Code).

In other words, the law may indeed provide for the cancellation of the disciplinary action due to the infringement of the terms under Article 55-bis, section 2 and, instead, its annulment due to the violation of section 4 of Article 55-bis (read in conjunction with section 1 of Article 1418 of the Italian Civil Code).

4 – Confirmation of the annulment of the disciplinary dismissal in question covers examination of the other ground of annulment (which is asserted in the second submission of the appeal) in the judgement under discussion (namely that the termination was decided by a body – the Consortium's Special Commissioner – which was not competent to do so).

5 – There is no basis for the third submission, albeit corrected pursuant to Article 384 of the Code of Civil Procedure, final section, as stated in the reasoning adopted by the Court of first instance on the matter.

It is also true that the unequivocal tenor of Legislative Decree no. 165 of 2001, Article 51, section 2, provides for its application also to contract-based public sector employees pursuant to Act no. 300 of 1970 "and subsequent amendments", regardless of the number of employees.

It cannot, therefore, be denied that the new text of Act no. 300 of 1970, Article 18, as laid down by Act no. 92 of 2012, Article 1, applies *ratione temporis* to the dismissal for which it was conceived, and this regardless of the legislative initiatives regarding harmonization provided for by the Fornero law as stated in the impugned decision.

Indeed, the new text of Article 18, section 1 of the Workers' Statute, as amended by Act no. 92 of 2012, specifically links (as well as the other cases provided for) the remedy of reinstatement (and not solely of compensatory damages) also to other cases of annulment provided for by law.

And there is no doubt that the cases for annulment provided for by law also include breach of imperative norms (see, in addition, Article 1418, section 1 of the Italian Civil Code,) and this also means, as has been stated, Article 55-bis, section 4 of Legislative Decree no. 165 of 2001.

On the other hand, a compensatory award of damages is provided for by the new text of Article 18 of the Workers' Statute in situations which differ from those of the case in question (such as when a dismissal is ruled to be invalid due to violation of the requirement pursuant to Article 2, section 2 of Act no. 604 of 15 July 1966 and subsequent amendments, on procedural grounds under Act no. 300 of 1970, Article 7 or of the procedure under Article 7, and subsequent amendments of Act no. 604 of 15 July 1966).

6 – The objections in the third submission cover the question of constitutional lawfulness raised in the fourth submission, since the applicability of the new text of Article 18 of the Workers' Statute has been affirmed (albeit in the form of reinstatement).

7 – The appeal must, as a result, be rejected.

[Source: Diritto delle relazioni industriali, 2016, page 247]

ANNOTATION

The decision of the Court of Cassation concerns the applicability of the regulations governing dismissal pursuant to Act no. 92 of 28 June 2012 (the so-called Fornero reform) to public sector employees. This law amended Article 18 of Act no. 300 of 20 May 1970 (the Workers' Statute).

Following this major reform, the remedy for unlawful dismissals is no longer always to be the reinstatement of the employee. This remedy applies in the case of dismissals on discriminatory grounds (in addition to reinstatement, a compensatory award covering the period of pay between the date of dismissal and the date of reinstatement is due). It also applies in the more serious cases of unjustified dismissal (but with a maximum compensatory award of twelve months' pay). In other cases, including unlawful dismissal on disciplinary grounds due to a flaw of form or procedure, a claim can only be made for a compensatory award, with no entitlement to reinstatement.

However, it is not clear whether the reform also applies to public sector workers, or whether the previous version of Article 18 (that is to say, with the right to reinstatement as well as a full compensatory award) continues to apply.

Decisions on the matter, also those handed down by the Court of Cassation, are conflicting.

According to one line of decisions (for example, Cass., Labour Division, decision no. 11868 of 9 June 2016) the 2012 reform does not apply to public sector employees. This is supported by sections 7 and 8 of Article 1 of Act no. 92/2012 (see the text quoted under Law Applied above). This would suggest that the legislature intended to refer the reform of dismissals in the public sector to a subsequent law. Moreover, it has been argued with specific reference to dismissals on disciplinary grounds, that these are regulated by a specific law, which is not compatible with the law regulating employment in the private sector. Finally, on the basis of Italian Constitutional Court Decision no. 351 of 24 October 2008, it has been stated that in the public sector the principles of impartiality and good functioning of public administration (under Article 97 of the Constitution) always require the Court to reinstate a public sector employee who has been unlawfully dismissed.

According to an opposing line of decisions, shared by the decision being commented on here, the 2012 reform is applicable. On the one hand, sections 7 and 8 do not clearly exclude public sector employment.

This would therefore mean the applicability of the principle laid down by Legislative Decree no. 165 of 2001 (the consolidated law on public sector employment), whereby the provisions concerning private sector employment also apply to the public sector, unless expressly provided for. Secondly, Article 51 of Legislative Decree no. 165 of 2001 provides for the application of Act no. 300/1970 (and so also Article 18 and subsequent amendments) to public sector employment. Hence, it must also be considered applicable to the reform of 2012. Lastly, although disciplinary procedures in the public sector are regulated differently from the private sector, this does not exclude the applicability of the remedies laid down by Article 18, including the amendments of 2012.

Finally, it should be pointed out that the regulation of dismissals was amended once again and even more radically by Legislative Decree no. 23 of 4 March 2015, even if only applying to the case of employment contracts signed as of 7 March 2015, the date on which the Decree came into force. This Decree now makes the remedy of reinstatement in the event of unjustified dismissal an exception, while generally providing for the payment of a compensatory award.

In the absence of specific legislation on the issue, the question of whether this reform is applicable to public sector workers has once again been raised. The Italian Government has signalled that Article 18 of the Workers' Statute will continue to apply to public sector workers, thereby confirming its more favourable disposition towards this category of workers.

PART FIVE

COLLECTIVE LABOUR
RELATIONS

UNITED STATES OF AMERICA

Court of Appeals for the Fifth Circuit
Associated Builders and Contractors of Texas v. NLRB

Timing of representation elections – timing of hearing to challenge voter eligibility – providing unions with information for contacting individual employees – privacy

HEADNOTES

Facts

The National Labor Relations Board (NLRB) modified its rules for electing bargaining representatives. This included decreasing the normal duration between filing an election petition and the date of the election, delaying a hearing on challenges to a voter's eligibility until after the election, and expanding the types of employee contact information that employers must provide to the NLRB and that the NLRB transmits to labor organizations. Employer organizations [ABC of Texas entities] sued to enjoin implementation of the new rules.

The issues were: Do the new rules inadequately safeguard the right to a fair hearing regarding disputed facts? Do the new rules improperly impede opportunities to persuade employees regarding election choices or unduly interfere with the privacy of employee contact information?

Decision

The new rules on their face are sufficiently within the scope of the NLRB's reasonable exercise of discretion and do not violate employee privacy rights.

JUDGMENT*

Before CLEMENT and HAYNES, Circuit Judges, and GARCIA MARMOLEJO, District Court.

CLEMENT, Circuit Judge:

Appellants [...] are Texas-based trade and advocacy associations that represent construction employers and small business owners. The ABC entities brought a facial challenge to enjoin enforcement of a final rule issued by the National Labor Relations Board (the "Board" or "NLRB") that modifies procedures relating to union representation elections. [...]

I.

The challenged NLRB rule amended the procedures for determining whether a majority of employees wish to be represented by a labor organization for purposes of collective bargaining. See Representation—Case Procedures, 79 Fed. Reg. 74308–10 (Dec. 15, 2014). Intended to decrease the time preceding union elections, the rule allows for employees to take a vote on union representation as soon as eleven days after a petition for representation is filed. Among other changes, the rule defers employer challenges to voter eligibility issues until after an election is held; removes the standard twenty-five day delay that normally occurs between the time a regional director directs an election and the actual election; and requires expanded disclosure of employee contact information.

Before the rule became effective, the ABC entities filed this action, arguing that the rule exceeds the Board's statutory authority under the National Labor Relations Act ("the Act" or "NLRA") and violates the Administrative Procedure Act ("APA"). The ABC entities, in a motion for summary judgment, requested that the district court vacate the rule changes as facially invalid and enjoin enforcement. In response, the Board filed a combined partial motion to dismiss and cross-motion for summary judgment, contending that deference is owed to decisions of the Board and that the rule changes are reasonable and consistent with the NLRA and the APA. The district court ruled in favor of the Board, and this appeal followed.

II.

[...] We analyze an agency's interpretation of its authorizing statute using the two-step procedure set forth in *Chevron, U.S.A., Inc. v. Natural*

---

* Footnotes are numbered as in the original. Deleted footnotes are not indicated.

Resources Defense Council, Inc., 467 U.S. 837 (1984). First, we ask "whether Congress has directly spoken to the precise question at issue." Id. at 842. If it has, "that is the end of the matter," and we "must give effect to the unambiguously expressed intent of Congress." *Id.* at 842–43. If it has not, we defer to the agency's reasonable interpretations of the statute. See *NLRB v. Ky. River Cmty. Care, Inc.*, 532 U.S. 706, 713 (2001).

The APA also authorizes us to set aside agency actions if "arbitrary, capricious, an abuse of discretion" or otherwise "not in accordance with law, or unsupported by substantial evidence on the record taken as a whole." *Tex. Clinical Labs, Inc. v. Sebelius*, 612 F.3d 771, 775 (5th Cir. 2010); see 5 U.S.C. § 706(2). Our task is to determine whether the agency examined the pertinent evidence, considered the relevant factors, and articulated a "reasonable explanation for how it reached its decision." *Tex. Office of Pub. Util. Counsel v. FCC*, 183 F.3d 393, 410 (5th Cir. 1999); see *Motor Vehicles Mfrs. Ass'n of U.S. v. State Farm Mut. Auto. Ins. Co.*, 463 U.S. 29, 43 (1983). This standard is highly deferential; we apply a presumption of validity. [...]

Because the ABC entities bring a facial challenge, they "must establish that no set of circumstances exists under which the [Rule] would be valid." *Center for Individual Freedom v. Carmouche*, 449 F.3d 655, 662 (5th Cir. 2006) (quoting *United States v. Salerno*, 481 U.S. 739, 745 (1987) [...]

III.

The NLRA grants employees the right "to bargain collectively through representatives of their own choosing [...] and to [...] refrain from [...] such activities." 29 U.S.C. § 157. Section 9 of the Act gives the Board authority to resolve questions of representation, and sets forth the basic steps for that process. When a petition for representation is filed, the Board is required to investigate the petition and "provide for an appropriate hearing upon due notice" before the election is held. *Id.* § 159(c)(1). [...] A union may represent employees in collective bargaining if the union is "designated or selected for the purposes of collective bargaining by the majority of the employees in a unit appropriate for such purposes." *Id.* § 159(a). In each case, "the Board shall decide" the "unit appropriate for the purposes of collective bargaining" in order to "assure to employees the fullest freedom in exercising the rights guaranteed by [the Act]." *Id.* § 159(b).

Aside from these general requirements, the statute says little about specific procedures for processing election petitions. The Board has authority to proscribe rules for processing such petitions, 29 U.S.C. §§ 156, 159(c)(1), and has repeatedly amended these procedures, usually without notice and comment. 79 Fed. Reg. 74310. Here, the final rule followed an extensive comment period, totalling 141 days and four days of hearings. *Id.* at 74,311. Overall, the Board implemented twenty-five amendments to the procedures for processing representation petitions. 79 Fed. Reg. 74, 308–10. [...]

III A. The ABC entities contend that the rule exceeds the Board's authority [...] by allowing regional directors to preclude employers from contesting voter eligibility issues in pre-election hearings. The Board argues that the Act's requirement that the Board hold an "appropriate hearing" on questions of representation does not demand pre-election litigation of all voter-eligibility issues. The Board has the better argument.

Section 9 of the NLRA states that "[t]he Board shall decide in each case [...] the unit appropriate for the purposes of collective bargaining." 29 U.S.C. § 159(b). The Act mandates that the Board investigate representation petitions "and if it has reasonable cause to believe that a question of representation affecting commerce exists shall provide for an appropriate hearing upon due notice." *Id.* § 159(c)(1).

Prior versions of the regulations neither expressly stated the purpose of the hearing nor specifically limited the evidence that could be introduced. [...] In the new rule, the Board addressed the administration of the pre-election hearing and emphasized that the purpose of the hearing "under Section 9(c) of the [NLRA] is to determine if a question of representation exists." 29 C.F.R. § 102.64(a).[4] Employers are now required to submit a written "Statement of Position" that identifies any basis for contending that the proposed bargaining unit is inappropriate, any challenges to voter eligibility, and "all other issues the employer intends to raise at the hearing." 29 C.F.R. § 102.63(b)(1)(i). In accordance with the rule's purpose, however, hearing officers and regional directors may decline to hear evidence on issues "that need not be decided before the election," including issues of individuals' eligibility to vote. 79 Fed. Reg. 74,384; see also C.F.R. § 102.64(a) ("Disputes concerning individuals' eligibility to vote or inclusion in an appropriate unit ordinarily need not be litigated or resolved before an election is conducted."). But even if a voter's eligibility or inclusion is not contested at the pre-election hearing, a party may later challenge the eligibility of any voter. *Id.* § 102.66(d).

---

[4] A question of representation exists "if a proper petition has been filed concerning a unit appropriate for the purpose of collective bargaining or concerning a unit in which an individual or labor organization has been certified or is being currently recognized by the employer as the bargaining representative." 29 C.F.R. § 102.64(a).

[T]he ABC entities argue that these rule changes impermissibly restrict the scope of the pre-election hearing. [...] Relying on the legislative history of the Taft-Hartley amendments to the NLRA and remarks of Senator Taft [a single sentence contained in a supplemental analysis produced after the Act was passed], they maintain that the "function of hearings in representation cases [is] to determine whether an election may be properly held at the time, and if so, to decide questions of unit and eligibility to vote." [...] By impermissibly preventing employers from litigating these issues at the hearings, the ABC entities argue, the rule violates the purpose of Section 9 and therefore is an unreasonable interpretation of the statute.

But this reading of the rule and the legislative history is unpersuasive. The actual language of the rule neither "precludes" nor "prevents" the presentation of evidence regarding voter eligibility. The rule simply indicates that "[d]isputes concerning individuals' eligibility to vote or inclusion in an appropriate unit *ordinarily* need not be litigated or resolved before an election is conducted." 29 C.F.R. § 102.64(a) (emphasis added); see 79 Fed. Reg. at 74,390 (explaining that the Board "expect[s] regional directors to permit litigation of, and to resolve, [individual eligibility or inclusion] questions when they might significantly change the size or character of the unit"). [...] The rule neither eliminates the possibility that a hearing officer could address these issues at an earlier stage nor prohibits an employer from ever raising such issues. [...]

[...] Section 9 specifies that the purpose of the pre-election hearing is to determine whether a question of representation exists, which is a different inquiry from the question of which specific individuals will vote in the ensuing election. The ordinary meaning of the statutory language cannot support the ABC entities' construction. [...]

In support of its argument that the rule conforms to the statutory text, the Board points to *Inland Empire District Council, Lumber & Sawmill Workers Union v. Millis,* 325 U.S. 697, 706 (1945). The Supreme Court, in *Inland Empire,* interpreted Section 9 to grant the Board wide discretion in devising the procedures employed in deciding whether a question of representation exists. The Court explained that the phrase "appropriate hearing upon due notice" is deliberately expansive and noted that Congress intended to "confer[] broad discretion upon the Board as to the hearing which [Section] 9(c) required before certification." *Id.* at 708. [...] (Congress has entrusted the Board with a wide degree of discretion in establishing the procedure and safeguards necessary to insure the fair and free choice of bargaining representatives by employees.").

The ABC entities counter that *Inland Empire* preceded the Taft-Hartley amendments, which "fundamentally rewrote the entire section of the Act in which the hearing requirement appears." The "appropriate hearing" language, however, remained the same pre- and post-amendment. In the absence of any change to the phrase, the Court's interpretation remains controlling. [...]

III B. The ABC entities also challenge provisions of the rule that require disclosure of personal-employee information both before and after the pre-election hearing. They argue that the provisions conflict with federal privacy law and thus constitute an impermissible interpretation of the NLRA. And they assert that the broader disclosure requirements are an arbitrary and capricious invasion of the privacy rights of employees in violation of the APA. The Board maintains that the disclosures are consistent with the purpose of the NLRA, and asserts that it carefully weighed the privacy rights of employees in accordance with the requirements of the APA. Because the NLRA does not prohibit these disclosures and because the Board offers a rational explanation for its decision, we defer to it.

The NLRA directs the Board to decide the "unit appropriate for the purposes of collective bargaining" so as to "assure to employees the fullest freedom in exercising the rights guaranteed by [the Act]." 29 U.S.C. § 159(b). Employees are also granted the "right" to "refrain from" engaging in union activity. *Id.* § 157. In its *Excelsior Underwear, Inc.* decision, the Board first required an employer to disclose the names and addresses of employees eligible to vote in representation elections. 156 N.L.R.B. 1236 (1966). The Board found that a lack of information in a representation election impedes employee's exercise of choice and determined that providing employee's personal information maximizes the "likelihood that all the voters will be exposed to the arguments for, as well as against, union representation." *Id.* at 1240–41. Upholding the validity of the disclosure rule, the Supreme Court endorsed this rational in *NLRB v. Wyman-Gordon Co.*, 394 U.S. 759, 767 (1969) ("The disclosure requirement furthers this objective [to ensure the fair and free choice of bargaining representatives] by encouraging an informed employee electorate and by allowing unions the right of access to employees that management already possesses.").

Here, the new disclosure provisions expand *Excelsior Underwear* by requiring two separate disclosures of employee information. First, within two days of a direction of election, employers must produce a voter list that contains "the full names, work locations, shifts, job classifications, and contact information (including home addresses, available personal email addresses, and available home and personal cellular ('cell') telephone numbers) of all eligible voters." 29 C.F.R. § 102.67(l). Employers must disclose this information about all employees who are deemed to be part of an appropriate bargaining unit, as well as those employees whose status is not yet determined. *Id.* §§ 102.62(d) & 102.67(l). Under the prior rule, employers were required only to produce a list of names and addresses within seven days of the direction of an election. *Excelsior Underwear*, 156 N.L.R.B. at 1239–40. Second, employers must disclose the names and job duties of employees to a petitioning union before any determination that the petition is supported by a sufficient showing of interest to proceed to an election. *Id.* § 102.63(b). Notably, however, before disclosing employee information to a union, the regional director must find that there is "reasonable cause to believe" that a question of representation exists. 29 C.F.R. § 102.63(a)(1).

III B 1. The ABC entities assert that these requirements conflict with federal laws that protect employee privacy. They suggest that federal law has moved away from *Excelsior Underwear*'s justification for disclosure and towards increasing privacy protections, citing, as support, the Privacy Act, the privacy exemption to the Freedom of Information Act, the Telemarketing and Consumer Fraud and Abuse Prevention Act, and the Controlling the Assault of Non-Solicited Pornography and Marketing Act. And they note generally that the disclosure requirements are "at odds" with congressional intent to "limit the number of intrusions into individual privacy." They fail, however, to identify any federal law that restricts the disclosure of employee information to unions by employers. They similarly fail to note any change in circumstances that would undermine the Board's concern for encouraging an informed employee electorate by allowing unions the right of access to employees. See *Wyman-Gordon Co.*, 394 U.S. at 767 (concluding that the Board was within its authority to order disclosure of employee information). Because the disclosure requirements reasonably further this valid objective, the rule change does not violate the NLRA.

III B 2. The ABC entities also contend that the disclosure provisions are arbitrary and capricious under the APA because the rule disregards employees' privacy concerns, exposes employees to union intimidation and harassment, enables union misuse of the voter list, and imposes a substantial burden on employers. They insist that employees' privacy rights "should outweigh the desire of unions to use the latest technology to facilitate their organizing efforts." [...]

The rule changes adopted by the Board were "intended to better advance the two objectives articulated by the Board in *Excelsior*"; namely, to ensure fair and free choice by maximizing voter exposure to non employer party arguments and to resolve questions of representation by facilitating knowledge of voters' identities. 74 Fed. Reg. at 74,335. As an initial matter, the ABC entities contend that the disclosure requirements place an undue, substantial burden on employers. In adopting the rule, the Board considered comments that the two-day turnaround was impractical and unduly burdensome. 79 Fed. Reg. 74,353. The Board concluded, however, that "advances in record keeping and retrieval technology" warranted reducing the time period for production of the voter list. *Id.* Noting that federal employment law already requires businesses to maintain employee records, the Board also pointed out that the regional director may "direct a due date for the voter list beyond two days in extraordinary circumstances." *Id.* at 74,354. Because the rule accords such deference to the regional director, the ABC entities' facial challenge to the turnaround time fails.

The ABC entities next charge that disclosure of personal information provides increased opportunity for union abuse and misconduct. But the language of the rule accounts for that concern, mandating that the parties "shall not use the [voter] list for purposes other than representation proceeding, Board proceedings arising from it, and related matters." 29 C.F.R. §§ 102.62(d) & 102.67(l) . [...] Moreover, the Board noted several remedial options for union misconduct, and concluded that it would continue to leave the "question of remedies to case-by-case adjudication." 79 Fed. Reg. 74,359.

With regard to the employee privacy concerns, the Board reviewed the "revolution in communications technology" between when *Excelsior* was decided and the present day. The Board cited evidence of the decline in traditional means of communication—including United States mail and "face- to-face conversations on the doorstep"—and analyzed the increasing use of digital communications technology, observing that home and cellular phones, as well as email, have become "a universal point of contact." *Id.* at 74,337. The Board considered "employee privacy concerns" and weighed the benefits of expanding disclosure of voter contact information against the privacy risk. [...] As the Board explained, however, the privacy risks associated with this disclosure is "part of our daily life," and requires only the release of information that the employee has already shared with his or her employer. *Id.* at 74,343 n.169.

The ABC entities predict that disclosure of such information exposes employees to identity theft. But the ABC entities fail to identify any evidence that disclosure of an email address and a cell phone number presents either a greater risk of identity theft or a greater possibility of privacy infringement than a home address. Indeed, virtual contact in the form of a phone call or email is routinely and readily ignored. Face-to-face contact with a union representative at an employee's home is significantly more intrusive and more difficult to avoid. [...]

Again, as this is a facial challenge, the ABC entities carry the burden of demonstrating that no set of circumstances exists under which this regulation would be valid. Exposing employees to a potentially increased risk of identity theft and data breach so as to ensure an informed electorate does not rise to the level of arbitrary and capricious agency action. [...] [I]t is within the Board's discretion to weigh competing interests and promulgate rules that advance the goals of the Act. Its reasoning is not irrational and it is not the province of this court to inject a contrary policy preference. The Board extensively considered the burden on employers and the privacy concerns of employees when determining the necessity of the expanded disclosure requirements. [...]

III C The ABC entities also argue that the rule violates the NLRA by interfering with protected speech during election campaigns. They contend that the cumulative effect of the rule change improperly shortens the overall pre-election period in violation of the "free speech" provision of the Act.

The NLRA protects the rights of both employers and employees to engage in "uninhibited, robust, and wide open debate in labor disputes." *Chamber of Commerce of U.S. v. Brown*, 554 U.S. 60, 67–68 (2008). [...] Prior versions of the regulations stated that the regional director "will normally not schedule an election until a date between the 25th and 30th days after the date of the decision, to permit the Board to rule on any request for review which may be filed." 29 C.F.R. §101.21(d) (2014). Under the new rule, "[e]lections will no longer be automatically stayed in anticipation of requests for review," 79 Fed. Reg. at 74,309, and instead, "[t]he regional director shall schedule the election for the earliest date practicable" consistent with the NLRA and the relevant regulations. 29 C.F.R. § 102.67(b).

III C 1. Again relying on legislative history, the ABC entities point to the 1959 amendments to the Act to demonstrate congressional opposition to "quickie" union elections. They point to comments by then-Senator

John F. Kennedy, sponsor of the 1959 bill, declaring the necessity of a 30-day waiting period as a "safeguard against rushing employees into an election." Notably absent from their argument, however, is any citation to a provision of the Act or other statute that mandates a specified waiting period prior to an election. This court refers to legislative history only when the statutory text is ambiguous. See *Rainbow Gun Club, Inc. v. Denbury Onshore, LLC*, 760 F.3d 405, 410 (5th Cir. 2014). This statutory text is unambiguous on its face, so we need not refer to legislative history to discern its meaning. [...]

III C 2. Moreover, to the extent the ABC entities argue that the timing provisions violate the APA, they fail to explain how or why—aside from repeatedly characterizing the elections as "quickie elections"—the rule change inhibits meaningful debate or qualifies as arbitrary and capricious. In declining to create a specific deadline for elections, the Board addressed concerns about impairing speech rights. The Board found that many employers begin speaking to employees about union representation well before a petition is filed, "often as soon as [the employees] are hired." 79 Fed. Reg. 74,320–21. [...] And as the Board pointed out, employers "can compel attendance at meetings at which employees are often expressly urged to vote against representation." 76 Fed. Reg. 74,323. The Board also charged regional directors, in setting the election, with taking into account "the desires of the parties, which may include their opportunity for meaningful speech about the election." *Id.* at 74,318. This discretion afforded to the regional director effectively precludes the ABC entities' facial challenge. [...] Because the Board considered the potential burdens on speech and afforded the regional director discretion in setting an election date, the ABC entities' challenge to the timing rule fails.

III D [...] Reframing their earlier arguments, the ABC entities contend that the rule is arbitrary and capricious because it is based on factors that Congress did not intend the Board to consider, including speed in scheduling elections, delay of voter eligibility issues, disclosure of employee information, and facilitation of organized labor.

The Board agrees that it considered speed in scheduling elections. But increasing the efficiency and effectiveness of regulatory programs is well within the Board's purview. See *Decker v. Nw. Envtl. Def. Ctr.*, 133 S. Ct. 1326, 1340 (2013) (Scalia, J., concurring in part, dissenting in part) ("Making regulatory programs effective is the purpose of *rulemaking*."); *Abbott Ambulance of Ill. v. NLRB*, 522 F.3d 447, 451 (D.C. Cir. 2008) noting that the Board rule promoted efficiency in union elections and finding that the Board could reasonably weigh delay and uncertainty in election results in altering rules. [...]

The Board also reasoned that the final rule was necessary to further a variety of additional permissible goals and interests. 79 Fed. Reg. 74,315. In adopting these changes, the Board explained that the rule was designed not only to increase the speed and efficiency of the election process, but also to reduce unnecessary barriers to elections, to modernize processes so as to reduce cost, and to "make effective use of new technology." *Id.*

[...] As a last-ditch effort, the ABC entities complain that representation elections were delayed in only a small number of cases and there was "no demonstrated need to make the sweeping changes adopted by the Board." But an agency does not act in an arbitrary and capricious manner simply because it attempts to improve a regulatory scheme. "[I]f the agency considers the factors and articulates a rational relationship between the facts found and the choice made" and gives "at least minimal consideration to relevant facts contained in the record," it is not the role of the court "to weigh the evidence pro and con." *Delta Found., Inc. v. United States*, 303 F.3d 551, 563 (5th Cir. 2002). Here, the Board identified evidence that elections were being unnecessarily delayed by litigation, see 79 Fed. Reg. 74,317–18, and that certain rules had become outdated as a result of changes in technology, see *id.* at 74,308. It conducted an exhaustive and lengthy review of the issues, evidence, and testimony, responded to contrary arguments, and offered factual and legal support for its final conclusions. Because the Board acted rationally and in furtherance of its congressional mandate in adopting the rule, the ABC entities' challenge to the rule as a whole fails.

[...]

[Source: 826 F.3d 215 (2016)]

ANNOTATION

The discussion regarding eligibility to vote could have and should have noted that if a party challenges a person's eligibility to vote in an NLRB representation election, that person is given a special double envelope with the ballot being placed in an unmarked interior envelope and the voter's name placed on the outer envelope. The outer envelope is opened only if the vote count for unchallenged ballots makes it possible for challenged ballots to change the election result. In that event, the inner challenged ballot envelope of a voter whose eligibility has been upheld is placed in a common pile with similar envelopes, opened after all challenges have been resolved by the Board, and then counted with the result being added to the count of the unchallenged ballots.

The NLRB's access to the disputed additional information about alleged bargaining unit members should facilitate its ability to more completely investigate what work specific employees actually do, regardless of their job titles; what contacts they have with each other; the extent of their common supervision and work environment; and the like. This information is weighed by the Board in assessing whether they share a "community of interests"—the test of whether a bargaining unit is appropriate and which individuals are within that unit.

On the one hand, one might ask why employers should want to delay when the NLRB holds its election. After all, the distraction and possible animosities of employees embroiled in debating the merits and demerits of union representation can be expected to interfere with productivity. On the other hand, studies have shown that the more time that lapses between the beginning of a union organizing campaign and the holding of an NLRB election, the less likely it is that the result will favor the union. Weiler, "Promises To Keep: Securing Workers' Rights To Self-Organization Under The NLRA", 96 *Harv. L. Rev.* 1769, 1778 (1983).

American law allows employers to communicate their point of view regarding which way their employees should vote in an NLRB election so long as they do so in a manner that is not coercive. As the court notes, both at the workplace and through other means of communication, employers have a distinct advantage in contacting each employee to communicate its viewpoint. The issues of employee privacy could be avoided if, instead of giving petitioning unions the employee name, phone number, address and email contact information, union organizers were given reasonable access to communicate with employees on the enterprise premises—something the U.S. courts have resisted on the ground of an undue infringement of the employer's property rights. Of course, with increased work performed at employees' homes in many industries, access to employees at the employer's premises may be meaningless. At least as to such employees, giving unions the same contact information as possessed by an employer may be the only way to ensure adequate opportunity to communicate with all prospective NLRB election voters.

ITALY

Constitutional Court
Decision no. 5126 of March 2015

Collective agreement – worker members of cooperatives – minimum wage – reference to collective agreements signed by the comparatively more representative organizations – Art. 39 of Italian Constitution requiring commensurate and sufficient remuneration

HEADNOTES

Facts

A member and worker of a cooperative lodged a complaint against the cooperative enterprise of which he was a member and employee, to obtain a ruling to order it to pay the difference in remuneration with respect to the national collective agreement signed by the sectoral trade unions belonging to the three main confederations in place of the collective agreement actually applied by the respondent cooperative, on the basis of Article 7, section 4, of Legislative Decree no. 248 of 31 December 2007.

The respondent cooperative claimed that Article 7, section 4, of the Decree was constitutionally unlawful because it violated Article 39 of the Italian Constitution.

The Court of Lucca sought a ruling on the constitutional lawfulness of section 4 of Article 7 of Legislative Decree no. 248 of 31 December 2007, declaring it to be material and not manifestly unfounded.

Decision

The Constitutional Court ruled that the question was not founded.

Law Applied

Constitution of the Italian Republic
Article 36, section 1
Workers shall be entitled to a remuneration commensurate with the quantity and quality of their work, and in any case sufficient to ensure to them and their families a free and honourable existence.

Article 39
The organization of trade unions is free.

No obligation shall be imposed on trade unions except that of registering at local or central offices according to the provisions of the law.

Trade unions shall only be registered on condition that their by-laws shall establish internal organizations based on democratic principles.

Registered trade unions shall have legal personality. Being represented in proportion to the number of their registered members, they may jointly enter into collective labour agreements, which shall be mandatory for all those who belong to the industry to which the said agreements refer.

Italian Civil Code
Article 2099
The remuneration of a worker may be decided according to time or piece rate and the amount paid shall be determined by corporatist laws, in the manner and terms in use in the place where the work is performed.

In the absence of corporatist laws or an agreement between the parties, the remuneration shall be established by a court, after having taken into account, where necessary, the opinion of the associations of professionals.

A worker may also be remunerated in whole or in part with a share of the profits or of the products, or with commissions, payment in cash or through the performance of work in kind.

Legislative Decree no. 248/2007, converted into Act no. 31/2008
Article 7, section 4
Until the full implementation of the law on member workers of a cooperative enterprise, in the case where there are a number of collective agreements covering the same sector of workers, and pursuant to Article 3, section 1, of Act no. 142 of 3 April of 2001, a cooperative enterprise which performs activities that are subject to the application of those sectoral agreements shall pay its worker members gross sums not less than those established by the collective agreements signed by the comparatively more representative employer and trade union organizations at the national level in the sector.

Act no. 142/2001
Article 3, section 1

Without prejudice to Article 36 of Act no. 300 of 20 May 1970, a cooperative enterprise shall remunerate a cooperative member worker gross sums commensurate to the quantity and quality of the work performed and, in any case, not less than the minimum set by the national collective agreement of the industry or similar sector for the performance of similar work, or, in the case of employment relationships differing from subordinate work, in the absence of specific collective agreements or arrangements, not less than the prevailing average remuneration applicable for similar work performed in the form of independent work.

JUDGEMENT

(*omissis*)

5.2. This is the legal background to Article 7, section 4, of Legislative Decree no. 248 of 2007, which, as already mentioned, reads "Until the full implementation of the law on member workers of a cooperative enterprise, in the case where there are a number of collective agreements covering the same sector of workers, and pursuant to Article 3, section 1, of Act no. 142 of 3 April 2001, a cooperative enterprise which performs activities that are subject to the application of those sectoral agreements shall pay its worker members gross sums not less than those established by the collective agreements signed by the comparatively more representative employer and trade union organizations at national level in the sector". This provision was adopted following the memorandum of understanding signed on 10 October 2007 by the Ministry of Labour, the Ministry of Economic Development, AGCI, Confcooperative, Legacoop, CGIL, CISL, UIL, in which the Government pledged to launch "a suitable administrative initiative so that cooperatives adopt gross pay rates for subordinate work, pursuant to Article 3, section 1, of Act no. 142 of 3 April 2001, that are no less than those set by the national collective agreement signed by the comparatively more representative employer and trade union organizations at the national level in the sector of reference" (point C). The signatories' common goal was to challenge the adoption of collective agreements signed by employer and trade union organizations of unproven representativeness, which adopt remuneration levels that are potentially in conflict with the concept of sufficient remuneration, under Article 36 of the Italian Constitution, as per the interpretation provided by case law deriving from Article 2099 of the Italian Civil Code.

Following the entry into force of Article7, section 4, of Legislative Decree no. 248 of 2007, a considerable number of inspections, promoted by the Ministry of Labour, were carried out, to ensure that: "in the presence of a number of national collective agreements in the same product sector, the remuneration rates set by collective agreements stipulated by the comparatively more representative employer organizations and trade union organizations shall be applied". This was in compliance with Article 7, section 4, of the Legislative Decree in relation to the types of employment relationships arising in the light of the internal regulation under Article 6, section 1, letter a), of Act no. 142 of 2001 (Ministry of Labour memoranda of 9 November 2010 and 6 March 2012) and consistent with specific indices of trade union representativeness identified in the Ministry of Labour memorandum of 1 June 2012.

Case law has re-iterated this interpretation and has argued that "in the case of a cooperative enterprise […] a cooperative worker member must be paid a gross remuneration (i.e. basic pay as well as other remuneration items) that may not be less than the minimum, for similar services, set by national collective bargaining of the sector or for workers of a similar sector, whose applicability, as for the contractual minimum, is not affected by the entry into force of the regulation under Article 6, of Act no. 142 of 2001, which, since it is essentially intended to regulate the manner of performing work by members and to indicate the applicable norms, including collective ones, cannot contain less favourable provisions derogating from the collective provisions for a sector" (Court of Cassation, Labour Division, Decision no. 17583 of 4 August 2014; similarly, Court of Cassation, Labour Division, Decision no. 19832 of 28 August 2013).

This Court too, which was recently asked to decide on the same issue of constitutional lawfulness as that under discussion today (what's more by the same judge) with regard to Article 7, section 4, of Legislative Decree no. 248 del 2007, with reference to Article 39 of the Italian Constitution, while ruling it to be inadmissible by virtue of the immaterial nature of the norm in question in relation to the *thema decidendum* of the referring court, pointed out, with regard to both the above-mentioned Article 7, section 4, and to the connected Article 3, section 1, of Act no. 142 of 2001, that "the objective of both laws is to ensure the extension of the minimum remuneration (so-called minimum wage) to members of a certain sector of workers, thereby ensuring equality of treatment among workers and among employers" (Decision no. 59 of 2013).

5.3. On the basis of what has been stated so far, it is clear that the reference made by the Court of Lucca is grounded on an erroneous interpretation.

Rather than attributing *erga omnes* effect to the above-mentioned collective agreements signed by the comparatively more representative trade union organizations in violation of Article 39 of the Italian Constitution, Article 7, section 4, of Legislative Decree no. 248 of 2007, together with Article 3 of Act no. 142 of 2001, through their enactment, make reference to the above-mentioned agreements, in particular to the minimum gross remuneration set, as an external parameter of measurement for a court to define the proportionality and sufficiency of the remuneration to be paid to the cooperative member worker, pursuant to Article 36 of the Italian Constitution. This parameter is referred to – and must therefore be complied with – regardless of the provisional nature of Article 7 itself, which refers to "pending the full implementation of the law on member workers of a cooperative enterprise". By making reference to the collective agreement which, more than others, reflects the changing wage patterns in the sectors in which cooperative enterprises operate, the Article seeks to combat downward wage competition, in line with the direction that, for some time now, case law has considered compatible with the requirements of proportionality and sufficiency (Article 36 of the Italian Constitution). This is the remuneration agreed in collective agreements signed by comparatively more representative associations (see, among others, the already mentioned Decision no. 17583 of 2014 issued by the Court of Cassation).

ANNOTATION

The decision being commented on here concerns the remuneration of a worker member of a cooperative. Under Italian law, work can also be performed on the basis of association agreements, which as such entails an entrepreneurial risk for the cooperative worker. This type also includes the case of a cooperative member of production and work, on the basis of which the cooperative member makes his/her contribution by performing work. However, some typical employment law protections are available also for this form of work. One such law is Act no. 142 dated 3 April 2001. This has created a so-called double relationship mechanism, on the basis of which a cooperative member not only has a membership relationship, but also an employment relationship (either independent or subordinate work) with the same enterprise, which is therefore subject to the application of the relevant legal regulations.

More specifically, in the case of remuneration the law states that cooperative enterprises are required to provide a remuneration that is commensurate to the quantity and quality of the work performed and, in any case, not less than the minimum set by the national collective agreement (Article 3 of Act no. 142/2001). Italian labour law commentators have identified in this law an attempt to limit the use of cheaper labour and guarantee fair competition among businesses, as well as ensure that the groups of workers involved are paid a fair remuneration, pursuant to Article 36 of the Italian Constitution for all employees.

However, this sector has seen the spread of "pirate bargaining", whereby worker trade unions and employers of unproven representativeness have signed collective agreements stipulating worse working conditions, and more specifically lower pay, than that agreed by the biggest trade unions. The Italian legislature therefore acted, requiring, pursuant to Article 7, section 4, of Legislative Decree no. 248/2007, that the gross remuneration of a cooperative member be based on collective agreements signed by the comparatively most representative organizations at national level, thereby giving general legal effect to these collective agreements on this specific issue.

Hence the purported incompatibility with Article 39 of the Italian Constitution, part two of which has never been implemented by lawmakers (see Court of Cassation Decision no. 11325/2005, reported in volume 25 of the ILLR), which lays down a specific procedure for trade unions to register and negotiate so as the sign collective agreements producing *erga omnes* effect. Given the inoperative status of the second part of Article 39 of the Italian Constitution, collective agreements are not endowed with such an effect, with the result that any law that attempts to achieve this objective by other means would be constitutionally unlawful.

Moreover, this is the conclusion that the Constitutional Court reached in a decision going back in time, but which is still of great importance for Italian trade union law, namely Constitutional Court Decision no. 196/1962.

However, in the judgement being commented on here, the Italian Constitutional Court has provided a different solution. The law in question is constitutionally lawful because it does not propose to extend the legal effect of collective agreements signed by the comparatively more representative organizations, or to impose the application *ex ante* regardless of an evaluation of their compliance with a fair remuneration, but only refers to remuneration as a parameter for measuring the commensurate and sufficient remuneration of cooperative member workers, in compliance with Article 36 of the Italian Constitution.

In other words, the Constitutional Court states that the intention of the legislature was, above all, to select the collective legal person which was best able to define the constitutionally protected remuneration to be paid to a cooperative worker member. Italy has no minimum wage legislation, which case law has remedied by making use of Article 36 of the Italian Constitution. Since, according to this provision of the Constitution, a worker is entitled to a commensurate and sufficient remuneration, the courts use the remuneration set by collective agreements as a parameter for a fair remuneration (see again Italian Court of Cassation Decision no. 11325/2005, reported in volume 25 of the ILLR).

In the presence of a number of collective agreements it is necessary to make a selection. It is reasonable for such a selection to be based on the criterion of trade union representativeness, which is better able to reflect the wage patterns in the sector where cooperatives operate. Such a selection is also compatible with the principle of trade union freedom under Article 39 of the Italian Constitution since, rather than imposing compliance with a given collective agreement, it makes reference only to the remuneration element, on the ground that the authorities regarding wages in the Italian legal order are the law and the social partners.

As the Constitutional Court notes, the provision in question is linked to combatting downward wage competition by pirate bargaining in the cooperative sector, and also serves the purpose of regulating the market. Commentators in Italy initially pointed to the possible consequences of such a decision. If the legislature's selection of applicable collective agreements, for the wage aspect, in the sector of the cooperatives, there would be nothing to stop the same phenomenon occurring in other sectors, again with the purpose of implementing the constitutional protection of a commensurate and sufficient wage. This could prove to be the "Italian path" to a minimum wage, provided, of course, it does not fall foul of Article 39 of the Italian Constitution.

Fin. 1

FINLAND

Supreme Court 2016:12
3.3.2016 (S2013/757)

Employment contract – employment benefits – bonuses – discrimination – industrial action

HEADNOTES

Facts

This case must be understood against the background of the important Finnish Supreme Court (SC) case from 2010 (2010:93, reported in ILLR volume 30). In that case the Court found that discrimination on grounds of trade union activity existed when an employer refused to pay so-called results-based bonuses to employees who had participated in unlawful industrial action during the period when bonuses were earned. In the case SC 2010:93 the industrial action had been undertaken and decided on by the trade union to which the employees belonged. In the present case SC 2016:12 the trade union had not in any way taken part in or supported the unlawful industrial action, which had been a spontaneous "wild cat" action undertaken by a group of individual employees. These actions had taken place on 31 May 2010, 1 to 3 September 2010 and 4 September 2010.

As a consequence of these industrial actions, which had been found unlawful by the Labour Court and for which the trade union therefore had to pay fines for breach of its active peace obligation (the obligation to make sure that its members do not resort to unlawful industrial action during the period a collective agreement is in force), the employer decided not to pay bonuses to those employees who had taken part in these "wild cat" actions. The decision was based on the explicit condition, unilaterally introduced by the employer, in the bonuses scheme according to which employees who take part in unlawful industrial action lose their entitlement to results-based bonuses.

The main issue on which the Supreme Court had to decide in this case was whether the assessment from the old case SC 2010:93 applied also in this case, which would mean that such a condition for payment of bonuses was to be regarded as discriminatory on the ground of trade union activity or whether the fact that the trade union had not decided upon these industrial actions that were initiated by individual employees would lead to a different outcome.

Furthermore this case was about the employees' liability for damages. Here the question was whether the restrictions regarding the liability for damages, which are applicable to employees, were applicable in this case. The plaintiff argued that the employer's withholding of the economic benefit had the consequence of being equivalent to liability for damages and that the restrictions under the Employment Contracts Act Chapter 12 section 1 para. 3 should apply.

Decision

The Supreme Court reaffirmed the conclusion from the first instance court according to which the industrial action in this case did not have any connection with trade union activity or the principle of freedom of association since the trade union was not involved in any way in the industrial action undertaken.

The preconditions for receiving bonuses had been laid down in the bonuses scheme on which the employer may decide unilaterally within the limits of mandatory law. There were no obstacles laid down in law in the present case for applying the clauses concerning the bonuses scheme according to which an employee who took part in an unlawful industrial action would loose his or her entitlement to bonuses for the period in question. The employees therefore were not entitled to the bonuses.

Law Applied

Finnish Constitution

Section 13 – Freedom of assembly and freedom of association

Everyone has the right to arrange meetings and demonstrations without a permit, as well as the right to participate in them.

Everyone has freedom of association. Freedom of association entails the right to form an association without previous authorization, to be a member or not to be a member of an association and to participate in the activities of an association.

The freedom to form trade unions and to organize in order to look after other interests is likewise guaranteed.

More detailed provisions on the exercise of the freedom of assembly and the freedom of association are laid down by an Act.

Non-Discrimination Act (1325/2014)

Chapter 3 Prohibition of discrimination and victimization
Section 8 Prohibition of discrimination.

(1) No one may be discriminated against on the basis of age, origin, nationality, language, religion, belief, opinion, political activity, trade union activity, family relationships, state of health, disability, sexual orientation or other personal characteristics. Discrimination is prohibited, regardless of whether it is based on a fact or assumption concerning the person him/herself or another.

(2) In addition to direct and indirect discrimination, harassment, denial of reasonable accommodation as well as an instruction or order to discriminate constitute discrimination.

Employment Contracts Act (55/2001)

Chapter 2, Section 2
[*This section was applied in its previous form, which was substantially equal to the Non-Discrimination Act, Section 8 below.*]

Section 2 (1331/2014) Prohibition of discrimination and equal treatment.

An employer must treat all employees equally, unless deviating from this is justified in view of the duties and position of the employees.

Without proper and justified reason less favourable employment terms than those applicable to other employment relationships must not be applied to fixed-term and part-time employment relationships merely because of the duration of the employment contract or working hours.

Provisions on equality and on the prohibition of discrimination are laid down in the Non-Discrimination Act (1325/2014). Provisions on equality and on the prohibition of discrimination based on gender are laid down in the Act on Equality between Women and Men (609/1986).

Chapter 12, Liability for damages
Section 1, General liability.

If the employer intentionally or through negligence commits a breach against obligations arising from the employment relationship or this Act, it shall be liable for the loss thus caused to the employee.

In derogation from the provisions of section 1 above, liability for termination of the employment contract contrary to the grounds laid down in Chapter 1, section 4, or in Chapters 7 or 8 is determined under section 2.

If the employee intentionally or through negligence commits a breach against, or neglects obligations arising from, the employment contract or this Act or at work causes a loss to the employer, the employee shall be liable to the employer for the loss thus caused in accordance with the grounds laid down in Chapter 4, section 1, of the Tort Liability Act (412/1974).

The compensation for neglecting to observe the period of notice is determined under Chapter 6, section 4. Chapter 5, section 7(3) lays down provisions on the entitlement of an employee who has been laid off for a minimum of 200 days, and who terminates the employment relationship, to receive compensation equivalent to pay or part of it for the period of notice.

Chapter 13, Miscellaneous provisions

Section 1 Freedom of association.

Employers and employees have the right to belong to associations and to be active in them. They also have the right to establish lawful associations. Employers and employees are likewise free not to belong to any of the associations referred to above. Prevention or restriction of this right or freedom is prohibited.

Any agreement contrary to the freedom of association is null and void.

JUDGEMENT

The Supreme Court noted that, in accordance with the bonus scheme that had been introduced unilaterally by the employer, an employee that took part in unlawful industrial action would lose his or her right to performance-based bonuses for the actual period of time on strike.

A number of employees had undertaken industrial action 31 May 2010, 1 to 3 September 2010 and 4 September 2010. The Labour Court found that the two first actions were unlawful under the Finnish Collective Agreements Act since the trade union had not fulfilled its duty to make sure that its members respect the peace obligation.

The Supreme Court held that there was a presumption of discrimination since those employees who had undertaken industrial action had been treated differently regarding their right to bonuses due to their exercise of the right to strike.

The Supreme Court made it clear that it had to decide on two issues. The first issue was whether this term regarding bonuses was to be regarded as discriminatory on the ground of trade union activity, and the second issue was has the employer – by these bonuses rules – introduced a liability scheme which goes too far in introducing a liability for the employees for damages caused by industrial action.

The Supreme Court argued that in the present case a presumption of discrimination has been established since the employees were treated differently due to reasons relating to trade union activities. The Court continued by asking the question whether the freedom of association principles protect individual employees who undertake industrial action without any participation by any trade union. The Supreme Court made a thorough analysis of the question and it went through a number of international instruments protecting freedom of association (European Union Social Charter, Article 12:1, the UN Human rights instruments, the ILO Conventions Nos 87 and 98, and the European Council instruments). The end result was that the Finnish Constitution and the international instruments only protect decisions and action undertaken by a trade union, but that there is no international obligation to protect single employees undertaking industrial action as individuals if there is an adequate protection in place for trade unions. In many cases the instruments leave an option for Member States to protect at least either individual employees or trade unions. Therefore and taking also into account some specific clauses in Finnish legislation, there is no obstacle in Finnish law against a clause in a bonuses program which restricts the access to bonuses for those who have undertaken unlawful industrial action. The presumption of discrimination can therefore be lifted by these circumstances.

Finally the SC stated that the issue at stake in this case was the preconditions for payment of performance-related bonuses. Since these bonuses and the loss of them has no relationship to the damage caused by the unlawful action towards the employer, there is no linkage to the liability for damage for the employer and this term in the bonuses scheme.

ANNOTATION

This is the first case from the Finnish Supreme Court limiting the application of the right to freedom of association as codified in the Constitution in Finland and several international instruments, so as to cover organized employees and trade unions, but not individual employees acting on their own behalf.

This is not surprizing taking into account that the Finnish labour market is highly organized and the trade unions are the legitimate actors within the collective bargaining system of Finland.

The case however clearly leaves some questions unanswered. In many cases it might not be very straight forward to establish whether the employee is acting on his or her own behalf or as a trade union member or even representative. The present system is in this regard actually slightly contradictory. On the one hand, the trade union can escape liability for breach of its peace obligation if it can show that its members were not involved. On the other hand, the trade union members need to be able to prove that they were acting on behalf of the trade union in order not be individually "liable" for an industrial action in the form of some negative economic consequences and in the most extreme cases loss of job in the form of lawful dismissal.

Another unsolved issue is whether a significantly "individual" benefit such as a bonus is of a different nature than a clearly collective benefit related to the collective agreement. It seems possible that differences might occur between these categories.

In summary, what we know so far about Finnish case law (SC 2010:93 and SC 2016:12) is that individual employees do not carry responsibilities for what trade unions do and that individual trade union members have a kind if immunity as long they follow instructions from a trade union. When acting on their own behalf there is no immunity to protect them.

S.A. 1

SOUTH AFRICA

Labour Appeal Court of South Africa
ADT Security (Pty) Ltd
v. National Security & Unqualified Workers Union and Others
[2012] ZALAC 52; [2014] 11 BLLR 1096; (2015) 36 ILJ 152 (LAC)

Demonstration outside of working hours aimed at placing pressure on an employer in a collective bargaining dispute – union not exercising rights under the Labour Relations Act but under the constitutional right to demonstrate – constitutes a circumvention of the dispute procedures of the Labour Relations Act – accordingly unlawful

HEADNOTES

Facts

The company and the trade union were in dispute over the trade union's organisational rights in the workplace. The Labour Relations Act (LRA) provides a procedure for the resolution of such disputes and two alternative remedies – the right to refer the dispute to arbitration or to strike. The trade union however decided to hold a public march to the premises of the company's head office to hand over a memorandum to management. The union informed the company that only those employees who were night shift or not on duty would engage in the march. Permission for the public demonstration was sought by the union and granted by the municipal authorities in terms of the Regulation of Gatherings Act (RGA). The company approached the Labour Court for an urgent injunction on the grounds that the march was unlawful.

Decision

The Labour Court dismissed the application for the injunction, principally for two reasons: first because the union did not rely on the LRA but on the constitutional right to protest and petition as that right had been given effect to by the Regulation of Gatherings Act; and secondly because the employees were off duty and accordingly not on strike nor in breach of their contracts of employment.

On appeal to the Labour Appeal Court, the critical issue was whether 'the exercise by the …[union] and its members of their constitutional protected right (s 17 of the Constitution) to assemble, march, demonstrate, picket and present petitions through the mechanisms of the RGA prohibited by the LRA was against public policy or in conflict with the LRA'. After noting with favour a number of related judgements by the Constitutional Court, particularly those that asserted the relative autonomy of labour law, the Labour Appeal Court held that a trade union could not circumvent the provisions of the Labour Relations Act. The dispute concerned organisational rights in the workplace in respect of which the Labour Relations Act had devised carefully crafted rules to deal with the resolution of these kinds of disputes, and accordingly the union ought to have made use of those procedures. Accordingly the appeal was upheld.

Law Applied

1996 Constitution

Section 17 Right to assembly, demonstration, picket and petition.

Everyone has the right peacefully and unarmed, to assemble, demonstrate, to picket and to present petitions.

Labour Relations Act, No. 66 of 1995

Section 21 Exercise of rights conferred by this Part.

(1) Any registered trade union may notify an employer in writing that it seeks to exercise one or more of the rights conferred by this Part in a workplace.

(2) The notice referred to in subsection (1) must be accompanied by a certified copy of the trade union's certificate of registration and must specify –

(a) the workplace in respect of which the trade union seeks to exercise the rights;

(b) the representativeness of the trade union in that workplace, and the facts relied upon to demonstrate that it is a representative trade union; and

(c) the rights that the trade union seeks to exercise and the manner in which it seeks to exercise those rights.

(3) Within 30 days of receiving the notice, the employer must meet the registered trade union and endeavour to conclude a collective agreement as to the manner in which the trade union will exercise the rights in respect of that workplace.

(4) If a collective agreement is not concluded, either the registered trade union or the employer may refer the dispute in writing to the Commission.

(5) The party who refers the dispute to the Commission must satisfy it that a copy of the referral has been served on the other party to the dispute.

(6) The Commission must appoint a commissioner to attempt to resolve the dispute through conciliation.

(7) If the dispute remains unresolved, either party to the dispute may request that the dispute be resolved through arbitration.

(8) If the unresolved dispute is about whether or not the registered trade union is a representative trade union, the commissioner –

(a) must seek –
 (i) to minimise the proliferation of trade union representation in a single workplace and, where possible, to encourage a system of a representative trade union in a workplace; and
 (ii) to minimise the financial and administrative burden of requiring an employer to grant organisational rights to more than one registered trade union;

(b) must consider –
 (i) the nature of the workplace;
 (ii) the nature of the one or more organisational rights that the registered trade union seeks to exercise;
 (iii) the nature of the sector in which the workplace is situated;
 (iv) the organisational history at the workplace or any other workplace of the employer; and
 (v) the composition of the work-force in the workplace taking into account the extent to which there are employees assigned to work by temporary employment services, employees employed on fixed term contracts, part-time employees or employees in other categories of non-standard employment; and

(c) may withdraw any of the organisational rights conferred by this Part and which are exercised by any other registered trade union in respect of that workplace, if that other trade union has ceased to be a representative trade union.

(8A) Subject to the provisions of subsection (8), a commissioner may in an arbitration conducted in terms of subsection (7) grant a registered trade union that does not have as members the majority of employees employed by an employer in a workplace –

    (a) the rights referred to in section 14, despite any provision to the contrary in that section, if –
- (i) the trade union is entitled to all of the rights referred to in sections 12, 13 and 15 in that workplace; and
- (ii) no other trade union has been granted the rights referred to in section 14 in that workplace.

    (b) the rights referred to in section 16, despite any provision to the contrary in that section, if –
- (i) the trade union is entitled to all of the rights referred to in sections 12, 13, 14 and 15 in that workplace; and
- (ii) no other trade union has been granted the rights referred to in section 16 in that workplace.

(8B) A right granted in terms of subsection (8A) lapses if the trade union concerned is no longer the most representative trade union in the workplace.

(8C) Subject to the provisions of subsection (8), a commissioner may in an arbitration conducted in terms of subsection (7) grant the rights referred to in sections 12, 13 or 15 to a registered trade union, or two or more registered trade unions acting jointly, that does not meet thresholds of representativeness established by a collective agreement in terms of section 18, if –

    (a) all parties to the collective agreement have been given an opportunity to participate in the arbitration proceedings; and

    (b) the trade union, or trade unions acting jointly, represent a significant interest, or a substantial number of employees, in the workplace.

[…]

Section 65 Limitations on right to strike or recourse to lockout.

(1) No person may take part in a strike or a lockout or in any conduct

in contemplation or furtherance of a strike or a lockout if –
  (a) that person is bound by a collective agreement that prohibits a strike or lockout in respect of the issue in dispute;
  (b) that person is bound by an agreement that requires the issue in dispute to be referred to arbitration;
  (c) the issue in dispute is one that a party has the right to refer to arbitration or to the Labour Court in terms of this Act or any employment law;
  (d) that person is engaged in –
    (i) an essential service; or
    (ii) a maintenance service.

(2)(a) Despite section 65 (1) (c), a person may take part in a strike or a lockout or in any conduct in contemplation or in furtherance of a strike or lockout if the issue in dispute is about any matter dealt with in sections 12 to 15.
  (b) If the registered trade union has given notice of the proposed strike in terms of section 64 (1) in respect of an issue in dispute referred to in paragraph (a), it may not exercise the right to refer the dispute to arbitration in terms of section 21 for a period of 12 months from the date of the notice.

Case law
– *In re Certification of the Constitution of the Republic of South Africa,* 1996 [1996] ZACC 26; 1996(4) SA 744 (CC); (10) BCLR 1253 (CC)
– *Gcaba v. Minister for Safety & Security & others* [2009] ZACC 26; 2010 (1) SA 238 (CC); (2010) 31 ILJ 296 (CC); [2010] 1 BCLR 35 (CC)

JUDGEMENT

"[30] Section 1 of the LRA states that the primary object of the LRA is 'to give effect to and regulate the fundamental rights conferred by section 23 of the Constitution' […] [A] litigant cannot avoid dispute-resolution mechanisms provided for in the LRA by alleging a possible violation of a constitutional right as that would undermine and frustrate the very primary objects of the LRA, unless […] the litigant is challenging the constitutionality of the legislation […] however, this is not applicable in the current matter. The present dispute is one to which the approach adopted by the Constitutional Court in *Gcaba v. Minister for Safety &*

Security & others 2010 (1) SA 238 (CC); (2010) 31 ILJ 296 (CC); [2010] 1 BCLR 35 (CC) at para 56 is clearly applicable:

> 'The legislature is sometimes specifically mandated to create detailed legislation for a particular area, like equality, just administration action (PAJA) and labour relations (LRA). Once a set of carefully crafted rules and structures have been created for the effective and speedy resolution of disputes and protection of rights in a particular area of law, it is preferable to use that particular system [...] If litigants are at liberty to relegate the finely tuned dispute-resolution structures created by the LRA, a dual system of law could fester in cases of dismissal of employees. The dispute here is one concerning organisational rights and should accordingly be dealt with in accordance with the procedure contemplated in s 22 of the LRA.'

[...]

[32] In conclusion [...] [the union] in relying on the provisions of the RGA in participating in the gathering, was in fact circumventing the provisions of the LRA, even though the participation of off-duty employees in the march did not amount to a breach of contract as they did so at their time. The [union] ought to have made use of the procedures afforded to it by the LRA, which contains carefully crafted rules to deal with the specific kind of activity engaged in by the respondents."

ANNOTATION

Although the judgement gives a strong message in favour of the autonomy of labour law, it circumscribes the exercise of economic power beyond the traditional economic weapons of strike and lockout.

In its judgement in *re Certification of the Constitution of the Republic of South Africa, 1996* 1996 (10) BCLR 1253 (CC), the Constitutional Court held that the constitutional right to bargain collectively contained within it the right to exercise economic power against bargaining partners: "[C]ollective bargaining implies a right on the part of those who engage in collective bargaining to exercise economic power against their adversaries [...].

Once a right to collective bargaining is recognised, implicit within it will be the right to exercise some economic power against partners in collective bargaining." (at paragraph 64.)

In determining whether or not the right to lockout ought to be constitutionalised, the Constitutional Court recognised the inequality of economic power inherent in the employment relationship, the voluntary nature of collective bargaining and the legitimate exercise of economic power as its principle operating mechanism. The employer's theoretical armoury included a "range of weapons, such as dismissal, the employment of alternative or replacement labour, the unilateral implementation of new terms of conditions of employment." In other words, the employer's economic power is not based on a right to lockout as the workers' economic power is on the right to strike. But if these forms of economic power can be exercised by employers, it should follow that the economic weapons of public protest, boycott of products or services, media campaigns should similarly be open to workers and their unions. Just because these forms of economic power are not specifically regulated by the LRA should not mean that they may not be capable of being exercised by workers and their unions.

SPAIN

Supreme Court Social Chamber
Decision No 961/2016 of 16 November 2016

*Strike, contractor and main company – forbidden cases
of strikers' replacement by hiring another contractor*

HEADNOTES

Facts

The firm Altrad Rodisola S.A.U. is a company whose activity consists of the assembly, dismantling and renting of metallic scaffolds, thermal insulation, protection against corrosion and medium-sized construction works, oriented to the chemical, petrochemical and nuclear sectors.

On 13 July 2015 the management of the company informed the workers' representatives of the company's decision to undertake a process of business restructuring consisting of a reduction of costs so as to ensure the future viability of the company, which would affect all of its work centers. Therefore, and according to Article 41.4 of the Workers' Statute, the establishment of a bargaining commission was required, in order to maintain the mandatory period of consultations provided for in the event of a substantial change in working conditions of a collective nature.

In the framework of the negotiation process regarding the company's decision to cut wages, in view of the disagreement between the company and the workers' representatives, and after a mediation failed, the assembly of workers decided to call a strike from 20 August. The trade union confederations *Confederación General de Trabajadores* (CGT), *Comisiones Obreras* (CC.OO) and *Unión General de Trabajadores* (UGT) joined the strike. The workers' representatives decided not to provide minimum services to the contractors considering that there was no obligation to do so because the company did not perform public or essential services for the community.

During the strike, two Altrad contractor companies (Dow Chemical Ibérica S.L. and Basell Poliofelinas Ibérica S.L.) hired a new contractor (Kaefer Aislamientos S.A.U. in the case of Dow, and Planifico Montajes SL by Basell) to meet their productive needs, given that the Altrad workers were on strike.

Once the consultation period was concluded without agreement, Altrad made effective its decision to cut wages.

The CGT filed a collective suit against Altrad Rodisola S.A.U., requesting that the company decision to cut wages be declared null and void or, alternatively, unfair, and that the company be ordered to replace workers in the working conditions that had existed before the adoption of the measure. On the understanding that the hiring of new contractors by the clients of the employer to carry out the work left undone by the strikers, violated their right to strike, the National Audience Decision 30 November 2015 (Rec. 278/2015), declared that the modification of their wage conditions was null.

Altrad Rodisola S.A.U. then approached the Supreme Court (Social Chamber), by means of an "appeal in cassation", alleging that there was no direct intervention on its part in the replacement of striking workers, since it was the clients who hired third party contractors to complete those services that Altrad Rodisola S.A.U. itself could not carry out because of the strike. Thus, the complainant could hardly have weakened the position of the workers' representatives during the negotiations regarding the pay reduction. On the contrary, Altrad Rodisola S.A.U. did not obtain any benefit from the fact that the work had been completed by contractor third parties, since not having made any contract with them itself, it could not charge for them either.

Decision

The Supreme Court's Decision of 16 November 2016 upholds the appeal, and revokes the Decision of the National Audience. It states that Altrad Rodisola S.A.U. did not violate its workers' right to strike and, to the extent that its decision to reduce wages had been justified during the trial on economic grounds, this measure could not be regarded as void but as valid.

Law Applied

Spanish Constitution of 27 December 1978
Art. 14.
Spaniards are equal before the law and may not in any way be discriminated against on account of birth, race, sex, religion, opinion or any other personal or social condition or circumstance.
Art. 28.
1. All persons have the right to freely join a trade union. The law may restrict or excempt the exercise of this right in the Armed Forces or Institutes or other bodies subject to military discipline, and shall lay down the special conditions of its exercise by civil servants. Trade union freedom includes the right to set up trade unions and to join the union of one's choice, as well as the right of trade unions to form confederations and to found international trade union organizations, or to become members of them. No one may be compelled to join a trade union.
2. The right of workers to strike in defence of their interests is recognized. The law governing the exercise of this right shall establish the safeguards necessary to ensure the maintenance of essential public services.

Workers' Statute (Royal Legislative Decree 2/2015 of 23 October)
Article 41. Substantial modifications of working conditions.
1. The company's management, if there are proven economic, technical, structural or production reasons, may approve substantial modifications in the working conditions. Such causes shall be deemed to exist where the measures are related to competitiveness, productivity or technical or work organization in the company. [...]
2. [...] A substantial modification of a working schedule shall be considered collective, where, within a ninety-day term, it affects at least:
(a) Ten workers, in companies employing less than one hundred workers.
(b) 10% of the number of company workers, if the company employs between one hundred and three hundred workers.
(c) Thirty workers in companies that employ three hundred or more workers.
[...]
4. [...] Any decision to carry out a substantial modification of collective

working conditions must be preceded by a consultation period with the workers' legal representatives lasting no more than fifteen days. [...]

During the consultation period the parties shall negotiate in good faith with the aim of reaching an agreement. [...]

5. The decision on the collective modification of working conditions will be notified by the employer to the workers after the consultation period has ended without agreement and will take effect within a period of seven days following notification.

The decisions adopted further to this section may be challenged by means of a collective dispute proceeding, notwithstanding the individual action foreseen in section 3 above. The filing of collective dispute proceedings will stop the proceedings of any individual actions initiated, until these are resolved. [...]

Act 36/2011 of 10 October, for social jurisdiction
Art. 138.7

The judgement shall declare the business decision justified or unjustified, depending on whether the reasons invoked by the company have been established or not, in respect of the workers concerned. [...]

The judgement declaring the measure unjustified will recognize the right of the worker to be replaced in his previous working conditions, as well as the payment of damages that the business decision could have caused during the time it has produced effects.

The judgement shall declare null and void the fraudulent decision adopted so as to circumvent the rules relating to the consultation period provided established in Arts. 40.2, 41.4 and 47 of the Workers' Statute, as well as when the employer's decision has been motived by any of the grounds of discrimination prohibited by the Constitution and the Law, or when it has been adopted in breach of workers' fundamental rights and public freedoms, including, as the case may be, other cases involving the declaration of nullity of dismissal in Article 108(2).

Royal Legislative Decree 17/1977 of 4 March, on labour relations
Art. 6.5.

During the strike, the employer shall not replace strikers with other substitute workers that were not employed by it on the date when the strike was called, except in the case of infringement of their duties envisaged by subsection 7 of this Article.

JUDGEMENT

ANTECEDENTES DE HECHO [...]
FUNDAMENTOS DE DERECHO [...]
TERCERO. La sentencia recurrida, apoyándose en la doctrina plasmada en las sentencias de esta Sala antes mencionadas (Grupo Prisa y Coca-Cola) llega a las siguientes conclusiones, en las que fundamenta la declaración de nulidad del despido por vulneración del derecho fundamental de huelga:

"1ª. En primer lugar, porque de lo arriba expuesto cabe concluir que los actos vulneradores del derecho de huelga pueden ser realizados por terceros empresarios distintos del titular de la empresa o centro de trabajo en cuyo ámbito se produce la huelga, si tales empresarios tienen una especial vinculación aquel, como sucede en nuestro caso, en el que la demandada presta servicios para los mismos, y tal vulneración se produce mediante los actos del empresario principal que acude a contratar los servicios de una nueva empresa contratista para realizar los trabajos que debían ser desarrollados por los trabajadores que ejercen su derecho a la huelga."

"2ª. En segundo lugar, porque también de lo ya dicho se deduce que cuando la vulneración tiene como efecto, neutralizar el legítimo derecho a la huelga como medio de presión en la negociación propia de un periodo de consultas vicia la medida que se adopte de nulidad, en nuestro caso la modificación sustancial de condiciones de trabajo comunicada a los representantes legales de los trabajadores el día 1/9/2015."

"3ª. Finalmente, porque constando dos indicios acreditativos de la vulneración a la que hacíamos referencia y de su trascendencia en el desarrollo de las consultas - de un lado, la actuación llevada a cabo por la Inspección de Trabajo y de la Seguridad Social previa denuncia del sindicato actor, y de otro lado, las referencias a dichos comportamientos que obran en las actas del periodo de consultas- , el empleador ni ha practicado prueba alguna que enerve tales indicios, ni ha dado una explicación razonable a las medidas adoptadas por sus clientes. En lo tocante a este último punto, refiere el empresario que únicamente se contrató con terceras empresas la ejecución de trabajos urgentes que de no haber sido ejecutados hubieran causado perjuicios irreparables para la comunidad. Sin embargo, el empresario ni siquiera intentó negociar servicios mínimos, lo que hubiera sido lógico si pudieran ocasionarse tan graves perjuicios, ni consta que adoptase en los periodos que median desde el anuncio de la huelga -14/8/2015- hasta el inicio de la misma- 20/8/2015, actuación alguna tendente a evitar los supuestos daños inminentes para la población que el paro pudiera ocasionar, antes al contrario, de la lectura de las actas, en concreto de la de 18 de agosto, parece inferirse que lo único que hizo fue comunicar en dicha fecha a sus clientes la huelga para que pudieran subcontratar temporalmente los trabajos que los empleados de Altrad Rodisola SAU hubieran desarrollado durante el transcurso de la huelga, sin oponerse a que fuera manipulado por terceros su propio material operativo."

Pero no podemos estar de acuerdo con la valoración jurídica efectuada por la sentencia recurrida, y ello por las razones que exponemos a continuación:

1º. Conforme a los Hechos Probados, Altrad se dedica al montaje, desmontaje y alquiler de andamios metálicos, aislamiento térmico, protección contra la corrosión y las obras de mediana envergadura, orientadas al sector químico, petroquímico y nuclear.

2º. En el acta levantada en la sesión celebrada el 18/8/2015 durante el periodo de consultas de la modificación sustancial de condiciones de trabajo, ante la huelga convocada, la empresa manifiesta a los representantes legales de los trabajadores que tiene la obligación de informar a los clientes ese mismo día pues pueden surgir, por diferentes motivos, intervenciones de seguridad o urgencias de prestar servicio, sin que la parte social adquiera ningún compromiso sobre los servicios por estas posibles intervenciones por entender éstas que no existe obligación de prestar servicios mínimos porque la empresa no realiza servicios públicos ni esenciales para la comunidad.

3º. La Inspección de trabajo realizó el informe que consta en el Hecho Probado Décimo. Resumidamente: durante la huelga de los trabajadores de Altrad en Tarragona la empresa Dow encomendó a la empresa Kaifer un trabajo de montaje y desmontaje de andamios que tenía que haber hecho Altrad durante una parada de corta duración, llegando a modificar un andamio de Altrad. La empresa Basell, que tenía un contrato de servicios para andamiaje, aislamiento y pintura por tres años con Altrad, dada la urgente necesidad de montar un andamio, contrató a la empresa Planifico Montajes para realizar este trabajo.

Dada esta realidad fáctica, no puede aplicarse la doctrina establecida en las sentencias de referencia, como se hace en la recurrida, pues no existe una vinculación que justifique hacer responder a Altrad Rodisola de una conducta en la que no ha participado y en la que no ha podido intervenir para tomar la decisión. La condición de clientes de Dow y Basell tampoco determinan ninguna vinculación especial que pueda condicionar la decisión de dichas empresas clientes de contratar trabajos con otras empresas de la competencia durante la huelga y tampoco las referidas empresas clientes forman un grupo de empresas con Altrad, como pone de relieve el Informe del Fiscal de la Audiencia Nacional. Es un caso bien distinto del de la sentencia de 11/2/2015 (Grupo Prisa), en donde la parte demandante sostenía esa especial vinculación, ya que los recurrentes habían demandado, no solo a la empresa en la que se convocó la huelga, PRESSPRINT S.L., sino también a EDICIONES EL PAÍS S.L., DIARIO AS S.L. y ESTRUCTURA GRUPO DE ESTUDIOS ECONÓMICOS S.A., todas ellas pertenecientes al GRUPO PRISA, siendo el único socio de PRESSPRINT S.L., EDICIONES EL PAÍS S.L., que cuenta con el 100% de su capital social y actúa como administrador único y la empresa PRESSPRINT S.L. tiene al Grupo PRISA como cliente mayoritario en un porcentaje superior al 70 % según se recoge en el Fundamento Jurídico de la sentencia del Tribunal Supremo, aunque no formaran un grupo de los denominados patológicos. En el caso de Coca-Cola, incluso se calificaba así al grupo.

Por el contrario, en este caso fueron los propios demandantes quienes entendieron que las empresas Dow Chemical Ibérica, S.L. y Basell Poliofelinas Ibérica, S.L. no habían conculcado el derecho de huelga, ya que no las demandaron, y por lo tanto no apreciaron que existiera entre ellas y la demandada Altrad ninguna especial vinculación que las obligara a respetar la huelga y, consecuentemente, a no contratar con otros las obras que ya tenía contratadas Altrad, y que ésta no podía realizar precisamente por la existencia de la huelga declarada en ella.

En el caso ahora examinado, la actuación de la demandada Altrad consistió únicamente en comunicar a todos sus clientes que no podía realizar los trabajos comprometidos con ellas durante la realización de la huelga por sus trabajadores. No tiene vinculación con sus clientes que le permita codecidir con ellas la realización de esos trabajos por terceras empresas de la competencia, ni estaba en condiciones de impedir que sus clientes las contratasen con terceros, ni tampoco se benefició de ello, porque no realizó ni cobró tales trabajos, y sin que tampoco conste que hubiese colaborado en su realización, como pone de relieve el informe de la Inspección de Trabajo, por lo que no puede imputarse a la demandada Altrad una conducta que haya impedido o disminuido los efectos de la huelga, o menoscabado la posición negociadora de los representantes legales de los trabajadores. Y en cuanto a que se hubiese manipulado el andamio colocado por Altrad en la empresa Dow, aparte de que no consta si esta actuación se produjo durante la huelga, no parece que Altrad pudiera oponerse a su desmontaje, ya que ella no podía llevarlo a cabo, y en todo caso no se ve en qué tal actuación pudiera perjudicar la posición negociadora de los representantes legales de los trabajadores.

La apreciación que hace la sentencia recurrida sobre la supuesta vinculación de Altrad con sus empresas clientes es tan amplia que conduciría a consecuencias totalmente exorbitantes respecto de una adecuada protección del derecho de huelga, pues si se impidiese a los destinatarios de los trabajos, que no lo tengan prohibido por contrato, contratar con otras, llegaríamos a sostener, como señala en su informe el Fiscal de la Audiencia Nacional, que los consumidores habituales de un comercio no pudieran comprar en otro, en caso de huelga en el primero, o que, la empresa que tenga que realizar determinados trabajos no pudiera recurrir a otra empresa de servicios.

Procede por ello estimar el motivo y revocar el pronunciamiento sobre nulidad de la medida por vulneración del derecho de huelga.

CUARTO. Descartada la nulidad de la modificación sustancial de condiciones de trabajo acordada por la empresa, debemos declararla ajustada a derecho, pues, como indica el Ministerio Fiscal, han quedado plenamente acreditadas las causas económicas en el hecho probado duodécimo, dado que disminuyó el volumen total de ventas en el último ejercicio, comprobándose así por las ventas correspondientes a los últimos cuatro trimestres consecutivos en comparación a los cuatro trimestres del año anterior. Desde 2005/2006 el resultado global es de pérdidas, siendo el denominado resultado ordinario -deducidos los ingresos por venta de inmovilizado y aplicación de provisiones- de pérdidas por importe de 4.232.408'71 euros y la previsión de resultados en los años futuros también negativa en más de un millón de euros.

Además, las medidas propuestas siempre respetaban los salarios establecidos en los Convenios Colectivos aplicables (Hecho Probado Quinto) por lo que teniendo en cuenta que el porcentaje de gastos de personal sobre el volumen de ventas era superior a la media del sector (Hecho Probado Duodécimo), aparecen acreditadas las causas económicas relacionadas con la competitividad, como señala el art. 41 ET.

QUINTO. Las anteriores consideraciones conducen, de acuerdo con lo razonado en el Informe del Ministerio fiscal, a la estimación del recurso, casando y anulando la sentencia recurrida y con revocación de la misma y desestimación de la demanda.

FALLO

Por todo lo expuesto, en nombre del Rey, por la autoridad que le confiere la Constitución, esta Sala ha decidido

Estimamos el recurso de casación interpuesto por la representación letrada de la empresa Altrad Radiola S.A.U. contra la sentencia de fecha 30 de noviembre de 2015 dictada por la Sala de lo Social de la Audiencia

Nacional, en el procedimiento nº 278/2015. Casamos y anulamos la sentencia dictada por la Audiencia Nacional, que revocamos, desestimando la demanda. […]

[Source: CENDOJ, http://www.poderjudicial.es/search/ECLI:ES:TS:2016:5720]

ANNOTATION

The case dealt with by this Decision of 16 November 2016 raises the issue whether, in the event of a strike by employees who work for the contractor that routinely provides services for the main company, the hiring of another contractor by the main company in order to carry out the work left undone by the strikers, can be regarded as a case of external scabbing, which could involve an infringement of the employees' right to strike.

Before analysing the Supreme Court (Social Chamber) Decision, it is worth recalling that Article 28.2 of the Spanish Constitution of 1978 recognises the "workers' right to strike for the defence of their interests." The right to strike is enshrined as a fundamental right, for it is contained within division 1 of Chapter 2 of Spanish Constitution. Consequently, the exercise of the right to strike enjoys the most important guarantees under the Spanish legal system. As Constitutional Court Decision 11/1981 underlines, this means that workers have "the right to place the employment contract in a state of suspension and thus restrict the employer's freedom", limiting its management powers.

As a result, the employer is not allowed to replace the strikers. The scope of this prohibition has been enhanced by the courts, by refusing to allow the direct recruitment of other workers by the employer (expressly forbidden by Art. 6.5 of Royal Legislative Decree 17/1977), or the replacement by employees of the same workplace ("strike breakers") with the purpose of performing the job of those colleagues who are taking part in the work stoppage (Constitutional Court Decision 123/1992), and even the hiring of a contractor whose employees could carry out the work of the strikers (*Prisa* and *Coca-Cola* cases, referred to below). In the case commented on here, the Supreme Court had to decide whether the prohibition should also cover the replacement of strikers by another contractor's workers when the decision to so hire comes from the main company. As shown in the following analysis, the latter case is very different, which is reflected in the response of the Supreme Court.

1. The forbidden use of manpower in order to minimise the impact of a strike as an act of strike breaking.

(a) The replacement of strikers by other workers directly or indirectly recruited by the employer of striking workers.

As noted above, Article 6.5 of Royal Legislative Decree 17/1977 forbids substitution of strikers by other workers who did not belong to the staff before the employer is notified of the strike. The replacement with external workers either hired directly by the employer or provided by a temporary employment agency, as well as with employees who work in other workplaces of the same enterprise, constitutes a very grave administrative infraction [Articles 8.10, and 19.3.a) of Infractions and Sanctions in the Social Order Act (LISOS)], which renders the employer liable to pay a fine.

Constitutional doctrine has gone further, interpreting these prohibitions in a broad sense in order to ban the employer from ordering any substitution that implies diminishing the impact of a strike, even with workers of the same workplace. In coming to this position, Constitutional Court Decision 123/1992 of 28 September, and more recently Constitutional Court Decision 33/2011 of 28 March, have stated that the employer infringed the right to strike when it appointed other workers who usually perform functions in higher categories to fulfil those carried out by strikers.

Under exceptional circumstances, however, employers are explicitly allowed to replace strikers. Indeed, although Article 6.5 does not forbid the replacement of employees who take part in an unlawful strike, or of those who fail to comply with minimum services or with security and maintenance services, Spanish courts (for example, in Constitutional Court Decision 120/1983 of 15 December) and doctrine have stated unanimously that workers may be replaced in these specific circumstances.

(b) The impact of outsourcing on the right to strike: the forbidden cases of replacement by a contractor's workers.

Furthermore, the Supreme Court has also found that the right to strike was violated by the replacement of strikers by employees of other companies integrated in a group having internal links.

Hence, in the so-called *Prisa* case (Decision of 11 February 2015 (Rec. 95/2014)), the company affected by the strike was Presprintt, belonging to Grupo Prisa, which was also its mayor client (in a percentage higher than 70%). In addition, Ediciones el País, S.L., another company of Grupo Prisa, was the only partner of Pressprint, owning 100% of its share capital and acting as its sole administrator. In December 2012, the workforce of Pressprint went on strike against the employer's plan for collective dismissal.

In response to the announced strike, Grupo Prisa contracted external enterprises and entrusted them to print and distribute its publications. The Supreme Court held that both the contractor company Pressprint and the parent company Grupo Prisa had undermined the fundamental right to strike of Pressprint employees and condemned both companies to €100,000 compensation in favour of the appellant trade union, CC.OO.

Likewise, in the *Coca-Cola* case, the workers called a strike when Coca-Cola Iberian announced it would close four of its eleven Spanish factories, including Fuenlabrada, alleging that the plants were operating at about half of their production capacity. The company planned to lay off 1,190 of its nearly 4,600 workers in Spain. After protests, industrial action and strikes, the company said it would reduce the job cuts to 840 workers. Nonetheless, unions took the company to court. Finally, the Supreme Court (Decision of 20 April 2015 (Rec. 354/2014)) annulled the collective layoff decided by the company, arguing that it had not respected the workers' right to strike since the company continued to supply its clients with soft drinks made at other factories and used alternative distribution channels.

As the Constitutional Court Decision 75/2010 of 18 October (which the Supreme Court Decision does not quote) had already stated "the prohibitions, guarantees and safeguards established by labour law in relation to business activities to the detriment of the right to strike would be of little effect if it were admitted that they only reach to the direct employer but not the main company, which is ultimately the one that suffers the economic effects of a strike and which, therefore, can be equally or even more interested than the employer in fighting it".

2. A different case: the replacement not decided by the employer of the strikers but by the main company.

Precisely by invoking the doctrine established in the *Prisa* and *Coca-Cola* cases, the National Audience's Decision of 30 November 2015 had annulled the measure of wage reduction introduced by Altrad, considering that it had been adopted in breach of the right to strike. However, in the view of the Supreme Court, the circumstances analyzed in the current case differ considerably from those that led to the doctrine established in *Prisa* and *Coca-Cola*, for the following reasons:

– On the one hand, there is no link between the contracting company in which the strike was taking place (Altrad) and its clients or main companies (Dow and Basell) that allows them to codecide the accomplishment of the work left undone as a consequence of the strike, by contracting with third parties.

- Altrad had no possibility of preventing main companies from using the services of other contractors, nor did it collaborate in that outside hiring or encourage the main company to do so, as emphasized in the report of the Labor Inspectorate.
- On the other hand, Altrad did not benefit from the fact that the client companies hired other contractors, since in not completing the work due to the strike of its employees, Altrad could not charge them.
- Indeed, the very fact that the union (CGT) which claims the violation of the right to strike has not sued, nor reproached, the client companies (Dow and Basell) that have hired other contractors to perform the tasks left undone by Altrad's employees, implies that the union admitted that there was no special link between them and Altrad that forced them to respect the strike, preventing them from contracting with others to complete the work previously contracted with Altrad, which the latter could not perform precisely because of the existence of the strike.

Consequently, in the Court's opinion, Altrad cannot be considered to have diminished the impact of the strike, or impaired the negotiating position of the workers' representatives during the consultation period prior to its decision to cut wages.

3. Conclusion.

This judgement does not imply a change in the doctrine of the Supreme Court laid down in the *Prisa* and *Coca-Cola* cases, because the reported Decision here deals with different facts. In fact, the Decision of 16 November 2016 does not admit, as a general rule, that in the event of a strike being called, the activity of the striking workers may be carried out by subcontracting.

Rather, according to the case law cited above, the company which is the subject of a strike call cannot divert production by hiring a contractor. Neither is the employer allowed to force or encourages the client company to hire another contractor, when there is a "special link" between the employer whose employees go on strike and the client companies, so that there is the possibility of influencing the decision-making of their clients.

In conclusion, the key to determining whether or not there is a violation of the right to strike is the existence of a special link between the employer of strikers which acts as a contractor, and the main or client company that hires another contractor in order to perform the tasks that striking workers have left undone. Only in such cases, i.e. when both companies belong to a group or are linked in a way that they can codecide or influence each other with the aim of replacing strikers, can it be said that the right to strike has been infringed.

PART SIX

ADMINISTRATION – JUDICIAL AND GENERAL

INDIA

Supreme Court of India
Cardamom Marketing Corporation and Anr
v. State of Kerala and Ors

Whether additional court fees can be collected from litigants in order to finance social security benefits for persons in the legal profession

HEADNOTES

Facts

The legality of section 76(1) of the Kerala Court Fees and Suits Valuation Act, 1959 was challenged in the High Court of Kerala, following which an appeal was made to the Supreme Court on the same matter. The Kerala Court Fees and Suits Valuation Act, 1959 hasd been enacted to amend and consolidate the law relating to court fees and valuation of suits in the State of Kerala. Chapter VIII of the Act provides for a Legal Benefit Fund. Section 76(l) of the Act enables the State Government to levy additional court fees in respect of appeals or revisions lodged with Tribunals or appellate authorities, other than civil and criminal courts, at a rate not exceeding one per cent of the amount involved in the dispute in cases where it is capable of valuation and in other cases at a rate not exceeding one hundred rupees for each appeal or revision. All proceeds of the additional court fee are to go into the Legal Benefit Fund. Subsection (3) of section 76 states that the Fund constituted under subsection (2) shall be applied and utilised for the purpose of providing an efficient legal service for the people of the State and to provide social security measures for the legal profession. Subsection (4) of section 76 authorises the Government to prescribe rules for the efficient legal services and social security measures.

The Kerala Government accordingly framed the Kerala Legal Benefit Fund Rules, 1991. The Rules provide for the establishment of a Trustee Committee. The Rules further state that the funds available each year shall be equally apportioned for the purposes of providing efficient legal service and social security measures for the legal profession. The funds pertaining to the social security of the legal profession are entrusted to the Secretary of the Bar Council of Kerala who is the Convener of the Advocate Welfare Fund constituted under the Kerala Advocates Welfare Fund Act, 1980. The Fund constituted by the additional court fees is to be used in accordance with the provisions of that Advocates Welfare Fund Act. A member of the Fund is entitled to receive a certain sum of money on the cessation of practice due to retirement or death. The Rules also state that the funds earmarked for providing an efficient legal service for the people of the State may include "provision for working space for the Advocates' Clerks", "resting place and other facilities for the parties and witnesses attending the courts, conducting legal aid camps for people, expenditure for engaging advocates in special cases, publications relating to legal issues and important decisions of the Kerala High Court to create legal awareness among people of the State, and such other matters as the Committee may feel necessary for providing an efficient legal service for the people of the State."

The legislative competence of the State in enacting under section 76(1) of the Kerala Court Fees and Suits Valuation Act, 1959 and permitting the Government to levy additional court fees for the Legal Benefit Fund was challenged before the Single Judge of the Kerala High Court unsuccessfully. On appeal, before the Division Bench of the Kerala High Court it was contended that the levy of additional court fees was disproportionately high and did not reflect the quality of a 'fee'. This contention was rejected and the Division Bench of the High Court held that an additional levy of court fees on all litigants for the Legal Benefit Fund was legal and could not be termed a tax. This decision was challenged by one of the aggrieved parties before the Supreme Court.

Decision

The three judge Bench of the Supreme Court confirmed the decision of the High Court.

Law Applied
   Article 39-A of the Constitution of India
   Kerala Court Fees and Suits Valuation Act, 1959
   Kerala Advocates Welfare Fund Act, 1980
   Kerala Legal Benefit Fund Rules, 1991

JUDGEMENT

[Extracts from the unanimous judgement of the three judge bench of the Supreme Court delivered by A.K. Sikri, J follow]

The two appellants before us [...] are the registered dealers under the Kerala General Sales Tax Act, 1963 and/or the Kerala Value Added Tax Act, 2003 in the State of Kerala. They challenged the vires of S.R.O. No. 226 of 2002 dated 5 April 2002 issued by the Government of Kerala in exercise of powers under section 76(1) of the Kerala Court Fees and Suits Valuation Act, 1959 (hereinafter referred to as the 'CF Act') whereby the Government authorised the tribunals and appellate authorities constituted by or under special or local law, other than civil and criminal courts, to levy additional court fees in respect of each appeal or revision at the rate of 0.5% of the amount involved in the dispute in cases where it is capable of valuation, and at the rate of 50 Indian Rupees in other cases. This notification further provides that the amount so collected shall be credited to the Kerala Legal Benefit Fund constituted under subsection (2) of section 76 of the CF Act. The main contention of the appellants was that the aforesaid levy is in the nature of compulsory exaction/tax and the element of service/*quid pro quo* was absent and, therefore, such a fee cannot be charged. The High Court has repelled the challenge thereby upholding the validity of the said notification following its earlier judgement in *Chackolas Spinning & Weaving Mills Ltd.* v. *State of Kerala* [...]. This judgement of the High Court is challenged in this appeal on the same grounds.

Section 76 of the CF Act, under which the impugned notification is issued, deals with 'Legal Benefit Fund' and makes the following reading: *"76. Legal Benefit Fund. (1) Notwithstanding anything contained in this Act or any other law for the time being in force, it shall be competent for Government to levy an additional court fee, by notification in the Gazette, in respect of appeals or revisions to tribunals or appellate authorities, other than Civil and Criminal Courts, at a rate not exceeding one per cent of the amount involved in the dispute in cases where it is capable of valuation and in other cases at a rate not exceeding one hundred rupees for each appeal or revision. (2) There shall be constituted a legal benefit fund to which shall be credited (i) the proceeds of the additional court fee levied and collected under subsection (1); (ii) fifty per cent of the court fees levied and collected on mukhtarnama or vakalathnama under Article 16 of Schedule II of this Act. (3) The fund constituted under subsection (2) shall be applied and utilised for the purpose of providing an efficient legal service for the people of the State and to provide social security measures for the legal profession. (4) The mode and manner in which the legal service to the people may be made more efficient and social security measures for legal profession may be provided, shall be as prescribed by rules made by Government."*

[Continuing with its judgement, the Supreme Court held:]

The mode and manner in which legal services are to be made more efficient and social security measures for legal profession need to be provided can be prescribed by rules made by the Government. For this purpose, the State Government has framed the Kerala Legal Benefit Fund Rules, 1991. These Rules prescribe the manner in which the Fund is to be operated. Rule 3 thereof enumerates the sources of monies to the said Fund and reads as under: *"3. Depositing of certain monies to the Fund. (1) The amount to be credited to the Legal Benefit Fund shall be drawn from the head of account 2014-800-06 Legal Benefit Fund – Contributions by the Secretary, Board of Revenue (L/R) and may be made available to the Secretary to Government, Law Department for depositing it in the Fund. Government may make available in the first instance for deposit in the Fund such amount as it may deem necessary for the initial working of the Fund. This amount shall be adjusted against the actual amount payable to the Fund on consolidation of Statements regarding court fees actually levied from the year from which this [these] rules shall be brought into force. (2) The amount of additional court fees levied and collected under subsection (1) of S.76 of the Act shall be added to the Fund as and when such additional court fees are levied and collections are made. This amount will also be made available to the Law Secretary during the beginning of every financial year based on consolidated accounts of collection made in the previous year. (3) The fund shall be deposited in the Public Deposit account as 'Fund' in the District Treasury, Thiruvananthapuram in the name of the Legal Benefit Fund Trustee Committee constituted under rule 4."*

Under Rule 4, a Fund Trustee Committee is constituted and detailed provisions are made for operating the Fund by the said Trustee Committee as well as the functions which the said Trustee Committee is supposed to discharge.

We may point out at this stage that the Legislature of the Kerala State has also enacted a law known as the Kerala Advocates' Welfare Fund Act, 1980. Rules are also framed under the said Act which are called the Kerala Advocates' Welfare Fund Rules, 1981. The Welfare Fund Act is aimed at providing of a Welfare Fund *for the payment of retirement benefits to advocates in the State of Kerala and for the matters connected therewith or incidental thereto.* [Emphasis supplied]

[...]

It becomes clear from clause (e) of subsection (2) of section 3 that the amount set apart from the Legal Benefit Fund constituted under section 76 of the CF Act is to be credited to the Advocates' Welfare Fund, for providing efficient legal services for the people of the State and social security measures for the legal profession. In a nutshell, the additional court fees at the rate of 0.5% of the amount involved or 50 Indian Rupees in each case before the tribunals and appellate authorities constituted by or under any special or local laws, other than civil and criminal courts, is meant for the aforesaid Welfare Fund which is to be utilised in accordance with the provisions of the Welfare Fund Act.

From the reading of the aforesaid provisions it becomes clear that section 76 authorises the State Government to issue such a notification and notification has been issued in exercise of powers contained therein. This power extends to levy additional court fees by tribunals and other appellate authorities constituted by or under any special law. The impugned notification, therefore, is *intra vires* the provision of section 76 of the CF Act. Even the rate which is prescribed in the notification is within the outer limit prescribed under section 76(2) of the Act. To this extent, therefore, there cannot be any quarrel.

However, the main argument of the appellants is that the additional court fee which is to be paid on the appeals etc. which are to be filed either under the Kerala General Sales Tax Act or the Kerala Value Added Tax Act by virtue of the aforesaid notification, has no nexus with the object and, therefore, it does not have any character of a 'fee' as no services are provided to the litigants in return. To put it otherwise, it is submitted that since such additional court fee collected from the assessees like the appellants is used for the benefit of the advocates and no benefit thereof accrues to the litigants, the charging of such an additional court fee is clearly impermissible as it amounts to compulsory exaction of the money from the appellants [...] without giving any corresponding benefit to the appellants. It is more so when such an additional fee has to be paid at each and every subsequent level of statutory appeal and revision as well.

The aforesaid argument of the appellants is devoid of any merit. Insofar as the argument predicated on a fee vis-a-vis tax is concerned, i.e. the submission that the imposition in question is in the nature of tax inasmuch as this imposition has no nexus to any object sought to be achieved in relation to the service available to the appellants and there has no *quid pro quo*, the same is dealt with by the High Court elaborately. The High Court has referred to Entry 3 in List II (State List) of the Seventh Schedule of the Constitution as it stood in the year 1960 when the CF Act was enacted [...]. This Entry reads as under: "*3. Administration of justice, constitution and organization of all courts except the Supreme Court and the High Court; officers and servants of the High Court; procedure in Rent and Revenue Courts; fees taken in all courts except to the Supreme Court.*"

By the Forty-Second Amendment to the Constitution in the year 1976, administration of justice became a Concurrent Subject, having been included as Entry 11A in List III which resulted in requisite modification to Entry 3 in List II as well. At the same time, by the very same amendment, Article 39-A was also inserted in Part IV of the Constitution which relates to the Directive Principles of State Policy. This Article exhorts the State to provide equal justice and free legal aid and reads as under: "*39A. Equal justice and free legal aid. The State shall secure that the operation of the legal system promotes justice, on a basis of equal opportunity, and shall, in particular, provide free legal aid, by suitable legislation or schemes or in any other way, to ensure that opportunities for securing justice are not denied to any citizen by reason of economic or other disabilities.*" As per the High Court, the administration of justice, thus, becomes a distinct topic and Article 39A calls upon the State to ensure establishment of such legal system which promotes justice and provides free legal aid. [...]

We agree with the aforesaid approach of the High Court. First of all, the argument of the appellants ignores that as per section 76(3) of the CF Act, one of the purposes for which the Fund is to be utilised is for providing efficient legal services for the people of the State. This clearly amounts to *quid pro quo*. Another purpose is also for the benefit of the public at large. When we talk of a sound and stable system of administration of justice, all the stakeholders in the said legal system need to be taken care of. The legal community and advocates are an inseparable and important part of a robust legal system and they not only aid in seeking access to justice but also promote justice. Judges cannot perform their task of dispensing justice effectively without the able support of advocates. In that sense, advocates play an important role in the administration of justice.

[...] it becomes apparent that providing social security to the legal profession becomes an essential part of any legal system which has to be effective, efficient and robust to enable it to provide necessary service to the consumers of justice. Section 76 of the CF Act and the impugned notification via which additional court fees are imposed have a direct nexus to the objective sought to be achieved in relation to the service available to the appellants or others who approached the courts/tribunals for redressal of their grievances. We, thus, do not find any merit in the appeal and the writ petitions, which are accordingly dismissed.

[Source: (2017) 5 Supreme Court Cases 255]

ANNOTATION

The Supreme Court judgement has clarified that an additional fee or a cess (tax) can be levied on one set of persons (in this case, the litigating public) to finance social security benefits to another (and perhaps overlapping) set of persons and that such a means of financing social security and welfare benefits is legal and constitutional.

India has successfully used the idea of a 'cess' to finance social security and welfare benefits for workers in particular industries. Unlike the traditional form of social insurance where individual employers and workers contribute toward social insurance with the employer's contribution dependent upon the number of workers employed, in the industries that have a 'cess-type' financing system, the industry is levied a cess based on the output or turnover rather than the number of workers employed. The situations which have this form of financing are usually in those industries where large numbers of workers are directly or indirectly employed through a chain of sub-contractors, where it may be administratively difficult to locate each contractor or sub-contractor or home-based worker, and obtain such contributions. In such industries, the law requires the contribution of a specific sum based on its turnover/production/cost to a welfare fund that is constituted specifically to benefit the workers of that industry. Thus, for instance, a welfare fund that provides medical, maternity and other benefits to building and construction workers has been financed by levying a cess on those entities constructing buildings across India. Similar cesses have been levied by law on the non-ferrous mining industry and the beedi (hand-rolled cigarettes) industry for financing such social security/welfare benefits.

A constitutional issue has repeatedly been raised with regard to levying a specific cess on persons/parties who are not employers nor beneficiaries of the social security benefits, but who are nevertheless called upon by statute to contribute to such social security funds. In the cases of the cess levied in the beedi, non-ferrous mines, and building and construction industries noted above, it was the ultimate employers who were made to pay the cess based upon their output. A loose connection of employer and employee connected through a chain of contractors and sub-contractors can be established in such cases. In the present case, the members of the litigating public are not only under a duty to contribute towards improving legal services available to litigants, but are also to contribute to the welfare fund that exclusively benefits retired or deceased advocates. The judgement does not require that a litigant must have hired the services of an advocate in order to become liable to pay this additional levy towards the advocates' welfare fund. A very loose nexus between group of persons who benefit from the services (litigants) rendered by another set of stakeholders in the legal services provided (advocates) has been considered as sufficient to burden the former with the additional levy. In effect, the requirement for some form of an employer-employee relationship as a prior condition for contributing to the welfare benefits of a specific group of persons has been diluted by the Supreme Court. While such additional sources of funding towards welfare funds that provide important benefits are welcome, it is likely that the constitutional basis of such a cess/levy will continue to remain a matter of legal challenge in the future.

Ire. 1

IRELAND

The Supreme Court
Stephen Miley, Devil's Glen Equestrian Centre Ltd and
Devil's Glen Partnership v. Employment Appeals Tribunal,
Paul Bourke and the Attorney General

*Employment tribunal – judicial review of decision – applicant
securing order of certiorari – whether applicant entitled
to costs – whether tribunal acted mala fide or improperly*

HEADNOTES

Facts

Paul Bourke (PB) made a claim to the Employment Appeals Tribunal (EAT) under the Unfair Dismissals Act 1977. A hearing took place and the EAT issued a determination that PB had been unfairly dismissed by Stephen Miley and awarded him €7,095 compensation. Mr Miley applied to the High Court for a judicial review of the determination seeking to have it quashed on the basis that, *inter alia*, the EAT acted contrary to fair procedures and its decision was irrational and unreasonable.

Neither PB nor the EAT filed opposition papers and neither appeared at the judicial review hearing. The High Court made an order of certiorari quashing the EAT's determination and also ordered that Mr Miley recover the costs of the judicial review proceedings against the EAT. The EAT appealed the decision of the High Court to the Supreme Court insofar as it awarded costs against it.

Decision

The appeal was allowed. Where bodies such as the EAT do not participate in judicial review proceedings, costs should not be awarded against them unless there was proof that the body acted with *mala fides* or with impropriety. There was no evidence of the former and, although the standard of the hearing before the EAT was wanting, it did not amount to impropriety. Nor was this a case where Article 6 of the European Convention on Human Rights was engaged.

Law Applied

The Court did not refer to any statute in its judgement.

JUDGEMENT

Denham CJ (O'Donnell, Clarke and Laffoy JJ concurring) delivered her judgement on 10 May 2016 saying:

[...]

It is well-settled law that members of the judiciary have immunity from orders as to costs. However, that immunity is not absolute. [...] In *McIlwraith v. Judge Fawsitt* [1990] 1 I.R. 343, Finlay CJ stated at 345-346:

> "With regard to the first issue which arose, namely, the propriety of the order, on the facts of this case, awarding to the applicant costs of the motion for judicial review against the first respondent, there can be no doubt whatsoever that this order was quite contrary to the legal principles which are applicable in a case of this description. The learned Circuit Court judge had made an order which was in excess of the jurisdiction vested in him by the applicable statutory provisions in an error occasioned by the application made on behalf of the second respondent and, one must presume, upon the submissions made on its behalf that he had power to make such an order. When the motion for judicial review was served upon him he did not seek to justify or defend the making of that order nor did he seek to oppose the remedies being sought by the applicant. There can be no conceivable question of his having acted with any impropriety or that the error into which he fell was other than an error due to a mistake in regard to the law applicable. In these circumstances, for the High Court, upon the applicant and his employer settling the issue between them and the applicant no longer seeking any relief or remedy by way of judicial review, to award to him, the applicant, his costs against the first respondent was entirely incorrect...I am quite satisfied that...under no circumstances should the High Court upon application for judicial review with regard to either a decision of a District Justice or of a Circuit Court judge award costs to a successful applicant in a case where there is no question of impropriety or *mala fides* on the part of the judge concerned and where he has not sought to defend an order which apparently is invalid..."

[...]

The question is whether such immunity should apply to the EAT. [...] In this case the EAT did not act as a *legitimus contradictor*. It was a tribunal which acted in a manner analogous to the position of a District Judge in many judicial review proceedings – where no opposition to the review was filed.

[...]

As a matter of public policy, and arising from its function, the EAT should not primarily be liable for an order of costs in judicial review proceedings when it has not participated in such proceedings. This means that, while the EAT would not in the first instance be liable for costs, that immunity would be lost if the EAT acted with *mala fides* or with impropriety. Thus I would determine first that the EAT is entitled *prima facie* to immunity from costs.

The next question is whether the EAT lost that immunity by reason of *mala fides* or impropriety? [...] It is clear from a review of the facts that, whatever happened in the EAT, it was not a decision reached with *mala fides*. Thus the next issue is whether the actions of the EAT amounted to impropriety? [...]

The term "impropriety" is defined in the *Concise Oxford Dictionary* (10th edn) as: "improper behaviour or character".

This gives some guidance. As the term "*mala fides*" is part of the test, and goes to intent and motive, the concept of "impropriety" appears to address a different aspect of conduct, such as wholly unfit proceedings.

Errors of law or of fact are matters to be dealt with on appeal, and are not matters of impropriety.

On a review of the facts, as set out earlier in this judgement, it is clear that the standard of the hearing was wanting. It is not the type of behaviour to which the EAT would aspire. It is important that the EAT, by its behaviour, enhance confidence in the system. While the process was anticipated to be informal, that is no reason to depart from important legal values and standards.

It is clear that the conduct of the EAT was not what the EAT or anybody with adjudicative functions would aspire to in this day and age nor was it conduct which participants in proceedings should be required to accept. For that reason the proceedings were properly quashed. However, it was not "impropriety".

The issue of the European Convention for the Protection of Human Rights and Fundamental Freedoms 1950 (the "ECHR") was raised before the Court. The respondents argued that, having succeeded in their application for judicial review, they were entitled to their costs, as in general would apply. They submitted that the effect of the rule of immunity was to deny them an effective remedy, in a situation where the EAT had acted in a manner which was procedurally flawed.

The costs in issue were those of applying *ex parte* to the High Court for leave to proceed by way of judicial review. As the application was not opposed there was no necessity for any further hearing, until the applicants sought their costs.

Whether there is a right under the ECHR to recover costs in all cases was considered in the High Court by O Néill J in *F v. Judge O'Donnell* [2012] 3 I.R. 483, where he stated at 510-511:

> "From the above it is clear that the Convention does not require in all cases that there be provision in law for the recovery of costs by a successful party from the defeated party. Recovery of costs *per se* is not an essential feature of the right of access to courts or tribunals (Article 6) or of an effective remedy (Article 13). The costs issue only engages the Convention and invariably Article 6, rather than Article 13, at a point where the lack of a provision in law for the recovery of costs acts as an impediment to access to the courts. Thus the jurisprudence of the European Court of Human Rights requires that, first, there be a consideration of whether the particular litigation costs, having regard to the particular circumstances of the case, constitute an obstacle to the applicant's right of access to the courts resulting potentially in a breach of Article 6(1), and, if the answer to this question is in the affirmative, secondly, does the prohibition on making a costs order satisfy the proportionality test?"

The European Court of Human Rights (the "ECtHR") considered the issue of costs and Article 6 in *Stankiewicz v. Poland* (2007) 44 E.H.R.R.47. In that case, the applicants complained that the decision of the respondent state to refuse to reimburse them the costs of civil proceedings which the prosecuting authorities had unsuccessfully brought against them was in breach of their rights under Article 6. Under Polish domestic law, the party losing a civil case was normally obliged to reimburse the litigation costs to the successful party, however that principle was not applicable when a public prosecutor participated in his or her capacity of guardian of legal order.

The ECtHR noted that the prosecuting authorities enjoyed a privileged position with respect to the costs of civil proceedings and it was accepted that such a privilege might be justified for the protection of the legal order. However, the court held that the principle was not applicable in that case as it would put the applicants at an unfair disadvantage, thus the court found there had been an infringement of Article 6.

The English Court of Appeal considered Strasbourg jurisprudence on the issues of costs and Article 6 in *Eastenders Cash and Carry Plc v. Commissioners of Her Majesty's Revenue and Customs* [2012] EWCA Civ 689. Elias LJ stated:

> "As to the Article 6 point, I accept that *Stankiewicz* supports the submission that there will be situations where differential rules on costs may engage the requirements of Article 6, although I confess that I have difficulty in understanding from the decision precisely when that will be the case. I can understand an argument that the denial of costs might in some cases inhibit access to the courts in a similar way to the denial of legal aid or the imposition of court fees [...]. However the court in *Stankiewicz* said [...] that these were not the relevant principles in play [...].
>
> In any event the claimants in this case were not in fact denied access. So if Article 6 is engaged, it must be for some other reason. Paragraph 60 of *Stankiewicz* goes on to recognise that there may be such situations
>
>> '...There may also be situations in which the issues linked to the determination of litigation costs can be of relevance to the assessment whether the proceedings in a civil case seen as a whole have complied with the requirements of Article 6(1) of the Convention.'
>
> The court noted that the prosecution in that case had a privileged position with respect to costs. That of itself would not, however, necessarily involve a breach of Article 6 because the privilege might be justified (para 69):
>
>> 'It is true that such a privilege may be justified for the protection of the legal order. However, it should not be applied to put a party to civil proceedings to unfair disadvantage *vis-à-vis* the prosecuting authorities.'
>
> The court concluded that Article 6 was infringed by the particular application of the rule in that case. As Mummery LJ has pointed out, the facts in *Stankiewicz* were unusual and very different from those arising here. In particular, the successful litigant was taken to court by the prosecutor in what he found to be a complex matter warranting legal representation. He did not choose to engage in the litigation.
>
> It is difficult to avoid the conclusion that the court found Article 6 to be engaged because the costs orders operated in what the court considered was a manifestly unfair and disproportionate way. How that creates an 'unfair

disadvantage' in relation to the trial process is more difficult to discern but we must assume that there are exceptional cases, of which *Stankiewicz* itself is one, where it does so and involves a breach of Article 6."

Elias LJ held that, even assuming that there may be exceptional situations where Article 6 is infringed by unfair discrimination in costs rules, the case before them was not such a case.

> "I would echo that approach so that, even assuming that there may be exceptional situations where Article 6 is infringed by unfair discrimination in costs rules, this is not such a case. I would also observe that risk of costs which cannot be recovered under the approach in *McIlwraith v. Judge Fawsitt* [1990] 1 I.R. 343 is by definition very limited. If a decision making body defends judicial review proceedings then it may be liable for costs if it loses. If it does not take part in the proceedings, then it is still open for the party who benefitted from the challenged ruling to defend the proceedings, in which case it will be responsible for costs if the claim succeeds. It is only if neither party seeks to stand over the conduct or ruling, that the applicant will succeed in the judicial review but not recover the costs of so doing. Those costs can only amount to the drafting of the application and the *ex parte* application for leave, and the uncontested application for judicial review. These costs are necessarily limited. There are other features of the legal system where parties can be successful but fail to recover some or all of the costs they incurred, often more substantial than the costs involved here.

> "In conclusion, I am satisfied that the EAT should not primarily be liable for costs in judicial review proceedings, when it has not participated in those proceedings. A rule similar to that stated in *McIlwraith v. Judge Fawsitt* [1990] 1 I.R. 343 should apply. Thus, while the EAT would in the first instance not be liable for costs, that immunity would be lost if the EAT acted with *mala fides* or with impropriety. I am satisfied that the EAT did not act either with *mala fides* or with impropriety in this case. Consequently, I would allow the appeal."

[Source: [2016] IESC 20; [2016] E.L.R. 177]

ANNOTATION

There is no doubt that, on the evidence before the High Court, the hearing before the EAT was "entirely unsatisfactory". Consequently, it was understandable that the employer opted to challenge the EAT's determination by way of judicial review, a remedy which focuses on the manner in which the decision was made. The employer, however, had the alternative option of appealing the EAT's determination to the Circuit Court where he would have been entitled to a *de novo* hearing of PB's unfair dismissal complaint, with the Circuit Court being empowered to award costs against the unsuccessful party on appeal.

In this case, the High Court (Hedigan J) was satisfied that the determination should be quashed and the matter remitted to the EAT for a determination in accordance with law. On remittal, the complaint was settled.

On the issue of costs, the Supreme Court endorsed the policy normally followed by decision making bodies such as the EAT in judicial review challenges, which is that they do not take part in the proceedings. The reason for this is that the *legitimus contradictor* is the employee or employer (as the case may be) and that any issue of costs is a matter between the parties and not, in this case, the EAT.

The Supreme Court did recognise, however, that there may be cases where a decision making body will decide to take part in judicial review proceedings; in which case they become liable for costs: see *Ryanair Ltd v. Labour Court* 27 I.L.L.R. 317 and *McGowan v. Labour Court* 33 I.L.L.R. 291 where the Labour Court fully participated in both proceedings.

The EAT is a statutory tribunal originally established in 1967. Its jurisdiction includes hearing redundancy, minimum notice and unfair dismissal claims as well as payment of wages and other appeals. It is a tripartite body which operates in divisions with a legally qualified chair and members drawn from panels nominated by the social partners. It was one of a number of bodies entrusted with the task of adjudicating on employment disputes; the others being the Equality Tribunal, the Rights Commissioner service and the Labour Court.

Following the establishment of the Workplace Relations Commission (the Commission) with effect from 1 October 2015, the EAT no longer accepts direct complaints or appeals. Instead all complaints and disputes under employment and equality legislation are referred to the Commission with appeals from adjudication officers being heard by the Labour Court *de novo*. Any further appeal is to the High Court and is confined to a point of law.

The EAT remains in place to deal with "legacy" complaints and appeals, on completion of which it will be dissolved. The Circuit Court will then cease to have any role in hearing unfair dismissal appeals: see Annotation to *Bank of Ireland v. Reilly* 35 I.L.L.R. 301, 313-314 and Kerr "The Workplace Relations Reform Project" (2016) 7 *European Labour Law Journal* 125.

This change to the dispute resolution machinery will not affect the Supreme Court's ruling in this case. A party who is dissatisfied with the conduct of proceedings before one of the Commission's adjudication officers will have the options of a *de novo* appeal to the Labour Court or a judicial review application to the High Court. The general attitude of that Court, however, is that the former remedy is more appropriate: see, most recently, *Sam Dennigan and Company v. Rights Commissioner O'Connell and the Workplace Relations Commission* [2016] IEHC 665 (Humphreys J) where leave to apply for judicial review was refused.

U.S.A. 2

UNITED STATES OF AMERICA

Court of Appeals for the District of Columbia Circuit
HTH Corp. v. NLRB

Remedies for unfair labor practices – public reading of notice of wrongdoing – wrongdoer's liability for costs of enforcing the law

HEADNOTES

Facts

An employer that refused to recognize a labor organization which had majority employee support, committed a series of unfair labor practices, including violation of a court injunction seeking to cure violations. The National Labor Relations Board (NLRB) eventually ordered that a notice recounting the violations and stating the employer's duty to obey the law, be read to assembled employees and executives and that the employer pay the NLRB and the labor organization for the costs of legal representation incurred to remedy the unfair labor practices.

The issues were: 1) Does the NLRB have authority to order that a notice be read to workers by a Board agent or by a designated manager announcing that their employer was guilty of specified violations of the National Labor Relations Act, will not again engage in these violations, and will provide restitution to those wronged?

2) If an employer has repeatedly committed serious unfair labor practices does the charging party NLRB have the authority to require the employer to pay the Board and the charging party for the costs of obtaining legal redress for those violations?

Decision

1) The remedial authority of the NLRB includes requiring a public reading of a notice to workers by a Board agent or by a designated manager

stating that the employer was guilty of specified violations of the National Labor Relations Act, will not again engage in these violations, and will provide restitution to those wronged.

2) The NLRB does not have authority to require an employer that repeatedly committed serious unfair labor practices to pay the Board and the charging party for the costs of obtaining legal redress for those violations.

Law Applied

National Labor Relations Act

Section 10(c) – "If upon the preponderance of the testimony taken the Board shall be of the opinion that any person named in the complaint has engaged in or is engaging in any such unfair labor practice, then the Board shall state its findings of fact and shall issue and cause to be served on such person an order requiring such person to cease and desist from such unfair labor practice, and to take such affirmative action including reinstatement of employees with or without back pay, as will effectuate the policies of [the Act]."

JUDGMENT*

Before HENDERSON and ROGERS, Circuit Judges, and WILLIAMS, Senior Circuit Judge.

Williams, Senior Circuit Judge

The National Labor Relations Board determined that petitioners HTH Corporation and various affiliates (collectively "HTH" or the "company") committed a host of severe and pervasive unfair labor practices, a finding that HTH does not here dispute. HTH does, however, petition for review of [...] extraordinary remedies imposed by the Board. [...]

The company [...] operates the Pacific Beach Hotel in Honolulu. [...] Time and time again, the Board and the courts have concluded that the company violated the law in its dealings with the International Longshore and Warehouse Union, Local 142. [...]

---

* Footnotes are numbered as in the original. Deleted footnotes are not indicated.

Starting as early as 2002, the company unlawfully interfered with a representation election [...] and then with an election held to replace that election. [...] The union prevailed in the latter and was duly certified. There followed various efforts to derail the union and two sets of unfair labor practice charges. The first set led to a Board order, [...] and to a court injunction under § 10(j) of the National Labor Relations Act. [...] The company violated that injunction, leading to compensatory contempt citations against it and its Regional Vice President, Robert Minicola. [...]

The second set of charges ultimately resulted in the extraordinary remedies contested here. In September 2011 an administrative law judge [ALJ] determined that the company had violated the Act by disciplining and firing a union activist [...] (who had been unlawfully fired once before), unilaterally increasing housekeepers' workloads, unreasonably withholding information from the union, surveilling union activities, banning two union representatives from the hotel and then announcing the ban to employees, threatening to remove a union agent who was distributing union literature from a public sidewalk, and halting its matching contributions to employees' 401(k) plans. [...] Several of these actions, including Villanueva's second termination, were in violation of the § 10(j) injunction and formed the basis of the district court's later imposition of contempt sanctions. [...] The ALJ recommended a set of remedies, only two of which are relevant for our purposes: requirements of (1) notice-posting and (2) notice-reading.

The ALJ's proposed notice-reading remedy required either the company's CEO and its President, or Minicola (the Regional Vice President), to read to employees a "notice" drafted by the Board. In the "notice" the officials are to say that "we" have violated the National Labor Relations Act and the employees' rights and to state 15 specific assurances in the form, "We will" adhere to specified NLRA obligations and remedy various breaches, or "We will not" violate the Act in a wide range of specified ways.

The company filed various exceptions to the ALJ's decision. Only one is relevant here—an objection to the notice-reading remedy on the ground that extraordinary remedies were unwarranted because there had been no showing that traditional remedies were insufficient to cure the company's unfair labor practices. The company didn't object to the ALJ's notice-posting remedy.

In October 2014 the Board issued the Order on appeal here. [...] The Board agreed with the ALJ that the company had committed each of the alleged violations but found the ALJ's recommended remedies insufficient. Accordingly, it *sua sponte* ramped up the notice-posting and notice-reading requirements and imposed three additional extraordinary remedies.

[…] [The NLRB] mitigated the order by allowing the company to have a Board agent read the notice rather than requiring that Minicola or the CEO and President do so. It toughened the remedy by (1) removing the option of having the CEO and President read the notice (i.e., if a company manager is going to fulfill this obligation, it must be Minicola); (2) requiring that an Explanation of Rights be read at the notice-reading event; (3) requiring that all company supervisors and managers attend the reading; and (4) specifying that a union representative be allowed to be present.

The new Board remedies […] consisted of (1) awarding litigation expenses to the General Counsel and the union; (2) awarding bargaining and other expenses to the union; and (3) subjecting the company for three years to Board "visitation" throughout company premises and files to assess compliance with the Board's more conventional orders. The Board tripled the length of the "notice" to be read aloud by including, among other things, assurances that "We will" implement each of the Board's remedial requirements. […]

Two members of the Board, Members Miscimarra and Johnson, dissented.

[The court ruled that for procedural reasons, only two objections to the remedy were before it for review: The notice reading requirement and the imposition of attorney's fees.]

We turn now to the merits of […] the mandated notice-reading first, [and] recall that the ALJ recommended an order requiring specified high-level company officials to read out the notice acknowledging the company's violations and committing not to indulge in such behavior in the future. The Board […] narrowed the choice of persons to one, Minicola, but then broadened the company's choices by giving it the option of having a Board employee read the notice in the presence of company management.

[…]

Given the company's long history of unlawful practices and the severe violations the Board found in this case, we uphold the Board's exercise of discretion in ordering notice-reading in the modified form, i.e., with the company having the option of punting the task to a Board employee. […] Further, given the option of having the notice read by a Board employee, we have no need to address the validity of an employee-specific notice-reading mandate unaccompanied by such an option.

We turn next to the Board's award of litigation expenses to the General

Counsel and the union. In *Unbelievable, Inc. v. NLRB*, 118 F.3d 795, 800-06 [...] (D.C. Cir. 1997), we held that the Board lacks authority to shift litigation expenses under § 10(c) of the Act, which empowers the Board "to take such affirmative action including reinstatement of employees with or without back pay, as will effectuate the policies of [the Act]," 29 U.S.C. § 160(c). In ordering fees in this case, the Board recognized the holding in *Unbelievable* but claimed that, like a federal court, it has "inherent authority to control and maintain the integrity of its own proceedings through an application of the bad-faith exception to the American Rule." *HTH Corp.*, 361 N.L.R.B. No. 65, Amended Deferred Appendix ("App.") 3-4. See *Chambers v. NASCO, Inc.*, 501 U.S. 32, 45-46 [...] (1991) (recognizing that although the American rule prohibits fee shifting in most cases, federal courts have inherent power to assess attorney's fees "when a party has 'acted in bad faith, vexatiously, wantonly, or for oppressive reasons'" [...]).

As a creature of statute the Board has only those powers conferred upon it by Congress. [...] To be sure, we have recognized that agencies enjoy some powers that were not *expressly* enumerated by Congress. See, e.g., *Ivy Sports Med., LLC v. Burwell*, 767 F.3d 81, 86 [...] (D.C. Cir. 2014) (power to reconsider prior decisions); *Polydoroff v. ICC*, 773 F.2d 372, 374, [...] (D.C. Cir. 1985) (power to police the behavior of practitioners); *Howard Sober, Inc. v. ICC*, 628 F.2d 36, 41 [...] (D.C. Cir. 1980) (power to correct clerical mistakes). Although we have often described these powers as "inherent," the more accurate label is "statutorily implicit." See *Ivy Sports*, 767 F.3d at 93 (Pillard, J., dissenting). Therefore, unlike a federal court, the Board may apply the bad-faith exception to the American rule only if some provision or provisions of the Act explicitly or implicitly grant it power to do so.

In deciding to award litigation expenses on a bad-faith theory, the Board relied solely on its "inherent authority to control and maintain the integrity of its own proceedings." *HTH Corp.*, 361 N.L.R.B. No. 65 [...]. Neither in its Order nor on appeal has the Board argued that the power to shift fees in cases of bad faith is implicit in the Act. Given that it is wrong to speak of agencies as having *any* inherent authority, it would under many circumstances be quite appropriate for us to say that the Board has cited no pertinent authority at all, to vacate this part of the Order under review, and to have done with it.

There are several reasons to reject that approach and consider whether § 10(c) implicitly authorizes fee shifting based on bad faith. First, the distinction between inherent authority and implicitly granted authority is a subtle one—so subtle that this court generally overlooked it until Judge Pillard pointed it out in *Ivy Sports*. Second, considering § 10(c) does not take us into refined linguistic nuances; § 10(c) simply authorizes the Board to take "such affirmative action [...] as will effectuate the policies" of the Act. Third, and closely related to the purely linguistic point, the decisive considerations resolving the issue stem not from the exact language of § 10(c) but from contextual concerns that were at the heart of *Unbelievable* and the subject of intense discussion at oral argument.

The controlling contextual concern arises from two propositions: first, that nothing in § 10(c) grants the Board punitive powers, and, second, that application of the American rule's bad-faith exception is punitive. On the first, as we said in *Unbelievable*, "The Supreme Court has consistently invalidated Board orders that are not directly related to the effectuation of the purposes of the Act *or* are punitive." 118 F.3d at 805 (emphasis added). We cited several decisions in support of that proposition, starting with *Consolidated Edison Co. v. NLRB*, 305 U.S. 197, 235-36, [...] (1938), which held that the Board's purported cancellation of bargaining agreements that were not causally derived from the alleged unfair labor practices was punitive and therefore not within the Board's § 10(c) powers, even if the Board should "be of the opinion that the policies of the Act might be effectuated by such an order." *Id.* at 236. Similarly, once we found in *Capital Cleaning Contractors, Inc. v. NLRB*, 147 F.3d 999, 1009-12 [...] (D.C. Cir. 1998), that the Board's imposition of contract terms on a successor employer based on terms negotiated by its predecessor was punitive in the circumstances, we held it beyond the Board's powers. A § 10(c) remedy, we said, "must be truly remedial and not punitive." *Id.* at 1009.

This authoritative ban on punitive remedies by the Board is triggered here: the Supreme Court has consistently classified application of the bad-faith exception to the American rule as punitive. *Hall v. Cole*, 412 U.S. 1, 5 [...] (1973). Such fee shifting is akin to a fine for civil contempt: both serve the purpose of vindicating the tribunal's authority over a recalcitrant litigant. *Chambers*, 501 U.S. at 53.

The Board doesn't dispute that it may not adopt punitive remedies but argues instead that its award of litigation expenses is "clearly compensatory in nature." *HTH Corp.*, 361 N.L.R.B. No. 65, App. 4. According to the Board, the General Counsel and the union were forced to squander resources on this case, and the fee award merely "helps restore the parties to where they would have been but for the [company's] unlawful conduct." *Id.* Of course we recognize that compensation and punishment are not inherently mutually exclusive goals. But in the context of the American rule, any attempt to rest on the compensatory character of a fee award runs into the basic underpinning of the American rule, namely, the idea that the compensatory functions of fee shifting collide, in the litigation context, with other values, particularly broad freedom to assert rights and defenses. See *Summit Valley Indus. Inc. v. Local 112*, 456 U.S. 717, 724-25 [...] (1982). Thus we said in *Unbelievable*, "To the extent that the Board is relying upon the idea that a party is not made whole unless it recovers its attorney's fees, [...] that is but a criticism of the American Rule—indeed, a criticism that the Supreme Court has heard and rejected." 118 F.3d at 805. As the Supreme Court declared in *Chambers*, "That the award ha[s] a compensatory effect does not in any event distinguish it from a fine for civil contempt, which also compensates a private party for the consequences of a contemnor's disobedience." 501 U.S. at 53-54 [...].

The Board's opinion also says that the fee award "protects the integrity of our processes, serving as a deterrent to violations" of its Order and protecting the parties' rights (presumably by way of deterring further unfair labor practices). *HTH Corp.*, 361 N.L.R.B. No. 65, App. 4. But in the context of identifying the powers granted the Board, the Court has rejected deterrent purposes precisely on the ground of their overlap with punitive goals. When the Board tried to order an employer to compensate government relief agencies whose expenditures had been increased as a result of the employer's violations, the Court firmly rejected the Board's reliance on deterrent effect. If "a deterrent effect is sufficient to sustain an order of the Board, it would be free to set up any system of penalties which it would deem adequate to that end." *Republic Steel Corp. v. NLRB*, 311 U.S. 7, 12 [...] (1940).

With respect to the award of litigation expenses, we grant the company's petition and deny enforcement. As to all other portions of the Order, we deny the petition and enforce the Order, either on the merits or because of HTH's failure to meet the requirements of § 10(e).

Henderson, Circuit Judge, concurring in part and concurring in the judgment: I agree with my colleagues that we should uphold the Board's notice-reading remedy and strike its award of litigation expenses. We differ, however, in how we reach that result.

[...] In my view, the Board-agent alternative "creates a problem more severe than the one it supposedly solves." *Int'l Union of Elec., Radio & Mach. Workers, AFL-CIO v. NLRB (IUE)*, 383 F.2d 230, 233 n.5 [...] (D.C. Cir. 1967); see also *Teamsters Local 115 v. NLRB*, 640 F.2d 392, 402 n.11 [...] (D.C. Cir. 1981) ("We [...] continue to doubt the propriety of having a Board representative perform the reading."). As we explained in *IUE*, a Board representative reading the notice "put[s] the imprimatur of the Board on both a particular union's activities, as well as on union activities in general," 383 F.2d at 233 n.5, thereby compromising the Board's role as labor-law referee.[1]

Judge Williams characterizes the imprimatur concern as "weak" because "the *substance* of the notice will make employees fully aware of how the Board has ruled" and "of which 'side' the Board has taken." Maj. Op. 16-17 (emphasis in original). But even if the notice's substance indicates "which 'side' the Board has taken" *in this case*, see *id.* at 17, when a Board agent stands up to castigate an employer in front of unionized employees, those employees are inevitably left with a perception of the Board as union enforcer, not neutral arbiter. A referee calling a foul is one thing; a referee calling a foul while wearing one team's uniform is quite another. In short, *who* reads the notice matters.

That said, I believe we are without jurisdiction to consider the validity *vel non* of the Board-agent option. The alternative is not part of the remedy the ALJ recommended and to which HTH originally excepted. Further, HTH did not move for reconsideration, objecting to the Board's modification of the remedy. [...]

My reasoning diverges from my colleagues' on a second point as well. After concluding "that it is wrong to speak of agencies as having any *inherent* authority," [...] (emphasis in original), my colleagues then analyze "whether § 10(c) implicitly authorizes fee shifting based on bad faith," see *id.* They ultimately conclude that section 10(c) does not by implication authorize fee shifting because fee shifting is punitive and the Board's power is exclusively remedial. *Id.* at 19-21.

In my view, analyzing whether section 10(c) "implicitly" authorizes fee-shifting is unnecessary—and jurisprudentially out of bounds—to resolve this case. The Board relied exclusively on its purported "inherent authority" to award litigation expenses, not on section 10(c) or any other

---

[1] It is true that since *IUE* and *Teamsters* we have upheld a notice-reading remedy that included a Board-agent option and that we did so "without even a nod to IUE." Maj. Op. 16 (discussing *Federated Logistics & Operations v. NLRB*, 400 F.3d 920, 929-30 [...] (D.C. Cir. 2005)). My colleagues fail to mention, however, that we gave no "nod" to the Board-agent option, *period*. [...] Indeed, the *Federated* court had no reason to do so inasmuch as the general validity of an "any-responsible-officer" notice-reading was not in question. We also acknowledged its validity in *Teamsters*, 640 F.2d at 404 (enforcing public reading only with "a responsible officer" of employer as reader), and even then-Judge Ginsburg, in her emphatic dissent in *Conair*, would have upheld the notice-reading remedy at issue there had "a responsible officer" been required to read the notice rather than a specific person, see 721 F.2d at 1401. Accordingly, the *Federated* court had no reason to comment on the propriety of the Board-agent option and I believe we should not read its failure to do so as a *sub silentio* endorsement thereof.

statutory authority. See *HTH Corp.*, 361 N.L.R.B. No. 65, at 4 & n.16 (Oct. 24, 2014) ("Because the Board may award litigation expenses against a party who engages in bad-faith conduct based on its inherent authority to control its own proceedings, it is unnecessary to pass on whether it may alternatively do so under its Sec. 10(c) remedial authority to effectuate the policies of the Act."). And as my colleagues recognize [...] no such extra-statutory "inherent authority" exists [...]. Contrary to the Board's apparent belief, it is *not* a court of law or equity; it exercises only the powers granted by the Congress. [...] Accordingly, I would hold that the Board has no "inherent authority" to award attorneys' fees, period; in my view, that is all that need be said to justify granting HTH's petition on this issue.

Rogers, Circuit Judge, concurring in part, concurring in the judgment. [...]

The Board's order directing that either a company Vice President or, at HTH's option, a Board representative read the Board's order is a permissible exercise of the Board's broad remedial authority. See *Federated Logistics & Operations v. NLRB*, 400 F.3d 920, 929-30 [...] (D.C. Cir. 2005).

[The Board in time adopted the position] that in some instances the public reading served a permissible purpose. This change was addressed in *Teamsters Local 115 v. NLRB* (Haddon House), 640 F.2d 392, 402-03 [...] (D.C. Cir. 1981). The Board, while acknowledging judicial doubts about the propriety of such an order, had concluded that where the employer had carried out an anti-union campaign there were circumstances where the employer itself must give its employees "reassurances that this campaign will end." *Id.* at 402. Although other circuits generally approved the public reading order once the Board representative option became routine, see *id.*, the Board concluded that would not suffice in these circumstances. The court acknowledged the Board's broad remedial powers and the court's limited review, see *id.* at 399 (citing *NLRB v. Gissel Packing Co.*, 395 U.S. 575, 612 n.32 [...] (1969); *Fibreboard Paper Prods. Corp. v. NLRB*, 379 U.S. 203, 216 [...] (1964)). [...]

The court declined to enforce a "highly unusual" feature of the public reading order, however. It noted that the Board had singled out a company's chief executive officer to perform a public reading only once before, where the Board had emphasized the personal participation of the company president in the unfair labor practices. The court observed that, although "it was unnecessary to decide whether [such circumstances], or any circumstances whatsoever, could justify the startling innovation of the Board reading order directed at a specific individual," here "the Board did not make a careful analysis of the necessity for [the company owner and president] to undertake the reading, and the record suggests no such necessity." *Id.* at 403. The company president had personally performed only one unfair labor practice while other members of management engaged in numerous others. See *id.* The court concluded the negative aspects of the order, as identified in this court's opinion in *IUE*, overwhelmed "the marginally greater impact" of having the company president read the order, and found it was "unjustified." *Id.* at 403-04.

Since *Teamsters*, the court, like our sister circuits, has enforced a Board order that required a notice reading where the employer was afforded the option of having the notice read by a Board representative. See *Federated Logistics & Operations*, 400 F.3d at 929-30. Alternatively, the court has enforced notice-reading remedies that single out a high official of the employer where the record indicates "a particularized need does exist and that the reading is necessary 'to dispel the atmosphere of intimidation created in large part by [the singled-out officer's] own statements and actions.'" *United Food & Commercial Workers Int'l Union v. NLRB*, 852 F.2d 1344, 1348 […] (D.C. Cir. 1988) (quoting *Conair v. NLRB*, 721 F.2d 1355, 1386-87 […] (D.C. Cir. 1983), and citing *IUE*, 383 F.2d at 234). […]

As this history indicates, there is no need to impugn the court's reconciliation of its precedent with the congressional design granting the Board broad power and discretion to devise remedies to effectuate the policies of the National Labor Relations Act. See *Gissel Packing Co.*, 395 U.S. at 612 n.32; *Fibreboard Paper Prods. Corp.*, 379 U.S. at 216. […] The record supports the Board's conclusion that a notice-reading remedy was warranted by the egregious conduct of HTH and its Vice President's pervasive unlawful conduct over an extended period of time. […] Accordingly, I concur in part and concur in the judgment.

[Source: 823 F.3d 668 (2016)]

ANNOTATION

In some cultures an agency's or court's pronouncement of wrongdoing may be enough to ensure that the wrongdoer will take corrective actions. Voluntary compliance is common in the U.S. because of both respect for the rule of law and awareness that non compliance will be accompanied by serious financial or other costs such as impaired public reputation. Yet in some segments of American society, including portions of the business community, resistance to government regulation is considered a virtue. Accordingly, the rule of law often is dependent upon the availability of remedial devices that increase the likelihood of future compliance and provide substantial restitution to those injured by violations of that rule.

Providing awareness of rights and explaining the availability and means for obtaining redress of wrongs long has been an important characteristic of labor protective laws in the U.S. This is accomplished through a number of approaches. One is to require the posting at work places of a standard notice explaining the protections of a particular set of laws and regulations. Another is for administrative agencies to issue public announcements through various news media describing the protected rights afforded to employees. Still another is to announce publicly the results in litigated disputes involving employee rights. Finally, there is the sort of notice at issue in the case under discussion. It is a notice specifically designed to reach the attention of the affected work force (or labor organization members) specifying the findings of wrongdoing, the commitment to obey the law, and the resulting remedies that have been imposed on the wrongdoers. Although the remedial use of mandatory notices of wrongdoing and the law's protection of rights is not specified in Section 10(c) of the National Labor Relations Act, the courts long have accepted the notice requirement as properly within the NLRB's remedial authority "to take such affirmative action . . . as will effectuate the policies of [the Act]."

Normally, when the NLRB directs that a notice be addressed to a specific group of workers, it is in the form of a written posting for a specified duration in a prominent location at the workplace. That approach leaves the risk that some workers or most workers may not bother to read the notice. As discussed in the *HTH* case, in the event of more egregious or persistent violations, normally the Board additionally requires that it be read aloud to the workers. Although this increases the prospect that all of the workers will in fact learn of the contents, it also involves a more emphatic form of public shaming. Although such shaming is an important law enforcement tool in some cultures, and was an accepted aspect of law enforcement in the U.S. a couple of hundred years ago, many Americans regard it as an inappropriate affront to the human dignity of the pronounced wrongdoers. Not only is the public shaming heightened if the wrongdoer is personally required to read the notice, but also, arguably, compelling the reading violates a broad understanding of freedom of expression as including the right to remain silent. The NLRB's solution to both objections is to provide the option of having the notice read publicly by an agency employee. Although one member of the court panel suggested that this practice undermines the Board's stature as an impartial party, that point of view has not prevailed inasmuch as it is generally understood that impartiality is not impaired if, after a full evidentiary hearing and presentation of arguments on the merits, a public decision is made and announced as to which litigant should prevail.

The second issue, whether the expenses of the NLRB litigation should be paid by a party that had posed a frivolous defense, had been resolved previously by a panel of the circuit's judges. Therefore, under American judicial practices it was to be expected that the court in the *HTH* case would apply the precedent of the earlier decision.

American courts are aware of the fact that in many other legal systems the losing party normally is required to pay the victor's litigation expenses. However, the judicially derived "American Rule" adopts the approach that in order to ensure against persons being discouraged from seeking vindication of their legal rights, each party should bear its own litigation expenses regardless of the outcome. Although the NLRB's remedial authority includes restitution of those injured by an unfair labor practice, the court of appeals decided that, due to the American Rule, the restitution of litigation expenses is not within the scope of the NLRB's remedial authority because the Act lacks clear statutory language or history demonstrating that Congress intended to override the American Rule for such cases.

Several federal statutes that protect employees, such as Section 16 of the Fair Labor Standards Act, the federal minimum wage and overtime pay law, expressly provide for recovery of litigation expenses, including a reasonable attorney's fee, by employees who prevail in their claims. Another example is the law providing for recovery by employees who are victims of employment discrimination. (See, for example, Title VII Section 7(k).)

Interestingly, when the NLRB has proceeded against a person or business, the Equal Access to Justice Act (5 US Code §504, 28 US Code §2412) allows that party to seek recovery from the NLRB of reasonable litigation expenses, including a reasonable attorney's fee, if the party is an individual who has a net worth not in excess of $2,000,000 or is a business that has a net worth not in excess of $7,000,000 or more than 500 employees. In order to sustain its litigation expenses claim, the party must have prevailed "in a significant and discrete substantive portion of the proceeding" and shown that the NLRB's position in the proceeding was not substantially justified.

In contrast with the decision in *HTH* commented on here, weeks later the same panel of judges agreed that if an employer bargains in bad faith the Board has the authority to require it to reimburse the union for the expenses incurred in attempting to negotiate a collective agreement: *Camelot Terrace, Inc. v. NLRB*, 824 F.3d 1085 (D.C. Cir. 2016).

U.S.A. 4

UNITED STATES OF AMERICA

Court of Appeals for the Eleventh Circuit
Suazo v. NCL (Bahamas) Ltd.

Suit for non resident employee's maritime claims barred by arbitration agreement

HEADNOTES

Facts

Suazo, a Nicaraguan citizen, signed an employment contract to work aboard one of NCL's cruise ships that was registered in the Bahamas. He was injured while lifting heavy garbage bins as part of his duties and was flown home to Nicaragua on medical leave. Eventually, NCL referred Suazo to an orthopedic surgeon who diagnosed him with a herniated disc that was compressing a nerve in his spine and prescribed physical therapy and epidural steroid injections. He received treatment but his medical care was terminated before he was healed. NCL ignored requests to reinstate his medical care.

Suazo's employment was covered by an individual agreement that provided for arbitration of all unsettled shipboard claims. It was also covered by a collective agreement providing that if a dispute between a represented seafarer and NCL is brought to arbitration, the union will represent the claimant in the proceeding unless the seafarer elects to be represented by his own attorney.

Suazo's own attorney sued NCL in a state court asserting claims under U.S. maritime law. The suit was transferred to a federal trial court where, on NCL's motion, it was dismissed based on the Convention on the Recognition and Enforcement of Foreign Arbitral Awards. Suazo was ordered to arbitrate his claim. He asserted that he was financially unable to do so.

The issue in this case was: when a foreign cruise ship employee is injured on the job, and his employment contract contains an arbitration agreement, can he nevertheless sue in court to vindicate his maritime law claims if high costs of arbitrating may prevent him from effectively pursuing his claim in that forum?

Decision

The assertion that the financial burden prevents the claimant from vindicating his claim in arbitration likely cannot be heard at the stage at which a court is asked to order the parties to arbitrate. Even assuming it can be raised at this stage, Suazo has not proffered proof of such financial inability and his assertion is unpersuasive because the collective agreement allows him to receive free representation from his union in the arbitration proceeding.

Law Applied

United Nations Convention on the Recognition and Enforcement of Foreign Arbitral Awards (known as the "New York Convention")

Art. II(3)– A court, at the request of one of the parties to an arbitration agreement involving the territory of a State other than the State where the recognition and enforcement of such awards are sought, shall "refer the parties to arbitration, unless it finds that the said agreement is null and void, inoperative or incapable of being performed."

JUDGMENT

Before MARCUS, JORDAN and WALKER, Circuit Judges.
Marcus, Circuit Judge:

In this appeal, we address a question of first impression in the Circuit: whether a cruise ship employee who is injured on the job, and whose employment contract contains an arbitration agreement governed by the New York Convention and Chapter 2 of the Federal Arbitration Act, can bar arbitration by showing that high costs may prevent him from effectively vindicating his federal statutory rights in the arbitral forum. Our [prior decisions suggest (but do not hold)] that a party may only raise this type of public-policy defense in opposition to a motion to enforce an arbitral award <u>after</u> arbitration has taken place, and not in order to defeat a motion to compel arbitration. However, we need not definitively answer this question today because, even if we were to assume that the plaintiff-appellant Willman Suazo could raise a cost-based (public policy) defense in response to defendant-appellee NCL's motion to compel arbitration, on this record he has plainly failed to establish that the costs of arbitration would preclude him from arbitrating his federal statutory claims. Thus, we affirm the district court's order compelling the parties to arbitrate. [...]

I

[The Convention on the Recognition and Enforcement of Foreign Arbitral Awards, the "New York Convention", to which the U.S. became a signatory in 1970, recognizes both non-domestic agreements to arbitrate and provides for enforcement of non-domestic arbitration awards.]

[...] The Convention provides that certain defenses may be raised in response to each cause of action. Article II of the Convention ... applies at the "initial arbitration-enforcement stage." *Escobar v. Celebration Cruise Operator, Inc.*, 805 F.3d 1279, 1286 (11th Cir. 2015). [Article II (3) of the Convention requires a signatory nation to enforce a non domestic arbitration agreement "unless it finds that the said agreement is null and void, inoperative or incapable of being performed."]

"Importantly, Article II contains no explicit or implicit public-policy defense at the initial arbitration-enforcement stage." *Escobar*, 805 F.3d at 1287. We have held that the Convention requires that a motion to compel arbitration must be granted "so long as (1) the four jurisdictional prerequisites are met and (2) no available affirmative defense under the Convention applies." *Lindo v. NCL* (Bahamas), Ltd., 652 F.3d 1257, 1276 (11th Cir. 2011) (citing *Bautista v. Star Cruises*, 396 F.3d 1289, 1294-95 (11th Cir. 2005)) [...] An arbitration agreement falls within the jurisdiction of the New York Convention if: (1) the agreement is "in writing within the meaning of the [New York] Convention"; (2) "the agreement provides for arbitration in the territory of a signatory of the [New York] Convention"; (3) "the agreement arises out of a legal relationship, whether contractual or not, which is considered commercial"; and (4) a party to the agreement is not an American citizen or the commercial relationship has some reasonable relation with one or more foreign states. *Bautista*, 396 F.3d at 1294 n.7.

Article V of the Convention governs only the "award-enforcement" stage, and provides for a substantially broader set of defenses that may be raised in response to a motion to confirm an arbitral award. [...] One of Article V's seven permitted defenses is a "public policy" defense:

Recognition and enforcement of an arbitral award may also be refused if the competent authority in the country where recognition and enforcement is sought finds that:

[...]

(b) The recognition or enforcement of the award would be contrary to the public policy of that country. *Id.*, art. V(2).

Notably, this public-policy defense, like the other Article V defenses, "applies only at the award-enforcement stage." *Lindo*, 652 F.3d at 1263. Therefore, parties must "wait until the award-enforcement stage to assert an Article V public-policy claim." *Escobar*, 805 F.3d at 1287.

Chapter 1 of the FAA governs domestic arbitration, and provides a broad array of defenses to the enforcement of arbitration agreements in the cases that it governs. See 9 U.S.C. § 2 (Courts shall enforce agreements governed by Chapter 1 of the FAA "save upon such grounds as exist at law or in equity for the revocation of any contract."). However, the broad defenses applicable in the context of domestic arbitration are not generally available in cases governed by the New York Convention [...]

Domestic defenses to arbitration are transferrable to a Convention Act case only if they fit within the limited scope of defenses [contained in Articles II and V of the Convention]. Such an approach is required by the unique circumstances of foreign arbitration [where] concerns of international comity, respect for the capacities of foreign and transnational tribunals, and sensitivity to the need of the international commercial system for predictability in the resolution of disputes require that we enforce the parties' agreement, even assuming that a contrary result would be forthcoming in a domestic context. *Mitsubishi Motors Corp. v. Soler Chrysler-Plymouth, Inc.*, 473 U.S. 614, 629 ... (1985).

[...]

The "effective vindication doctrine" is one defense that the federal courts have recognized in the context of domestic arbitration. [...]

[W]e are aware of no court that has even applied the effective vindication doctrine to invalidate an arbitration agreement in the context of a New York Convention case. See *Escobar*, 805 F.3d at 1291.

II

A

[...] Suazo, a Nicaraguan citizen, signed an employment contract (the "Employment Agreement") with NCL to work aboard one of its cruise ships. The Employment Agreement plainly requires arbitration of any dispute arising out of his employment with NCL:

> ARBITRATION – Seaman agrees, on his own behalf and on behalf of his heirs, executors, and assigns, that any and all claims, grievances, and disputes of any kind whatsoever relating to or in any way connected with the Seaman's shipboard employment with Company [...] shall be referred to and resolved exclusively by binding arbitration pursuant to the United Nations Convention on Recognition and Enforcement of Foreign Arbitral Awards [(the "New York Convention")], except as otherwise provided in any government mandated contract [...]
>
> The place of the arbitration shall be the Seaman's country of citizenship, unless arbitration is unavailable under The Convention in that country, in which case, and only in that case, said arbitration shall take place in Nassau, Bahamas. The substantive law to be applied to the arbitration shall be the law of the flag state of the vessel. [...]
>
> The arbitration referred to in this Article is exclusive and mandatory. Lawsuits or other proceedings between the Seaman and the Company may not be brought except to enforce the arbitration provision of this Agreement or to enforce a decision of the Arbitrator.

The Agreement is silent as to who must bear the costs of arbitration. However, it says that "the employment relationship established hereunder shall at all times be subject to and governed by the [Collective Bargaining Agreement ("CBA")]."

The CBA in turn provides:

> 7. Arbitration [...]
>
> e. In the event a dispute between the [Norwegian Seafarers' Union ("NSU")] and NCL, or between NCL and a Seafarer represented by the NSU, cannot be resolved through good faith negotiations and either party commences an arbitration proceeding, NCL shall bear the reasonable costs related to the arbitration process from beginning to end including, but not limited to fees charged and expenses incurred by arbitrators, and any costs related to proceedings brought by the NSU necessary to enforce a decision. The NSU and NCL shall each bear the costs of their own attorney fees and legal representation.
>
> f. If the Seafarer rejects the representation appointed by the NSU at arbitration or thereafter, or if he or she initiates arbitration independently, then he or she will cover the cost of his or her own

legal representation, if any. Where the Seafarer is not represented by the NSU, the arbitrator shall seek the NSU's opinion as to the interpretation of this Agreement before making a decision.

Thus, the CBA provides that, if the Seafarer is represented by the Norwegian Seafarers' Union in arbitration, NCL will bear the "reasonable costs related to the arbitration process from beginning to end." However, the CBA is silent as to who bears the cost of arbitration if the "Seafarer rejects the representation appointed by the NSU." In this situation – which the parties agree is applicable here – both NCL and the International Center for Dispute Resolution, which performs the arbitrations between NCL and its employees, have taken the position that the employee and NSU must each bear one-half of the costs until the arbitrator decides who will pay the costs.

Suazo worked for NCL aboard the Bahamian vessel Norwegian Epic, where his duties consisted of frequent heavy lifting. In April 2011, he was injured while lifting heavy garbage bins as part of his duties onboard the ship. He went to the ship's doctor complaining of back pain, was prescribed pain medications, and was sent back to work. His pain continued to worsen until he could no longer work. On August 24, 2011, Suazo was flown home to Nicaragua on medical leave. NCL did not make arrangements for his medical care in Nicaragua until after Suazo contacted the local hiring agency requesting medical attention. On August 31, 2011, NCL referred Suazo to an orthopedic surgeon, who diagnosed him with a herniated disc that was compressing a nerve in his spine and prescribed physical therapy and epidural steroid injections. Suazo received treatment throughout 2012, but his medical care was terminated in December 2012 before he was healed. NCL ignored requests to reinstate his medical care.

B

[…] Suazo, represented by private counsel, brought suit against NCL in Florida circuit court in Miami-Dade County. The four-count complaint asserted claims for negligence under the Jones Act, 46 U.S.C. § 30104, and under general maritime law. NCL timely removed the case to the United States District Court for the Southern District of Florida pursuant to 9 U.S.C. § 205, which allows for the removal of state court actions relating to an arbitration agreement that falls under the New York Convention "at any time before the trial thereof." After removing the case to federal court, NCL filed a motion to dismiss and compel arbitration.

Suazo opposed NCL's motion to compel arbitration. He noted that, although the employment agreement was silent as to who would bear the costs of arbitration for individuals who forego representation by the Norwegian Seafarers' Union, NCL had said that it would require him to pay half of the costs of arbitration. He claimed that he was too poor to bear that cost and, therefore, that the district court should refuse to compel arbitration in the first place. Suazo submitted an affidavit in support of his opposition, which stated, in pertinent part [that he is from a poor rural community in Nicaragua where it is not easy to find work, he is the main source of his family's income and does not have money to pay for an arbitration or for an arbitrator, he does not have the means to pay for thousands of dollars to an arbitrator, and to do so would deprive his family of support].

On November 4, 2014, the district court granted NCL's motion and compelled the parties to arbitrate, retaining jurisdiction of the case in order to enforce the arbitration award "if appropriate." The court reasoned that Suazo's argument that he could not afford to pay the costs of arbitration invoked the "effective vindication doctrine," which was a "public policy" defense that could not be considered at the arbitration-enforcement stage under the New York Convention. This timely appeal ensued.

Suazo raises a single question on appeal: whether he may defeat NCL's motion to compel arbitration by showing that he is too poor to afford the costs of arbitration.

[...]

III

[...] The district court was required to compel arbitration if the arbitration agreement satisfied the four jurisdictional prerequisites found in the New York Convention [...] It is undisputed that the four jurisdictional prerequisites have been met. The parties agree that: the employment agreement is in writing; the agreement provides for arbitration in Nicaragua, which has signed the Convention; Suazo's employment with NCL was a commercial relationship; and Suazo is not an American citizen. [...] Suazo argues, nevertheless, that the district court erred in compelling him to arbitrate because he cannot afford the costs of arbitration that he will be required to pay and, therefore, he will be unable to effectively vindicate his federal statutory rights in the arbitral forum.

A

We have not squarely decided whether a party can raise a cost-based effective vindication defense at the arbitration-enforcement stage under the New York Convention, and we are aware of no other federal circuit court that has done so. Nevertheless, three of our decisions provide substantial guidance.

In *Bautista v. Star Cruises*, 396 F.3d 1289 (11th Cir. 2005), several cruise ship employees who were injured at work brought suit in federal district court against their employers, asserting claims under the Jones Act [...] and under the general maritime law of the United States. *Id.* at 1292. The district court [...] compelled the parties to arbitrate the dispute under the New York Convention. *Id.* at 1294. The plaintiffs appealed the order compelling arbitration, arguing, among other things, that the arbitration provision was unconscionable. *Id.* at 1301-02.

We affirmed the order compelling arbitration. [...] We adopted the First Circuit's view that Article II's "'null and void' clause [...] limits the bases upon which an international arbitration agreement may be challenged to standard breach-of-contract defenses," and that the clause "must be interpreted to encompass only those situations – such as fraud, mistake, duress, and waiver – that can be applied neutrally on an international scale." *Id.* at 1302 (internal quotation marks omitted) (quoting *DiMercurio v. Sphere Drake Ins*. PLC, 202 F.3d 71, 79-80 (1st Cir. 2000)). We observed that unconscionability could provide a defense to arbitration enforcement in the domestic context, but that "[d]omestic defenses to arbitration are transferrable to a Convention Act case only if they fit within the limited scope of defenses" contained in the Convention. [...] Because we "doubt[ed] that there exists a precise, universal definition of [unconscionability] that may be applied effectively across the range of countries that are parties to the Convention," we refused to consider the plaintiffs' unconscionability defense and affirmed the order compelling arbitration. *Id.*

[...]

[...] *[I]n Lindo v. NCL (Bahamas), Ltd.*, 652 F.3d 1257 (11th Cir. 2011) [...] a Bahamian cruise employee sued his employer, NCL, in Florida circuit court in Miami-Dade County, alleging that he had injured his back while lifting trash bags at work, bringing a claim under the Jones Act. *Id.* at 1260-61. The employment agreement between NCL and the employee required all such claims to be arbitrated in the employee's country of citizenship, which was Nicaragua, and that the law of the vessel, which was the Bahamas, would apply. *Id.* NCL removed the case to federal court and moved to compel arbitration; the district court granted the motion. *Id.* at 1261-62. Lindo appealed and [...] argued that the application of Bahamian law in the arbitral forum would prevent him from effectively vindicating his United States statutory rights under the Jones Act. He also asserted that the arbitration agreement was unconscionable and, therefore, unenforceable. *Id.* at 1276.

We affirmed the district court's order compelling arbitration. First, we explained, we were required to "start our analysis with a strong presumption in favor of the arbitration agreement in Lindo's Contract," and that presumption was unaffected by the fact that Lindo was seeking to litigate federal statutory claims. *Id.* at 1275-76. Because Lindo conceded that the four jurisdictional prerequisites to the New York Convention were met, *id.* at 1276 & n.17, we needed only to decide whether Lindo's effective vindication argument constituted an available affirmative defense under the Convention. Citing *Bautista*, 396 F.3d at 1302, we held that Lindo had not made any "claim – much less any showing – of fraud, mistake, duress, or waiver," and he therefore could not avoid arbitration under Article II. *Id.* at 1276.

[…] Furthermore, Lindo could not raise any public policy defense under Article V because "Article V applies only at the arbitral award-enforcement stage and not at the arbitration-enforcement stage." *Id.* at 1280. Moreover, we noted that it was likely Bahamian law would permit Lindo to pursue the same types of claims as American law. Thus, Lindo's "public policy" defense was "premature" at the arbitration-enforcement stage, since Lindo could challenge the manner in which the arbitration was conducted under Article V at the arbitral award-enforcement stage, when "the arbitrator […] will have ruled and the record will show what legal principles were applied and what Lindo recovered, or did not recover, and why." *Id.* at 1284. [...]

Most recently, in *Escobar v. Celebration Cruise Operator*, 805 F.3d 1279 (11th Cir. 2015), we confronted the precise question presented in this case: whether a cost-based effective vindication defense could be raised at the arbitration-enforcement stage under the New York Convention. In *Escobar*, the plaintiff – a cruise ship employee who had been injured on the job – brought suit in state court against his employer, who removed the case to federal court and moved to compel arbitration. *Id.* at 1282-83. The plaintiff had signed an employment agreement that contained an arbitration clause, which stated: "[a]lthough [the employer] shall bear the initial cost of the arbitration, each [party] shall be responsible for one half of the cost of arbitration." *Id.* at 1282. Escobar argued that his arbitration fees would be $20,000 for even a short, three-day arbitration, and he submitted an affidavit stating that he had no money to pay the fees. *Id.* at 1283. Nevertheless, the district court granted the motion to compel arbitration. *Id.* Escobar appealed, arguing under the effective vindication doctrine that the cost-splitting provision in the arbitration agreement "effectively denie[d] him access to the forum because he is indigent." *Id.* at 1291.

We affirmed. We began by observing that we had found no court that had ever applied the effective vindication doctrine to a New York Convention case. *Id.* at 1291. Yet we found it unnecessary to decide whether Escobar's cost-based effective vindication defense could be raised at the arbitration-enforcement stage, in as much as Escobar's effective vindication claim failed for three other reasons. "First, to the extent Escobar could make [an effective vindication] claim in a New York Convention case," it was "premature for Escobar to do so at this arbitration-enforcement stage." *Id.* at 1292. We reached this conclusion because the cost-splitting clause in the arbitration agreement required the employer to pay the initial fee to "open the doors to begin the arbitration and begin the proceedings," *id.* at 1292 & n.16, meaning that "Escobar has access to the forum," *id.* at 1292.

Second, we determined that the "most reasonable reading" of the cost-splitting clause was that the employer would "initially pay for the cost of the arbitration itself," and that Escobar "ultimately [would] be responsible for his one-half share." *Id.* Recognizing that "the precise application of the cost-splitting clause [was] an issue properly for the arbitrator to consider," we found that Escobar had failed to show that he was likely to incur "any costs due prior to the arbitrator's decision." [...] Third, we determined that Escobar had not provided any evidence of how much arbitration actually would cost him, and, therefore, had failed to carry his burden to prove that he would be denied access to the forum. *Id.* Thus, we observed that based on the arbitration clause language and his own filings, Escobar had "wholly failed to establish that he would be denied access to the forum." *Id.* We indicated that "the appropriate time for Escobar to raise any argument relating to the payment of fees would be at the award-enforcement stage, if and when [his employer] attempt[ed] to collect arbitral costs from him." *Id.*

B

Because Suazo is attempting to defeat a motion to compel arbitration, he can only raise his cost-based effective vindication defense if it falls within the defenses enumerated in Article II of the New York Convention. See *Lindo*, 652 F.3d at 1263. [...] Suazo has fallen far short of establishing that enforcing the arbitration agreement in this case will effectively deny him access to the arbitral forum.

In order to prevail on a cost-based effective vindication defense in a domestic arbitration case – assuming such a defense can be raised under Article II – a party seeking to avoid arbitration must "demonstrate that he faces such 'high costs' if compelled to arbitrate his claim [...] that he is effectively precluded from vindicating his [federal statutory] rights in the arbitral forum." *Musnick v. King Motor Co. of Fort Lauderdale*, 325 F.3d 1255, 1259 (11th Cir. 2003) (quoting *Green Tree*, 531 U.S. at 90). […]

[…] In the district court, Suazo submitted no evidence concerning "the amount of the fees he is likely to incur." *Escobar*, 805 F.3d at 1291 (internal quotation mark omitted). His counsel simply opined that arbitration costs could exceed $20,000, but he cited no evidence in support of that claim. […]

Suazo's factual foundation for regarding his "inability to pay [the arbitration] fees," *Escobar*, 805 F.3d at 1291, is insufficient. The only record evidence offered is Suazo's affidavit, which states, in sum, that he lives in a poor community where it is "not easy to find work," that he "do[es] not have money to pay for an arbitration, much less for an arbitrator's salary," and that he "do[es] not have the means to pay for thousands of dollars to an arbitrator." These conclusory statements do not establish that Suazo could not afford to pay even $3,750, a figure he claims he might incur in arbitration. […]

We recognize that the arbitration agreement in this case is distinguishable from the agreement at issue in *Escobar*. While "application of the cost-splitting clause is an issue properly for the arbitrator to consider," *id.* at 1292, it seems likely that Suazo will be required to bear half of the cost of initiating arbitration and "may" also become responsible for some other costs prior to the arbitrator's decision. Even so, on this almost barren record, Suazo has not carried his burden of proving that it is likely that unaffordable costs will deny him "access to the forum." *Id.*

We hold that Suazo cannot prevail on his effective vindication defense for a second and independent reason. The CBA between Suazo and NCL provided that, as long as Suazo was represented by the Norwegian Seafarers' Union, NCL "shall bear the reasonable costs related to the arbitration process from beginning to end." However, if Suazo chose to initiate arbitration "independently" of the NSU, the CBA is silent as to who must bear the costs of arbitration. On this record, it appears that the only reason Suazo would be required to bear any cost in arbitrating his dispute with NCL is because he opted to retain private counsel instead of proceeding to arbitrate with union-appointed counsel. The agreement gave him a choice: arbitrate for free with your union-chosen representation, or pay your own way with counsel of your choice. Having chosen the latter course of action, we will not second-guess the bargain struck in the contract and let Suazo eat his cake and have it too. Because the arbitration agreement and the

CBA gave him the ability to arbitrate for free and thereby "vindicate[e] his [federal statutory] rights in the arbitral forum," *Musnick*, 325 F.3d at 1259, his effective vindication defense is unmeritorious.

[Source: 822 F.3d 543 (2016)]

ANNOTATION

One might ask on what basis a Nicaraguan seafarer injured while employed by a Bahamian registered ship could seek redress in a U.S. court. The ship on which Suazo was injured operates cruises between Florida and the Bahamas. We are not told where the ship was located when the injury occurred or where Suazo was when he was recruited by NCL. Nevertheless, his right to sue in a U.S. court is established by the Jones Act, 46 U.S. Code § 30104, which states: "A seaman injured in the course of employment […] may elect to bring a civil action at law, with the right of trial by jury, against the employer. […]" Although choice of law rules may require the suit to be governed by foreign law, it is sufficient for the seafarer to be able to serve process on the employer to bring the suit in a U.S. court. *Lauritzen v. Larsen*, 345 U.S. 571 (1953).

If after all of the relevant facts are ascertained, it is determined that U.S. law is the appropriate substantive law to apply, the plaintiff will benefit from the fact that the Jones Act incorporates a very relaxed statutory standard of negligence liability as well as the maritime recovery doctrines of the duty of maintenance and cure plus liability for injuries resulting from unseaworthiness. Moreover, the remedies can include damages for pain and suffering and permanent disability. *Ferguson v. Moore-McCormack*, 352 U.S. 521, 523 (1957); *In re RJF Int'l Corp.*, 354 F.3d 104, 106 (1st Cir. 2004); *Evich v. Morris* ("*Evich II*"), 819 F.2d 256, 258 (9th Cir. 1987). All of these grounds for recovery and the scope of recovery should be weighed by an arbitrator. However, because a jury trial is available under the Jones Act, a court suit might be favoured by the plaintiff on the assumption that juries are more sympathetic and generous than an arbitrator whose selection for future cases is dependent on being acceptable to both the claimant's and the ship's representatives. The election to have the case heard by a jury is, of course, barred by the court's decision that Suazo must take his claims to arbitration.

Had this suit involved a U.S. seafarer and U.S. registered vessel, the employer's effort to force the matter into arbitration would have been thwarted by a provision of the Federal Arbitration Act that explicitly excludes employment contracts of seafarers from the Act's coverage. *Circuit City Stores v. Adams*, 532 U.S. 105, 113 (2001).

Because the parties agreed that Suazo's employment with NCL was a commercial relationship, the Court's discussion did not address two other sources of law that arguably require that the NY Convention be construed so as to not apply to employment agreements.

In describing the scope of its coverage, the NY Convention specifies that "the agreement arises out of a legal relationship, whether contractual or not, which is considered commercial." However, both U.S. and international law have acknowledged that employment is not a commercial activity. The Clayton Antitrust Act, 15 U.S. Code § 17, states: "The labor of a human being is not an article of commerce." Similarly, the International Labour Organization's Constitution incorporates by reference the principles set forth in the Declaration of Philadelphia of 10 May 1944, which states as a fundamental principle that "labour is not a commodity." Accordingly, because both under U.S. law and international law the employment relationship should not be "considered commercial", it is not within the scope of the New York Convention.

U.S.A. 5

UNITED STATES OF AMERICA

Federal Supreme Court
Tyson Foods v. Bouaphakeo
136 S.Ct. 1036 (2016)

Employer failed to keep certain worktime records – damages awarded to a certified class – can court rely on expert evidence estimating the time worked under Federal Rules of Procedure

HEADNOTES

Facts

Plaintiff employees sought to bring a collective action under the Fair Labor Standards Act (FLSA; the principal federal wage and hour regulatory statute) and under an Iowa State wage recovery law to recover wages for time spent in donning and doffing clothing that served as protective gear for the performance of their duties in carrying out various tasks in butchering pork. Some of this activity occurred at the beginning and end of the workday, some at mealtimes. The employer had not maintained records that would show with precision the amount of time involved. The defendant employer argued that this was not a proper case to be brought as a collective action because the amount of time spent by individual workers varied substantially. To counter this, plaintiffs submitted expert testimony with respect to time worked. An industrial relations expert conducted over 700 videotaped observations of employees in different departments. On the basis of those observations he concluded that the time required in the "cut" and "retrim" departments was 18 minutes a day, and the time required in the "kill" department was 21.25 minutes a day. The trial court certified the class, applying the provisions of the Federal Rules of Civil Procedure and section 16 of the FLSA. During the trial, another expert took the estimate provided by the first expert witness and the pay records for all employees in the relevant departments. This witness performed mathematical manipulations of those data that ultimately gave a figure of US$ 6.7 million due to the 3,334 members of the class. The jury found for the plaintiff class and gave judgment for US$ 2.9 million. The district court had not yet made an attempt to disburse the judgment when the case was appealed. The United States Court of Appeals for the Eighth Circuit affirmed, and the defendant sought relief from the Supreme Court of the United States.

The issue was: When the failure of an employer to keep records makes the determination of precise hours worked impossible, is it permissible to use studies conducted by experts to estimate likely times worked by groups of workers in order to certify a class action under the Federal Rules of Procedure or a collective action under the Fair Labor Standards Act for those workers?

Decision

The expert studies conducted in this case were sufficient to permit the court to certify this as a class action under the Federal Rules of Civil Procedure and as a collective action under section 16 of the Fair Labor Standards Act.

Law Applied

See judgment.

JUDGMENT

Justice KENNEDY delivered the opinion of the Court.

The employer [...] makes two arguments. [...] First, the employer argues the class should not have been certified because the primary method of proving injury assumed each employee spent the same time donning and doffing protective gear, even though differences in the composition of that gear may have meant that, in fact, employees took different amounts of time to don and doff. Second, the employer argues certification was improper because the damages awarded to the class may be distributed to some persons who did not work any uncompensated overtime. [...]

Until 1998, employees at the plant were paid under a system called "gang-time". This compensated them only for time spent at their workstations, not for the time required to put on and take off their protective gear. In response to a federal-court injunction, and a Department of Labor suit to enforce that injunction, Tyson in 1998 began to pay all its employees for an additional four minutes a day for what it called "K-code time." The 4–minute period was the amount of time Tyson estimated employees needed to don and doff their gear. In 2007, Tyson stopped paying K-code time uniformly to all employees. Instead, it compensated some employees for between four and eight minutes but paid others nothing beyond their gang-time wages. At no point did Tyson record the time each employee spent donning and doffing.

[…]

Tyson […] contended that, because of the variance in protective gear each employee wore, the employees' claims were not sufficiently similar to be resolved on a class-wide basis. The District Court rejected that position. It concluded there were common questions susceptible to class-wide resolution, such as "whether the donning and doffing of [protective gear] is considered work under the FLSA, whether such work is integral and [in]dispensable, and whether any compensable work is *de minim[i]s.*" […] The District Court acknowledged that the workers did not all wear the same protective gear, but found that "when the putative plaintiffs are limited to those that are paid via a gang-time system, there are far more factual similarities than dissimilarities." *Id.*, at 899–900. As a result, the District Court certified [two] […] classes.

The only difference in definition between the classes was the date at which the class period began. The size of the class certified under Rule 23, however, was larger than that certified under [section 16 of the Fair Labor Standards Act]. This is because, while a class under Rule 23 includes all unnamed members who fall within the class definition, the "sole consequence of conditional certification [under section 16] is the sending of court-approved written notice to employees … who in turn become parties to a collective action only by filing written consent with the court." […] A total of 444 employees joined the collective action, while the Rule 23 class contained 3,344 members.

Since the employees' claims relate only to overtime, each employee had to show he or she worked more than 40 hours a week, inclusive of time spent donning and doffing, in order to recover. As a result of Tyson's failure to keep records of donning and doffing time, however, the employees were forced to rely on what the parties describe as "representative evidence". This evidence included employee testimony, video recordings of donning and doffing at the plant, and, most important, a study performed by an industrial relations expert, Dr. Kenneth Mericle. […]

Although it had not kept records for time spent donning and doffing, Tyson had information regarding each employee's gang-time and K-code time. Using this data, the employees' other expert, Dr. Liesl Fox, was able to estimate the amount of uncompensated work each employee did by adding Mericle's estimated average donning and doffing time to the gang-time each employee worked and then subtracting any K-code time. [...]

Using this methodology, Fox stated that 212 employees did not meet the 40-hour threshold and could not recover. The remaining class members, Fox maintained, had potentially been undercompensated to some degree.

[...] The District Court submitted both issues of liability and damages to the jury.

II

[...] This opinion assumes, without deciding, that [...] if certification of respondents' class action under the Federal Rules was proper, certification of the collective action was proper as well, [and] that, in order to prove a violation of the Iowa statute, the employees had to do no more than demonstrate a violation of the FLSA.

A

Federal Rule of Civil Procedure 23(b)(3) requires that, before a class is certified under that subsection, a district court must find that "questions of law or fact common to class members predominate over any questions affecting only individual members." [...]

Here, the parties do not dispute that there are important questions common to all class members, the most significant of which is whether time spent donning and doffing the required protective gear is compensable work under the FLSA. [...] To be entitled to recovery, however, each employee must prove that the amount of time spent donning and doffing, when added to his or her regular hours, amounted to more than 40 hours in a given week. Petitioner argues that these necessarily person-specific inquiries into individual work time predominate over the common questions raised by respondents' claims, making class certification improper.

Respondents counter that these individual inquiries are unnecessary because it can be assumed each employee donned and doffed for the same average time observed in Mericle's sample. Whether this inference is permissible becomes the central dispute in this case. Petitioner contends that Mericle's study manufactures predominance by assuming away the very differences that make the case inappropriate for classwide resolution. Reliance on a representative sample, petitioner argues, absolves each employee of the responsibility to prove personal injury, and thus deprives petitioner of any ability to litigate its defenses to individual claims.

Calling this unfair, petitioner and various of its *amici* maintain that the Court should announce a broad rule against the use in class actions of what the parties call representative evidence. A categorical exclusion of that sort, however, would make little sense. A representative or statistical sample, like all evidence, is a means to establish or defend against liability. Its permissibility turns not on the form a proceeding takes—be it a class or individual action—but on the degree to which the evidence is reliable in proving or disproving the elements of the relevant cause of action.

It follows that the Court would reach too far were it to establish general rules governing the use of statistical evidence, or so-called representative evidence, in all class-action cases. [...]

In many cases, a representative sample is "the only practicable means to collect and present relevant data" establishing a defendant's liability.

One way for respondents to show, then, that the sample relied upon here is a permissible method of proving classwide liability is by showing that each class member could have relied on that sample to establish liability if he or she had brought an individual action. If the sample could have sustained a reasonable jury finding as to hours worked in each employee's individual action, that sample is a permissible means of establishing the employees' hours worked in a class action.

This Court's decision in *Anderson v. Mt. Clemens* explains why Mericle's sample was permissible in the circumstances of this case. In *Mt. Clemens*, seven employees and their union, seeking to represent over 300 others, brought a collective action against their employer for failing to compensate them for time spent walking to and from their workstations. The variance in walking time among workers was alleged to be upwards of 10 minutes a day, which is roughly consistent with the variances in donning and doffing times here.

The Court in *Mt. Clemens* held that when employers violate their statutory duty to keep proper records, and employees thereby have no way to establish the time spent doing uncompensated work, the "remedial nature of [the FLSA] and the great public policy which it embodies ... militate against making" the burden of proving uncompensated work "an impossible hurdle for the employee." [...]

In this suit, as in *Mt. Clemens*, respondents sought to introduce a representative sample to fill an evidentiary gap created by the employer's failure to keep adequate records. If the employees had proceeded with 3,344 individual lawsuits, each employee likely would have had to introduce

Mericle's study to prove the hours he or she worked. Rather than absolving the employees from proving individual injury, the representative evidence here was a permissible means of making that very showing.

Reliance on Mericle's study did not deprive petitioner of its ability to litigate individual defenses. Since there were no alternative means for the employees to establish their hours worked, petitioner's primary defense was to show that Mericle's study was unrepresentative or inaccurate. That defense is itself common to the claims made by all class members. [...]

Petitioner's reliance on *Wal–Mart Stores, Inc. v. Dukes*, 564 U.S. 338 (2011), is misplaced. *Wal–Mart* does not stand for the broad proposition that a representative sample is an impermissible means of establishing classwide liability.

Wal–Mart involved a nationwide Title VII class of over 1.5 million employees. In reversing class certification, this Court did not reach Rule 23(b)(3)'s predominance prong, holding instead that the class failed to meet even Rule 23(a)'s more basic requirement that class members share a common question of fact or law. The plaintiffs in *Wal–Mart* did not provide significant proof of a common policy of discrimination to which each employee was subject. [...]

While the experiences of the employees in *Wal–Mart* bore little relationship to one another, in this case each employee worked in the same facility, did similar work, and was paid under the same policy. As *Mt. Clemens* confirms, under these circumstances the experiences of a subset of employees can be probative as to the experiences of all of them.

[...] Once a district court finds evidence to be admissible, its persuasiveness is, in general, a matter for the jury. Reasonable minds may differ as to whether the average time Mericle calculated is probative as to the time actually worked by each employee. Resolving that question, however, is the near-exclusive province of the jury. The District Court could have denied class certification on this ground only if it concluded that no reasonable juror could have believed that the employees spent roughly equal time donning and doffing. [...]

The Court reiterates that, while petitioner, respondents, or their respective *amici* may urge adoption of broad and categorical rules governing the use of representative and statistical evidence in class actions, this case provides no occasion to do so. [...]

B
[...]

Petitioner's [other] argument is that, "where class plaintiffs cannot offer" proof that all class members are injured, "they must demonstrate instead that there is some mechanism to identify the uninjured class members prior to judgment and ensure that uninjured members (1) do not contribute to the size of any damage award and (2) cannot recover such damages." *Ibid*. Petitioner contends that respondents have not demonstrated any mechanism for ensuring that uninjured class members do not recover damages here.

Petitioner's new argument is predicated on the assumption that the damages award cannot be apportioned so that only those class members who suffered an FLSA violation recover. According to petitioner, because Fox's mechanism for determining who had worked over 40 hours depended on Mericle's estimate of donning and doffing time, and because the jury must have rejected Mericle's estimate when it reduced the damages award by more than half, it will not be possible to know which workers are entitled to share in the award.

As petitioner and its *amici* stress, the question whether uninjured class members may recover is one of great importance. See, *e.g.*, Brief for Consumer Data Industry Association as *Amicus Curiae*. It is not, however, a question yet fairly presented by this case, because the damages award has not yet been disbursed, nor does the record indicate how it will be disbursed.

Respondents allege there remain ways of distributing the award to only those individuals who worked more than 40 hours. [...]

Whether [...] some [...] methodology will be successful in identifying uninjured class members is a question that, on this record, is premature. Petitioner may raise a challenge to the proposed method of allocation when the case returns to the District Court for disbursal of the award.

Finally, it bears emphasis that this problem appears to be one of petitioner's own making. Respondents proposed bifurcating between the liability and damages phases of this proceeding for the precise reason that it may be difficult to remove uninjured individuals from the class after an award is rendered. It was petitioner who argued against that option and now seeks to profit from the difficulty it caused. Whether, in light of the foregoing, any error should be deemed invited, is a question for the District Court to address in the first instance.

[...]

ANNOTATION

This case deserves attention for four reasons. First, it provides a clear illustration of why enforcement of the Fair Labor Standards Act's overtime provisions can be challenging. Consider the incentives. Suppose an employee at this location spent an extra 18 minutes donning and doffing every day for 50 weeks for two years in a row. If his or her hourly rate was US$ 12.00, then his unpaid overtime would add up to US$ 2,100, a nice sum but not one to lead one to hire counsel and engage in time-consuming litigation. On the other hand, the jury here found that the large corporate employer saved roughly US$ three million by its non-payment of overtime. Even in a firm that large, multiple millions of dollars matter for the bottom line. Thus, the only likely avenue of enforcement is either an action brought by the government in the name of the Secretary of Labor, or a class (or collective) action. Both were used at this workplace.

Second, the Court's opinion makes clear the reasons why allowing the use of "representative evidence" is appropriate and significant. One can readily understand why the employer did not choose to keep track of "donning and doffing" time, but the failure to do so made the prosecution of any claim for that time challenging. To require an employee-by-employee presentation would require an immense amount of time and, as a practical matter, make pursuing these claims almost impossible. The use of an expert analysis of the sort done here is immensely more efficient but still affords a defendant employer the opportunity to challenge the proof or to submit its own expert testimony in rebuttal.

Third, the case makes clear the importance of having both State and Federal law available to such workers. The Federal statute was enacted nearly seventy years ago, at a time when collective actions were far less common. It is little wonder the drafters of that law chose to use an "opt-in" method for forming the claimant class. However, time has demonstrated that often it is difficult to gain the participation of many workers in the prospective class. Difficulties in communication arise, and many individuals are reluctant to respond for a variety of reasons, ranging from lack of understanding through to indifference to fear of reprisal. That the State law here could be used in tandem with the Federal law brought the opt-out procedures of Rule 23 of the Federal Rules of Civil Procedure into play and more than tripled the size of the class.

Finally, there is the point that remains unsettled: How much uncertainty about whether undeserving class members will benefit would justify denying a remedy to the class in general? On remand in this proceeding, the trial court found it possible to minimize that chance enough to justify entering a disbursement order in October 2016. One of the claimants' expert witnesses returned to use what wage and hour data the employer had made available to eliminate a substantial number of individual claims, and the court found that minimized the chance of "windfall" payments sufficiently. Further motions, however, continue in this case, with respect to expenses and fees. Thus a proceeding that began in February 2007 lingers at least into the summer of 2017.

U.S.A. 6

UNITED STATES OF AMERICA

Federal Supreme Court
Heffernan v. City of Paterson, N.J
136 S.Ct.1412 (2016)

Demotion of a public employee in the mistaken belief that the employee has exercised a right protected by the United States Constitution – a wrongful act for the purpose of federal law

HEADNOTES

Facts

Plaintiff, a police officer, was working in the office of the Chief of Police of Paterson, New Jersey, at a time when a political campaign for election of a mayor of the city was going on. The incumbent mayor was a candidate. So also was a personal friend of the plaintiff. The plaintiff, however, did not engage in any campaign activity for that candidate. The plaintiff's mother asked him to go to the campaign headquarters of the incumbent's opponent to obtain a sign bearing his name, to place in her front yard as a replacement for a damaged one. The plaintiff did so, and was observed there talking to a member of the campaign staff. The observer(s) reported plaintiff's presence at the campaign site to his superiors. Plaintiff was demoted from the rank of detective to patrol officer and sent back onto those duties. Plaintiff brought this action against the City as well as his supervising officers in the police department alleging a violation of a Federal statute, 42 U.S.C. §1983, which states: "Every person who, under color of any statute, ordinance […] or usage of any State […] subjects […] any citizen […] to deprivation of any rights […] secured by the Constitution and laws […] shall be liable to the party injured in an action at law […]." Plaintiff argued that his demotion was a response to what his supervisors mistakenly thought was his participation in the campaign of a political candidate, an activity that would be protected under the First Amendment to the United States Constitution. The trial court dismissed the case on the ground that the plaintiff had not in fact engaged in protected activity, but was only mistakenly believed to have done so. The United States Court of Appeals for the Third Circuit affirmed.

The issue was: If a public officer retaliates against a public employee in the mistaken belief that the employee has exercised a right protected by the United States Constitution, is that a wrongful act for the purpose of federal law?

Decision

If a public employer demotes an employee out of a desire to inhibit that employee from engaging in political activity that the First Amendment to the United States Constitution protects, that employee is entitled to challenge that unlawful action under 42 U.S.C. §1983, even though the employer has made a factual mistake in believing that the employee engaged in that activity.

Law Applied

See judgment.

JUDGMENT

Justice Breyer delivered the opinion of the Court.
[…]
With a few exceptions, the Constitution prohibits a government employer from discharging or demoting an employee because the employee supports a particular political candidate. […] The basic constitutional requirement reflects the First Amendment's hostility to government action that "prescribe[s] what shall be orthodox in politics." […] The exceptions take account of "practical realities" such as the need for "efficiency" and "effective[ness]" in government service. [Thus a] neutral and appropriately limited policy may prohibit government employees from engaging in partisan activity, and [a] political affiliation requirement [is] permissible where affiliation is "an appropriate requirement for effective performance of the public office involved."

In order to answer the question presented, we assume that the exceptions do not apply here. […] We assume that the activities that

Heffernan's supervisors *thought* he had engaged in are of a kind that they cannot constitutionally prohibit or punish, [...] but that the supervisors were mistaken about the facts. Heffernan had not engaged in those protected activities. Does Heffernan's constitutional case consequently fail?

The text of the relevant statute does not answer the question. The statute authorizes a lawsuit by a person "depriv[ed]" of a "right ... secured by the Constitution." 42 U.S.C. § 1983. But in this context, what precisely is that "right?" Is it a right that primarily focuses upon (the employee's) actual activity or a right that primarily focuses upon (the supervisor's) motive, insofar as that motive turns on what the supervisor believes that activity to be? The text does not say.

Neither does precedent directly answer the question. In some cases we have used language that suggests the "right" at issue concerns the employee's actual activity. In *Connick v. Myers*, 461 U.S. 138 (1983), for example, we said that a court should first determine whether the plaintiff spoke " 'as a citizen' " on a " 'matter[ ] of public concern,' " *id.*, at 143, 103 S.Ct. 1684. We added that, if the employee has not engaged in what can "be fairly characterized as constituting speech on a matter of public concern, it is unnecessary for us to scrutinize the reasons for her discharge." [...]

These cases, however, did not present the kind of question at issue here. In *Connick*, for example, no factual mistake was at issue. The Court assumed that both the employer and the employee were at every stage in agreement about the underlying facts: that the employer dismissed the employee because of her having circulated within the office a document that criticized how the office was being run (that she had in fact circulated). The question was whether the circulation of that document amounted to constitutionally protected speech. If not, the Court need go no further. [...]

Waters v. Churchill, 511 U.S. 661 (1994), is more to the point. In that case the Court did consider the consequences of an employer mistake. The employer wrongly, though reasonably, believed that the employee had spoken only on personal matters not of public concern, and the employer dismissed the employee for having engaged in that unprotected speech. The employee, however, had in fact used words that did not amount to personal "gossip" (as the employer believed) but which focused on matters of public concern. The Court asked whether, and how, the employer's factual mistake mattered.

The Court held that, as long as the employer (1) had reasonably believed that the employee's conversation had involved personal matters, not matters of public concern, and (2) had dismissed the employee because of that mistaken belief, the dismissal did not violate the First Amendment. [...] In a word, it was the employer's motive, and in particular the facts as the employer reasonably understood them, that mattered.

In *Waters*, the employer reasonably but mistakenly thought that the employee *had not* engaged in protected speech. Here the employer mistakenly thought that the employee *had* engaged in protected speech. If the employer's motive (and in particular the facts as the employer reasonably understood them) is what mattered in *Waters,* why is the same not true here? After all, in the law, what is sauce for the goose is normally sauce for the gander.

We conclude that, as in *Waters*, the [...] reason for demoting Heffernan is what counts here. When an employer demotes an employee out of a desire to prevent the employee from engaging in political activity that the First Amendment protects, the employee is entitled to challenge that unlawful action under the First Amendment and 42 U.S.C. § 1983—even if, as here, the employer makes a factual mistake about the employee's behavior.

We note that a rule of law finding liability in these circumstances tracks the language of the First Amendment more closely than would a contrary rule. Unlike, say, the Fourth Amendment, which begins by speaking of the "right of the people to be secure in their persons, houses, papers, and effects ...," the First Amendment begins by focusing upon the activity of the Government. It says that "Congress shall make no law ... abridging the freedom of speech." The Government acted upon a constitutionally harmful policy whether Heffernan did or did not in fact engage in political activity. That which stands for a "law" of "Congress," namely, the police department's reason for taking action, "abridge[s] the freedom of speech" of employees aware of the policy. And Heffernan was directly harmed, namely, demoted, through application of that policy.

We also consider relevant the constitutional implications of a rule that imposes liability. The constitutional harm at issue in the ordinary case consists in large part of discouraging employees—both the employee discharged (or demoted) and his or her colleagues—from engaging in protected activities. The discharge of one tells the others that they engage in protected activity at their peril. [...] Hence, we do not require plaintiffs in political affiliation cases to "prove that they, or other employees, have been coerced into changing, either actually or ostensibly, their political allegiance." [...] The employer's factual mistake does not diminish the risk of causing precisely that same harm. Neither, for that matter, is that harm diminished where an employer announces a policy of demoting those who, say, help a particular candidate in the mayoral race, and all employees (including Heffernan), fearful of demotion, refrain from providing any such help. [...] The upshot is that a discharge or demotion based upon an employer's belief that the employee has engaged in protected activity can cause the same kind, and degree, of constitutional harm whether that belief does or does not rest upon a factual mistake.

Finally, we note that, contrary to respondents' assertions, a rule of law that imposes liability despite the employer's factual mistake will not normally impose significant extra costs upon the employer. To win, the employee must prove an improper employer motive. In a case like this one, the employee will, if anything, find it more difficult to prove that motive, for the employee will have to point to more than his own conduct to show an employer's intent to discharge or to demote him for engaging in what the employer (mistakenly) believes to have been different (and protected) activities. We concede that, for that very reason, it may be more complicated and costly for the employee to prove his case. But an employee bringing suit will ordinarily shoulder that more complicated burden voluntarily in order to recover the damages he seeks.

[...] We have assumed that the policy that Heffernan's employers implemented violated the Constitution. There is some evidence in the record, however, suggesting that Heffernan's employers may have dismissed him pursuant to a different and neutral policy prohibiting police officers from overt involvement in any political campaign. See Brief for United States as *Amicus Curiae* 27–28. Whether that policy existed, whether Heffernan's supervisors were indeed following it, and whether it complies with constitutional standards [...] are all matters for the lower courts to decide in the first instance. Without expressing views on the matter, we reverse the judgment of the Third Circuit and remand the case for such further proceedings consistent with this opinion.

ANNOTATION

Discipline wrongly imposed because of poor fact-finding is routine grist for the mill of labor and employment law arbitrators. Only rarely does it become a matter of concern for the federal courts. That the specific facts of this case are unlikely to recur with any frequency, does not take away its importance, however. What the Court majority accomplish here is to focus the attention of trial courts applying this post-Civil War statute on the motivation of the public officers who have allegedly injured an individual. Public employees are particularly open to this sort of abuse, although they are not the only potential victims of prejudice or – as possibly here – the desire to maintain political power.

Protecting the power of public employees to speak out on a variety of issues has a particular importance. Those workers are often peculiarly well situated to discern problems in the functioning of governance, such as inefficiency, cronyism, favoring of special interests, and so on. If the lips of public employees are sealed, the likelihood that the public may learn of such improper conduct is significantly reduced.

As the final paragraph of the Court's opinion indicates, the Court has been ready to permit governments to institute limits on certain types of political activity, provided that those are "neutral" with respect to particular parties or candidates. It is no doubt sensible to say that police officers should not wear campaign badges on their uniforms, so long as that applies across the board to all candidates and parties. Not giving the voting public a reason to think that one candidate is the "official" one is a decent objective. However, facially neutral rules of this sort can be administered in ways that serve particular political interests, with enforcement largely limited to cases involving support of a particular party or candidate. Presumably, the decision in this case will provide an impetus for trial courts to look with care at whether such rules have been enforced even-handedly. Whether that was true in the instant case is not a matter of record, since on remand the plaintiff's claim was resolved in mediation.

Printed in the United States
By Bookmasters